MORE·FAITH·THAN·FEAR
The Los Angeles Stake Story

MORE·FAITH·THAN·FEAR
The Los Angeles Stake Story

Chad M. Orton
With a Foreword by Paul H. Dunn

BOOKCRAFT
Salt Lake City, Utah

Library of Congress Catalog Card Number: 87-72307

ISBN 0-88494-646-0

First Printing, 1987

Printed in the United States of America

Contents

Foreword

Every member of The Church of Jesus Christ of Latter-day Saints must start sometime somewhere to come to a realization of life and experience in the Church program as well as the gospel itself; to put down both physical and spiritual roots, to start building relationships and a foundation for religious training and living. This time in life occurred for me when in 1939 my family moved from a small Little Rock, Arkansas branch of the Church in the Southern States Mission to Hollywood Ward in the Los Angeles Stake. I was fourteen years old. One of my first recollections of this great ward and stake was the time Bishop Raymond L. Kirkham, a powerful but gentle and understanding man, asked me to give a talk in the stake priesthood meeting at the stake center, which was the Wilshire Ward meetinghouse. This was to be my first public talk as a Latter-day Saint, and the subject assigned to me was how to honor my priesthood.

When I announced to my parents that I was going to be a speaker at this meeting, they both reacted with expressions of surprise and concern, because up to that point in my church exposure and development I had had no experience standing before a group. In Hollywood my family owned and operated a small grocery business in which I worked with my father and brothers. Now with the announcement of this talk my father recognized that the family name was on the line and, knowing how badly I needed preparation and practice, suggested that I go over my planned remarks in the back room of the store. He even suggested that I pretend the cans on the back room shelves were my audience. This was good counsel. I have since learned that there is a great similarity between surplus canned goods and some of the expressions on the faces of people in congregations. The day finally came for the talk to be given and I managed to do a reasonably good job. Following this inaugural address I soon began to realize the wonderful opportunities and potential for spiritual growth and development and for the giving of service in a ward and stake such as these. From that time until my call by President David O. McKay to the First Council of the Seventy I have spent many rewarding years of association with the great leaders and members of the Los Angeles Stake. When our family first arrived in Hollywood, President Wilford Edling was the stake president, and it has been my pleasure since that time to work with each succeeding stake president. As a General Authority of the Church I have had the privilege of returning to my home stake on several occasions for conference visits. It has been a wonderful experience to observe the growth and development of this stake over the years.

Prior to my call as a General Officer I had an additional privilege of directing the Institute of Religion program in southern California. It was at the University of Southern California that the Church began, as part of the institute program, its first student ward outside of the state of Utah, which ward was immediately assigned to the Los Angeles Stake.

It is a personal honor to be associated with this publication of the historical record of the Los Angeles Stake, and I am impressed with and proud of its impact on thousands of Church members throughout the years. It has been particularly uplifting and enlightening to travel the Church and find that many early-day members of this stake have had a tremendous influence on other units scattered worldwide through the Church.

Thus with deep gratitude and much nostalgia I salute the great leaders and teachers of this stake who have done so much for so many in developing faith and commitment to the gospel of Jesus Christ. May all of us who read this book be inspired and encouraged to accept the Savior's admonition to "Go, and do . . . likewise."

PAUL H. DUNN

Preface

Addressing the 1980 World Conference on Records, President Spencer W. Kimball stated: "Whether we recognize it or not, we are connected with our past, and we can fashion a better future if we draw upon the inspiration of the past and the lessons of history, both as a people and individually. . . . People who care nothing for the past usually have no thought for the future and are selfish in the way they use the present. Where there is proper regard for the past and its people, we enrich the present as well as the future." To help ensure a "proper regard for the past," President Kimball asked each stake to write its history. It is appropriate, therefore, that as the Los Angeles California Stake celebrates its sixtieth anniversary in 1987, it evidences its obedience to this prophetic counsel with the publication of this book.

When approached in March 1986 to write this history, I envisioned a history consisting of detailed lists of roadshows, officers, and biographical sketches, important in themselves, but which failed to raise in me the perspective envisioned by President Kimball—this because of my Utah upbringing and my academic training in the pioneer period of Church history. But the zeal of stake president William W. Tanner was contagious, and I accepted the task. Time has since shown that his enthusiasm was well founded, for I have learned that the stake and its members have also been pioneers in the Church.

When the Los Angeles Stake was formed in 1923, it was the first stake in a large urban area. Its membership, composed largely of transplanted Utahns, had to meet the challenge of establishing the Church in a new environment where Latter-day Saints were a minority. Four years later the Los Angeles Stake was divided and the Hollywood Stake was created. In 1939 the name of the Hollywood Stake was changed to the Los Angeles Stake and in 1974 to the Los Angeles California Stake. As changes took place within the city, beginning with the Great Depression of the 1930s and continuing to the present through an increasingly diversified ethnic population, the Los Angeles California Stake has continued to be on the forefront of a worldwide Church.

Consequently, the stake has been very important to the Church, not just in Los Angeles but also far beyond stake boundaries. Several of the programs introduced to meet stake needs have been later implemented on a Church-wide basis. The stake has also been a training center for many local leaders in southern California and throughout the world of Church operations. Five of the present General Authorities received part of their training there.

Because this has not been the typical stake, its history has not lent itself to being the typical stake history. Here is a story of how one stake has progressed by meeting the varied challenges of its urban setting. I have focused my efforts on that story and have tried to present a history which gives proper understanding to the period and is also as applicable to those who lived through the time as to those who come later. It is with regret that in my attempt to achieve that manageable focus some people and events were necessarily omitted, not because they lacked importance but rather because the project required limits of space and time. Thus, I have tried to write a history in the dual language of faith and scholarship.

This work briefly covers the history of the Church in California before the creation of the Los Angeles Branch and the history of that branch and subsequent stake to the beginning of 1987. In some respects it is more than just a stake history; it is also a history of the Church in southern California and a case study of how one group of Saints has flourished in its twentieth century environment. The majority of information has been gathered from stake records, newspapers, particularly the *California Intermountain News*, and Leo J. Muir, *A Century of Mormon Activity in California*. To limit the number of endnotes, these sources, whose information can easily be checked, have only been noted when directly quoted or when the source is not readily apparent. In the main, endnotes have been limited to ideas and information gathered from other not so easily recognized sources.

There are those who might wonder about the title. Specifically, it refers to an important decision made by stake leaders. Generally, it is one of the few titles which describes the entire stake experience and explains why it has progressed. Thus, the title could as easily apply to Joseph E. Robinson and Eliza Woollacott as to John K. Carmack and Ella Farnsworth and to all stake members whose actions, small or great, have demonstrated their faith. To them this work is dedicated.

I am indebted to many people without whose assistance this work would never have been accomplished. President William W. Tanner gave freely of his insights and time, but more important were his timely words of encouragement. Arthur Wallace and the stake history committee identified areas which needed to be covered and gathered materials from which to work, aided by former and present stake members who willingly furnished information, reviewed the manuscript, and provided financial assistance. Two of my professors at Brigham Young University, James B. Allen of the History Department and G. Wesley Johnson of the Center for Family and Community History Studies, recognized the value of this project and generously provided assistantships and secretarial help. Dr. Allen also sacrificed countless hours refining the manuscript. Gordon Irving and Ron Watt of the Church Historical Department continually provided encouragement and support as did the staff of the Historical Department. Russell Orton, Cory Maxwell, and the editorial staff at Bookcraft kept a sense of humor in spite of missed deadlines and provided technical direction. My father-in-law, C. Bailey Sainsbury, lent me his new computer for this work, thereby setting aside a dream, then died with his dream unrealized. My father, Bryce B. Orton, provided unlimited access to his printer. Finally, a very special thanks to my wife, Elizabeth, and to Amy, Laura, and Spencer for their untiring support.

One of the Great Fields in Which the Church Would Thrive

Outside Utah, the greatest concentration of members of The Church of Jesus Christ of Latter-day Saints is found in California. At the beginning of 1987, Church membership in the state exceeded 650,000 and the number of stakes exceeded 140. Such a presence would have astounded pioneer Saints in California who despaired that the Church would ever grow significantly within the state's boundaries.

The prominent role the Latter-day Saints played in the settlement of Utah and the Great Basin has been justly celebrated. However, the important role Latter-day Saints played in the history of California is not as well known. They were among the first Anglos in Los Angeles, San Francisco, San Diego, and San Bernardino, and were present when gold was discovered at Sutter's Mill. Through their experiences in California from 1846–57, Latter-day Saints contributed to the heritage of the state an interesting history of individual and group struggles, successes, and failures. As a result of the several early failures associated with efforts to establish itself in California, the Church made little progress for a period of about thirty years; when formal activity resumed in the 1890s, the heritage of the past played an important role in a renewed determination to build up the kingdom in California.

This chapter briefly outlines the history of the Church in California prior to the establishment of a branch in Los Angeles, some of the problems associated with establishing a foothold in the state, and the legacy which early California Saints left to the Saints of a later time.

The history of the Church in California begins on 29 July 1846, one year before Brigham Young called Salt Lake Valley "the right place." On this date a group of 231 Latter-day Saint emigrants under the direction of Samuel Brannan arrived at the small Mexican settlement of Yerba Buena, now San Francisco, on the ship *Brooklyn*. By coincidence, this group of Saints had left New York on the same day that Brigham Young left Nauvoo; the *Brooklyn* party was to rendezvous with the main body of Saints in the West following an ocean voyage around Cape Horn. This sea journey lasted almost six months, during which time ten members of the company died and two children, named "Atlantic" and "Pacific," were born. Upon arrival in California, which at that time was under the control of Mexico, part of the *Brooklyn* colony stayed in Yerba Buena, while Brannan sent the remainder east to the San Joaquin Valley to establish an agricultural colony, which they called "New Hope." At these two sites the *Brooklyn* Saints spent the winter of 1846–47, establishing schools, a newspaper, a saw and grist mill, a store, and successful agricultural concerns, but no formal Church organization. Because the number of Saints who arrived on the *Brooklyn* was greater than the number of inhabitants of Yerba Buena, the Saints were also instrumental in changing the name of the settlement to San Francisco, in honor of a mission in the vicinity.[1]

After a winter of prosperity in the relatively mild California climate, Sam Brannan hoped that California would be "the right place" for the Saints in the West and left San Francisco to meet with Brigham Young concerning that possibility. Brannan, a young man of twenty-seven and a relatively new member of the Church, met Brigham Young on the banks of the Green River, but failed to persuade the prophet to move his followers to California. Brannan remained with President Young's party and was with the first company that entered the Salt Lake Valley in July 1847; after remaining there for a few discouraging days, he returned to San Francisco and his successful business ventures.

In June 1847, while Brannan was meeting with Brigham Young, Addison Pratt landed at San Francisco on his way home from a mission to the Society Islands, to which the Prophet Joseph Smith had called him in 1843. Upon arrival in San Francisco, Pratt noticed evidence of spiritual degeneracy among the colony and noted that "mammon was making decisive inroads."[2] Although he had been away from his family for nearly five years, Pratt determined to stay with the colony for a time to try to provide its members with spiritual guidance and to rejuvenate faith among them. His task was made easier as Brannan's influence in the colony was beginning to decline and dissensions began to arise.

Pratt, with the permission of Brannan, organized a branch among the Saints in December 1847. Brannan, whose business ventures were occupying most of his time, wished only to retain the title of "first elder" and was only too happy to let Pratt run the affairs of the branch. Brannan was not only neglecting the spiritual welfare of the Saints but also setting a questionable example and teaching doctrines incompatible with Church teachings. He opposed the call for the colony to gather to Zion, advised his followers against preaching religion to non-Mormons, and encouraged marriage outside the Church. There even seems to be evidence that Brannan's major interest in the Church was collecting the Saints' tithing for his own personal gain.[3] In the spring of 1848, following the discovery of gold, Addison Pratt closed down the branch and, along with many of the colony, moved to Utah.

Following the disbanding of the branch, Brannan went throughout the gold region, trying to get gain from the Mormons who had joined in the gold rush. Clearly in a state of apostasy from gospel teachings, Brannan was later disfellowshipped by Elder Parley P. Pratt during his mission to California. One of the activities leading to his disfellowshipment was Brannan's organizing of the first vigilante committee in San Francisco. Having been a Mormon in name only these many years, Brannan's only tie with the Church was now severed. He would eventually go on to help establish Sacramento and Yuba City; own large tracts of land in Los Angeles, San Francisco, and Sacramento; establish a lucrative trade with China; build the first great wharves in San Francisco and the state's first two railroads; and become California's first millionaire. He would also die one of its paupers.

In March 1849 Elder Amasa M. Lyman of the Council of the Twelve Apostles was sent to San Francisco to save those Saints who remained in the city from the intoxication of the gold rush and to direct missionary efforts in the state.[4] He was replaced by Elder Charles C. Rich of the Council of the Twelve, who arrived in February 1850 and stayed in San Francisco until October. However, their efforts were unsuccessful, as most California members by this time were dissatisfied with the Church and few would listen to the message. The two Apostles became convinced that there was no place for a Church colony in northern California, although they held some hope for the Church in southern California.[5]

In July 1851 Elder Parley P. Pratt arrived in San Francisco, and in addition to disfellowshipping Brannan, he re-established the branch when eight converts were made in the city. In July 1852 Elder Pratt was replaced by George Q. Cannon, who later became a member of the First Presidency. Cannon stayed in San Francisco until 1857, not only providing spiritual guidance to the colony but also directing the Church's missionary efforts in California, partially through publishing a newspaper, *The Western Standard*. When Brigham Young recalled all the Saints to Utah in September 1857 as a result of the Utah War, the faithful in San Francisco left. For thirty years after that, no official attempt was made to re-establish Church activity in the city. Most of those who stayed in San Francisco eventually fell into inactivity, and many joined the Reorganized Church of Jesus Christ of Latter Day Saints when it began formal organization in the city.

On 26 June 1846, one month before the *Brooklyn* landed in California, Captain James Allen of the U.S. Army arrived at the Mormon settlement of Mt. Pisgah, Iowa, with orders to raise a battalion of five hundred men to assist in the war with Mexico. Captain Allen's request for volunteers was in part the national government's response to Brigham Young's efforts to find means of helping the Saints finance their migration west. In 1844 President James K. Polk had run on a platform which called for the annexation of the Republic of Texas to the United States and the resolution of the dispute with Great Britain regarding ownership of the Pacific Northwest.

President Young, knowing of Polk's desire to populate the Oregon Territory—thereby reinforcing America's claim to the area by sheer numbers—felt he might be able to secure a government contract to build stockades and blockhouses along the Oregon Trail. Building these stockades would help the government by providing protection to settlers heading for Oregon, and at the same time provide badly needed funds for the Saints. To build these forts would slow down the progress of the pioneers, but not force them to deviate greatly from their intended route, which ran parallel to the Oregon Trail. With this idea in mind, President Young wrote Jesse Little, then on a mission in New Hampshire, asking him to go to Washington to let government officials know of the Saints' financial difficulties and to "embrace any facilities for emigration to the western coast" that "our government shall offer."[6]

However, by the time Little presented the plan to Polk, the crisis with great Britain concerning the Oregon Territory was nearly resolved. Since populating Oregon was no longer a vital aspect of resolving the conflict with Great Britain, President Polk rejected the Saints' offer to build forts but accepted their offer of assistance. Polk suggested to Little that the Saints could be of assistance with America's more pressing concern—a war with Mexico that had begun over the annexation of Texas.

The Republic of Texas had been created ten years earlier—in October 1836—after a war of independence with Mexico. By 1830 ten times more Americans than Mexicans had settled in this Mexican state. When the Mexican government began to assert more control over them, the Texans began seeking independence. In 1835 the movement had escalated into a full-scale rebellion and Mexican President Santa Anna brought an army of six thousand men to Texas to subdue the rebellion. In February 1836 Santa Anna's army killed 187 Texans under the command of Colonel William B. Travis at the Alamo. Two months after the fall of the Alamo, Sam Houston and a greatly outnumbered Texan army—with their battle cry "Remember the Alamo!" —routed the Mexican Army and won Texas independence. Although most Texans desired annexation by the United States, U.S. officials recognized that to annex Texas would likely lead to war with Mexico; therefore, Texas remained an independent republic for ten years.

Texas was finally annexed in 1845, but in 1846 war broke out over the question of whether its border was the Rio Grande or Nueces River. An unsuccessful attempt was made to purchase the disputed land, but shots were fired in April 1846 after Polk ordered the U.S. Army to advance to the Rio Grande. Polk had tried to purchase not only that area from Mexico, but also New Mexico and California, which Americans perceived to be rightfully theirs by "Manifest Destiny."

To Jesse Little, Polk suggested the possibility of the Mormons' raising an army of two thousand men to help take possession of California from Mexico.[7] When Polk presented his plan to cabinet members, they suggested that only five hundred Mormon volunteers be recruited.

At first many Mormons viewed the call for volunteers as unfair and unreasonable in light of past difficulties with the government and of the desperate need for all able-bodied men to assist in the westward migration. However, when Church leaders appealed for volunteers throughout the Mormon settlements in Iowa and at Nauvoo, the response was favorable. While calling the Battalion was not the type of government assistance they had hoped for, Church leaders realized that the pay the Battalion members would receive would greatly assist in financing the westward migration.

On 16 July 1846 the Mormon Battalion was mustered into the U.S. Army for a period of twelve months. Four days later it began the longest infantry march in recorded history, a march that would take the recruits to San Diego and Los Angeles before they were discharged from the service. Accompanying the Battalion were thirty-five women and several children. From the government, members of the Battalion had received assurance that they would remain together for their period of service; from Brigham Young they received assurance that "not one of those who might enlist would fall by the hands of the nation's foes, that their only fighting would be with wild beasts and that there would not be as many bullets whistle around their ears as did around Dr. Willard Richards' in Carthage jail."[8]

After a two hundred–mile march to Fort Leavenworth, the Battalion was outfitted for the remainder of its journey to California. At Fort Leavenworth each Battalion member was given a forty-two–dollar clothing allowance for the year. Instead of purchasing clothing, however, most of them sent the money back to help support their families and to assist the migrating poor and seriously ill. The fact that every Mormon volunteer knew how to sign his name to the payroll surprised the paymaster, for only one in three of the Missouri volunteers could do so. Before the volunteers left Leavenworth, they received a communication from Brigham Young urging the officers to be as fathers to their soldiers, to be prayerful, and to be kind and courteous at all times. He advised the soldiers to be respectful, obedient, and trustworthy to their superiors. He urged all members of the Battalion to avoid profanity and base language and to keep themselves clean in thought and act. The records show that when the Battalion was released, these men had been true to the instructions of Brigham Young and their religious ideals.

From Leavenworth the Battalion headed south along the Santa Fe Trail. By the time they reached the Arkansas River, several men had taken sick and were ordered to Pueblo, Colorado, while the rest of the Battalion continued the march towards Santa Fe. At Santa Fe eighty-six of the more infirm and almost all of the women and children were also dispatched towards Pueblo under the leadership of Captain James Brown. As the Battalion left Santa Fe, its numbers had been diminished to around four hundred.

At that point the Battalion had only sixty days' supply of food. To ensure that there would be enough rations to last until they reached California, the men were placed on three-quarters rations, or worse, for the remainder of the trip. The roads along this stretch of the journey were almost impassable; the sand was so deep in places that the men, already burdened with heavy packs, had to help pull the wagons. Because of these conditions, another group of fifty-five sick and worn out men were sent to Pueblo.

On 9 December 1846 the Battalion fought the first and only battle of its journey. This battle was, in accord with Brigham Young's prophecy, with wild bulls and lasted under an hour. As the column passed a herd of wild cattle, around one hundred of the bolder bulls attacked it, goring to death several pack mules and draft animals and throwing several wagons about. The men fired at the bulls, killing sixty before driving off the rest.

Finally, after six months and nearly two thousand miles of marching through hot deserts, the Mormon Battalion reached San Diego on 27 January 1847. Daniel Tyler, a Battalion member, recorded his feelings, probably typifying those of the others, upon seeing the Pacific:

> The joy, the cheer that filled our souls, none but worn-out pilgrims nearing a haven of rest can imagine. Prior to leaving Nauvoo we had talked about and sung about the great Pacific sea, and we were now

upon its very borders, and its beauty far exceeded our most sanguine expectation. Our joy, however, was not unmixed with sorrow. The next thought was, where, oh where were our fathers, mothers, brothers, sisters, wives and children whom we had left in the howling wilderness, among savages, or at Nauvoo, subject to the cruelties of the mobs?[9]

To the members of the Battalion, Colonel Philip St. George Cooke, their government appointed commander, issued a commendation upon arrival at San Diego:

> History may be searched in vain for an equal march of infantry. Half of it has been through a wilderness where nothing but savages and wild beasts are found, or deserts where for want of water, there is no living creature. There with almost hopeless labor we have dug wells, which the future traveler will enjoy. Without a guide who had traveled them, we have ventured into trackless table-lands where water was not found for several marches. With crowbar and pick ax in hand, we have worked our way over mountains, which seemed to defy aught but the wild goat, and hewed a passage through a chasm of living rock more narrow than our wagons. To bring these first wagons to the Pacific, we have preserved the strength of our mules by herding them over large tracts, which you have laboriously guarded without loss. . . . Thus marching half naked and half fed, and living upon wild animals, we have discovered and made a road of great value to our country.[10]

On 1 February 1847 the Battalion was ordered to the mission San Luis Rey where they began twenty days of intensive military drills. Although the war had ended on 16 January 1847, eleven days before their arrival in San Diego, this training was carried out in case the terms of surrender should be disregarded by the local residents.

On 19 March 1847 the main body left San Luis Rey for Los Angeles, the former Spanish California capital. Arriving at their destination on 23 March, the Mormon soldiers camped on the eastern edge of Los Angeles.

In the latter part of April, as rumors of a possible Mexican uprising and attacks by Indians became prevalent, the order was given for the Battalion to build a fort on a hill overlooking the city—the first public structure in Los Angeles. Work continued on Fort Moore, named after a U.S. Army captain who had recently died, until it was completed by 1 July. On the Fourth of July, at the Fort's formal dedication, the Battalion raised the American flag for the first time over Los Angeles on a "liberty pole" made from the tallest tree that could be found in the mountains near San Bernardino. The men then gave nine cheers for the Stars and Stripes.

At the same time that the main company had left San Luis Rey for Los Angeles, Company "B" had left the mission for San Diego. These men made such a favorable impression upon the local citizens through their hard work, moral living, and community service, that a group of San Diego residents wrote the commander of the military district requesting that another company of Mormons be raised to take the place of Company "B" and stating "that they did not wish any other soldiers quartered there."[11]

On 9 July 1847 Company "B" was reunited with the main force in Los Angeles, and on 16 July the Mormon Battalion was mustered out of the United States Army after a year of service. Following their release, most Battalion members prepared to rejoin their families, whom they had left on the plains or at Nauvoo. After organizing themselves as the Israelites of old into hundreds, fifties, and tens, they bade farewell to Los Angeles on 21 July. Few, if any, had any reluctance to leave the city which they "had found to be a 'sink of iniquity,' a cesspool of profligacy, drunkenness, debauchery, thievery, gambling, cruel bullfights and other forms of degeneracy."[12]

Once they left Los Angeles, the former Battalion members headed north through the San Joaquin Valley, with the idea of heading across the Sierras to Salt Lake City. At Sutter's Fort the Mormon volunteers camped overnight with a disappointed and disgruntled Sam Brannan, who was returning from his meeting with Brigham Young. Brannan presented a gloomy picture of the Salt Lake Valley and recommended that the volunteers stay in California, for, he predicted, the Mormons in Salt Lake would soon be forced out by the harshness of the land.

After Brannan had left for San Francisco, Battalion members also met Captain James Brown, who had led the Pueblo sick detachment to the Salt Lake Valley and was on his way to Monterey to collect the back pay of that detachment. Brown brought an official direction from Church leaders advising that only those with means of subsistence in Utah should continue the journey and that the remainder should stay in California until spring. About half the company wintered at Sutter's Fort, while the other half moved on to Utah. While at Sutter's Fort, some of these former Battalion members were involved in the discovery of gold on 24 January 1848, thus helping to set off the famous California Gold Rush.

Those who left for Salt Lake arrived there on 16 October 1847 and spent the first winter with the Saints in the valley. For thirty-two of them, however, their joy at reaching Salt Lake was short lived as they found their families were still on the plains. Tired from their long journey and ill equipped for another, these men nevertheless headed across the plains to be with their families. Near Laramie, Wyoming, they were greeted by the first snows of winter. On 18 December 1847, the march of the Mormon Battalion finally ended for this little band of frozen and hungry men as they were reunited with their families at Winter Quarters.

The men of the Mormon Battalion have left a legacy of faith, determination, and good will both within and outside the Church. In 1905 the Daughters of the Mormon Battalion began a campaign to perpetuate the memory of the Battalion through the erection of a monument. May Belle T. Davis, of the Wilshire Ward in Los Angeles, and a granddaughter of battalion member Thomas Karren, joined in raising funds for the monument that was dedicated on the Utah State Capitol grounds in 1927. Davis also felt that one should be erected in Los Angeles on the site of Fort Moore, which had long since been torn down. She began a fund-raising campaign for such a memorial in the 1930s. The Daughters of the War of 1812 and the Daughters of the American Revolution acknowledged the contribution of the Battalion by placing a flag pole and bronze plaque on the site of the fort. While Davis appreciated the recognition these groups had given the Mormon Battalion, her dream had been to have an imposing memorial erected on the site.

As construction began around the Los Angeles Civic Center, however, part of her dream diminished as all except the northwest portion of the hill on which the historic fort stood was removed. As part of the project, the city had indicated it wished to place a historical monument in the downtown area in honor of the California centennial, which would occur in 1950. The suggestion was made that a statue of Father Junipero Serra be placed in the area. Upon hearing this, Davis called the stake Relief Society president exclaiming, "I'm infuriated! The idea! Father Serra did nothing for downtown Los Angeles. It's all unhistorical and all out of place."[13] She then called the *Los*

Angeles Times, which, after hearing her case, gave its full support to the monument, telling her that many had expressed regret over the destruction of Fort Moore Hill. The support given by the *Times* brought additional pleas for the memorial, and the Los Angeles city and county councils donated the land located on Hill Street and an additional $600,000 for construction of the memorial.

On the remaining portion of the hill, a forty-foot sculptured frieze was erected, which contained the "figures of men whose names and achievements are written in the history of the state and the nation," along with tablets listing the names and accomplishments of the men of the Battalion.[14] In 1954 the Fort Moore Memorial was finally dedicated, over twenty years after May Belle T. Davis began raising money for its construction. For a period of time the Los Angeles Stake Primary held a flag raising ceremony at the memorial in celebration of the Twenty-fourth of July, a tradition which has recently been revived by the Los Angeles Stake.

Once the Saints were headquartered in Salt Lake Valley in 1847, Brigham Young began laying plans for the creation of the State of Deseret, whose territory would encompass all of present-day Utah and Nevada and parts of Colorado, Wyoming, Idaho, Oregon, New Mexico, Arizona, and the southern portion of California. Small groups of Saints were called to settle areas outside the Salt Lake Valley as Brigham Young began colonizing his imposing State of Deseret. At the same time, a constitution was drafted, and Almon W. Babbitt was selected to petition Congress for statehood.

Unfortunately, the State of Deseret was doomed from the start. By the time Babbitt reached Washington, the slavery issue was again occupying the attention of the nation. As part of the Compromise of 1850, Congress admitted California as a state, and organized the New Mexico and Utah territories with the right to decide for themselves whether they would be slave or free states. As a result of the Compromise, Utah Territory was half the size of the State of Deseret, occupying the present states of Utah and Nevada and portions of Wyoming and Colorado. But even without the slavery controversy, it is unlikely that the State of Deseret would have been approved by Congress. The proposed state embraced almost one-sixth of the nation's territory, including parts of California, which conflicted with the claims of its inhabitants. In addition, the population of the State of Deseret was below the figure required for statehood.

Important to Church plans for the State of Deseret was the so-called Mormon Corridor to the Pacific, through southern Utah and Nevada to the ports of San Diego and San Pedro. By establishing a series of Mormon settlements between Salt Lake and the coast, Church leaders hoped to provide a more convenient way for immigrants to migrate to Salt Lake City than across the overland trail, and also to develop a useful trade route. Even after the state of California was created, Church leaders still tried to make their plan work by establishing communities, such as Las Vegas, as resting points along the route. Although the Mormon Corridor never materialized, a Mormon colony was planted near the shores of the Pacific at San Bernardino.

In 1851 Brigham Young called Apostles Amasa M. Lyman and Charles C. Rich to lead a company of Saints to California and settle the San Bernardino Valley. One of those who volunteered for the duty was Jefferson Hunt, formerly a captain in the Mormon Battalion who had scouted the valley east of Los Angeles during his stay in that city. While a member of the Battalion, he wrote Brigham Young that the Saints had an opportunity to purchase land in the San Bernardino Valley if they wanted it. He also promoted the idea that it would be to the benefit of the Church to establish a Latter-day Saint colony in southern California, an idea with which Church leaders agreed. President Young desired a party of approximately twenty to fifty men to establish the settlement. To his great alarm 437 men, women, and children volunteered to go to California. After the company had left Payson, Utah, for California, President Young wrote, "I was sick at the sight of so many saints going to California."[15] The reason for this feeling was clear: he saw these men as going "after the God of this world."[16] Church leaders had encouraged the Saints to stay in Utah and avoid the gold fields of California. In spite of these pleas, many Saints went searching for gold, and many, as a result, were lost to the Church. The great number of volunteers for San Bernardino convinced President Young that the same spirit existed among many in that group.

Among the members of the San Bernardino company were Parley P. Pratt, recently called as president of the Pacific Mission, and eight missionaries on the first mission to the non-Mormons of the state. The missionaries journeyed with the group to San Bernardino and then headed to Los Angeles, arriving in the city on 16 June 1851. There they spent two weeks preaching the gospel with their efforts rewarded on 26 June when Pratt baptized and confirmed James Warren as a member of the Church.[17] From Los Angeles these missionaries went by boat to San Francisco where, as noted earlier, Elder Pratt reorganized the San Francisco Branch. Most of the missionaries went on from San Francisco to labor in the South Pacific islands.

After the missionaries had left the main body at San Bernardino Valley, the Saints there were able to obtain title to the Rancho del San Bernardino's 35,000 acres for $77,500. They immediately set out to improve the land. They planted 1300 acres in wheat, dug canals, built roads, erected a bowery that served as both school and chapel, and built grist and saw mills. They also laid out a city in accordance with Joseph Smith's plat of the city of Zion, with the center site set aside for a temple, and they established the San Bernardino Ward and the San Bernardino Stake of Zion, the first in California. Additionally, they were instrumental in the creation of San Bernardino County from the western half of Los Angeles County.

By 1853 the colony had grown to almost nine hundred, but factions were arising among the Saints and problems were developing with the non-Mormons in the area. In April 1857, the days of the colony seemed numbered as Elders Lyman and Rich were called on missions to Europe. The end for San Bernardino as a Church colony came in the fall of 1857 when Brigham Young recalled the settlers after President James Buchanan sent an army to Utah to put down a rumored Mormon rebellion. On 24 July 1857, the Saints were celebrating their tenth anniversary in the Salt Lake Valley when they received word that an army was en route to "invade Utah territory."[18] Brigham Young, having received no official word on why troops had been sent and remembering the Missouri and Illinois persecutions, had the Saints prepare for war. Martial law was declared; the Territorial militia, the Nauvoo Legion, was mobilized; supplies were stockpiled; and missionaries were recalled from the eastern states and Europe. In addition, the call went forth for all the Saints to abandon outlying colonies and return to Salt Lake. However, only fifty-five percent of the Saints in San Bernardino answered the call, showing that almost half the colony would rather abandon the Church than their homes.[19] The preparations for war proved unnecessary as the Utah War was brought to a peaceful end in the early months of 1858.

Following the end of the Utah War, Church leaders made no effort to re-establish the California Mission; nor did they make an official effort to re-establish the San Bernardino colony, for the losses—especially of Church members—far outweighed the gains of keeping the colony.

Instead, leaders' efforts were concentrated on establishing the Church in the Intermountain area as Church leaders encouraged members to gather to Utah. Missionary efforts continued to be centered in Europe and the eastern United States where the Church's ventures had not cost more members than it had gained, as was the case in California. Nevertheless, there continued to be a sizeable Mormon presence in the state.

Beginning in the summer of 1858 and continuing for a number of years, many families returned to join those who remained at San Bernardino, often bringing new arrivals with them. Those who arrived at San Bernardino did not always make that valley their home. The *Los Angeles Star* in January 1860 reported that "San Bernardino has received a considerable accession to its population with a few weeks past. A large number of families from Utah have arrived and are locating in different parts of California."[20] However, a majority of these were members in name only as most faithful members had caught the spirit of the gathering and returned to Utah. In San Bernardino there is no evidence that religious services were held after Brigham Young gave the call to gather to Utah in 1857.[21] Most of those who stayed behind in California had developed a negative attitude towards the Church and its teachings, especially polygamy, and viewed Brigham Young as a high-handed authoritarian.

Even if those who stayed in the state had maintained their faith, the lack of Church-sponsored religious activities for over thirty years further contributed to the loss to the Church of a generation of California Mormons. The one notable exception to the lack of religious organization was in Sacramento, where a small branch was organized in 1871 by a group of Utah Mormons who had joined with the Reorganized Church and later became dissatisfied. However, the branch was not begun with official Church approval.

Another reason why the Church failed to establish itself in California during these years—in addition to its emphasis on establishing the Saints in the Great Basin and the mostly negative experience of attempting to establish the Church in the state—was the practice of plural marriage. During this time opposition mounted not only in public outcries, but also in Congressional legislation that threatened the Church's practice of plural marriage and the Church itself.

Probably as early as 1831, Joseph Smith had received a revelation on the practice of plural marriage in this dispensation.[22] In the early 1840s this law was shared with a few leading Church members, and these practiced it secretly until 1852, when it became an official doctrine of the Church. Almost immediately an outcry was heard throughout the nation, as many came to believe that the subjugation of women through plural marriage was little different from the subjugation of blacks through slavery. In 1856 the Republican Party incorporated this perception into its platform by calling upon Congress to use its power over the territories to prohibit "those twin relics of barbarism—polygamy and slavery."

In 1862 Congress passed the Morrill Anti Bigamy Act, which prohibited the practice of polygamy in the territories, but made no provisions for its enforcement, largely because of the Civil War then preoccupying the nation. Following the war, the nation's efforts at reconstructing the South continued to allow the Saints to live with minimal outside interference. In the 1870s, however, a cry was again raised against the Mormon practice, and several federal officials attempted to initiate a crusade against plural marriage in Utah. As a result, Church leaders, believing that the Anti-Bigamy Act would be stricken down because it violated the Constitution's provision guaranteeing religious freedom, wished it to be tested in the courts. In 1874, George Reynolds, Brigham Young's personal secretary, volunteered to go on trial for practicing plural marriage. After the Morrill Act was upheld in the lower courts, the case was appealed to the Supreme Court, which unanimously sustained the law's constitutionality in January 1879. In 1882 Congress passed the Edmunds Act, which declared polygamy a crime and polygamous living a misdemeanor, and power was given to enforce the law. In October 1884 the first of many convictions for plural marriage was handed down. Rather than obeying what they felt was an unjust man-made law, however, many Mormons followed President John Taylor's policy of passive resistance and went "underground" into hiding.

Because the Saints continued to practice plural marriage, Congress passed the Edmunds-Tucker Act in 1887. This bill increased the government's power to enforce the law by disincorporating the Church and allowing the government to escheat Church property in excess of $50,000. By June 1888 most of the Church's property, including the nearly finished Salt Lake Temple, was in receivership. Inasmuch as Church members' continued practice of plural marriage threatened the very existence of the Church, President Wilford Woodruff, after much consideration and prayer, and under inspiration from God, issued his famous Manifesto in September 1890 declaring his intention to obey the law of the land and advising all members to do the same, stating that he did so "under the necessity of acting for the temporal salvation of the Church."[23] With this announcement, many of the problems with the federal government ended, and the Church began a renewed emphasis on missionary work.

It was the government's attempts to end plural marriage that helped bring about the expansion and growth of the Church in California prior to the issuance of the Manifesto. During the "raid" on polygamists in the 1880s, several Saints went to California to hide from the U.S. marshals. Because of the anti-polygamy prosecutions and the ill feelings which existed towards the Mormons during this time, most Saints in California found it advantageous to keep their religious affiliation quiet. Joining with a few faithful members already there, they would form the nucleus for Church activity and missionary work when it was re-established in the state.

One man who left Utah for California to escape the law was Mark Lindsey. In July 1890, two months before the Manifesto, Lindsey, described as an "elderly man," moved with a wife and two children to Oakland "for his health" and because he was "in hiding."[24] A native of England, Lindsey was responsible for the first baptisms in northern and southern California as the Church was re-established in the state.

While walking the streets of Oakland looking for a place to stay, he saw a man of whom the Spirit said, "He is a saint; follow him."[25] The man, a Bishop Cutler from Lehi, Utah, had also come to California to escape prosecution for plural marriage. Bishop Cutler informed Lindsey that "there were several of us in

California on the 'Underground' and did not want to be known too extensively."

Among these Saints was J. W. Pickett, who had made acquaintance with Alfred and Charlotte Nethercott, their son Charles, and daughter-in-law Rebecca. The Nethercotts were members of the Church who had left Utah for the California gold fields. Because there was no Church organization in the mining districts, Alfred had became associated with the Reorganized Church of Jesus Christ of Latter Day Saints, although never fully accepting its tenets. However, as a result of Alfred's outspoken opposition to aspects of the RLDS Church and his attempts to make converts to the LDS Church from among the RLDS congregation, he was excommunicated. The family then began associating with the small Latter-day Saint colony in Oakland which had started holding meetings following the Manifesto. Alfred Nethercott also wrote an old friend, Seymour B. Young of the First Council of the Seventy, asking what his family must do to be rebaptized.[26]

In addition, Lindsey also wrote the First Presidency concerning the Nethercotts. To this letter, President Woodruff replied that Lindsey and Pickett were authorized "to act as missionaries in the midst of the people who you have sojourned among, and to baptize and confirm any who by sincere repentance show they are worthy of these blessings."[27] On 6 December 1890, Lindsey rebaptized the Nethercotts into The Church of Jesus Christ of Latter-day Saints in the font in the RLDS chapel in Oakland.

From the Nethercotts, Lindsey learned of Norman B. Phillips, a recent RLDS convert, whom Alfred Nethercott had tried to convert to the beliefs of the Utah Church. By this time, however, Norman Phillips had moved to Los Angeles for the winter and then decided to make Redondo Beach his home. In June 1891 Lindsey took his family on a vacation to Redondo Beach where he hoped to contact Phillips. Of his first Sunday in Los Angeles County, Elder Lindsey wrote in his journal: "There being no Saints in this place where we can meet together and worship God we spent the day on the beach."[28] Unknown to Elder Lindsey there was indeed a small group of Saints in Los Angeles County who had been living there for several years and were anxious for the kind of contact with the Church that he could have provided.

On 2 July 1891 Norman B. Phillips was baptized into the

Church in the ocean at Redondo Beach, the first convert in the new era of the Church in southern California. Because of his baptism, Phillips's wife left him, and, unaware of the small Mormon colony in Los Angeles, he shortly thereafter returned to Oakland to be with the branch of Saints in that city. Elder Lindsey returned to Utah also without making contact with the Saints in the county.

A year later, in August 1892, the California Mission of the Church was officially reestablished as John L. Dalton of Ogden, Utah, was called to work with the Saints at Oakland. Before the year was over, three other missionaries were called to California, and John Dalton was appointed president of the mission. Most missionary efforts were centered in the Oakland and Sacramento areas, where most of the Saints in California were known to reside. A branch was established in Oakland and another was reorganized in Sacramento. By 1893 President Dalton knew there were in Los Angeles three LDS families, totaling twelve baptized members, including two priesthood holders and three children under eight.[29] But the lack of numbers prohibited him from sending missionaries to assist them.

President Dalton continued to preside over the California Mission until he was replaced by Dr. Karl G. Maeser, a former president of Brigham Young Academy, in January 1894. Dr. Maeser was sent to California primarily to arrange and direct a Latter-day Saint educational exhibit for the Church at the San Francisco Mid-Winter Fair. Through the exhibit at the fair, Church leaders hoped to overcome some of the prejudices against the Mormons. *Campbell's Illustrated Magazine* of Chicago reported that "the exhibit made by the Mormon schools of Utah is a very interesting and attractive one. The work done by pupils in this display is, if anything, far superior to that shown in other exhibits and speaks well for the system of education prevailing among the disciples of Brigham Young."[30] During the fair the numbers attending the Oakland Branch were increased by visitors from Utah, but, as the mission historian recorded, "the seeming impetus given the work here by this increased attendance only served to intensify the loneliness of the few Saints" in the city.[31] While the fair helped to overcome prejudices, it failed to bring in the hoped-for converts.

On 26 July 1894, Henry S. Tanner of Ogden, Utah, received a call from the First Presidency to take over the leadership of the

California Mission on 15 August. President Tanner was barely past his twenty-fifth birthday when given this heavy responsibility. He was, however, not without mission experience. A week following his marriage to Laura Woodland on 5 March 1890, he left for a mission to the southern states, on one occasion being driven out of town by a South Carolina mob. In June 1894 he was called on a six week mission to the mining camps around Park City, Utah. Prior to his mission to the mining camps, Tanner had graduated from Brigham Young Academy with a Bachelor of Pedagogy [teaching] degree.

When the call came to go to California, the finances of the Church, the California Mission, and of the young President Tanner—who had spent most of his four-and-one-half years of marriage in school or on a mission—wouldn't allow him to take his family with him. Leaving his wife Laura and two children with her parents in Idaho until they were financially able to follow him to California, Tanner left on his mission. He arrived in Oakland and was greeted by Elder Henry B. Williams, a missionary who had served under both Presidents Dalton and Maeser and had agreed to extend his mission until President Tanner became acquainted with his duties.

From the time Henry Tanner set foot in California, he felt that the adversary was determined that he should not fulfill his mission.[32] Two days after his arrival he was stricken with a case of typhoid fever. At first he thought it was a return of the malaria he had contracted while in the southern states. With the help of Elder Williams and George Hyde, a member attending medical school, Tanner treated the illness the best he knew how. He remained sick for nearly two weeks when, finally, the fever made him delirious. Elder Williams called for a doctor, who diagnosed the illness as typhoid in its most advanced form and moved him to a hospital.

Three days later the doctor recommended that the next of kin be notified to be prepared for the worst, as there was no hope for President Tanner's recovery. The First Presidency was notified of his condition and quickly telegraphed Laura Tanner with the news. On 10 September she left the railroad depot in Ogden, arriving in Oakland 12 September. When she went to the hospital she found her husband "strapped to his bed, as in his delirious condition it was impossible for two strong men to handle him."[33]

Norman B. Phillips, the first convert in the Southland, remembers the concerns of the Saints when their new mission president was placed in the hospital:

> The Brethren obtained permission to administer to [President Tanner], after which they came to church and reported his condition. The Saints gathered there were filled with gloom and downhearted. We talked of his case and of the condition under which he was placed. It was suggested that we hold a prayer meeting and plead to our Heavenly Father in his behalf. We chose Brother Charles Nethercott to be mouth.
>
> It was one of the most eloquent prayers in behalf of the sick that I have ever heard. I want to testify that during and after that prayer there was the greatest outpouring of the spirit of God that I ever saw. When we rose from our knees, there was not a sad face, nor gloom in the building. The spirit testified to us each and all that all would be well with Brother Tanner. That he would get well and be amongst us again shortly, notwithstanding the unfavorable report given by the Doctors. I will never forget that meeting, and the calm, soothing and peaceful influence that filled our souls and gave to our minds an assurance of his recovery. At the hospital the Doctors were surprised at his rapid recovery, in fact they were surprised at his recovering at all.[34]

On 14 September 1894, President Tanner regained consciousness. Three weeks later, on 8 October he was released from the hospital, sufficiently strong to continue his mission. Laura Tanner was given a Church calling to take care of the mission home, and she remained with her husband until the time of the birth of their third child the following year.

On 15 November 1896, after two years and three months of service, Henry S. Tanner was released as president of the California Mission. When he had assumed the leadership of the California Mission, the only functioning branches were in Oakland and Sacramento. By the end of his administration, branches had been organized in Stockton, San Diego, Fowler, Latrobe, and Los Angeles. Church membership in the state had grown from less than 120 to over 400.

Before returning to Utah, President Tanner wished to leave a debt-free mission to his successor, but did not have money enough to settle with the mission's creditors. Accordingly, he went to his Heavenly Father in fervent prayer asking for the help he so desperately needed to leave the mission free of debt. The next morning, around 4:00 A.M., there was a knock at the door. When he answered the door, there stood a Brother Smith, a chemist from a nearby town who had recently joined the Church. After Brother Smith came in he asked, "President Tanner, do you need some money?" When President Tanner answered yes, Brother Smith told him that he had been awakened by a voice telling him to take the young mission president a certain sum of money. He then presented a check for the amount needed to leave the mission free of debt.[35]

Following their release, the *Deseret News* commented on the mission experience of the Tanners:

> When Elder Tanner arrived in California, the outlook for proselyting among the people was anything but encouraging. Indeed it looked as though Mormonism, of all religions, would receive a very cold reception and but little or no consideration from the people. So much prejudice existed against the Mormons, that the very mention of the name, was sufficient to bring out abuse and to make it next to impossible to be given a hearing. But things changed in time.[36]

And change they did. Not only did the feelings of the people in California change concerning the Church, but also the Church's attitude towards California changed. Gone were the days when many Saints feared that the Church and California were incompatible and that to move to the state meant spiritual death. Now it was felt that the Church could not only survive in California, but also thrive. Nowhere would this be more evident than in the Los Angeles area in general and the Los Angeles California Stake in particular.

Perhaps Laura Tanner best summed up the feelings of those who helped establish the Church in the state:

> None, except those who took part in the early missionary experiences of breaking down the prejudices and the indifferences of the people toward the Church in California can appreciate the struggle and sacrifices made by the Elders and the Saints. . . .
>
> Through the struggle, we felt confident that in time the Mission would be one of the great fields in which the Church would thrive and develop.[37]

A Sunday School, a Branch, and a Mission Conference

During the first few months of 1895, the number of missionaries serving in the California Mission climbed to sixteen. With the increase in missionaries, President Tanner opened new cities to missionary work, including Los Angeles. The first two missionaries assigned to Los Angeles, Elder John R. Smith of Sugar City, Utah, and Moroni H. Thomas of Ogden, Utah, arrived in that city on 16 March 1895. They brought with them the name and address of Eliza W. Woollacott, who had written mission headquarters requesting that missionaries be sent to Los Angeles.

Eleven years previously, on 5 July 1884, Henry J. and Eliza W. Woollacott had arrived in Los Angeles. With them were two of their daughters, Nellie and Winnifred, and two grandsons, Albert Henry Thomas and William Howard Thomas. They had moved from Salt Lake City so that their family might be together, as their oldest son, Henry, Jr., had moved to Los Angeles eight years earlier to make his fortune.

Both Henry, Sr., and Eliza were natives of England where they were converted to the Church. In the early 1850s both immigrated to America and made their way to Salt Lake City.

Eliza's trip is likely representative also of Henry's journey. After a six-week ocean voyage, she landed at New Orleans. From there, she spent three months traveling, mostly by ox team and foot, until she reached the Great Salt Lake Valley.

On 3 November 1855 Henry and Eliza were married in Salt Lake City. Nine children were born to their marriage, although only three would survive their parents. For thirty years the Woollacotts were active members of the Salt Lake Fourteenth Ward. Henry, a stone cutter by profession, spent twenty-five years working on the Salt Lake Temple before moving to California.

Much of the credit for the beginnings of the Church in Los Angeles belongs to the Woollacotts. When Henry and Eliza moved to Los Angeles in 1884 there were only two other known Latter-day Saints in the city, August L. and Freda H. Hedberg, Swedish immigrants who had moved from Ogden, Utah, the year before. Within five years, however, several other Mormons were engaged in business enterprises in the city. On the same block where Henry Woollacott, Jr., ran a wine-importing and exporting business at 245 South Spring Street, Hans C. Jacobson, later to be first president of the Los Angeles Branch, opened a bakery. In the northeast part of the city, John Johnson ran a pigeon farm on Riverside Drive, just east of Elysian Park. In the Boyle Heights area, a family named Rothlessberger operated a dairy. It was also during this time that Eliza was left a widow, Henry having died in May 1888 after a long illness.

Because of a lack of records, almost nothing is known concerning the Church in Los Angeles during the years prior to 1895. What is known is that because of limited contact with the Church resulting from a lack of missionary activity in California, the emphasis placed on the "gathering," and the federal government's crusade against polygamists, these families were mostly left to provide for their own spiritual needs.

The first stop Elders Smith and Thomas made in Los Angeles was at Eliza Woollacott's home. Elder Thomas wrote in his journal that when Eliza saw that missionaries had been sent to Los Angeles, she wept tears of joy and told them that "she had been praying to the Lord that He would send missionaries to her home."[1]

With her prayers answered, Eliza worked to assist the missionaries in their work. The Woollacott home at 220 North

Grand Avenue became the "cradle and refuge" for members and missionaries during the infancy of the Church in Los Angeles; its doors were always open for missionary cottage meetings. Eliza's encouragement of the missionary program and her influence and enthusiasm paid dividends as Elders Thomas and Smith were able to baptize eleven people during their first six months in Los Angeles and located a number of Saints who had migrated from Utah.

In addition to being open for missionary work, the Woollacott home was also used for Sunday School and sacrament services, as well as for social activities. With the increase in Church membership and with the growing number of investigators, larger quarters were soon needed. Accordingly, the elders rented a small storeroom at 516 W. Temple, the rear portion of which was used as a missionary apartment.

By June 1895, however, these quarters also were outgrown. Eliza, therefore, gave to Elder Thomas a letter of introduction to her son, Henry, Jr. As a result, Thomas was able to obtain at no cost the use of a large third story room in Henry's business on Spring Street. Thus this building, known as the Foresters' Lodge Hall, became the third meeting place in three months for the small Los Angeles Mormon colony. While the Foresters' Lodge could be used only on Sunday and only occasionally on a weekday evening, it could seat more than one hundred comfortably and provided space for socials.

Only seven months after Elders Thomas and Smith had arrived at Eliza Woollacott's door, a branch of the Church was organized in Los Angeles. On 18 October 1895 President Henry S. Tanner arrived in the city to attend the first meeting of the Southern California Conference of the California Mission and to organize the Los Angeles Branch of the mission. Of this first conference in Los Angeles, held 20 October 1895, Elder Thomas informed the readers of the *Deseret News*:

> It affords me much pleasure as clerk of the Southern California Conference to report to you the proceedings of our meetings held in [Los Angeles]. Friday afternoon Elder Henry S. Tanner, President of the California Mission, arrived from San Francisco . . . and arrangements were made for a Sunday School, a Branch and a Conference organization.
>
> This morning [Sunday] we met and organized a Sunday School with about twenty pupils. Elder William N. Woodland was appointed superintendent of the Los Angeles Sunday School, and Miss

Winnifred Woollacott as secretary and treasurer, and Oscar Berg, assistant.

At 2 p.m. the meeting was called to order. After a devotional exercise Elder Parley T. Wright was chosen president of the Southern California Conference, and Moroni H. Thomas as clerk. A branch of the Church was also organized with Hans Jacobson as president and Emile Berg as clerk. There were forty at our afternoon services. . . .

There were eighty at our evening services who listened attentively to Elder Tanner depict the rise and progress of the Church. . . .

Sister Woollacott will give an entertainment for the Saints in this city next Thursday evening. She deserves special mention for her extensive hospitality. She has done everything in her power to make this part of the mission a success.[2]

No auxiliary organizations were established at this time as they were not then part of the prescribed Church program. Membership in the Relief Society did not automatically come with Church membership.[3] Only those who wished to belong were enrolled in the organization, although all women were encouraged to join. Membership of youth in the Mutual Improvement Association and of children in the Primary was likewise discretionary. However, with the establishment of the Los Angeles Branch, the framework was in place for the eventual organization of these auxiliaries when numbers would justify it.

With a branch of the Church established in Los Angeles, membership continued to grow; by the end of 1895 seventy members, including children, were listed on the mission records. Within a year of its organization, membership in the branch had reached 120, and the Los Angeles Branch was the largest in the state. In large part, this increase was the result of migration from the Intermountain area to California for its expanded educational and economic opportunities, and its warmer climate, which often aided in the recovery from illnesses. Also, the missionaries laboring in Los Angeles were meeting with good success. In the five months following the organization of the Los Angeles Branch, forty-seven cottage meetings were held, eight hundred tracts and five thousand Articles of Faith cards were handed out, and several new converts were made.

In November 1896, thirteen months after he organized the Los Angeles Branch, Henry S. Tanner was replaced by Ephraim H. Nye as president of the California Mission. Like Eliza Woollacott, President Nye was born in England and joined the

Church there before immigrating to Utah. He later returned to serve a mission in his native England prior to being called to preside over the Saints in California.

One of the first actions taken by President Nye was a change in missionary policy to accord with a passage in the Doctrine and Covenants that encourages missionaries to go forth without "purse or scrip." (D&C 24:18.) As a result, missionaries moved out of their apartments and began traveling their areas, relying upon the good will of local residents for food and lodging. To implement this policy, missionaries were no longer assigned specifically to a city but were assigned two to a county. Elder A. G. Bowman reported in a meeting of the Southern California Conference of "kind treatment and high prospects" in Los Angeles County.[4] He and his companion "had traveled entirely without purse or scrip and God had manifested His power to them in many ways."[5] However, missionaries in other parts of the mission were not treated as well, and the number of baptisms diminished as more missionaries were now working in less populated areas. The decline in baptisms led to the discontinuance of this program; within a year missionaries were once again assigned to the cities, and the number of converts again began to rise.

Unlike many other areas of the world where missionaries labored and the Church expanded during this time, Californians seldom, if ever, displayed open hostility to the Church. In England missionaries were tarred and feathered, mobs gathered against the Mormons, and rocks were thrown at chapels as vicious stories circulated concerning Mormon polygamy and mythical tunnels leading to Salt Lake City. The strong opposition, however, did not hamper missionary efforts, and many converts continued to be made in Britain. Similarly, the Southern States Mission, where anti-Mormon feelings ran high, was the most productive mission in the Church at the time. However, while the Church grew in California, the numbers were far fewer than in areas where open opposition brought the Church to the foreground of people's attention. The problem in California was one of indifference to the missionaries' message. One missionary informed those at home that the greatest opposition the missionaries were experiencing was "the cold indifference on the part of the people generally in regard to what we have to tell them. . . . If we were to judge from apparent apathy manifested in religious matters, we would be compelled to say that the 'honest in heart' are extremely scarce."[6]

When missionary work resumed in earnest in the cities of California, street meetings became the normal means of preaching the gospel, with special emphasis placed upon reaching those attending holiday events like the annual Los Angeles celebration, "La Fiesta." In a typical street meeting the missionaries gathered on a street corner, sang a hymn to attract attention, and then delivered sermons to those who would listen. As a missionary tool, these meetings were successful, for "large, intelligent audiences, approaching the hundreds" would often gather with the results that friends of the Church were made, many prejudices disappeared, sacrament meeting attendance increased, and "some baptisms" were realized.[7] During one four-month stretch eight baptisms resulted from street meetings. The influence of Los Angeles street meetings, however, was not limited to the city, but extended throughout the nation since many of those reached by the missionaries were vacationers from the East who then returned home with better impressions of Mormonism, often asking for missionaries to be sent to their homes.[8]

City officials would occasionally force the missionaries to hold their meetings on a particular street corner by refusing them permission to use other streets in the city. President Nye related in general conference one of his experiences at a meeting on this street, which he called "the lowest spot in Los Angeles."[9] In this area of saloons where the "riffraff" met, the missionaries often could hardly hear themselves because of the "lewd songs that were being sung inside of the saloons."

President Nye recalled that the listening crowd, composed mainly of blacks, Hispanics, Orientals, American Indians, and a few whites, was "about the hardest looking lot that [he] ever gazed upon." As he stood at the edge of the "motley crowd" waiting his turn to speak, he thought, "if we could baptize this whole lot they are not worth having." He told the general conference audience: "My soul sank down to my boots. . . . I felt so disheartened, so discouraged to think that here was one of the great cities of the country and a fine people, but the rules of the city councilors were such that we could not go upon the better streets; we had to take that corner, and here we had to stand and speak to such a lot of people." However, as he began to address the crowd:

> The Spirit of the Lord rested upon me more and more, and it seemed as though they became beautiful before me. It seemed to me as though, instead of having the thought that I wouldn't do anything for them, I was filled with the feeling that I could not only preach the Gospel to them, but if necessary I could lay down my life for them. I continued on until the Spirit of the Lord rested upon me so abundantly that it seemed as though I did not stand upon the ground. It seemed as though a mighty power surrounded me and caused me to see the value of their souls to the Lord. . . . I spoke on, filled with the Spirit, overcome with the joy, that I had known under no other circumstances in human life.[10]

Like Peter in New Testament times, President Nye learned a lesson that day about all of God's children, a lesson that would, several years down the road, become a dominant theme and force in the Los Angeles California Stake.

President Nye and his missionaries served the Lord and the Saints in California not without personal difficulties. In April of 1897 Elder James Christensen was released early from his mission on the account of the death of one of his children, the second who had died since his mission began. Elder Alonzo E. Wall was transferred to Los Angeles from San Francisco after returning from a trip to Utah to bury one of his children. A short time later Elder William Beecher was found dead at the conference headquarters at 522 Temple Street, having been asphyxiated by a leak in a gas heater. In spite of these tragic events, the Church in Los Angeles continued to progress, and by 1897 three missionaries were laboring in the city, with two more laboring in the unincorporated areas of the county.

Under the direction of President Nye the Los Angeles Branch moved ahead. On 21 April 1897 George L. Matthews and Frederick Brown were sustained as counselors to President Jacobson in the branch presidency. The following month, on 7 May 1897, a Relief Society and Mutual Improvement Association were organized in the branch. Eliza Woollacott was called as the branch's first Relief Society president, with Freda H. Hedberg, Harriet Rand, and Sarah A. Matthews as counselors, and Nellie Woollacott Howland as secretary. H. E. Peterson was sustained as MIA president with Oscar Berg and Robert Rand as counselors.

As branch membership continued to increase, the branch once again outgrew its quarters, and a small chapel was acquired on 10th Street, just east of Grand Avenue. This building had been used by a Scandinavian Lutheran congregation until they also outgrew their quarters and offered them for rent.

Beginning in 1908 priesthood meetings in the wards and branches throughout the Church were held on a weekly basis, usually on a week night.[11] Prior to this time, they were held on an irregular, although usually monthly, basis. This change was brought about in part because Church leaders were concerned that priesthood holders should seek brotherhood in the priesthood rather than in fraternal lodges.[12]

In the early days of the Los Angeles Branch, priesthood holders in the city were always invited to the Southern California Mission conferences, and since all the missionaries at the time were male, these were usually referred to as "priesthood meetings." A social given by the members of the branch always followed these meetings. One social was held in the Grand Army of the Republic Hall, with two hundred people present. A short program preceded the dancing and ice cream. Another was held in the Marmonial Hall with 175 present. At 7:30 P.M., according to mission records,

> Elders, Saints and friends met at the hall to participate in a grand sociable that had been arranged by the local Saints. After a short program consisting of speeches of welcome, songs, recitation and instrumental music, all hands sat down to a beautifully decorated and heavily loaded table. After partaking of the bounties and luxuries of the board, the musical instruments gave signal for the dance which was much enjoyed.[13]

Other favorite socials included picnics at East Lake Park or Terminal Island Resort and trips to Catalina Island.

In 1899 Hans and Margaret Jacobson returned to Utah and George L. Matthews became the new branch president. Also, Freda H. Hedberg replaced Eliza Woollacott as the Relief Society president. Records show that as the twentieth century approached, branch membership fell to 107, including children, with attendance at meetings ranging from forty-five to eighty-seven persons. Membership declined as many Saints, like the Jacobsons, were caught up in the spirit of the "gathering" and moved to Utah.

    This spirit of gathering to Zion presented a real problem for
the growth of the Church in California. At the 1903 general conference, Joseph E. Robinson addressed this issue: "We can only
make converts fast enough to replace those who come to Zion, in
spite of the fact that we do not preach to them to gather. We
would rather have them stay with us to strengthen the
branches; but . . . the spirit of gathering comes upon them
when they have taken upon them the name of the Lord Jesus
Christ."[14]

    While branch members were few in numbers, they pos-
sessed a great deal of musical and dramatic talent. Recognizing
that Mormonism advocated a well-rounded life, they did not
hide their talents, but presented many musical and dramatic
productions in the early days of the branch. The first recorded
musical and dramatic evening occurred on 20 July 1900, when
the elders and Saints in Los Angeles presented "an entertainment to the public that would have been a credit to many
stronger organizations." The program consisted of "two one act
dramas, interspersed with solos, quartets, and recitations, etc.
. . . Many strangers were in attendance and expressed themselves as being pleased both with the entertainment and the
association of the Saints." It was concluded that "not only will
the branch be benefited in a financial way" by the entertainment, but good would also come "from getting a few more interested in the work being done by the Elders."[15]

    In the spring of 1901, President Nye was released as the
California Mission president after four years of service to become
president of the Southern States Mission. The responsibility for
the work in California then fell upon thirty-three-year-old
Joseph E. Robinson.

    Born in Pinto, Utah, and raised in Kanab, Utah, Robinson
was a merchant by profession and was active in Utah politics.
He served in the Utah State Legislature and was a member of the
Utah Constitutional Convention which drafted the state's constitution in 1895. He was called as a missionary to California in
June 1900, and then called and sustained as president of the
California Mission in May 1901, a position he would occupy
until April 1919—a total of nearly eighteen years. As revealed
through his letters, he was a kind and loving man who had inter-
nalized the covenant of baptism as set forth by Alma in that he
was "willing to bear [others'] burdens," "mourn with those that

mourn," and "comfort those that stand in need of comfort." (Mosiah 18:8–9.) When one of the members of the mission became pregnant out of wedlock he wrote her mother:

> I have seen so much of the world . . . in this mission that my heart is full of sympathy for the girl who has had to go out into the world to make a living and has come in contact with the men of the world. No one not acquainted with the conditions . . . can appreciate how determined the adversary is to undo them. . . . I advise you to write in love and not reproach her too much for she might be driven to worse things than she has in her present state of mind. . . . Her punishment is very sore and it will be a long time before it grows less.[16]

When another member of the mission needed money, Robinson sent him all the money he had and wrote that he "only wished it could have been two hundred" rather than two dollars.[17]

Following his call as mission president, Elder Robinson moved his family from Kanab to the mission headquarters situated in San Francisco. Here the family remained until 1906, when the mission headquarters were moved to Los Angeles following the San Francisco earthquake and fire. When the great earthquake rumbled through San Francisco at 5:13 A.M. on 18 April 1906, the mission home at 609 Franklin Street survived with little damage, but did not escape the resulting fire. On 28 April 1906 President Robinson moved his family to Los Angeles and initiated construction of a mission home on West Temple near conference headquarters. President Robinson did not make clear the reason for the move, but like many in the city he probably worried about future earthquakes. Additionally, life in San Francisco had been disrupted and would remain so for some time. Therefore, a new location would provide the most conducive environment for continuing missionary work. Furthermore, by the time of the earthquake, there were more Saints in Los Angeles than in San Francisco, and within a dozen years Los Angeles would experience what President Heber J. Grant called "the greatest [Church] growth of any city in the history of the world."[18] With the mission headquarters in Los Angeles, the way was opened for the Church to have the necessary local leadership in the city when migration from the Intermountain West, then a trickle, became a flood following World War I.

After a short period of time on West Temple, the mission home and office were moved to a house on 10th Street, next door to the Los Angeles Branch chapel. Rooms in the mission home were then available for use as Sunday School classrooms by the branch.

In 1906 George and Julia Handy moved to Los Angeles from Idaho and introduced the first parents' class into the Los Angeles Branch Sunday School; prior to this time Sunday School instruction had been only for children. At the same time that changes were being made in the Los Angeles Branch Sunday School program, President Joseph F. Smith was optimistically looking to the day when every priesthood council would not only understand its duty, but also magnify its responsibility. "When that day shall come," he stated, "there will not be so much necessity for work that is now being done by the auxiliary organizations, because it will be done by the regular quorums of the Priesthood. The Lord . . . has made provision in the Church whereby every need may be met and satisfied through the regular organizations of the Priesthood."[19] Such a vision began to be fulfilled as reforms, such as weekly priesthood meetings and revitalized ward teaching, were implemented.

Prior to the turn of the century, ward teaching was the responsibility of the Aaronic Priesthood. Beginning in 1902, the Presiding Bishop authorized the calling of Melchizedek Priesthood holders to accompany priests and teachers on their visits to the homes of the members. These men were dubbed "acting priests" and "acting teachers" inasmuch as they were acting in the duties of the Aaronic Priesthood and were helping train the young men in their duties. The change not only helped improve the quality of ward teaching, but in urban areas such as Los Angeles, it also improved the quantity of home teaching not only by making available more ward teachers, but also by providing transportation for youth who might not otherwise have been able to visit their scattered families. Because most members were isolated from other Church members and contacts outside of Sunday meetings were few, visits to each home were viewed as extremely important. Thus, in spite of unpaved roads and the great distances between families, ward teaching percentages were seldom lower than those of later periods when ward boundaries were smaller and better transportation was available.

Also during this time, Church leadership began evaluating the lessons of the various organizations in the hopes of better correlating them. As part of this effort, George D. Pyper, General Church Sunday School superintendent, wrote President Robinson regarding the viability of Sunday School instruction in the California Mission. Robinson replied that he found Sunday School to be "the best *organized* missionary, if I may be permitted to designate it that way" as throughout the mission non-Mormons attend the meetings "because of the very atmosphere of genial fellowship."[20] He also found the manuals to be, for the most part, very profitable for the instruction of nonmembers as well as members.

However, he identified two problems in using Sunday School manuals written mainly for the majority of Church members, who lived in rural Utah, and in trying to adapt them to urban California in particular and the mission field in general. First, these manuals often "dealt with many questions peculiar to our people in their own villages, etc.," such as taking care of city parks, which could not easily be applied outside of Utah. Second, many of those in attendance were either new converts or investigators who usually "had not graduated from anyone of the lower grades of the Sunday School" and did not have the background to "jump from Nephi to Helaman, then Alma, Mormon or Moroni for some doctrinal point . . . for they do not know who these men are nor the conditions of the people of their day and time." As a result, the Saints in California studied the standard works chronologically to improve their background knowledge and then seized "upon the doctrinal points as they have been met."

During these early years visits by General Authorities of the Church to Los Angeles were common and helped strengthen the Mormon community. Frequent visits were made possible by the completion of a railroad line in 1905 directly connecting Salt Lake City and Los Angeles. Often the brethren visited the branch on their way to other areas, and at other times they came primarily for the healing effects of the ocean breezes. The Church even purchased a retreat home in Santa Monica in 1913 where members of the First Presidency could go to relax. Five years earlier, in 1908, President Joseph F. Smith and several of the Brethren made a tour of the California Mission and while in Los Angeles they were entertained at the prestigious Jonathan Club. Most of the Brethren on this visit expressed great optimism concerning the possibilities for the Church in the state.

In 1910 Hyrum G. Smith, the President of the Los Angeles Branch, became one of the General Authorities of the Church. Smith had moved from Salt Lake to Los Angeles to attend the

University of Southern California Dental School and following graduation had remained in the area to establish his practice. When George L. Matthews was released as branch president in 1911, Hyrum Smith became the new branch president, serving until he was released to become the Patriarch to the Church the following year.

In 1912 the Church's membership in Los Angeles received a boost from Pancho Villa and the Mexican Revolution. Before Wilford Woodruff issued the Manifesto forbidding the practice of plural marriage in the United States, many Saints had moved to Canada and Mexico to continue this practice. Several Mormon communities were established in northern Mexico. When these families were forced to flee Mexico and the revolution, some returned to Utah, while others helped lay the foundation for the establishment of the Church in Arizona and Texas—and several families migrated to Los Angeles.

Even though the Church was growing, its numbers were still relatively small. In 1912 it was estimated that there were only three hundred Church members in all of southern California and these were spread over large distances. The Los Angeles Branch embraced an area extending from Orange County to the San Fernando Valley. Because of the distances involved in going to Church and because relatively few members owned automobiles, those who did seldom went to Church without picking up others and taking them to meetings. For those without access to cars, attending Sunday services often involved a real journey. Elise Connover Dyer's family, for example, lived near Griffith Park; to attend Sunday services, her father drove their horse and buggy to Western Avenue and Hollywood Boulevard, where the family caught the red street car downtown and then the yellow street car to a stop near the meeting place —a trip that took nearly two hours. Because of the distances involved, it is hardly surprising that no attempt had been made to organize a Primary and that the Relief Society and MIA met irregularly. For a period of time, sacrament meeting and Sunday School were even scheduled back to back.

By 1912 there was a measurable Church membership in the southern portion of the county. As a result, a Sunday School was established at Long Beach. Sixteen members attended the first meeting held in the home of Sussana D. Morrison. Subsequent meetings were held in the Morrison and Lars J. Larson homes.

Two classes were taught, one in theology for the adults and the other in Primary instruction. A Relief Society was organized in December 1914 with Christina Larson as president, and the following month an MIA was organized. While the Saints met in Long Beach for these meetings, they came to Los Angeles Sunday evenings for sacrament service. These organizations dependent upon the mother branch not only allowed local leadership to more fully develop in preparation for the day when an independent branch would be established, but also assured that the mother branch still had sufficient strength to thrive.

In 1913 a Sunday School was established in Ocean Park and Santa Monica. Unlike the Long Beach organizations, however, it was dependent upon the California Mission and not the Los Angeles Branch. Therefore, missionaries, rather than members, filled the leadership positions, and continued to staff whatever positions they could. The one position usually filled by local members was Relief Society president because of the lack of sister missionaries. In July 1918 a Relief Society was established in Ocean Park with Adelaide Snyder as its president.

Because of the creation of the Ocean Park and Long Beach Sunday Schools, the Sunday schedule of the Saints in these areas became much more convenient. Instead of traveling to Los Angeles twice each Sunday (once for Sunday School and again in the evening for sacrament meeting), they now could stay home for Sunday School and had to go downtown only once. This also relieved some of the overcrowding at the Los Angeles Branch Sunday morning.

Nevertheless, Church membership in 1913 was still greater than the South Spring Street facilities could support, and the decision was made to build the first LDS meetinghouse in Los Angeles. Robert Taylor was given the assignment to draw up the plans, and President Robinson appointed Samuel Dailey, a building contractor and recent convert, to supervise construction. A large piece of land was purchased on Adams Boulevard for $5,500, and construction of the Los Angeles Branch chapel began.

Early in 1913, a cornerstone containing a brief history of the Los Angeles Conference of the California Mission and the standard works of the Church was laid in the right front corner of the new building by President Anthon H. Lund of the First Presidency and Elder George Albert Smith of the Council of the Twelve

Apostles. On 4 May 1913 President Joseph F. Smith dedicated the building, which was referred to as the Los Angeles Branch chapel or the Adams chapel.

Construction of the chapel cost $20,000, with most of the funds being donated by the Church and only a minor portion being raised locally. It was built of red brick, accentuated with red sandstone imported from President Lund's hometown of Manti, Utah. Prior to the completion of the chapel, baptisms were performed in a covered municipal swimming pool on the corner of Third and Vermont, which the city let the missionaries use on the fourth Saturday of each month.[21] The Adams chapel served as an important focal point for the Church in the Southland for many years, as the first two stakes in California (following the discontinued stake in San Bernardino) were created within its walls. Immigrants from Utah in the 1920s would often make it one of their first stops in Los Angeles.

A prominent feature of the building was a large stained-glass window in the back of the chapel depicting Joseph Smith's first vision. This window cost $600, financed mainly by a contribution from Adam Petterson of Ogden, Utah, a friend of President Robinson. Another important feature was the chapel's size; it was built to accommodate four times the branch's population and was believed adequate to the needs of the Saints for many years to come. Yet, in spite of such foresight, local leaders did not anticipate the growth to come, and the chapel still was not large enough to handle the membership of the Church in Los Angeles following World War I. Within ten years a building ten times the size of the Adams chapel would have overflowed. North of the chapel a new mission home and missionary quarters were also built.

Nevertheless, these structures not only provided adequate facilities for Church activities for the time being, but also served as a valuable missionary tool. The Adams chapel was an attractive place where members could bring their non-Mormon acquaintances, and it functioned as a visible symbol of the presence and viability of Mormonism to the larger Los Angeles community. Of this point, President Robinson remarked:

> We have been able to erect a most beautiful chapel in Los Angeles, with a home for the presiding authority of the mission, and also a mission home and office for our office force and elders. Commercially speaking, since this has been done, our stock has advanced a hun-

dred percent and more. People who before were indifferent towards us, when they see what we have done, have been led to interest themselves and to seek our society, to ask advice and counsel at our hands, and they want to know what we think of various conditions other than that which we call religious. This offers an opportunity for telling something of the Gospel; and it is good to know that the man who thinks, sees the hand of the Lord in our success in reclaiming the waste places of Zion and in building up in the great centers of the land an evidence of the fact that God is with this people.[22]

For years these structures stood in Los Angeles as monuments to the vision and sacrifice of those who established the Church in Los Angeles. They were monuments not just to Joseph Robinson and Samuel Daily, but to Henry and Laura Tanner, Henry and Eliza Woollacott, Hans Jacobson, Henry and Freda Hedberg, Moroni Thomas, and all the others who helped ensure that the gospel would find a place in the Southland.

Prior to 1919, there is no record that Primary was held in Los Angeles. However, with permission of branch and mission leaders, Ada Gygi Hackel organized the first Primary Association at her home on East Santa Barbara. There is no mention in Church records that this primary was part of the official organization of the Los Angeles Branch, but primary would be included as part of ward organizations following the creation of the Los Angeles Stake.

In January 1919 Elder Joseph McMurrin of the Church's First Council of the Seventy was appointed President of the California Mission to succeed President Robinson, who was to be released after nearly nineteen years of service to the residents of California. On 21 April 1919 a testimonial was held in honor of President and Sister Robinson. In attendance were President Heber J. Grant and Elder Rudger Clawson of the Council of the Twelve.

At this testimonial, President and Sister Robinson were presented a cashier's check for the sum of $3,838 by President William J. Reeve of the Los Angeles Branch, as a token of the love and esteem of the Saints for his years of service to the Church in California. This money had come from the Saints throughout the mission and was given with the suggestion that it be used to build a home, preferably in California. Those who spoke about President Robinson praised his influence as a preacher of righteousness, his sensitivity to the needs of people, and his love.

To the many tributes President Robinson replied:

> In my childhood it was always my desire to be of service. . . . I have
> loved to serve and to be with you under all circumstances, and have
> rejoiced in it all, for it was service to the children of God. . . . I have
> loved and will always love the people of the California Mission, as
> you have loved me, and only because I feel that it is a gift of love can I
> accept the fund you have tendered me.[23]

This gift would eventually be used to purchase a home in Los
Angeles, where the Robinsons resided until they died. In the
meantime, however, as President Robinson told *Liahona: The
Elder's Journal*, "Whilst it is not expected that one could leave a
life's work without some heart throbs and pangs of regret at
separating from friends and loved ones; yet it is with joy I turn to
face homeward to the Stakes of Zion where the house of the Lord
is and his holy servants preside."[24] In this brief statement,
Robinson underscored the importance of extending not only the
blessings of Zion and its stakes to the Saints in California, but
also those blessings that can be had only in a temple.

During President Robinson's administration, the California
Mission, which covered California, Nevada, and Arizona, had
experienced remarkable growth. From 1901 to 1919 Church
membership had grown from less than 600 to 5,000 located in
fifteen branches presided over by local leaders and four
branches presided over by the elders. Church possessions had
grown from "some meager pieces of household furniture and
furnishings" to "real estate and buildings with furnishings
valued at more than $100,000."[25] In addition, the Saints had
experienced a rich outpouring of the spirit.

As President Robinson reported in the *Liahona*, through the
power of the priesthood, miracles and miraculous healings were
performed as "men have been called back from the very jaws of
death; the dumb have been made to speak; the deaf to hear; the
paralytic to arise and walk."[26] Through the fellowship of the
Saints and the gospel of Jesus Christ, "the discouraged have
been encouraged, the despondent filled with cheer; the fearful
made courageous; the weak given strength; the froward have
been recalled and the wicked reclaimed from their evil ways; the
mourner has been comforted and the dead appropriately
buried"; and through untiring missionary efforts, "the name of
God has been acclaimed upon the highways and byways of
country, town and city." Concluded President Robinson, "God

has magnified us beyond our deserts and given inspiration and wisdom exceeding our experience and knowledge. Praised be His name forever!"

At the close of President Robinson's administration, it was indeed apparent that remarkable progress had been made in California. Not only were Church members moving to the state, but most immigrants were also viewing California as an ideal location for permanent residency, whereas before that many would only stay for a short time before "gathering" to Utah. To these Saints were added a growing number of converts who helped the Church to become viable. The members of the Church who resided in California were not the less faithful Church members as in the past, nor were they necessarily perceived to be; the prevailing feeling was that Zion could also exist outside the intermountain area. This feeling was fostered by the new pioneers of the Church in California, such as Eliza Woollacott, who showed that Church members could indeed live in the world and not be of it. Their examples paved the way for the first steps in the extension of Zion in California: the creation of branches and the building of chapels, which in turn were the motivation for Saints to come and the impetus for those already there to stay. Partially as a consequence of the faithfulness of those living the gospel in California, Church leaders—while not encouraging the Saints to leave Utah—were no longer publicly encouraging them to gather there.

During the twenty-four years between the creation of the Los Angeles Branch and the time that Joseph Robinson was released as mission president, the number of Saints in Los Angeles grew tenfold from around forty to nearly 400. Not only were they enjoying the blessings of California, but they were also enjoying many of the blessings of the Church and laying a foundation to build upon. Few members could have anticipated the remarkable growth of the Church upon that solid foundation laid by the faithful Saints of the Los Angeles Branch and the California Mission.

Exodus and Promised Land

F ew periods of growth in the Church have paralleled its expansion in California during the first eight years of Joseph W. McMurrin's leadership of the California Mission. When President McMurrin took over the mission in 1919, there were eighty-five Church organizations (conferences, branches, Relief Societies, MIAs, Primaries, and Sunday Schools) in California. Within a year, that number had increased to 115 organizations and by 1921 to 162. The significance of this growth can be seen in the fact that between 1919 and 1927, nearly one third of the branches established in the missions of the Church were created in the California Mission.[1] Between 1923 and 1927, over sixty percent of all wards and branches created in the stakes of the Church were created in California, most of them in the Los Angeles area.[2] By 1923 the membership in the Los Angeles County alone mushroomed from a 1919 level of around four hundred to nearly four thousand, necessitating the creation of a stake. In 1927, the eighth year of President McMurrin's administration, nearly eight thousand Mormons lived in the Los Angeles area, requiring the creation of a second stake in the city. In addition to the nearly eight thousand Latter-day Saints living in Los Angeles in 1927, another four thousand lived in the Bay Area and a stake was organized in San Francisco. There were also sizeable Mormon communities in San Diego, Sacramento, and Gridley. In the space of eight years the number of Mormons residing in California had grown from less than two thousand to nearly twenty thousand.

This remarkable growth of the California Mormon community came not so much from convert baptisms as through migration from Utah and surrounding states following the end of World War I. Between 1900 and 1920 Utah's population grew from 276,749 to 449,396. This growth was the consequence of the state's larger-than-average family size, the Mormon "gathering" to Utah, and an influx of non-Mormons coming to work in Utah's expanding mining and smelting industries. With the outbreak of World War I, Utah's economy was able to absorb this increased population as greater demands were created for the state's minerals, manufactures, and agricultural products. Almost all areas of the economy doubled as compared with the pre-war years, and even marginal farm land became profitable.

When the war ended in 1918 and demands for its products were reduced, Utah, along with almost all states in the Union, suffered a depression. Unlike most states, however, where the down-swing was severe but short, Utah and other Intermountain states would experience only a partial recovery. These states were far removed from the nation's major population centers and the cost of moving goods long distances over underdeveloped transportation networks prevented them from competing with products grown and manufactured near those centers. As a result, farm income in Utah declined to less than one half the level of the war years, retail sales dropped even below the average experienced a decade later during the Great Depression, and the number of Utah businesses that failed during 1921–1925 was greater than the number of failures ten years later.

Because of such conditions at home, many Utahns, like others in the nation hard hit by the depression, looked to other areas of the country for better opportunities. Mormons went east to Washington, D.C.; New York; Chicago; and other major cities where they helped form the nucleus of Church membership in those areas. California, because of its climate, proximity to Utah, and resilience in the face of depression, was viewed by many migrants as the ideal place to seek work; no community in California better combined these factors than did Los Angeles.

Following the war and for years afterwards, thousands of Mormons from the Intermountain West joined the tide of migration to the shores of the Pacific. Almost every Sunday new arrivals from Utah and the Intermountain states would join with the California Saints, who, having been in a similar position a short time before, not only welcomed them with open arms, but also sought them out to discover where they were from, to learn what was happening in their former residences, and to share news of those who had previously moved to the Southland. This growing body of Saints, anxious to keep informed, eventually led to the creation of a Mormon newspaper, *The California Intermountain News*, which was published "in the interest of former residents of the intermountain states now living in southern California." Its masthead showed a plane, car, and train leaving the Rocky Mountains for California.[3] Originally it published both news of the Church in California and information on who was visiting from the Intermountain West, who was going to the Intermountain West, who was getting married back home, who bagged a buck in the Utah deer hunt, and what changes were taking place back home, such as a chapel dedication in Firth, Idaho. Later, the paper became more oriented towards California news.

The large Mormon migration to Los Angeles carried with it major challenges. It was no small task to assimilate new arrivals, both spiritually and temporally, as rapidly as possible into their new environment, to procure meeting places for the rapidly increasing Church population, and to provide effective leadership for the new units which had to be created. The responsibility of addressing these new problems of mission management in Los Angeles and throughout California, and at the same time overseeing missionary work in California, Nevada, and Arizona fell to Joseph W. McMurrin.

In many respects a leader better able to meet these challenges scarcely could have been found. Not only was he the mission president, but as one of the General Authorities of the Church he also had full authority to accomplish his task. One acquainted with President McMurrin described him as a man who "knew Church procedure and was tactful and methodical in dealing with people. . . . Aside from [his] authority, and perhaps transcending it, this man was in his own right a great leader of men. He possessed tremendous spiritual vigor. He had a profound and unfaltering faith."[4]

Joseph McMurrin was born 5 September 1858 in Tooele, Utah, and as an infant moved with his family to Salt Lake City. As a young man he worked as a teamster in Utah's mining camps. At seventeen he was called on a mission to Arizona to help colonize the town of St. Joseph. Following his release from that mission he married Mary Ellen Hunter on 1 April 1879. Two years later he was again called on a mission, this time to the British Isles where he served in the Scottish Conference for two years.

In November 1885 Joseph McMurrin was accidently shot twice through the abdomen by a United States marshall on a raid looking for polygamists violating the Edmunds Act. His wounds were believed to be fatal, but Elder John Henry Smith of the Council of the Twelve visited his bedside and asked him if he desired to live. When he assured Elder Smith that he had a strong desire to live and to enjoy his family and to serve the Lord, the Church leader blessed him that he would live.

Joseph McMurrin went on a second mission to the British Isles in 1886, this time to England, returning to Utah four years later. In 1896 he was called to serve in the presidency of the European Mission. While on this, his fourth mission, he was called and sustained as a member of the First Council of the Seventy. In January 1919 he was appointed President of the California Mission, a position he held until January 1932 when illness prevented him from continuing in that calling. He passed away in Los Angeles in October of that same year at the age of seventy-four.

By the later part of November 1919, the Saints in Los Angeles County had outgrown the Los Angeles Branch chapel on Adams Street and the decision was made to create a second independent branch of the California Mission—at Long Beach— to help relieve the overcrowding. At least three factors favored the creation of the Long Beach Branch. First, the Church population in the southern portion of the county was sufficient to sustain a branch organization. Second, by 1919 a Sunday School, Relief Society, and MIA were functioning in the homes of members located in Long Beach. While it was difficult for auxiliaries to function on a large scale in an urban area such as Los

Angeles County, they functioned well on a smaller scale. Thus, these organizations formed the nucleus of a branch with members experienced in administering the programs. Finally, the Saints had prepared themselves for a branch by making arrangements for building a chapel. They had begun a fundraising campaign, and by September 1919 had purchased a chapel site on Atlantic Boulevard. The only thing lacking was authority from Church leaders to hold their own sacrament services and the appointment of a branch president to oversee the spiritual and temporal affairs of the Saints in the area.

On 23 November 1919, the Long Beach Branch of the California Mission was established under the direction of Joseph McMurrin with George M. Tonks as branch president. The following week, on 30 November, the cornerstone was laid for a chapel. By early autumn 1920 the new building had been completed at a cost of $22,000 and dedicated to the Lord as a house of worship. In 1921, the branch organized a primary with Pearl Miner as president.

By the spring of 1920 there were enough members in the northwest portion of the county to justify the creation of an independent branch there. On 16 May 1920, therefore, President McMurrin organized the third independent branch of the California Mission in Los Angeles County. Although the Saints met at the Masonic Hall in Santa Monica, they unanimously agreed that the name of the branch should be Ocean Park. Otto J. Monson was sustained as the first branch president.

As Church membership continued to grow over the next two years, branches and Sunday Schools were established throughout Los Angeles County. Branches were organized in Alhambra, Garvanza, Hollywood, Huntington Park, and Inglewood; Sunday Schools were established in Belvedere, Boyle Heights, Glendale, and San Pedro. Unlike the independent branches at Long Beach and Ocean Park, these new organizations were dependent branches and Sunday Schools. However, the strength of the Los Angeles Branch was such that these organizations were dependent on the branch and its president, William J. Reeve, rather than directly upon the California Mission.

As the number of Latter-day Saints increased throughout the county, they began to express a desire for a temple in their area. Church leaders in Salt Lake City listened to their request and investigated the possibilities of building one in Los Angeles. During the latter part of 1920, Harry Culver, developer of Culver City, offered the Church a six-acre tract for a temple. At first this offer was considered favorably by Church authorities, but after pursuing the matter during the winter of 1920–21, they declined it.[5] Evidently, the Brethren in Salt Lake City felt that building a temple at this time would only increase what was seen as an already alarming migration from Utah to California, which large migration, while strengthening the mission, was also adding a great burden to the mission's leadership. They were also concerned that accepting this gift would later involve the Church in obligations not then foreseen.

One monumental building erected during this time, however, was the Ocean Park chapel. In October 1920 the Saints in Ocean Park began laying plans for a fund-raising campaign to build a chapel. In February 1922 these plans were undertaken in earnest when a letter was received from the Masonic Lodge informing the branch that it could no longer use lodge facilities.[6] On 15 February a meeting was held at the First Presidency's retreat home in Santa Monica to discuss purchasing a building site. Present at the meeting were President Heber J. Grant, Presiding Bishop Charles W. Nibley, Apostle John A. Widtsoe, and President Joseph W. McMurrin; President Otto Monson, his counselors George F. Harding and James Thomas, and clerk N. C. Christensen of the Ocean Park Branch presidency were also present. There it was agreed that the branch should purchase a lot on the corner of Washington and Strand in Santa Monica for $4,000.

Only seven months elapsed from the purchase of the lot to the dedication of the Ocean Park chapel on 24 September 1922 by President Grant. The chapel cost $41,600 to build, with the local Saints contributing $12,000 and almost all the labor. Like the beautiful Adams Street chapel, the Ocean Park chapel was projected to be the finest the Saints could build. Also, as with the Adams Street chapel and several others in the Southland, a prominent feature was a beautiful stained-glass window. The Ocean Park window depicted Moroni delivering the gold plates to Joseph Smith and was a gift of Mrs. A. W. McCune of Ogden, Utah.

There were at least three reasons why these new pioneers working to establish the Church in Los Angeles and California tried to make their chapels and their activities the finest possible. First, all the buildings and activities were dedicated to the Lord, and they desired to give him their best. Second, while the stereotypical view of the Mormons as ignorant, backward people was disappearing, the Saints in California wished to show the world that those images had little basis in fact and that Mormons did not take a back seat to any other denomination. Finally, through these buildings and activities Church members were able to attain a sense of community among themselves as they enjoyed the beautiful setting and felt pride in their collective accomplishments.

The need to create and maintain a sense of community was especially important in an area such as Los Angeles where members were few. It was often difficult to achieve a sense of identity with the Church and as a Church when there was only one Latter-day Saint for every three hundred residents in the city, especially after coming from areas where Mormons were in the majority. In Utah, where people had constant contact with the Church and its members, and ward boundaries often encompassed only a few blocks, a sense of community was relatively easy to achieve. Ward buildings, socials, activities, such as plays, dances, and choirs, served to reinforce that sense of community. As the Church expanded into California, the needs of the Church members were different from those of the Utah Saints; therefore, they approached socials, activities, and chapels in a different way. The Saints felt that as pioneers for the Church they could not approach anything half-heartedly.

Chapels built in urban areas where Latter-day Saints were a minority gave Church members something in which to take pride because of their beauty. They also served to unite the Saints socially in a common goal as they labored together to build chapels that, when finished, served as symbols that the Saints were, indeed, a community and that the Church had made a commitment to remain in the area. A chapel also helped to legitimize the existence of the Church in the eyes of non-Mormons by providing a visible representation of its presence. As a result, these structures built during the early years of Church expansion in California were often more ornate than those in Utah, a fact which many in the Intermountain area saw as an extravagance. The need for chapels as symbols diminished over time, however, as the Church became more well known and especially when a more lasting and more impressive symbol—a temple—was built in the area.

Socials and activities serve the needs of Church members in much the same way as chapels do. While dances had been a regular part of the Mormon experience in Utah, they became even more important in the urban centers and were always of the finest quality. In southern California these activities helped assimilate new arrivals into the LDS community by giving members of the group a sense of identity with each other and with the Church. Activities and socials were also missionary tools and, as such, the quality of the event was always emphasized.

While socials and other activities were important for all members, they were viewed as particularly important for the youth to help ensure that they married within the faith. Because there was seldom even a handful of Mormons at school, the only major contacts with other Latter-day Saints for most youth of dating age came on Sundays and at socials and activities. Therefore, to help instill the values of Church leaders concerning temple marriage, it was important for young people to socialize in large gatherings with those holding similar values.

One important activity that served as an effective symbol of the Mormon community was the Los Angeles Conference Choir. Much of the credit for its success goes to William Salt, a Salt Lake City native who came to Los Angeles shortly after the end of World War I. A builder by trade, he was also both a musician and a musical director of outstanding ability. Shortly after his arrival in Los Angeles, Salt organized and directed this choir, composed of members of the Los Angeles, Long Beach, and Ocean Park branches. The choir often provided music for mission conferences, and during the summer of 1922 it presented Evan Stephens's cantata, "The Martyrs," which portrays the lives of Joseph and Hyrum Smith, at a concert in Balboa Park, San Diego. Nearly twelve thousand people attended the concert, which received favorable coverage in the southern California press. A few months later the choir provided a further public relations opportunity, at the same time enhancing the sense of community among the Saints, when it performed "The Martyrs" and another Evan Stephens cantata, "The Vision," written to commemorate the centennial of Joseph Smith's first vision, in the Long Beach auditorium.[7] Between five and six thousand people attended each performance, including President Heber J. Grant, who also addressed the gathering.

William Salt also organized a larger choir, the Young People's Chorus, to help meet the social needs of the youth.

Members of the Young People's Chorus were drawn largely from the M Men and Gleaners, and in time the Los Angeles Conference Choir was disbanded and Salt put all his energy into the new choir. He had such a great love for the Young People's Chorus and such a strong belief in the need for it, that even after he moved to Phoenix he continued as its director, frequently making the long drive to Los Angeles. The Young People's Chorus helped many LDS youth of Los Angeles to identify more fully as members of the Church and also to find marriage partners within the faith.

One of the major concerns of the Latter-day Saints has always been that of keeping family members active in the Church, and as the Saints moved from Utah to gentile southern California, that concern was magnified. Parents and Church leaders were especially concerned because they were a minority group and the values they had shared with their fellow Saints in rural Utah were not shared to the same degree by the majority in urban Los Angeles. Church leaders, therefore, gave added emphasis to the importance of the family in combating those forces that came in conflict with Church standards.

One recognized way of strengthening the family was the implementation of regular family-oriented activities. As early as 1915 the First Presidency had encouraged the Saints to implement such a program, declaring: "If the Saints obey this counsel, we promise that great blessings will result. Love at home and obedience to parents will increase. Faith will be developed in the hearts of the youth of Israel, and they will gain power to combat evil influences and temptations which beset them."[8] While it would be many years before the Church would undertake an official weekly family home evening program, there were many members who followed the advice of President Joseph F. Smith and his counselors and implemented this program for themselves. Shortly after his arrival in Los Angeles, President McMurrin was encouraging the Saints in Los Angeles to set aside one night a week for the family.

One family in Los Angeles who had been holding weekly family home evenings and had found a successful way to implement the program was the Joseph and Lois West family. For a Los Angeles District Conference in 1922, President McMurrin invited the Wests and their children, Jack, Venice, Lois, and Edna, to demonstrate how to hold a family home evening.[9] The program consisted of an opening prayer and hymn; a song by Lois (the mother), who accompanied herself on the guitar; a lesson from the Bible by Joseph; a song and dance by Lois (the daughter), "I'm Forever Blowing Bubbles;" two popular songs sung by the whole family and accompanied by Jack on the banjo and Edna on the ukulele; a song and dance by Joseph and Lois, "Have You Seen My New Shoes?"; and a closing hymn and prayer. This was the first such demonstration ever to be made in the Los Angeles area, and it set an impressive standard indeed for other families to emulate.

While Church leaders worked to minimize the problems associated with belonging to a minority religion in an urban environment, their expressed concerns led to a rumor spreading through the Ocean Park Branch that the Brethren in Salt Lake City desired all Church members to return to Utah. Even though the Church had publicly discouraged gathering to Utah for several years and had encouraged the Saints to build up Zion wherever they resided, the Saints in Ocean Park asked Branch President Otto J. Monson during the summer of 1921 to write President Heber J. Grant concerning the "sentiment among the leaders of the Church against the movement of the Mormons to California."[10] When President Grant visited the Ocean Park Branch in October 1921 he assured the Saints that the day of the gathering to Utah was over and that "the idea of a permanent Mormon settlement at Santa Monica was in full accordance with Church policy."[11] Thus, from the prophet himself, the Saints in the Southland received word that Los Angeles in the 1920s was as much "the right place" as Salt Lake City and Utah had been in the nineteenth century.

Not only did the Saints in Santa Monica stay in this promised land, but so did most of the Saints in Los Angeles County, and new arrivals continually added to their numbers. In the April 1922 general conference, President McMurrin reported on the migration and spoke of what it meant to the Church in Los Angeles:

> These newcomers are strengthening, to a very wonderful degree, the branches of the California Mission. I suppose the largest branch that has ever been known in the Church is located in Los Angeles. This branch has a membership of about three thousand souls. The Los Angeles Branch is divided into a number of subdivisions. . . . where Sabbath schools are being held, where a preaching service is

conducted every Sabbath, and where Relief Societies have been organized.[12]

With this rapid growth it became apparent that the needs of the individual Saints in Los Angeles, as well as of the Church, would be better served by the creation of a stake. As Richard O. Cowan has pointed out, "The scriptures have identified 'stakes' as sources of strength. The prophet Isaiah, seeing the latter-day glory of Zion, wrote figuratively about her preparation for rejoicing: 'Enlarge the place of thy tent, and let them stretch forth the curtains of thine habitations: spare not, lengthen thy cords, and strengthen thy stakes.' "[13] Unlike mission organizations, "which generally must receive strength and leadership *from* the Church, a stake is able to *give* strength and stability *to* the Church, just as stakes support a tent."[14]

Thus, early in 1922 President McMurrin sent a recommendation for a stake to Church officials in Salt Lake City, who, after studying the proposal, concurred with it. During the month of April 1922, President Grant visited with George W. McCune, soon to be released as president of the Eastern States Mission, in the mission offices in New York City. President McCune's diary for 14 April noted, "I saw President Grant and received first hand word of my call to preside over a Stake of Zion to be established in Los Angeles."[15] He accepted the new call and made preparations to move to California. Although his home was in Ogden, Utah, McCune had previously expressed the possibility that following his release his family would join the thousands of Utahns who were moving to Los Angeles.

Shortly before President McCune was released from his mission, President Grant wrote him of his conviction that the step they were taking was the right one: "I believe that the organization of a stake in Southern California will do an immense amount of good. The more I think of this organization the better pleased I am with the conclusion that we came to, to have it organized."[16] Following his release at the end of June and a short visit to Utah, McCune moved with his wife, three sons, and a daughter to Los Angeles. By September 1922, four months prior to the stake organization, the McCunes had settled into a new home in Santa Monica, which had a reputation as a strong family community.

When the McCunes moved to Los Angeles they were not unfamiliar with the area, having visited the city on family vacations. However, the Los Angeles they moved to was drastically different, so far as the Church was concerned, from the one they had previously known. As President McCune became acquainted with the stake over which he would preside, he could not help but notice the differences among the Saints since he had last visited the area three years earlier. While the members of the Los Angeles Branch were faithful members in 1919, McCune found them even more so in 1922 and admitted that he was "astonished . . . at the wonderful devotion and interest shown by our people in the gospel of our Redeemer in that portion of the vineyard."[17] He further noted that these "people are taking a very active interest in the gospel, a keener interest even than they had taken at home." McCune also noted the remarkable growth of the Church evident during his visits to the various branches, which verified the need for a stake organization and larger facilities to accommodate the many Saints. On his first Sunday in Los Angeles he attended the Sunday School at Ocean Park and noted that "the little hall would not wholly hold our Sunday School children. As many as twenty-five children had to stand." That same day he also attended the services at the Los Angeles Branch:

> When I left that place a little over three years ago, their chapel was ample to accommodate them all. When I returned I found that little chapel was wholly inadequate for the Sunday night meeting, and every available space was taken for standing room. On the next Sabbath I visited another branch where the chapel was built about a year ago [Long Beach]. In that time the building had become inadequate. The next Sunday I attended services in our little chapel in Ocean Park. It is estimated that about 1200 attended our services there, and the new chapel was inadequate to hold the people.[18]

As indicated in this passage, McCune used the four months between his arrival and the stake organization to visit every branch in Los Angeles County to become acquainted with the members who would be in his stake and identify those men and women qualified to be stake officers and ward leaders. Not only were there sufficient numbers to justify a stake organization, but there was also sufficient leadership to run it effectively.

While McCune attempted to observe others for their leadership abilities, he himself was also being observed for his ability. Apparently, President McMurrin had not been apprised that George McCune was to be the stake president, but recognizing McCune as a strong leader, he called him to be the Ocean Park

Branch president in December 1922. Although realizing that his calling would only be temporary, President McCune gladly accepted it in the same spirit in which he had accepted all Church assignments throughout his life.

As with Joseph Robinson, George W. McCune was well suited to the task of leading the first stake in a metropolitan area. Born in Nephi, Utah, in 1872, he spent his boyhood in that city before graduating from the University of Utah. In January 1896 he was called on a two year mission to England where he first became acquainted with Joseph McMurrin, then a member of the European Mission presidency. During the latter part of his mission McCune joined with other conference presidents in England in drafting a resolution urging the General Authorities to secure better places of worship for the Saints in the British Isles. Because he was soon to be released, McCune was designated to present the resolution to the First Presidency. After hearing the resolution, the First Presidency invited him to present the matter before the priesthood session of the April 1898 general conference. McCune accepted the invitation and made an appeal for Church members to help provide better meeting places for the Saints in Europe.[19] From his experience in England, he learned the importance of the meeting place, and as president of the Los Angeles Stake he would insist that the Saints seek out the best possible environment in which to worship.

Following his mission to England, McCune moved to Ogden, Utah, where he was employed by John Scowcroft and Sons, a dry goods firm. He married Sara Alice Scowcroft and their union was blessed with four children. Sara passed away in 1931 and McCune married Florence Lysle Schofield, to whom was born one daughter. In 1919 he was called to preside over the Eastern States Mission, a position he held until he was released to preside over the Los Angeles Stake.

While McCune became acquainted with the Saints in Los Angeles, he also entered into successful banking, real estate, and insurance ventures. With a group of other Mormons in the Santa Monica area he formed the California Intermountain Investment Company, which purchased a sizeable tract of land in Mar Vista where the investors hoped to attract a large Latter-day Saint community. Many streets in this development were given Mormon names, with the main street originally to be named after President Heber J. Grant until the prophet asked the developers to change it.[20] McCune was also an organizer of the Bank of America and one of its directors for many years, which bank and its name were later merged with the larger Bank of Italy.

George McCune's success as a leader was not limited to the business world, for he was also a very successful Church leader. His philosophy as conference president, mission president, branch president, and stake president is summarized in the words of the James Edwin Markham poem he always carried in his pocket:

> He drew a circle that shut me out,
> Heretic, rebel, a thing to flout;
> But love and I had the wit to win,
> We drew a circle that took him in.[21]

Evarard L. McMurrin, a member of the first Los Angeles Stake high council and a son of Joseph McMurrin, later recalled President McCune's love, influence, and positive outlook:

> George McCune is a Christian gentleman of refining influence: gallant, jovial, companionable, his is a sanguine nature, a disposition to look on the bright side of things; to expect, to hope, and to work for the best. His cheery words spontaneously give cheer to others. His good humor radiates to all. Moreover, he possesses to a marked degree the power to imbue those among whom he mingles with a measure of his own amiability. To maintain an even disposition; to share with others the sunshine of life; to preserve the spirit of optimism which is the spirit of youth—these and other qualities are fairly indicative of the liberal and human principles to which George McCune has ever been an ardent subscriber.[22]

Just as the direction of the United States was shaped to a great extent by its first president, George Washington, so also was the Los Angeles Stake shaped largely by the example of its first president. Its achievements found their source of inspiration in the pattern of action instituted by George W. McCune, who has been characterized by almost all who knew him as "a refined gentleman." He would never give less than his best, and he refused to allow stake members to give less than theirs.

At the same time that McCune accepted the position as Ocean Park Branch president, President Heber J. Grant was visiting Los Angeles. Upon his return to Salt Lake City, he announced on 22 December 1922 that the time was right for the creation of a stake in California and that this momentous event would take place on 21 January 1923 at the next mission conference scheduled in Los Angeles. While President McCune continued to direct the affairs of the Ocean Park Branch, he also made quiet preparations for the organization of the stake. By the appointed day things were ready for the creation of the first stake in the Church in a major metropolitan area, and one of the first outside the Intermountain area.[23]

The Los Angeles Stake of Zion

On Friday afternoon, 19 January 1923, a meeting was held at the Los Angeles Branch chapel on West Adams Street as part of the quarterly conference of the Los Angeles Conference of the California Mission. In attendance were local and general Church leaders, including Presidents Heber J. Grant and Charles W. Penrose of the First Presidency, Elder George Albert Smith of the Council of the Twelve, Presiding Bishop Charles W. Nibley, President Joseph W. McMurrin of the California Mission and a member of the First Council of the Seventy, Axel Madsen and Preston Nibley of the YMMIA General Board, and George W. McCune. This meeting marked an important transition in the history of the Church, for its purpose was to discuss the creation of the Los Angeles Stake of Zion on the following Sunday. During the meeting George W. McCune's appointment as stake president was confirmed, as were those of Leo J. Muir and George F. Harding as counselors in the stake presidency. An important new era was dawning for the Church and its membership in southern California.

The next day, while the General Authorities and general Church officers made the final preparations for the conference sessions, the new stake presidency considered individuals to fill the high council and other leadership positions. Theirs was a herculean task, for in one day they had to create the framework for a stake organization where none had previously existed. By the end of the day, however, sufficient progress had been made that a stake could be organized with a majority of the presidencies, superintendencies, and high council positions filled.

Sunday morning, 21 January 1923, was a beautiful southern California winter's day as the Saints gathered at the Adams chapel for this historic occasion. A sense of excitement pervaded the Mormon community and in anticipation of the large numbers that would attend the conference, unsuccessful attempts had been made to secure a larger hall. However, as one of the newspapers reported, "an auditorium twice the size of the chapel could not have housed" the large congregation, for attendance at the two general sessions and priesthood session exceeded three thousand.[1] At the afternoon session alone, twelve hundred people crowded into the chapel. Lucille McMurrin Chipman later recalled that there had been few occasions when she had seen such a gathering of Saints: "Adams Ward was filled to overflowing. Even the balcony was jammed packed."[2] In addition, overflow meetings for the general sessions were held in the recreation hall.

President Heber J. Grant presided over and conducted all the sessions of the conference. Music was provided by the 110-voice Young People's Chorus under the direction of William Salt and accompanied by Louise Smith and Alexander Schreiner, a missionary assigned to the area who later achieved fame as Mormon Tabernacle organist.

During the first session on Sunday morning, a priesthood meeting, Presidents Grant and Penrose both reminded their audience of the momentous importance of the step they were about to take for both the Church and the Saints in southern California. President Penrose gave the opening address, telling those present that they were "assembled for a very important and exalted purpose, made necessary by the growth of the Church in this part of God's vineyard, to organize a stake of Zion. This should gladden the hearts of the people as it will give them the great opportunity of development in the activities of stake and ward organizations."[3] The value of the new stake organization, he said, would be in furnishing opportunities to serve to many California Saints who had not been able to take an active part. President Penrose also stressed the authority by which the work was done and recommended that everyone study Section 107 of the Doctrine and Covenants so as to better understand the priesthood. He closed by reminding those present that they were helping to lay "the foundation for the Kingdom of God broad and deep for that which is to come" and encouraged them to follow the Savior's command to "let every man learn his duty and do it."[4]

Following President Penrose, President Grant commented on the growth of the Church in the area. "No city in the history of the world has had the phenomenal growth of the city of Los Angeles," he said, "and to start out at this time with a great stake of Zion, I firmly believe, will lead to great development for the Church and its people in this district."[5] He then submitted to the priesthood for approval the General Authorities of the Church, the stake officers, and the name of the stake: the "Los Angeles Stake of Zion." The vote for approval was unanimous. In addition to the stake presidency, other officers sustained were James Thomas, stake patriarch; Alexander Nibley, stake Sunday School superintendent; and Vern O. Knudsen, YMMIA superintendent. Eight members of the high council, sufficient for a quorum, were also sustained: William J. Reeves, Samuel Dailey, Charles B. Stewart, Arthur F. Reddish, H. C. Healy, Bertram M. Jones, Everard L. McMurrin, and Thomas Lloyd.

President Grant announced that the stake would include Los Angeles County and the cities of Los Angeles, Ocean Park, Long Beach, and San Pedro, and noted that initially the stake would consist of seven wards: Ocean Park, Long Beach, Los Angeles, San Pedro, Huntington Park, Boyle Heights, and Hollywood. Alhambra, Belvedere, Garvanza, Glendale, and Inglewood would be branches of the new stake.

During the afternoon session President McMurrin addressed his remarks to the theme that "this is the work of God and not of men," reminding the congregation that "this is the Church of God and that it will never be given to another people."[6] The Church's Presiding Bishop, Charles W. Nibley, prophetically declared that the spirit had indeed testified to him that the stakes of Zion should be extended until Zion "shall cover the whole earth for the blessing of the people of the world. The prophecies in the Book of Mormon are being fulfilled, for it was said that the Saints would be scattered about the earth and yet they are being organized into stakes of Zion."[7] At the same meeting President Penrose declared that if "there was anyone who should feel like shouting 'Hosanna! Hosanna!' it was the people of this region, permitted to enjoy the blessings of nature in southern California and now to have the blessings of complete Church organization."[8]

President Grant again submitted the names of stake and general Church officers along with the name of the stake, this time for approval of the general membership. In addition to those officers submitted to the priesthood, Katherine R. Stewart was sustained as stake Relief Society president and Veda Savage as YWMIA president.

In the closing session of conference held Sunday evening, each member of the new Los Angeles Stake presidency was asked to speak. President George W. McCune addressed the subject of the work of God. He also advised the Latter-day Saints still in the Mountain West to consider carefully before leaving their homes for California in order to ensure that the numbers arriving in the state were not greater than employment opportunities. "Do not encourage members to come to California if there is nothing for them to do when they come here," he counseled.[9] President Leo J. Muir reminded all those present that because they were a minority group they must be the leaven of the loaf, and President George F. Harding urged the Saints to cultivate the Spirit of God.

President Grant closed the conference by speaking of the steadfast devotion and increasing testimony of the Latter-day Saints as they struggled to establish the work of the Lord. "Any work built upon a lie cannot endure," he assured the assembled Saints.[10] The expansion of the Church to California was, of course, one sign that it had endured.

With the close of the first Los Angeles Stake conference, a new era of Church history was inaugurated. Although the Los Angeles Stake was the eighty-eighth stake organized in the Church since the Saints moved to Utah in 1847, it was one of the first stakes outside the Intermountain West and the first in a major urban area since that time. As a result, the boundaries of Zion were officially extended to the Pacific Ocean, and, for the first time in the Church's history, a stake was created in an area where nonmembers overwhelmingly outnumbered members of the Church and continued to endure.

Although the Saints were excited that Zion had extended her borders, some worried that a stake might not survive in such an environment. The Church in Los Angeles has had to adapt to its environment, but its experience, especially during the early years, has shown that the Church could not only endure outside of Utah, but also flourish. Sixty years after the organization of the Los Angeles Stake, over 1600 stakes were located throughout the world, most of them in areas where Mormons were a small minority and many in the world's major urban centers. Daniel's prophecy that a stone cut out without hands would roll forth to fill the whole earth was being fulfilled. (Daniel 2:31–45.)

Following the organization of the stake there was still much work to be done before members could enjoy its full benefits. Stake organizations needed to be staffed and wards created, which would take several months to complete, and stake offices needed to be established. However, neither the Adams, Long Beach, nor Ocean Park chapels were equipped to be conveniently used as stake offices. As a result, stake offices were located in office space of the California Intermountain Investment Company on the third floor of the Hiberian Building, on the corner of Fourth and Spring Streets. Each Wednesday evening the stake presidency held its meetings there and on the second Wednesday of each month it met with the high council. Other stake organizational meetings and all stake conferences and conventions were held at the Adams Ward chapel.

Creating a stake organization where one did not formerly exist presented both problems and benefits to the California Saints. The major problem was that the entire stake leadership had to be chosen largely from among people who had no experience in running a stake organization. In addition, stake leaders often did not know each other and therefore faced special challenges in learning to work together.

At the same time, the new stake had some administrative advantages, for the new leaders were not tempted to make the situation fit too rigidly some preconceived understanding of how a stake should be run. Instead, they were able to create stake programs and positions to fit the special needs of the Church in their area. Most Church organizations then existing were geared for rural or small metropolitan areas, and many of the programs with a Utah orientation were unworkable in the huge urban setting where the Saints were a minority. Local

Church leaders, therefore, had to look to their own experiences and special circumstances to determine what would be best for the success of the Church in Los Angeles, since, in many cases, Church leaders in Salt Lake City could give little advice, having never had to address issues related to an urban Church organization. As a result, the early leaders of the Los Angeles Stake made the stake one of the most innovative in the Church. Recognizing the challenges that the stake was facing, the *Deseret News* predicted at the time of organization, "the Los Angeles Stake should prove itself one of the most progressive in the Church."[11]

Not only were the eyes of the Church upon the Los Angeles Saints in this new endeavor to see if a stake could survive intact in its urban setting but so also were the eyes of the people of Los Angeles, and the stake recognized the need to do things right. Because they were pioneers, stake members worked hard to ensure the stake's success. To help the Saints in their task, the stake presidency printed a message for the members of the stake to be delivered to each home by the ward teachers outlining those things necessary for the stake's prosperity. That message read in part:

> The Stake is well organized, well launched on its career. In many respects it has made marvelous progress, considering the wholly new and often bewildering problems that confronted us day by day. And even among the things which have seemed slow of accomplishment, we cannot think of one about which we are in any sense discouraged. Each objective will be attained in its own due time.
>
> Whence has come this success? It has come because the Spirit of God touched the hearts of a band of true Latter-day Saints—quickened them to action, and led them unitedly in a vigorous, enthusiastic effort to establish another unit of the Kingdom here in the Southland. Prayer, faith, loyalty—and action with a right good will behind it have brought us thus far on our road.
>
> We say all this in high joy, but also in deep humility. To have done what we have done has been a triumph—to stop where we are is failure. And every step in our progress is bringing with it new perplexities that make us, your Stake Presidency, yearn more ardently than ever for support from you and from On High. . . .
>
> [Your Ward Teacher] is instructed to exhort you to greater fidelity—great humility, greater self-denial. He will talk to you of family prayers, night and morning—of tithing—of attendance at sacrament meetings—of a 100% observance of the Word of Wisdom.
>
> Above all, he will urge you to keep alive in your hearts and in the hearts of your children a vigorous, powerful, definite faith in God

and in His goodness and justice and wisdom. And in your family circle, he will join in humble prayer by your side for Heavenly guidance and help in keeping true to that faith throughout all the years of your life. . . .

We want to feel that your response to [this message] is a renewal of your covenants and a firmer resolve to do your part in all things, great and small, that may contribute to the welfare of your people.

Certain that this is the spirit which this message will instill, we shall, as a Stake Presidency, go forward with renewed courage and happiness in serving you to the utmost of our ability.[12]

In an effort to meet the far-reaching challenges and opportunities of the new stake, the stake presidency established three goals for those engaged in Church service: (1) The cultivation of the cooperative spirit; (2) The adoption of the high standards attitude; (3) The development of the achievement habit.

Within a few weeks of the creation of the stake, most of the remaining leadership positions were filled. William G. Brown, a recently released California missionary who had helped organize the Ocean Park Branch, and a former mission secretary, became stake clerk. John S. Worsley, David W. Cummings, E. Fayette Marshall, and C. Don Harding were called to fill the vacancies in the high council. It was over three months, however, before Cora W. Leaver was sustained as president of the Primary Association and Lars J. Larson became president of the Los Angeles Stake high priests.

In addition to filling stake positions, the new stake presidency set about creating wards. On 11 February 1923, three weeks after the stake was organized, stake leaders met in the Ocean Park chapel to organize the first ward in California since the closing of the San Bernardino Ward in 1857. President Heber J. Grant presided at and conducted this meeting. David O. Stohl, who had recently moved to Los Angeles to establish California offices for Beneficial Life Insurance Company, was installed as the first bishop. He thus became not only the first bishop of the Ocean Park Ward, but also the pioneering bishop in the new era of the Church in California.

The formation of other wards quickly followed. On 26 February, the Huntington Park Ward, with Fred Baker as its bishop, was organized; and the following week, on 4 March, Hollywood Ward was created and Melbourne C. Stewart sustained as bishop. On 11 March the Adams and Boyle Heights Wards were organized with Hans B. Nielsen as bishop of the Adams Ward and David P. Cheney as bishop of Boyle Heights.

While most wards kept the name by which they were known as branches, the name of the Los Angeles Branch was changed to the Adams Ward after the street on which the chapel was located. Inasmuch as the stake covered all of Los Angeles City and County and the ward did not, the decision was made to identify the ward with the area it covered. This change also eliminated any possible confusion which might arise over whether the ward or the stake was being discussed.

On 2 April the sixth ward, San Pedro, was organized, with Joseph W. Covington as bishop. The last ward provided for when the stake was created, Long Beach, was organized on 29 April, and Willard Hansen was sustained as bishop. By the end of the year, however, Church membership had grown so rapidly that all five branches of the Los Angeles Stake had become wards. In addition, two new wards, two independent branches, and four dependent branches were formed out of existing wards with bright prospects for the creation of additional units. On 10 June 1923 the Alhambra Branch became the Alhambra Ward and the Garvanza Branch became the Garvanza Ward. Andrew O. Larson and Albin A. Hoglund, respectively, were the first bishops. On that same day the Adams Ward was divided, and the Florence Ward was created out of the portion of the Adams Ward south of 54th Street. With the creation of the Florence Ward, the stake presidency was hoping to "relieve the congestion at Adams Ward," which continued to be the gathering place for new arrivals. There were approximately 200 members in the new ward, and George T. Wride was sustained as bishop.

The Saints in the Florence Ward immediately laid plans for building a ward chapel. Their efforts were blessed in part through the generosity of George and Sarah Matthews, who presented to the ward two lots valued at $10,000 on the south side of Florence Avenue. They also contributed a house and lot which brought an additional $5,000 upon sale. In gratitude for the generosity of the Matthews, the name of the Florence Ward was changed to Matthews Ward.[13]

On 26 August the Glendale Branch was reorganized as the Glendale Ward and William G. Gough was sustained as bishop. The same day, Boyle Heights Ward was divided at the Los Angeles River and the Belvedere Ward created out of the eastern part. David P. Cheney became bishop of the new ward and Clawson N. Skinner was sustained as bishop of Boyle Heights.

During November 1923, the Inglewood Branch became the Inglewood Ward, with James McCardell as bishop, and a branch was established at Virginia City (now North Long Beach) with Walter R. Sant as the branch president. The following month the Huntington Park Ward was split and the Home Gardens Branch organized. It was an unusually cold day when fifty-four Saints met on the day before Christmas in the unfinished, unheated Dudlex Building on California Avenue for the organization of the branch.[14] Despite the cold, a relatively complete organization was set up with Samuel B. Dye sustained as branch president. Dependent branches were located at Monrovia, Pasadena, Lankershim (North Hollywood), and Redondo Beach. The Monrovia Branch was eventually transferred to the California Mission.

Like previous growth, most of this expansion was the result of migration. In spite of President McCune's plea at the organization of the stake, which was printed in the *Deseret News*, Church members kept coming to Los Angeles. While most eventually found work, few had guaranteed jobs upon arrival. As a result, stake leaders had to work to meet not only the spiritual needs of the newcomers, but often their physical needs as well. More than a decade before the Church officially established its famous welfare program, the Los Angeles Stake began to apply its own resourcefulness to meet the demands placed upon it.

One of the first actions taken by stake officials was the creation of an information bureau/employment office to help new arrivals in settling in their new home. At first the regular stake officers functioned in this capacity, but by July 1924 James A. Rasmussen was designated as manager of vocational direction and employment for southern California. Willard J. Anderson, a member of the Garvanza Ward, took it upon himself to gather surplus furniture, clothing, and other goods that could be given to the poor, and his efforts can be seen as foreshadowing the establishment of the Deseret Industries.

The stake Relief Society played an active role in meeting the welfare needs of the burgeoning Latter-day Saint community, and it also assisted in various city, county, and state welfare organizations. During the first part of the twentieth century, "auxiliary members tended to see their role as encompassing the larger society as well as the Mormon community."[15] Thus, when the Child Guidance Clinic was established in Los Angeles the stake Relief Society became a charter member. Relief Society President Katherine Stewart and her associates contributed generously to the Los Angeles Children's Hospital. Stake Relief Society members not only attended conventions of the state welfare societies, but also sponsored several of these conventions. This involvement provided opportunities to serve the larger Los Angeles community, to learn of various welfare programs which could assist Church members, and to teach the gospel. At one convention in Sacramento, the Los Angeles Stake Relief Society operated a booth where it displayed quilts, household textiles, and articles of clothing made by the sisters of the stake. The Relief Society also desired to establish a maternity home in the city, but while nearly $3,000 was donated by the sisters of the stake, the project was never brought to fruition.[16]

This same spirit of community involvement was also exhibited by the other auxiliaries in the stake. In some other areas where the Church was well entrenched, some of its members during this time "became dubious about the legitimacy of considering compassionate and social service outside wards and stakes as service in the Lord's kingdom."[17] This view would become widespread in the Church, especially following the adoption of the welfare program. However, members in Los Angeles, because of their lack of numbers and the need to draw strength from wherever they could, have not necessarily made that distinction, and they have found that in their service to the community they have also been serving the Church. As a result, stake leaders have emphasized that as members of the Lord's kingdom, the Saints' responsibilities extend beyond the immediate bounds of the Church and its members. Consequently, not only is the name of the Church held in high regard in Los Angeles, but baptisms have also resulted.

While the majority of those who came to Los Angeles in the 1920s were young adults just starting in life and seeking educational and vocational opportunities, many of the migrants were established members who had come for health reasons. Of these, a good number were over sixty; as a result, the stake continued a practice established in Utah and organized an Old Folks Committee under the direction of Orson Hewitt, which functioned to help with their social needs.

By working to meet the temporal needs of its members, the Los Angeles Stake was able to progress in its responsibility for the spiritual needs. In April 1924 the *Deseret News* carried a report, written by a member of the stake, David W. Cummings, on the stake's progress during its first year and the challenges it still faced. Cummings began by recounting some of the unusual conditions the Los Angeles Stake faced, and in so doing exemplified the true pioneering nature of the stake. While the unique characteristics of the stake were the exception rather than the rule in 1923, they now (1987) typify the majority of areas in which the Church is established: a ward that doubled in membership in a year; another ward that encompassed 200,000 people but only two hundred members; stake officers who had to travel fifty miles or more each Sunday largely through dense traffic; most members having to travel between one and fifteen miles to go to church. "These are but a few of the strokes one might use in painting a word picture of the Los Angeles stake—the only stake in the Church located within a large metropolitan area, and consequently, a stake that presents characteristics strikingly unique and interesting."[18]

While most large urban areas in America had had branches of the Church for several years, Cummings observed,

> when it came to forming a stake, the most intricate subdivision in the Church system, in a city which offers in the extreme the complexities of modern metropolitan life, there was encountered an entirely new set of problems, the working out of which is providing one of the most interesting experiences in Church history.
>
> It was quite a novelty, for example, to set ward boundaries in a city of a million people, when only a small fraction of that million were concerned with or even knew anything about these boundaries. It gave one somewhat the feeling of trying to make chalk marks on a pool of water.

Cummings further noted that widely lacking in the stake was that "force for permanence and stability which emanates from a ward owning its own meeting place. Only three chapels have been erected prior to the organization of the stake. . . . All the other wards are assembling in rented halls, scarcely any of which can be secured for all the meetings it is desired to hold. This fact has proved a stumbling block to the organization of several auxiliaries, including the Primary and Relief Society." In addition, these quarters were proving inadequate because of the phenomenal growth.

Another unique problem he identified was traffic. "It is not uncommon for a Church member to spend anywhere from 30 minutes to an hour and a half to get to Sacrament meeting, particularly if he must go by street car." Consequently, with the multiplied activities of a stake, this handicap became a serious obstacle to the efforts of stake members and leaders to travel to the many activities they needed to attend.

Cummings continues that the most complicated problem, however, was Los Angeles itself with its

> perennial spirit of play—its restlessness—its hordes of visitors and shifting population—its orgies of scandal and crime—its waves of reforms—its manifold allurements to Sunday amusement away from Religious observance—its dauntless optimism—its fads and fancies—its amazing opportunities for wealth—its constant excitement for greed—its streaks of Puritanism through its mass of worldliness—the flashing, fascinating, hectic, endlessly varied movement and color in the rushing currents of life.
>
> These influences all have deep reactions upon the minds and hearts of the Saints, which the stake as a church organization must deal with—some to temper and some to completely counteract.
>
> With these new problems in this untried field of Church organization, what success has been encountered? Measured in actual statistics it has been astounding.

In spite of these challenges, Cummings noted that during the first month of its existence, the Los Angeles Stake was the top stake in the Church in the percentage of members attending sacrament meeting, a position which it continued to hold nearly every month for a year.[19] The degree to which the members in Los Angeles participated that first year was remarkable, especially when compared with the average Church attendance. Cummings informed *Deseret News* readers that in December 1923, in spite of living "in the playground of America," the Saints "demonstrated a remarkable degree of personal loyalty" when they established a Church-wide attendance record at sacrament meeting with a 67 percent average throughout the stake. This percentage stood out in contrast to a Church-wide average of less than 20 percent attendance at the time.[20] This statistic reflects the fact that in such an environment where members were few, sacrament meeting attendance initially was a more vital part of the Church experience and commitment than it had been in Utah, although a reorientation to the importance of attendance at meeting was taking place throughout the Church.[21]

In addition to its high sacrament attendance, according to Cummings, the stake led the Church in the other two statistics published for December: 100 percent ward teaching and 77 percent of the ward teachers attending sacrament meeting.[22] "Moreover," he continued, "in the numerous ways which never appear in statistics, and yet which speak far more eloquently, they are demonstrating an aggressive fervor and solid unity that clearly explains the phenomenal success of the stake." This unity, he concluded, began with the challenging period of settlement when the members were part of the California Mission, and, he said, "today's harvest is the result of seeds faithfully and skillfully sown."

He also noted that in spite of what the stake had accomplished, there was still much work to be done, including the completion of organizations, finding quarters, providing amusements "under the proper influence," and furnishing opportunities for the youth to mingle with others of their religion. "Each of these problems is being dealt with earnestly and intelligently and with an interest perhaps all the keener because there are few precedents," he wrote. "The people were unanimous in their conviction that the establishment of the stake was divinely inspired and that it has already provided a great blessing to them. It may safely be predicted that during the next few years Los Angeles will be the scene of a development which will have a profound influence upon Church history." And through the efforts of stake members, it has.

Shortly following the creation of the stake, the Boy Scouts of America and the Los Angeles Stake became closely allied. What is believed to be the first LDS Boy Scout troop in southern California was organized in December 1923 under the direction of the Belvedere Ward MIA. Wallace E. Lund, who arrived a month earlier from Utah, organized the troop and served as its first scoutmaster. The creation of Scout troops not only helped provide activities for the boys of the stake but also served as an important missionary tool. In this first Scout troop non-Mormons outnumbered Mormons eighteen to fourteen.

In addition to Scout activities, a stake recreation committee was organized. Because there were so many worldly temptations in the city, such as pool halls and non-LDS dance halls, special emphasis was placed upon appropriate activities for the youth. Almost every Friday evening dances and parties were held. In addition, special dances were also held on such occasions as Christmas (usually on Christmas day itself) and Valentine's Day. These dances were often elaborate affairs organized and sponsored by the M Men and Gleaners of the stake.

Athletics also played a large role from the early days, with most wards fielding basketball teams each year, resulting in the need for a northern and southern division. In addition, a track meet was held each May. The young women of the stake were involved in these activities, serving as cheerleaders for their ward's team. Since the stake possessed no suitable hall for amusements, buildings had to be rented throughout the city for youth activities. The first hall to be rented was in the basement of the Masonic temple at the corner of Pico and Figueroa. Other halls used were the Masonic temple at the corner of Washington and Oak and, occasionally, the Friday Morning Club.

The Young People's Chorus served also as a vehicle for youth activities and excursions, in addition to its role in providing music. While the chorus initially performed only in the Los Angeles area, three trips were made to Salt Lake City to perform at the MIA's June Conference. The first trip came in June 1924 and included a concert at the California Day at Saltair, a resort on the south end of the Great Salt Lake.

Those who made the trip were expected to pay their own expenses, and a year prior to this time a thrift club was organized at a local bank to help the members save their money. Each person wishing to go to Salt Lake City had to deposit one dollar in the thrift club and then add a dollar each week until the time of the trip, which money was supposed to be earned by the members. The *Deseret News,* upon learning of this requirement, reported in amazement that the trip "was not accomplished, as many suppose, by a Chamber of Commerce drive, contributions by loyal ward and stake residents or other similar artifices usually resorted to in such a feat. The simple and amazing truth of the fulfillment of this undertaking, reveals a year's effort of diligent work, sacrifice and self-denial upon the part of each member of the chorus."[23] As a result of this experience, the choir became known as "The Thrift Chorus."

In 1925, for the fiftieth anniversary of the Mutual Improvement Association, the Los Angeles "Thrift Chorus" again made the trip to June Conference, with each member again paying his or her own expenses. During this conference, a girls' chorus under the direction of Hortense G. Steed, the group's accompanist, competed in the Young Ladies' Chorus Contest and was awarded first place. The following year, the chorus again made the trip.

When the Los Angeles stake was created, only the Adams, Long Beach, and Ocean Park wards had chapels. The building of new chapels, therefore, became one of the primary concerns of the stake. The need arose not only from the desire for "permanence and stability" within the stake, but also from the inadequacy of outside halls: few buildings rented by the wards could be secured for all activities such as Primary, Relief Society, MIA, and ward socials; most halls were also insufficient for the size of the wards. Within a few years, six new chapels were erected by the Matthews, Belvedere, Huntington Park, Home Garden, Lankershim, and Virginia City wards, and an additional chapel was purchased to house the Alhambra Ward.

The growth of the Latter-day Saint community in Los Angeles not only necessitated the obtaining of larger buildings, but also compelled the creation of additional wards. While no limits were placed on the size of wards, it was recognized that it was in the best interest of the members and the Church to keep them small. Some, like the Adams Ward, exceeded fifteen hundred Saints. For the individual, smaller units, both stakes and wards, allowed for greater personal attention from leaders, provided more opportunities for service, and created a more cohesive community; for the Church, it meant a greater chance of progress by giving more people responsibility for the success of the work. In December 1924 the Home Gardens Ward (later South Garden) was created with Samuel B. Dye as bishop, and Virginia City Ward was organized with William N. Horrick as bishop. Branches were organized at Pasadena and Torrance in 1926, and the Lankershim Branch became a ward in January 1927 with Edmund R. Paul, bishop.

At the April 1925 general conference, President McMurrin summarized the growth of the stake and then discussed a problem even more challenging than growth: the near constant turnover of membership. "I do not suppose," he commented,

> that in any other mission it can be said that there were received and recorded, during the year 1924, over thirty-six hundred Church members . . . who had come from other sections of the country. . . .
> There have also been a large number who have been trans-

ferred, probably thirteen hundred or fourteen hundred Church members have received their certificates of membership during the year, and have transferred to other communities. This, of course, causes changes in officers. There have already been in the Los Angeles Stake since its organization changes in four or five different bishoprics, and there have also been a number of changes in the high council.[24]

The problem of turnover has constantly plagued the Church in urban areas, and there are several reasons for it. For one thing, members who work for large corporations are continually being transferred. More significant, it appears, is the fact that many Saints in these areas do not own their own homes. When members have no tie to the community, which home ownership promotes, they often tend to move whenever things become rough or when even a slightly better opportunity presents itself. President McMurrin identified these problems as the major reasons for the outflux of Saints from the Los Angeles Stake:

> This is brought about by the fact that the Latter-day Saints who are in California as a general thing are not in the condition as home owners. . . . There is but a very small percentage of the members of the Church in the California mission who own their own homes. . . . It is an easy matter when one doesn't own a home if he hears that there is a little better prospect in some other section to pick up his grip and call for a drayman to take his trunk to the railroad station and go elsewhere.[25]

President McMurrin closed his remarks by reaffirming the plea made by President McCune when the stake was formed for members not to move to Los Angeles without being sure of the economic opportunities. Such a plea was given not only to discourage the Saints from moving into situations which may be no better than the ones they left, but also, hopefully, to ease the problems faced by authorities in connection with the constant growth and turnover as well as the welfare problems:

> I am glad to say, however, notwithstanding the large number of people who have come to California who are Latter-day Saints, there has been work as a general thing in the past for all of this great influx of people. . . . At the present time, however, conditions are not as desirable as they have been, from a working point of view in the past.
>
> I would recommend that if there are any Latter-day Saints who have the thought in their minds of coming to California for the purpose of finding employment they be a little slow in putting such thought into execution. I think I can safely say that there are more men in California at the present time than there is work, and there

are many idle men in California. Rents are very high. California is a wonderful state, a beautiful country, a desirable place for habitation in many respects, but it is not a very desirable place for men and women to come to who do not have money in their pockets, and I would like to say that Latter-day Saints without money will be altogether better off, and they will be altogether safer, in these well-established communities where the people own their homes, than to migrate to California.

In spite of such pleas, Church members kept arriving. In 1925 the membership of the Los Angeles Stake was nearly six thousand and by 1927 it was almost eight thousand.

The growth of the Church in Los Angeles was not limited to Anglo-Americans, for during this time missionary work began also among the city's Spanish-speaking people. It was estimated that some fifty thousand Hispanics lived in Los Angeles and another twenty-five thousand in adjacent areas. In August 1924, the first two Spanish-speaking missionaries were assigned to work among the Hispanics in Los Angeles. President McMurrin had arranged with President Rey L. Pratt of the Mexican Mission to transfer two missionaries to the California Mission. Elders Jessup W. Thomas and Frank Copening were selected by President Pratt for the new assignments in Los Angeles. They labored among the Spanish-speaking people until March 1925, when Elder Thomas was released to return home and Elder Copening was called to become mission secretary. No one, however, was assigned to replace them, and so the Spanish-speaking community of Los Angeles had no missionaries working full-time among them for over a year. Then, early in 1926, the Mexican government began to enforce the provision of its constitution that prohibited foreign missionaries from functioning in Mexico. This forced the Church to recall all missionaries from that country, and by August four of them had been reassigned to work with the Los Angeles Hispanic community, most of whom had immigrated from Mexico.

In August 1927 a conference was held for Mexican converts and investigators in Los Angeles, with Elder Joseph Fielding Smith of the Council of the Twelve in attendance. There were 103 people at this first Spanish-speaking conference, and President Pratt served as interpreter for Elder Smith. In February 1928 another conference was held with President Anthony W. Ivins of the First Presidency in attendance. Having been raised in Mexico, he was able to speak to over 120 people in their native language. Work continued in the Hispanic community and on 16 June 1929 the Los Angeles Branch of the Mexican Mission was organized with Juan Miguel Gonzales being sustained as branch president, a position he would hold until 1944. Earlier in 1929 the mission home of the Mexican Mission was transferred from El Paso to Los Angeles, but following the death of President Pratt in 1931, it was transferred back to El Paso as most of the mission's efforts were again directed towards Mexico and Texas.

In 1936 the Spanish-American Mission was created from the Mexican Mission with direct responsibility for missionary work among the Spanish-speaking within the United States. By this time, however, the Los Angeles Stake had been split and most of the work with Spanish-speaking people was carried on within the boundaries of stakes in the eastern portion of the city, where the Hispanic community resided. Missionary work among Hispanics in the Los Angeles California Stake remained nearly dormant until the 1960s, when revolutions in Central and South America brought a large number of Spanish-speaking refugees to western Los Angeles and helped re-establish the work among them.

Meanwhile, the growth of the English-speaking congregations reached a point where the creation of a second stake in Los Angeles became necessary if the stake was to remain manageable. With almost eight thousand members and nineteen wards and branches, the growth of the stake had outstripped its capacity for providing the kind of effective leadership, personal attention, and frequent contact between the leaders and the members that Church leaders deemed essential, especially in an area where Church contact was limited.

On Friday, 18 February 1927, Presidents Heber J. Grant and Charles W. Nibley of the First Presidency met with stake and mission leaders in the California Mission Home next door to the Adams Ward chapel. There the decision was reached to divide the Los Angeles Stake, then barely four years old. It was also decided that the division should take place during the next scheduled stake conference, which was in May, and that a campaign should be launched for raising funds to construct one building to serve the needs of both stakes following the division. The idea of using one building to serve two stakes was unusual in the early twentieth century, but was also reminiscent of the early days of the Church in Utah when a tabernacle was built for a city, rather than for the exclusive use of one group of Saints.

A fund-raising committee consisting of J. David Larson, Mathonihah Thomas, David W. Cummings, and George T. Wride was appointed by the stake presidency. On 27 February 1927, immediately upon receiving its assignment, the committee held its first meeting in an automobile parked in front of the Adams Ward chapel. There plans were drawn up for a fund-raising campaign, which called for pledges to be obtained from the individual members and the money to be collected in installments over a period of time. The plans were approved by the stake presidency and preparations went ahead for the new building.

In January 1927, in what President McCune called "a very remarkable deal," Bishop David P. Howells of the Adams Ward completed arrangements for the purchase of a parcel of land on the corner of Manhattan Place and Country Club Drive for $90,000, near the Los Angeles Country Club in one of the most exclusive areas of Los Angeles.[26] When President McCune first moved to Los Angeles he and his associates had set aside a four-acre tract of land in Mar Vista for the building of the tabernacle. It was the feeling of the brethren in Salt Lake City, however, that the Saints could best be served by a site more centrally located, and the land purchased by Bishop Howells served that purpose. They also recommended that a small tract of land be set aside for a ward meetinghouse in Mar Vista. This suggestion was followed, and later the Mar Vista chapel was built on this location.

Before the end of March the fund-raising drive began in earnest and by 6 April 1927 over $105,000 had been pledged towards the new building; a telegram was sent to President Grant telling of the success of the campaign. During a session of general conference, President Grant read the telegram and informed those in attendance that the Church would match whatever the Saints in Los Angeles raised towards the building of their tabernacle. As a result of the pledges of the local Saints, he told the congregation, "there will be in southern California quite a fine building, as a further evidence [to the Church's critics] of the 'decaying of the Church.' "[27]

Preparations for the new Los Angeles Tabernacle did not take priority over plans being laid for the creation of the new stake, the ninety-eighth in the Church. One of the first decisions made was the name for the new stake—Hollywood. The proposed creation of a Hollywood Stake provided the occasion for a bit of humor in the Eastern press. The *Washington Independent Herald* wrote: "If the Mormons start a Church at Hollywood they will find plenty of fellows there who have had a lot of wives already."[28] The *Brooklyn Times* of 29 March 1927 commented tersely: "Mormons announce they will establish a church in Hollywood: That's carrying coals to Newcastle."[29]

By May all arrangements had been completed for the creation of the second stake in Los Angeles. Other major metropolitan areas such as Washington, D.C.; New York; Chicago; and San Francisco were still preparing for their first stake while Los Angeles was preparing for its second. From one branch and approximately four hundred members in 1919 to two stakes and nearly eight thousand members eight years later, this was truly remarkable growth. More important than the growth itself, however, was the secure foundation for the Church that these Saints had built and were enlarging upon as southern California became one of the strongholds of the Church in the twentieth century.

5

Forward
Hollywood

On 22 May 1927, Elders David O. McKay and Stephen L Richards of the Council of the Twelve presided at an especially important quarterly conference of the Los Angeles Stake, held at the Adams Ward chapel. There the four-year-old stake was divided, resulting in the creation of the Hollywood Stake, the ninety-eighth in the Church and the second in a major metropolitan area. Outside Los Angeles Church members took little notice of what was happening, for, instead of wide publicity like that given the organization of the Los Angeles Stake, only one short report about the new stake in Hollywood appeared in the *Deseret News*.[1] Some thirteen years later the name of the Hollywood Stake was changed to Los Angeles, and the Los Angeles Stake became the South Los Angeles Stake. The Hollywood Stake, then, became the direct precursor of the present Los Angeles California Stake.

The boundary between the Los Angeles and Hollywood stakes, as drawn during a meeting of local leaders and General Authorities on Saturday, 21 May 1927, ran roughly east and west. It began at the Pacific Ocean north of the Redondo resort and ran in a northeasterly direction to 54th Street in Los

Angeles, then north along Vermont Avenue to 6th Street, east along 6th Street to the Los Angeles River, southward along the river to Industrial Way, east along Industrial Way to Indiana Street, north on Indiana Street to Alhambra Boulevard, then east to the Los Angeles–San Bernardino county line.[2] Those wards and branches north of this line became members of the Hollywood Stake; those south of the line remained in the Los Angeles Stake. The irregularities in the line accommodated the creation of a new ward—the Wilshire Ward. It was created as the Adams Ward was divided along Vermont Avenue, the western half of the ward becoming the Wilshire Ward of the Hollywood Stake (referred to in the *Deseret News* as the Adams Ward) and the eastern half retaining the designation of Adams Ward of the Los Angeles Stake (referred to in the *Deseret News* as the East Adams Ward).

Following the division, the Los Angeles Stake consisted of the Adams, Home Gardens, Huntington Park, Inglewood, Long Beach, Matthews, Redondo, San Pedro, and Virginia City wards and the Torrance Branch. The Hollywood Stake included the Wilshire, Alhambra, Belvedere, Boyle Heights, Garvanza, Glendale, Hollywood, Lankershim, and Ocean Park wards and the Pasadena Branch. The baptized membership of the stakes was listed at 3,401 for Los Angeles and 3,269 for Hollywood. Interestingly, almost one third of the Hollywood Stake's membership was listed in the new Wilshire Ward.

George W. McCune, former president of the Los Angeles Stake, was sustained as president of the new Hollywood Stake, while his former first counselor Leo J. Muir was sustained as president of the Los Angeles Stake. George F. Harding, former second counselor in the Los Angeles Stake presidency, was set apart as the new first counselor in the Hollywood Stake with John S. McCune becoming the new stake clerk. However, no second counselor was sustained at that time.

Members of the first Hollywood Stake high council sustained at the organization were Charles H. Norberg, Vern O. Knudsen, Charles B. Stewart, David W. Cummings, John S. Worsley, Espee T. Cannon, Louis K. Simms, and J. E. Williamson. William J. Reeve was sustained as president of the stake high priests, and seven elders quorums were organized for the ten units. Other officers sustained included Katherine R. Stewart as stake Relief Society president, Alex Nibley as superintendent of

Sunday Schools, Charles H. Norberg as YMMIA president, Winifred W. Poulton as YWMIA president and Cora W. Leaver as Primary Association president.

Although the Hollywood Stake was created in May, the final break was postponed until 1 July 1927 to allow for both stakes to begin with relatively complete organizations. Two days following the split, 3 July, the Wilshire Ward was officially organized at a meeting of the Adams Ward at the Adams chapel. Bishop David P. Howells was sustained as the first bishop of the new ward with Joseph A. West replacing him as bishop of Adams Ward. Until the Wilshire Ward could secure a place of its own, the two wards followed the unusual practice of meeting together, with each ward's bishopric presiding on alternating Sundays.

When the new stake was created, Elders McKay and Richards recommended that the two stakes in Los Angeles continue with the plan of building one stake center. However, the Los Angeles Stake soon expressed a desire to build its own stake center and requested a meeting with the First Presidency regarding the matter.[3] On 15 July a special meeting was held at which the First Presidency, Elders McKay and Richards, Leo J. Muir and Fred S. Hatch of the Los Angeles Stake, and George W. McCune of the Hollywood Stake were present. There the First Presidency endorsed the Los Angeles Stake's plan for separate stake tabernacles. It was agreed that the money pledged towards the single building be split according to the pledges received from the members residing in each stake. President Grant recommended that since the Los Angeles Stake had the beautiful Adams Ward chapel, which many members of the Hollywood Stake had helped to build, the Los Angeles Stake should give to the new stake an additional $10,000.[4]

When this plan was presented to the members of the Hollywood Stake high council, they unanimously agreed that the stake should build a joint stake house/ward house. They also authorized President McCune to begin conferring with the First Presidency regarding the acquisition of a building site. Because the site purchased by Bishop Howells for the two-stake tabernacle at the corner of Manhattan Place and Country Club Drive was within the boundaries of Wilshire Ward, President McCune approached the brethren for permission to use this property for the joint Hollywood Stake house and Wilshire Ward chapel, and it was granted. Until this new structure could be built, or other quarters located, the stake presidency and high council continued to meet in the Hiberian Building, with all other stake meetings held in the Ocean Park chapel.

The first Hollywood Stake conference was held 28 August 1927 at Ocean Park with Elders David O. McKay and Joseph Fielding Smith of the Council of the Twelve and Rey L. Pratt of the First Quorum of the Seventy and President of the Mexican Mission as the conference visitors. Their messages dealt with the opportunities and challenges of living the gospel in California and the changes in the Church that had taken place in Los Angeles over the previous few years. President McCune outlined for stake members the proposed building program for the stake tabernacle. An important matter of business was also undertaken when Arthur H. Sconberg was sustained as second counselor in the stake presidency and ordained a high priest and set apart in his new calling by Elder McKay. Stake Clerk John McCune recorded in the conference minutes a note that showed the wisdom of organizing two stakes on a smaller scale, thus allowing greater participation. There were 756 in attendance at the afternoon session and, except for the conferences when the Los Angeles and Hollywood stakes were created, "no larger crowd was ever recorded prior to the division of the Stake."[5]

The large attendance also reinforced the need to erect a structure that could comfortably accommodate the stake's membership. When the Hollywood Stake was organized, only four of the ten units (Lankershim, Ocean Park, Alhambra, and Belvedere) had their own buildings, and they contained no adequate facilities for stake offices, were not centrally located, and were not equipped to handle large crowds. Consequently, building the stake center became an important priority for President McCune, who later recalled that of the many challenges which faced the new stake, "the chief source of discouragement [was] the complete lack of a suitable place to hold our meetings. . . . [The Hollywood Stake] literally had no place to lay its head."[6] Although this was an urgent need, President McCune was a man of vision whose past experience with chapels in England would not allow him to settle for second best. As he recalled at the new stake center's dedication:

> A large, cheap structure could have been erected in a comparatively short time and satisfied this deficiency for the time being—but in

doing so the greatest opportunity that has yet been given the Church would have been completely lost—that is, to preach the Gospel to the world by means of a structure that would place Mormonism on a par with her sister churches. . . . Should The Church of Jesus Christ of Latter-day Saints take a back seat to any of these? Should we be satisfied with the commonplace when others are dwelling in marble halls?[7]

For President McCune and the members of the stake the answer was a resounding "no." Consequently, they would erect one of the finest edifices, outside of the temples, ever built in the Church. Although the stake had nearly $60,000 dollars pledged towards the tabernacle, which would finance a nice structure, President McCune envisioned a building for the Hollywood Stake of comparable magnitude to what had originally been planned for the two stakes.

An important element in this effort to erect the finest building possible was the enlistment of someone who could effectively translate the desire into reality. Fortunately for stake members, the junior partner in the Salt Lake City architectural firm of Pope and Burton, Harold Burton, had recently moved into the stake for health reasons and had opened a Los Angeles office of the firm. Among the many structures which Burton had designed prior to this time were the Cardston and Hawaiian temples. By September 1927 President McCune had engaged Harold Burton in drawing up the plans for the new stake center.

That the stake was even able to draw upon the talents of Harold Burton was the result of the efforts of Joseph Nielson, a Utah architect. In the early 1920s the Church began experimenting with an architectural department and standardized plans for meetinghouses. However, in 1924 Nielson had complained to President Grant that such a policy was unfair to local architects since what work they got on the local level often made the difference between success and failure. After considering the matter, President Grant changed the policy and announced that local units could hire local architects to design their buildings if they so desired.[8]

While Harold Burton worked to design the permanent home of the Hollywood Stake and Wilshire Ward, a temporary home was located by Harvey Sessions, first counselor in the Wilshire Ward bishopric, on the sixth floor of the Odd Fellows Hall, located at the corner of Oak Street and Washington Boulevard. There was one minor drawback to this temporary home, however. A radio station was located on the seventh floor, and this fledgling industry naturally created a great deal of interest. It was not unusual for some of the young people, therefore, to skip a meeting in order to watch the excitement behind the station's glass windows.[9] Nevertheless, these quarters so delighted President McCune that he inquired into the possibility of also moving the stake offices into the building. When it was discovered that the facilities could be used without cost on Tuesday evenings, the stake offices were moved there and the night for stake meetings was changed from Wednesday to Tuesday.

Stake leaders soon found it necessary to make a few adjustments among the units in the stake, and in September the decision was made to organize an independent branch at Edendale, which would eventually become the Elysian Park Ward. There were nearly three hundred members in the new branch, and Wallace Jackman served as the first branch president. In October the Belvedere Ward was transferred to the Los Angeles Stake and the Inglewood and Redondo Wards were transferred to the Hollywood Stake, bringing to twelve the number of units in the stake. This transfer made stake activities more convenient to members of the respective wards and was carried out only after receiving approval from the members involved.

Also in October 1927 the Mesa, Arizona, Temple was dedicated, and this brought considerable excitement to the Saints in Los Angeles. Since no railroad service connected Salt Lake directly with Mesa, the route taken by the Church leaders and others brought them to Los Angeles. The Hollywood and Los Angeles stakes entertained a party of more than one hundred General Authorities and guests on their stopover. After a morning of sightseeing in Los Angeles and Hollywood and a luncheon party at one of Hollywood's popular restaurants, Douglas Fairbanks directed the visitors from Utah on a tour of the United Artists movie studio. Following their day in Los Angeles, the members of the group continued on to Arizona.

The dedication of the Mesa Temple was also attended by the Los Angeles Thrift Chorus. On the Sunday morning preceding the dedication, the 150 choir members mounted the annex of the temple and gave a sunrise rendition of Evan Stephens's cantata, "The Vision." This would be one of the choir's last major performances, for a little over a year later the decision was made to disband the Thrift Chorus in favor of ward and stake choirs, and an important part of the early cultural history of the Church in Los Angeles came to a close.

In November preparations for the combined Hollywood tabernacle and Wilshire Ward chapel had progressed to the point where ground could be broken and the site dedicated. Since the property on the corner of Country Club Drive and Manhattan Place had become badly overgrown with weeds and barley, Harvey Sessions gathered the Wilshire Ward Boy Scouts together and cleared if off in preparation for this important event. On 13 November 1927 the Saints in the stake gathered for ground-breaking ceremonies for the new stake center. In attendance were Charles W. Nibley of the First Presidency, Elder Richard R. Lyman of the Council of the Twelve, and over two thousand members of the stake.[10] The following week, on 20 November, the site was dedicated.[11]

Major steps had been taken towards the construction of the stake house, but there was still much to be done. Fortunately, those who were overseeing the work—President George W. McCune, Bishop David W. Howells, and Adele Cannon Howells —all possessed great vision and none would settle for what they felt was second best. Thus, they were not willing to rush the process or sacrifice quality.

President McCune believed not only that the Saints in the Hollywood Stake were entitled to the finest facilities available, but also that their activities should be worthy of the chapel he envisioned and in the best of taste and, at times, even elegant. Perhaps the glamor of their Hollywood setting as well as the fact that many Saints in this area were both affluent and influential, contributed to these attitudes and practices that were not necessarily common elsewhere in the Church. A rumor even circulated in Salt Lake City that the General Authorities should take tuxedos with them when visiting the Hollywood Stake.[12] This rumor actually had some basis in fact, for many Church social activities, especially those involving stake leaders, were formal affairs requiring tuxedos for men and gowns for women.[13] Outside Hollywood, dressing one's best normally did not require more than a business suit, but since most major social affairs in that somewhat exclusive community required tuxedos, President McCune felt the Saints should do the same and not take a back seat to anyone. Not only did he feel that stake members should dress their finest, he also desired that all things be done in the best way, not just to help ensure that the Church would be held in the best light but also because the Lord and his Saints deserved the best. Thus the numerous cultural activities, including concerts and plays, and the many dances were planned to be something special, and they were carried out in a grand manner that exhibited a touch of class. Members of the stake such as Emily Simms, who shared the desires of President McCune, worked to transform these desires into action by making sure that at dances, for example, everything from the decorations to the manner of dancing was just right. LeGrand Richards would later say that he wished he could hold up the Hollywood Stake's dances as a model for all the Church.[14] In striving for the best, a sense of unity and a sense of satisfaction in belonging to the Hollywood Stake apparently was achieved among most of its members.

Some of the means implemented by President McCune to give stake members a feeling of identity and unity have seldom been used in other areas. A stake seal or emblem was created consisting of a beehive encircled with a holly wreath and the inscription "For the Glory of God." Of the significance of the emblem, the *Hollywood Stake Herald,* the stake's first publication, stated that the "bee is perhaps the most industrious creature. The holly has come to represent and commemorate the birth of the Lord Jesus Christ, so that we feel that it is a very appropriate emblem for the Hollywood Stake."[15] In addition, stake colors—green and red—were chosen, and a stake hymn and stake rally song were written. The stake hymn, "Forward! Hollywood!" was sung to the tune of "Men of Harlech":

> Hollywood, the dawn is breaking
> Lo, the world is slowly waking
> Men their slumbers are forsaking
>   Forward! Hollywood.
> Gone the night of sin and error
> Truth has shorn them of their terror
> Rally round the standard bearer
>   Forward! Hollywood!
>
> Chorus
> Hollywood, forever!
> We will fail you never
> Firm and true

Our love for you
That no power can dissever
Hark! the anthems we are singing
To the Heavens our praises ringing
Joy to every creature bringing—
Forward! Hollywood!

Hollywood, thy land is smiling
Here no discord nor reviling
Nature all our hearts beguiling
    Happy, Hollywood!
Lo! thy sons and daughters meeting
Gladly do we give thee greeting
Hark! the battle cry repeating
    Forward! Hollywood![16]

The stake rally song was set to the music of "Boola, Boola":

O, Hollywood Stake! O, Hollywood Stake!
Is the finest Stake in all the land.
We'll do what's right with all our might,
And we'll work for the Stake that is so grand.
We've hope and faith in Hollywood,
To win we cannot fail.
O, Hollywood! O, Hollywood!
To thee we sing All Hail.

    Chorus
Hollywood—da!
Hollywood—da!
Hollywood—da!
Hollywood—da!
O, we cheer thee,
And we hail thee,
For we love thee,
Hollywood![17]

The stake hymn was sung occasionally at stake conference, and both the hymn and the "Hollywood Stake Rally Song" were sung at large stake gatherings, such as fund raisings, where active participation was desired. They were especially popular during the time the stake center was being planned and built.

Bishop David P. Howells of the Wilshire Ward and his wife Adele Cannon Howells shared equally in the vision of President

McCune regarding the importance of a beautiful stake center and the proper place of the Church in Los Angeles. They, along with President McCune, were the leading forces behind the financing and building of the Wilshire Ward/Hollywood Stake tabernacle.

Bishop Howells, a native of Salt Lake City, graduated from the University of Utah in 1901 at the age of seventeen with a teaching certificate. From 1904 to 1907 he served a mission in New Zealand, and upon his return he worked in the life insurance business in Oregon, Washington, and other Western states. On 12 March 1913 he married Adele Cannon, a native of Salt Lake City and a graduate of the LDS High School and University of Utah, in the Salt Lake Temple.

Shortly following their marriage, the Howellses moved to San Francisco, where David attended the Hastings Law College of the University of California at San Francisco. While a student he accepted an offer to distribute World Film Company movies in Australia. Subsequently, the Howells family moved to New York where David's business grew to the point that he was the largest distributor of films in Europe. While in New York, David served as president of the Manhattan branch and Adele as president of the Relief Society.

In 1924 the Howellses sold their distributorship, followed the movie industry to Los Angeles, and entered into other movie-related businesses, including establishing the Los Angeles Costume Company. In March 1925 he replaced Hans B. Nielsen as bishop of the Adams Ward; when the Wilshire Ward was created, he served as its first bishop. Following the death of Bishop Howells in March 1939, Adele Howells was chosen as a counselor in the general Primary presidency and moved to Salt Lake City. In 1943 she became general Primary president, a position she held for many years.

While George W. McCune, David P. Howells, and Adele Cannon Howells were the driving forces behind the completion of the new building, their vision of a beautiful stake center could not have been realized without the financial and physical help of the members of the stake. The Wilshire Ward chapel was truly a stake effort.

As 1928 began, the architectural plans were nearing completion, arrangements were being made for fund raising, and President McCune was asking that the stake house be given a top priority in the hearts of stake members. In February work began on the new building with the Lynch-Cannon Construction Company as contractors, with a major portion of the labor performed by volunteers from the stake.

Unfortunately, when the drawings of the new stake center were unveiled, many stake members were less than enthusiastic. Harold Burton greatly admired Frank Lloyd Wright's simplicity and had designed a structure which was to be built of exposed concrete, a style gaining popularity at the time. Many in the stake felt that a more elaborate building was appropriate. When it was completed, however, it was apparent to almost all that Burton had designed an appropriate stake house whose beauty resulted, in part, from its simplicity. It was, in fact, a magnificent structure in which Church members could meet, and one which contributed to the beauty of the community. It received high praise from Church members and nonmembers alike. Indeed, when *Architectural Concrete* undertook a contest in 1933 to find the finest cement building in America, the Wilshire Ward Chapel was awarded first prize.

On 15 April 1928 the cornerstone for the new building was laid by President McCune with a "splendid crowd" in attendance and a "good spirit prevailing" among stake members.[18] Two equally important priorities faced the Saints of Hollywood Stake in their quest for a stake house—building the structure and raising the necessary funds. C. Fred Schade was made supervisor of the voluntary labor at the stake house, assisted by Preston D. Richards, who was given responsibility for Saturday volunteer work. Because Wilshire Ward members would receive the greatest benefits from the new building, they were asked to work two nights each week, while members of the other wards in the stake were asked to volunteer one night each week. A goal was set to have two hundred men and boys working each weekday evening and Saturday; usually this number was exceeded as almost everyone in the stake contributed labor. On many occasions stake members worked well into the night pouring the 86,400 cubic feet of concrete the building contains. Most evenings a limousine would arrive at the chapel site bringing Bishop Howells from work to preside at the cement mixer "in his shirt sleeves and his most jovial manner," where he made certain that the fifteen thousand bags of cement and the 640 five-ton trucks of sand and gravel were properly mixed.[19]

Pouring cement was only one of the many jobs performed by stake members who also helped to place the beams, level the ground, and do all the work that did not require skilled labor. The beams for the stage in the cultural hall weighed nearly a ton and required twenty-six men to lift into place. The work on the stake house was not limited to full-time stake members: on one occasion even President Heber J. Grant picked up a shovel while visiting the chapel site and did his part that day in landscaping.

Recalling the days of working on their chapel, the *Memory Book* for the 1945 Wilshire Ward reunion recounts the efforts of ward and stake members:

> Working in the evenings sometimes under the lights, was like a big family gathering. The women would serve food and refreshments while the men would alternately work and loaf and count the trips the different ones would make to the water bucket. Blisters and aching backs would soon turn into muscle and callouses as we dug the basement, drove the tractor, held the scraper, shovelled sand and gravel into the cement mixer while Bishop Howells would kid us on our feeble efforts. The hod carriers wore blisters on their shoulders, and the disposal of plaster refuse and scrap lumber seemed to be an endless task, but the real fun was in scraping the paint off the thousands of little glass panes in the doors of the recreation hall. When the work was done, we would be fed by the Relief Society and the Gleaners, and then we would build huge bon fires and have community singing. All seemed right with the world. The building of our great chapel was indeed a work of love.[20]

While building the chapel required great effort, in many respects it was less work than obtaining the money to purchase materials and to pay for the work of the contractors. During this period the Church usually built its chapels with "matches," that is, Church headquarters would match on a fifty-fifty basis what the wards and stakes contributed. However, the cost of the building the Hollywood Stake wished to construct was greater than Church authorities were willing to match, largely because of the increasing demands which were being placed upon Church resources. As a result, stake members had to come up with the bulk of $250,000 needed to construct the chapel. Consequently, the importance of fund raising was a constant theme during the time of construction.

Even though over $60,000 had been pledged, a good portion of this amount still had to be collected, in addition to considerably more money necessary to see the building to completion. A special fund-raising committee was established with Harvey Sessions as its chairman, and few methods were left untried to raise the needed money. On 1 April "a big pep rally" for all stake and ward members and workers "was held in the Wilshire Ward Hall under the auspices of the Stake President for the purpose of arousing enthusiasm for raising funds to go on with the work at the Stake House."[21] Every member of the High Council was asked to discuss fund raising on his visits to the wards. The Garvanza Ward responded by placing tin banks in every home in the ward to enable its members to save for the stake house. Elysian Park Branch held a fund-raising bazaar. Several of the wards sponsored fund-raising dinners. The children in the stake conducted newspaper drives in their neighborhoods trying to beat the record of a Los Angeles school that had earned two hundred dollars in one day collecting newspapers.

Additional help was provided by local businesses. Piggly-Wiggly and Safeway grocery stores offered a percentage of their sales to Church members towards the stake center. Safeway also offered additional donations if the stake would sell Safeway coupons, and Adele Howells was given responsibility to see that members took advantage of this opportunity. Blackstone Cleaners and Dryers on Union Avenue donated twenty percent of its profits from business brought in by stake members.

Stake members were also continually encouraged to make contributions and to pay their pledges. One man who paid his pledge early good-naturedly advised others against the practice since stake leaders would then ask for additional money.[22] The *Hollywood Stake Herald* included several notices reminding people to donate. From the July 1928 issue:

Budget and place the home on a sound economic basis
Unite the real luxury of giving with sacrifice
Deliberate in advance; insure getting what you want most
Get full co-operation of the family
Economize and keep within proper bounds
Take your full share of responsibility[23]

And from the October *Herald*:

Become a helper mighty quick
Use your strength and never kick;

Determination always wins
Get on the job with friendly grins.
Excuses never built a Church,
Try climbing down from your old perch.[24]

As 1928 drew to a close it looked as if the stake, in spite of these efforts, would have to go into debt to finish the chapel. However, Preston D. Richards argued persuasively against the idea, and stake leaders renewed their determination to complete the building without borrowing. Instead of going into debt, the stake created a special gifts committee, which included Adele Cannon; the committee drew up a special list of individuals to be approached whose financial situation might permit them to make special donations.

One of those on the list was Earnest R. Woolley. Helen Woolley Jackson recalls that one morning around 6:00 A.M., the family received a phone call from Adele Howells informing them she would be by in half an hour for breakfast.[25] Since this was not out of character for Adele Howells, Helen and her mother, Emeline, quickly prepared breakfast. At a little after 6:30 A.M., Adele Howells arrived at the home and asked Earnest Woolley over breakfast if he would be willing to contribute the cost of the stained-glass window that was anticipated for the front of the chapel. To this he agreed, with the understanding that the window was being donated in honor of his great-grandfather, Charles C. Rich, and Emeline's great-grandfather, Parley P. Pratt.[26]

As the time for the January 1929 stake conference approached, the decision was made to use the building itself to spearhead the drive to raise the last $25,000. On 27 January stake conference was held in the cultural hall of the unfinished tabernacle, and each session was filled to near capacity. President McCune told stake members that if the additional money could be raised, the building would be dedicated in three months, at the next conference.

During the months between conferences, the Hollywood tabernacle became the site of other fund-raising activities. On one occasion the MIA sponsored a fund-raising dance in the partially completed recreation hall with nearly one thousand in attendance. On another occasion, a turkey dinner was given in the unfinished hall. People came dressed up, many in tuxedos and evening dresses. For each table a host and hostess had been chosen ahead of time who not only furnished the meal, but also invited a group of their friends to enjoy the evening in return for a contribution to the stake center. On signal, the hosts emerged from the kitchen carrying the turkeys that their wives had cooked and circled the hall several times before going to their tables. This dinner proved so popular that more like it were held several times even after the fund raising campaign had ended.

So great was the struggle to raise funds that even President McCune, the eternal optimist, grew discouraged and asked Church leaders to release him.[27] At heart, however, was the difficulty he had experienced with Church officials in Salt Lake City over the whole matter of such a huge and costly stake center. From the beginning, even though they had allowed the Hollywood Stake to proceed, Church leaders had objected to President McCune's costly plans and refused to provide extra financing from Church funds.[28] Finally, on 9 April 1929, only two weeks before the dedication and with the stake still needing substantial funds to pay off the tabernacle, President McCune wrote President Grant recommending that he be released at the next conference because of the differences he had had with the brethren. President McCune still believed that his view was correct and told the prophet,

> Our people are very proud of the building they have erected and we feel that it will do estimable good for the Church in this locality. I regret very much that you brethren feel that we have spent too much money on its erection but I believe that within a short period of time the growth here will justify this expenditure and everybody will be happy with the matter.[29]

After receiving this letter, President Grant immediately wrote President McCune with the good news that, at least to some degree, he and his associates had softened:

> It seems to us that it would be a fine thing for you to remain in your present position for at least a few months after the completion of your building, to enjoy some of the fruits of your energetic labors. . . .
> The thought of you retiring just at the completion of your building has caused our hearts to soften, and we have decided to help you an additional $10,000.[30]

Even with this additional money, there was still not enough to buy an organ. Nevertheless, the stake had created something fine, and there were few who could deny it then—or now. The dedication program contained words of praise from both Church, state, and local leaders, and almost all who beheld the

Wilshire Ward/Hollywood Stake tabernacle raved about it. In spite of his concerns over the cost, when President Grant saw the finished building, he said: "I am paralyzed. I thought you were building something good, but it is far more elaborate and substantial than I ever dreamed of. It is splendid."[31]

At the front of the chapel, which faced east, was the stained-glass window donated by the Woolleys representing Christ as "The Light of the World." It was taken from the painting of the same name by Holman Hunt and based on Revelation 3:20, depicting Christ standing at a heavily paneled door in a garden at midnight. With his right hand he was knocking on the door, and in his left hand was a lantern. One critic, upon seeing Hunt's painting, told the artist that he had not finished the painting, for there was no handle on the door. "That," replied Hunt, "is the door of the human heart—it can be opened only from the inside."[32]

On the north wall of the chapel, smaller stained-glass windows depicted various Christian themes such as the Bible, the Anchor, the Sheaf of Grain, the Cup of Friendship, the Cluster of Grapes, the Dove of Peace, the Holly Wreath, the Lily, the Torch, and the Hand Clasp. Each was donated by individuals or organizations in the stake at a cost of $100 apiece, with the Gleaner Girls of the Wilshire Ward donating one window and Joseph W. McMurrin another.

The walls were covered with bright art-deco colors and patterns popular at the time. Splendid chandeliers hung in both the chapel and the cultural hall. Located above the cultural hall was a beautiful reception hall—furnished mainly through the generosity of the Howells family—which included a beautiful mirror on the east wall, six imposing hand-carved walnut armchairs, and a pair of French hand-carved benches, all of which had been previously used on movie sets. The seating capacity of the chapel was 860; an additional 1,250 could be seated with ease in the cultural hall. The classrooms could accommodate between thirty-five and seventy-five people.

By the time of the April 1929 stake conference, all but the organ was in readiness for the dedication of the permanent home of the Wilshire Ward and Hollywood Stake. The building had been finished and—at last—paid for.

The dedication activities were attended by President Grant and his first counselor, Charles W. Nibley, and continued over three days. Friday evening, 26 April, at 8:15 P.M., a concert was given in the chapel, following which a reception was held in the reception room and a ball held in the cultural hall. The next afternoon, a party was given for seven hundred children of the stake, at which time they donated a bushel of pennies toward the purchase of an organ for the chapel. In the evening, a general priesthood meeting was held.

During the general sessions of conference on Sunday, the huge congregation in attendance overflowed into the cultural hall. President Nibley, a native of Scotland, told those in attendance that for architectural beauty he could not think of an English or a Scottish word to describe it.[33] President Grant dedicated the building in the afternoon session with an "impressive dedicatory prayer" and congratulated stake members on their generosity and their beautiful building.[34] He also told them that outside the temples and the tabernacle in Salt Lake City it was the finest in the Church. Indeed, when the stake house was completed, only the temples had cost more to construct and few buildings other than the temples were as elaborate.

The feeling of some that a church "is judged very considerably by its buildings" may have been exaggerated, but the Mormon colony in Los Angeles wanted those who looked at the Wilshire Ward building to give the Church the consideration it deserved as the restored Church of Jesus Christ. Ultimately more important, however, was the fact that the new building was not just exquisite in appearance, but also fully equipped with the facilities necessary for housing and enhancing the activities of the Hollywood Stake. The beautiful, well-appointed chapel provided a setting conducive to worship, and the spacious cultural hall and very adequate classrooms provided a long-needed place for a variety of social, recreational, and instructional activities. Further, efforts to build a home for the stake and the Wilshire Ward were as much for the benefit of those who came after as they were for the Saints of 1929. The dedication program cited the English philosopher John Ruskin: "We have built forever not only for present delight and present use: our descendants will thank us. This place will be held sacred and men will say as they look upon this sincere effort, 'See! This our fathers did for us.' "

While the major emphasis of the Hollywood Stake during the first two years of its existence had been on finding a suitable home, the building of the kingdom did not give way to the building of the stake house. To ensure the success of the ward teaching program, one member of the high council was assigned to each ward to oversee that program. That same month, the stake presidency organized a stake mission, with the seventies in the stake being given the major responsibility for missionary work. In addition, the Church was growing rapidly enough that in early February, as construction began on the stake tabernacle, the decision was made to divide the Ocean Park Ward. The division took place on 26 February, under the direction of President McCune. The northern portion of the ward became the Santa Monica Ward and the Southern portion the Mar Vista Ward. Thus five years after becoming the first twentieth-century ward in California, the Ocean Park Ward was dissolved. John T. Corbridge was sustained as bishop of the Santa Monica Ward; Elick Joseph Sorensen was sustained as bishop of the Mar Vista Ward.

Inasmuch as the Ocean Park chapel was within the boundaries of the Santa Monica Ward, the Mar Vista Ward was without a place to meet. Although President McCune had requested at the first of the year that the building of the stake house be given number one priority, he gave permission for the ward to undertake a building project as long as it did not interfere with the building of the stake house. The land which the California Intermountain Investment Company had set aside in Mar Vista for a chapel was broken and dedicated in May 1928 and work began on the Mar Vista chapel that same month. Four months later, on 23 September 1928, President Heber J. Grant dedicated the completely-paid-for, Spanish-style structure which had cost nearly $70,000, excluding the land, doors, and windows, all of which were donated. Of this exceptional feat, accomplished by the less than four hundred members in the Mar Vista Ward, President Grant told a general conference audience:

> It is remarkable that in less than five months from the time the erection of the building was commenced, it was completed and paid for. Men, women and children worked on this building. The little children carried tiles to the roof; the good sisters nailed on laths; and some of our non-Mormon friends devoted time and attention to laboring there. The people did more than one-half of the total cost in erecting this building. I think it is the most remarkable accomplishment in that length of time of any building we have erected in the various wards.

> The spirit of the dauntless pioneers lives today in the heritage that inspires new leaders to do in this age, such deeds as may be done for the glory of their faith in the same spirit that these things were done when the early Mormon colonists found their way westward to Utah.[35]

While work was progressing on the Mar Vista chapel the decision was also made to divide the Redondo Branch. This decision was related to unspecified difficulties among members of the branch, and on 1 July 1928 the El Segundo Branch was created.

Unfortunately, disagreements among the Saints were not limited to El Segundo. In the Santa Monica Ward difficulties arose between several members of the ward and Bishop Corbridge over the release of Otto P. Monson as a Sunday School teacher. Consequently, the stake presidency called a special meeting of Santa Monica Ward members to discuss the matter, and the ward was reportedly left with a better spirit.

The appearance of difficulties in the wards and branches might be ironic evidence that many Church members were beginning to believe that the Church had indeed been established fully in Los Angeles, a fact reinforced by the building of the Mar Vista and Wilshire Ward meetinghouses. The fact that prior to this time the number of problems arising were amazingly few might be explained, in part, by the perceived need of the members to bury their differences and work hard to establish the Church in the area. But when these Saints began to feel that the Church had arrived, so to speak, many seemed to turn their focus inward to the frailties of leaders and other members, thus at least partly hampering their ability to work together effectively. Such human frailties were not, of course, limited to the Hollywood Stake, but they illustrate the continuing challenges faced by Church leaders and members alike in their efforts to build the kingdom.

In April 1929 the stake presidency and high council decided that the responsibility for overseeing the genealogical work in the stake should be given to the high priests. This assignment was undertaken with vigor. In June a Genealogical Union meeting was held to teach the members of the stake the importance of genealogical work. Shortly thereafter, members of the stake were called and set apart as genealogical workers in the Los Angeles Public Library.

At the October 1929 stake conference, a new ward in the

Westwood, Sawtelle, and Santa Monica area was carved out of the Mar Vista and Santa Monica wards. In an unusual move, Elder Melvin J. Ballard had taken this action at the request of President McCune but without the approval of the rest of the Council of the Twelve. A month later, the new ward did not even have a name or any definite boundaries, though Westwood Ward was the favored name. On 20 November Elder Ballard returned to Los Angeles and called a special meeting of the Hollywood Stake high council. There he reviewed the reason for forming the new ward, explaining that while it was unusual for a member of the Twelve to act without taking up the matter with the other members of the Council, it was not unprecedented. He then told stake leaders that when the matter was discussed among the brethren, it was decided that Elder Ballard should disband the newly created ward. The major reason was that the Church was experiencing a lack of funds and was not appropriating money for new meetinghouses. As a result, the creation of the new ward was postponed. Elder Ballard told stake leaders: "Good will come from this if we are patient. I made a mistake. I regret it but I am willing to do what will help the cause in any way."[36] Although disappointed in the outcome, President McCune pledged the stake's support of the decision.

The centennial of the organization of The Church of Jesus Christ of Latter-day Saints was observed on 6 April 1930. From six members, meeting in the Peter Whitmer home in Fayette, New York, the Church had grown in a hundred years to an organization with 104 stakes and 1,032 wards and branches, with all the stakes located west of the Mississippi River. Church membership stood at 700,000, with 6,511 of that number being converts in 1929 and over 10,000 residing in Los Angeles.

Celebrations commemorating the Church's centennial were staged wherever Saints were located. The Hollywood Stake's celebration was held 26–28 April in connection with stake conference. On each night a program was presented that depicted the first coming of Christ, the re-establishment and growth of the Church, its expansion into other lands and cultures, the gathering of Israel, and the second coming of Christ. Fourteen nations were represented by members in native costumes, though few were actually natives of other nations. The program closed as the Hollywood Stake Centennial Chorus sang the "Hallelujah Chorus" and the congregation and choir sang the "Doxology." Each evening the Wilshire Ward chapel was filled to capacity as almost 2500 attended the three-day event.

At the centennial celebration Wilshire Ward's new Austin organ was played publicly for the first time by Alexander Schreiner. Sale Lake Tabernacle organist for many years, Schreiner was on leave from his position, having been invited by UCLA to play the first twenty-five recitals on the Mudd Memorial Organ. As a result, he was retained as an organist and lecturer in music at UCLA until 1939, when he returned to his position as Tabernacle organist. During the time he resided in the Hollywood Stake, he served as a member of the high council and as director of music at the Wilshire Boulevard Temple, one of the largest Jewish congregations in the world.

As the Church's centennial year drew to a close, the stake records for 31 December 1930 indicated that the baptized membership stood at 5,871, an increase of 2,500 in a little less than three years. Most of the growth had come in the previous year when the nation had been plunged into the Great Depression, for stake membership had grown by less than one hundred its first year of existence. The membership of the stake included one patriarch, 203 high priests, 111 seventies, 597 elders, 247 priests, 192 teachers, 300 deacons, 3,107 lay members, and 1,112 children. This membership was located in fourteen wards and branches: Alhambra, Boyle Heights, Garvanza, Glendale, Inglewood, Lankershim, Santa Monica, Wilshire, Hollywood, and Mar Vista wards, and the El Segundo, Elysian Park, Pasadena, and Redondo branches. During March 1931 the fifteenth unit in the stake, the Burbank Ward, was created by a division of the Glendale Ward, and Nephi L. Anderson was chosen as the ward's first bishop.

The centennial year of the Church found the nation in the grips of a great depression, brought about in part by the stock market crash of October 1929. Thirty billion dollars in stock market assets vanished almost overnight, with an additional forty billion disappearing in the next two and a half years. Nearly a third of the nation's banks failed. Between 1929 and 1933 unemployment increased from 1,499,000 to 12,634,000, over one-fourth of the work force. Millions more earned only starvation wages, as almost all sections of the economy cut back production. There were those living in $100,000 homes who could not pay the utilities. A new car often could be bought for under one hundred dollars, but incomes barely covered the necessities, let alone luxury items.

As was the case following World War I, thousands of Latter-day Saints from the Intermountain area tried to escape the Great Depression and fled their homes for California in the hope of a better life. Like most areas of the country, however, Los Angeles was not completely immune from the effects of the depression. Apartment buildings near Wilshire Boulevard could be purchased for fifteen to thirty cents on the dollar, but few could afford this opportunity.[37] However, as with the depression following World War I, Los Angeles fared somewhat better than most of the nation, particularly the Mountain West. For the Saints in Los Angeles necessities were often scarce, and occasionally it was not certain where the next meal would come from. Nevertheless, as bad as the situation was in Los Angeles, for many Saints who stayed in Utah it was worse. While in some wards of the Hollywood Stake unemployment ran as high as 20 percent at the height of the depression, this was significantly lower than the high of 36 percent unemployment for the state of Utah in 1931, one of the highest percentages in the nation.

While few Church members in Los Angeles were immune from the effects of the depression, the consensus was that Latter-day Saints in general, and full-tithe payers in particular, were less affected by the depression than the general population. It was apparent to most members that the Lord had been mindful of his people in Los Angeles.

The rudimentary welfare program that had been implemented in 1923 to help meet the needs of the great influx of migrants from the Intermountain West was expanded during the early months of the depression, and means were provided for bishops and the Relief Society to help poor Church members. Among the first steps taken were efforts to help the unemployed. Once again a stake employment center was established; the Melchizedek Priesthood quorums gave a party to benefit the unemployed, which was reportedly very successful in both a social and financial way. Each of the wards worked to collect funds, above and beyond fast offerings, to help those less fortunate.

Where possible, county, state, federal, and voluntary organizations were used to supplement the assistance provided by the local stake and Presiding Bishop's office during these early days of the depression. For many new arrivals from Utah, assistance from the Church was of vital importance since state and county organizations would only help those who had been in Los Angeles for at least three years.

To escape the realities of everyday depression life, entertainment was especially important for both the nation and the Saints in Los Angeles. Throughout the nation, the movie industry, radio industry, and book industry did brisk business as people sought momentary escapes from their problems. The need for entertainment was strongly felt in the Hollywood Stake, as dances continued to be sponsored regularly, with the M Men and Gleaners hosting the majority of them. These dances had to pay for themselves; consequently they were well planned, presented, attended in the grand tradition of the Hollywood Stake—and more often than not, they broke even. In addition to Church sponsored dances, Mormon dance groups, with the Debonairs the most notable, were also organized. Other forms of entertainment, such as stage productions, were also popular. In March 1931, for example, the stake presented a grand opera in the Wilshire Ward under the direction of the stake MIA, which was well attended.

In spite of the good intentions of stake leaders, the desire to do things nicely was carried to an extreme by some stake members. For example, a social organization was started among some of the wives of high councilors called the Ladies of the High Council, who reportedly were the ones insisting upon tuxedos at the parties for stake leaders.[38] Following the dedication of the Wilshire Ward, many young people desired elaborate weddings in the beautiful chapel before they went to the temple, though a temple marriage usually followed. Such problems were hardly major, but they did raise some concerns, especially among some of the Brethren in Salt Lake City. Thus, when Church leaders acted upon President McCune's request to be released, they went outside the stake for the new stake president and selected a man capable of helping the stake maintain the high standards which President McCune had set while eliminating the excesses of some members.

Nevertheless, as the Hollywood Stake approached its fourth anniversary it may well have been said of the Saints in Los Angeles, as it was said of the early Saints, that they were "laying the foundation of a great work. And out of small things proceedeth that which is great." (D&C 64:33.) As with any new situation, of course, mistakes were made; but compared with the accomplishments, the mistakes were minor. These Saints and their leaders were trying their best to face the challenges involved in nourishing the Church in a new environment under changing circumstances and, at the same time, dealing with the myriad problems of unusually rapid growth. For the most part the Saints in the Hollywood Stake had met their challenges in a most commendable manner and left an important legacy for the Saints of a later day.

Hollywood Stake
Part II

E eight years after he had been sustained as the first stake president in Los Angeles and four years after the Hollywood Stake was organized, George W. McCune was released at the April 1931 stake conference. LeGrand Richards, later the Presiding Bishop of the Church and after that a member of the Council of the Twelve, was sustained as the new Hollywood Stake president.

The calling of LeGrand Richards as stake president, as with the calling of George McCune, suggests the concerns of Church authorities over providing outlying areas with leaders who could effectively nurture the Church in those areas and who would not allow questionable practices to get out of hand. It was not uncommon during those days of expansion in the early twentieth century to choose leaders for Church units outside the Intermountain area from among those most recently arrived from Utah, or, at times, from among Utah residents who were then asked to move to the locations involved.[1] Thus, when Elder George F. Richards, LeGrand's father and a member of the Council of the Twelve, entered his son's real estate office in Salt Lake City in late December 1929, sixteen months prior to the

April 1931 Hollywood stake conference, it was by assignment of the First Presidency and the result of concerns for the still youthful Mormon community in Los Angeles. "President Grant wants to know," George F. asked, "whether you would be willing to move to California and serve as the president of the Hollywood Stake."[2]

"Well, Father," the younger Richards responded, "I have my business here with a dozen people depending upon me for their jobs. I don't know what I'd do for a living in California. We have a lovely new home. . . . Our daughters are at the mating age and have many fine friends." Then he added, "You'd better tell the President that I think enough of the Lord, the Church, and him that if this is what he wants, I will go down and look around to see how I can earn a living."[3]

This willingness to help the Lord's work characterized the life of LeGrand Richards. Born in Farmington, Utah, he served a mission to the Netherlands, served as president of the Portland, Oregon Branch, and then returned to preside over the Netherlands Mission from 1913 to 1916. Following his release as mission president he returned to Salt Lake City and became bishop of the Sugarhouse Ward, went on a short-term mission to the Eastern states, and was serving as a member of the high council of the Granite Stake when he was approached about moving to Los Angeles.

Within a month of his new call, Richards had sold his business, put his house up for sale, and was heading by himself in the family car for southern California. Once in California, he joined with former Utah friends and fellow Church members Alex Nibley and Preston Cannon selling real estate in the Rossmoyne residential development. Within a couple of months he purchased a house in Glendale and moved his wife, Ina, and his children to California.

The reason for Richards's move to Los Angeles was not announced, and it was not until 1978 that most people became aware of the circumstances.[4] As a result, shortly after Richards's arrival, and unaware that he was to become the new stake president, President McCune recommended him for bishop of the Glendale Ward. When President Heber J. Grant became aware of the proposed call, he suggested to President McCune that before receiving such a demanding position Richards ought to be given time to settle in. When Richards learned of President

Grant's recommendation, however, he immediately wrote his father:

> Glendale Ward is down on everything, and I think I'd better be bishop while I'm getting acquainted. If I am appointed stake president now, there will be an insurrection on the part of the leaders down here to think that a man was sent down from Salt Lake when they have so many talented men here in the stake. If I could lift Glendale Ward up, that would be my approach to the other appointment.[5]

As a result of this letter, President Grant approved Richards as the bishop of the Glendale Ward, and he was sustained in absentia while on vacation with his family and father at San Diego in late June 1930. Bishop Richards worked hard to turn around the ward by restructuring programs, putting all members to work, and then showing them a good time through effective ward socials. Within six months, the Glendale Ward had become a model of unity and growing spirituality.

LeGrand Richards had demonstrated great insight into human nature as well as the situation in Hollywood Stake when he told his father that there would be an "insurrection" if someone were sent down from Utah to replace President McCune. His concerns were realized when, on 25 April 1931, he was called into a meeting with Elders George Albert Smith and Joseph Fielding Smith of the Council of the Twelve, who were in town to reorganize the stake. Members of the high council, he was informed, were circulating a petition against the release of President McCune.

Somehow, news of the impending reorganization had begun to circulate even before there was any discussion with President McCune himself, and he learned about it early in April from two Beehive girls who were staying at his home and had received the information at an MIA meeting. Deeply hurt at the fact that he seemed to be among the last to know, he wrote President Grant that he "would have been happy and satisfied if my labors could have been rewarded with just an honorable release coming in the proper way."[6] President Grant quickly replied that while the matter had not been handled in the best manner, President McCune would, indeed, be given an honorable release in the proper way.[7]

Several prominent stake members, however, discovered what had happened and, feeling that their beloved stake president was not receiving the respect he deserved, but was being removed from office as a result of differences with the Brethren over the cost of the Hollywood tabernacle, they began circulating a petition protesting his release. At the meeting with the two Apostles, Richards stated that if it would be better for someone else to serve as stake president, he "would be perfectly happy to continue as bishop of Glendale Ward." He further suggested that it might be wise to discuss the matter with the priesthood at its meeting the following evening to learn how priesthood members felt. The Apostles agreed to this proposal.[8]

At the priesthood meeting, Elder George Albert Smith announced that President George W. McCune had been given an honorable release by the First Presidency and Quorum of the Twelve. Elder Smith then told the priesthood brethren that they would be given a chance to express their choice for a successor. After a period of discussion, the matter was put to a vote and LeGrand Richards received nearly the same number of votes as the popular first counselor, Arthur Sconberg. This was a strong enough showing in favor of Richards that the Apostles decided they would reorganize the stake presidency with LeGrand Richards as the new president.

Following the meeting, President Richards was asked whom he would like as counselors. He replied that he wanted as his first counselor the "man who headed the petition." "I don't believe he would accept," responded Elder George Albert Smith. "I don't think he would either," was Richards's response, "but it would stop him from heading any activity against me."[9] The man did refuse, but the second man on the list, high councilor David H. Cannon, accepted the position of first counselor. Another member of the high council, Charles H. Norberg, became second counselor.

Since the petition protesting the release of President McCune had originated with the high council, the visiting authorities offered to release all its members in order that the new president might begin with a clean slate. Instead, Richards asked that they be retained, telling the brethren: "I don't want them standing on the bank saying 'Watch him swim.' Just give me the high council as they are, and within a year I will have them all for me or release them one by one."[10]

At the Sunday afternoon session, 27 April 1931, the Hollywood Stake presidency was officially reorganized. Elder George

Albert Smith reviewed the dedicated labors of President McCune, mentioning that two years previously he had asked to be released, but the General Authorities felt it best for him to continue to serve. Elder Smith's call for an expression of appreciation for the service of President McCune and his counselors was greeted with a heartfelt vote by stake members. Elder Smith then presented the new stake presidency for approval, with John McCune continuing as stake clerk. No mention is made in the minutes of how this proposal was accepted by the people, but it seems safe to say that most members put aside their differences and pledged their support.

Nevertheless, some observers felt that there was much work to be done in the Hollywood Stake, for almost no part of it had escaped the formation of factions. There were even those who threatened to resign their Church positions after the new presidency was put in. Understandably, the new stake president felt that changes were needed in attitude, organization, and social patterns, and with his counselors he identified four major areas of concern: first, to overcome rifts and factions among stake members; second, to unite the stake family; third, to harness the talents and abilities of stake members; and fourth, to build spirituality. Two slogans were adopted to help meet these goals: "Not failure, but low aim is often our greatest sin," and "Work for everyone, and everybody working."[11]

Under the direction of President Richards, some things that had been important were no longer emphasized and others that had not been as important were given greater emphasis. He applied the same methods he had used in the Glendale Ward to the Hollywood Stake. In high council meetings, for example, he would make penetrating inquiries into each high councilor's concept of various aspects of the gospel. For several members of the high council this resulted in a change in their whole concept of the gospel and its applications in their lives. This in turn was carried over to the members of the stake as the high councilors visited the various wards.

President Richards was able to accomplish this change because of his belief in the good in people, and he would always build them up in his legendary warm manner, causing them to seek to do their best. One example was in his calling of a man to lead the stake's genealogical and temple program. When he suggested the man to his counselors and the high council, they told him he could not make the call because the man smoked. To this, President Richards replied, "I know it, but we can clean him up." After the man had accepted his new position, the president told him: "Now, there's one little thing we'd have to ask you to do. We couldn't have a man at the head of our genealogy and temple work who is using tobacco, but I told the brethren that you'd quit to do this important work for the Lord."[12] The man, embarrassed that others knew about his cigar smoking, committed to quit. A short time later, this same man led the first busload of Saints from the Hollywood Stake to attend the Mesa Temple. He not only responded to his stake president's confidence and did an excellent job in coordinating temple and genealogical work, but also eventually became one of the stake's most beloved bishops.

Prior to President Richards's administration, some of the Brethren in Salt Lake City had criticized the stake for a tendency toward elitism. Parties for stake officers, for example, often reflected the social status of some stake members. Many were held in the beautiful lounge at the stake center and formal dress was required. Other instances of somewhat exclusive social activities were suggested in the organization of special clubs by wives of stake leaders.

One of the first changes undertaken by President Richards was to remove some of the "Hollywood" from the Hollywood Stake in the dress required for stake-sponsored socials. Admitting that he enjoyed wearing his tuxedo as much as the next person, Richards nevertheless declared that until every member in a stake leadership position or bishopric could comfortably afford to wear one, formal dress would be optional, and he would set the example by wearing his Sunday suit.[13]

Always a great believer in the need for parties and socials in the lives of Church members, President Richards fostered them on both a stake and ward level. Each month, two high councilors were assigned to plan an activity for stake officers and their companions, and at Christmas time a party was given for all stake and ward leaders and their spouses. These events, in a less formal setting, helped further to promote unity and closeness among stake leaders. The stake also continued to sponsor many activities for general members, and bishops were encouraged to raise the level of recreation in the wards to make sure that the Saints were more sociable and that all were entertained.

To further strengthen unity between ward and stake organizations, President Richards invited members of the high council and stake auxiliary board members to accompany the stake presidency to each ward conference. This was not general Church policy at the time, but as the bishops saw such support being given to their conferences, they gave greater support to quarterly stake conferences. Within the first eighteen months, attendance at stake conference had more than doubled. In addition, stake and ward leaders were no longer given preferential seating at conference, but all seats were opened to everyone who came.

Another area that received great attention was reactivating the inactive. As he visited each ward conference, President Richards called for the priesthood rolls and placed a check mark by the names of the inactive members. At the next conference he would ask for these rolls again, to see what had been done towards bringing people back into activity.

The youth were not forgotten by President Richards, who emphasized that their social contacts must be considered seriously and that more attention must be given to special entertainments in order to help strengthen them in the gospel. Under his leadership, buildings were considered not only as religious and social centers, but also as recreation centers where all the youth could mingle. In addition to regularly scheduled dances, an annual M Men and Gleaner banquet was held, and the young people assigned each year to preside over the event worked hard to make each banquet more successful and attractive than the last. Special emphasis was also placed upon having the youth speak in ward meetings and stake conferences concerning various aspects of the Church and what it meant in their lives.

Renewed emphasis was given to family nights as parents were encouraged to set aside one night a week for their children, either at home or in a family outing. Since earlier efforts had not been coordinated, few undertook the effort. However, the stake presidency and high council, with the approval of the bishops, recommended that each Monday night be set aside throughout the stake as family night, and that no meetings be held on that night.

Wilford Edling, a member of the high council who would later become stake president, said that under LeGrand Richards's direction, "There was a great change in the spirituality. As a result of what President Richards did, those of us that succeeded him found ourselves in friendships and conditions of understanding that never would have been there except that he had set the pattern and led the way."[14]

One of the first socials given by the new stake presidency was a dance and reception at the stake tabernacle in June 1931 in honor of the service rendered by the former presidency. At this reception, President McCune was presented with a Hamilton watch and Sister McCune a set of silver candelabra. Counselors Arthur E. Sconberg and Louis K. Sims were each given a silver plate.

For the October 1931 stake conference the stake center's cultural hall was equipped with permanent loudspeakers, and several hundred people seated there were able to hear the sessions of conference. That conference was a historic occasion for another reason, also: Katherine Higginbotham was sustained as stake clerk, possibly the only woman ever to hold that position. From the time the Wilshire Ward was dedicated, Katherine Higginbotham had served as receptionist at the stake house and had done much of the detailed work for the stake clerk. An employee of Bishop Howells, she worked full-time as a kind of "bureau of information" for the Church in Los Angeles, answering the questions of visitors who might visit the new building. An office was built for her just inside the east entrance. During the summer of 1931, President Richards obtained President Grant's approval to appoint her as stake clerk. Such approval was necessary, for Church policy usually requires that this position be filled by a Melchizedek Priesthood holder. Clearly, President Richards, who had great faith in the ability of women, was not one to let tradition interfere with practicality.

During the later months of 1931 the Religious Conference at the University of California, Los Angeles contacted stake officials recommending that the LDS students on campus form an organization to promote fellowship and religious identification and instruction, as other denominations had done. The lack of such an organization had been a matter of concern among stake leaders, who were fearful that the religious needs of students in this secular environment—many being exposed to worldly ideas for the first time—were not being adequately met. Since the Church had no regularly sponsored programs to handle the religious training of university students, the Hollywood Stake took it upon itself to ensure that these needs were met.

In 1932, two Latter-day Saints Deseret Clubs, forerunners of the institutes of religion in southern California, were organized in Los Angeles under the direction of the stake. The first was organized at UCLA, 13 January 1932. Two Latter-day Saint faculty members, Dr. Vern O. Knudsen, dean of graduate study, and Alexander Schreiner of the department of music, were instrumental in establishing this organization on campus, and fellow Hollywood Stake members Preston D. Richards and Adele Cannon Howells were assigned to organize the club. The stake originally paid the ninety-dollar yearly fee which was required of a member of the University Religious Conference Association. When a University Religious Conference was organized at Los Angeles Junior College, a Deseret Club was established there, too, in April 1932, under the encouragement of LDS faculty member Heber G. Harrison. Over the next several years, Deseret Clubs were established also at Pasadena and Compton Junior Colleges, at Woodbury College, and at the University of Southern California.

In 1936, jurisdiction of the Deseret Clubs was transferred from the stakes to the Church Educational System, with the leadership for these clubs and the responsibility for religious training being handled by CES personnel doing graduate work in the area. Shortly thereafter, a "federation" called "The Deseret Clubs of Southern California" was established to integrate the social activities of the students from the various colleges. Later, this "federation" became known as the Institute of Religion at Los Angeles, and still later individual institutes were organized on the various campuses. G. Byron Done was made responsible for overseeing religious instruction for students in the entire area.

During President Heber J. Grant's administration the brethren in Salt Lake City began placing renewed emphasis on various aspects of gospel living, and no doctrine was preached more diligently than the Word of Wisdom. In 1921 adherence to the Word of Wisdom became a requirement to attend the temple. During the early 1930s, as the nation moved towards the repeal of Prohibition and as the Church looked forward to the centennial of the Word of Wisdom in February 1933, the topic was given even greater emphasis. The Hollywood Stake also took up the same campaign, and few stake conferences passed without discussion of the Word of Wisdom. Unfortunately, some members of the stake even began to feel that too much emphasis was being placed on it and complained that it could hardly be distinguished from the gospel itself; one member of the high council eventually went inactive over the issue.

When the matter of implementing greater observance of the Word of Wisdom was discussed by members of the stake presidency, they decided to follow the course generally adopted throughout the Church. Concerning leaders of auxiliary organizations who used tobacco, it was recommended that the older members be labored with in kindness to help them overcome their habit, as was the case with the man who was called to head the temple and genealogical work in the stake. However, less leeway was given to younger members of the Church who had not been entrenched in their habits for so many years.

Less attention was given to alcoholic beverages for the eighteenth amendment had, theoretically, taken care of the problem of "strong drink" by limiting its supply. Unfortunately, however, a few stake members became caught up in the Hollywood environment by partaking of the liquor served at its many parties, as well as using other items forbidden in the revelation. A 1937 survey of active stake members revealed that 77 percent strictly obeyed the Word of Wisdom by never using tea, coffee, liquor, or tobacco, while nearly 18 percent reported that they were occasional users, and a little over 5 percent were frequent users of these items.[15]

To help those members who needed to overcome such habits, and to help ensure that other members, especially the youth, were educated as to their evils, the stake followed Church precedent and established an Anti-Liquor and Tobacco Committee which functioned for many years, initially under the direction of John T. Corbridge. The committee also tried to carry the message of the Word of Wisdom to non–Latter-day Saints. During the 1932 Los Angeles County Fair, for example, the California Mission and the Hollywood Stake sponsored a Word of Wisdom exhibit which was reportedly well attended.

Another emphasis throughout the Church at this time was on the payment of tithing. With the onset of the depression, the amount of tithing being paid by Church members had greatly decreased, and the Brethren noted that the majority of Hollywood Stake high councilors and stake officers were not on record for having paid tithing during the first three months of

1933. They urged that greater care be used in setting an example. As the depression continued, however, it seems that less attention was given to the commandment. A survey of active stake members found that 76.4 percent paid tithing, but only 38.1 percent could be classified as full-tithe payers.[16] Bishops were instructed to push this principle and see that temple recommends or priesthood advancements were not given to non-tithe payers.

Another topic receiving renewed emphasis was temple marriage. During the January 1933 stake conference, a special high council meeting was called at which Elder Melvin J. Ballard discussed one of the greatest challenges facing the youth—marrying outside of the Church. He stressed the continuing need for better social opportunities where LDS youth could meet and become acquainted, and he told stake leaders that one result of so many marriages outside the Church was "the problem of running a spiritual hospital."[17]

The need for Church-sponsored socials for the youth was apparent, but President Richards also noted that parents were shirking their duties if they relied entirely upon the Church to provide social activities for their children. He recommended, in one of his characteristic displays of wisdom, that parents with young people in their homes should also give parties at their houses to help introduce their children to other youth with similar values. The responsibility to see that socials were given to help their children find partners worthy of temple, or celestial, marriage was as much with the parent as it was with the Church, President Richards suggested.

With this renewed emphasis upon celestial marriage, it was also appropriate that stake leaders and parents set the example for the youth by attending the temple. Although a trip to the Mesa Temple required a fair amount of time and money, the Los Angeles Stake, under the direction of President Leo J. Muir, had achieved a remarkable record of temple and genealogical work and regularly sent busloads of stake members to the temple. During May 1933, the Hollywood Stake conducted its first excursion to the Mesa Temple. The cost was $5 for a round-trip bus ride and a week's stay, and the excursion was well supported by stake members. This was the first of many stake-sponsored trips to the Mesa and St. George temples until a temple was built within the boundaries of the stake.

President Richards also placed considerable emphasis upon missionary work in the stake. In connection with the January 1933 stake conference, Elder Melvin J. Ballard accepted an invitation from the stake to conduct four member-missionary meetings the following week. These meetings were designed to help teach non-members about the gospel and motivate the Saints to recognize the importance of doing missionary work. Attendance at the meetings averaged over one thousand per night. Nearly one-third were non-members, and the increased emphasis on missionary work soon paid dividends in converts. During 1933 486 cottage meetings were held in the homes of stake members and 140 converts made, all without the assistance of full-time missionaries. The following January these missionary meetings were held again, but attendance averaged only around three hundred.

During this time the Hollywood Stake received Church-wide recognition for some of its accomplishments. This was partly the result of a good-natured but sometimes overly intense rivalry between the two stakes in Los Angeles. This seems to have been more important initially to the Los Angeles Stake than to the Hollywood Stake, as the former was constantly issuing challenges and broadcasting its successes, but soon the latter was caught up in the spirit of competition. The 3 December 1933 Hollywood Stake *MIA News* reads: "The Hollywood Stake is nineteenth in the Church-wide drive for Improvement Era subscriptions according to a report received from Salt Lake City. Los Angeles has at last been exceeded by Hollywood but the desired goal of first place is yet to be obtained."

At a Primary convention in April 1932, Janette Bingham Dee of the Primary General Board reported that the Hollywood Stake led the Church in attendance at Primary. At the MIA Conference in Salt Lake that year, Hollywood Stake's Myron Pinkston was elected vice-president of the Church-wide M Men organization. In 1933, Paul Vorkink of the Glendale Ward represented the stake well by winning the Church-wide re-told story contest at June conference. Also in 1933 the Glendale Ward M Men team won the all-Church basketball tournament in Salt Lake, which called forth a victory ball for the champions given by the Hollywood Stake in the recreation hall at the Wilshire Ward.

It was also in 1933 that Elder George Albert Smith publicly stated that it was his opinion that the Hollywood Stake had led the Church in leadership during the past year, a comment elicited largely as a result of the renewed emphasis upon spiritual matters sparked by LeGrand Richards. By 1933, it was clearly evident that although the Hollywood Stake was the younger of the two, it no longer played second fiddle to the Los Angeles Stake.

At the October 1933 stake conference, Presidents Heber J. Grant and J. Reuben Clark were the visiting General Authorities, and over 1,900 stake members were in attendance. To have two members of the First Presidency attend a stake conference suggested that something important was in the offing, such as a division of the stake or the calling of a new stake president. Neither change took place, but between the Sunday sessions of conference the two Church leaders called President LeGrand Richards to preside over the Southern States Mission, beginning in January 1934. Having originally been called to the Southern states as a young man only to have his call changed to the Netherlands, President Richards was delighted that the call had come again. President Grant informed him that they would not make the announcement but that he was free to make it as he saw fit. On 25 October, therefore, at the first high council meeting following stake conference, President Richards told stake leaders of his new assignment. On 20 December the Richards family left California for a brief visit in Salt Lake City before going to Atlanta, Georgia. Until the stake presidency was reorganized in January, First Counselor David H. Cannon served as presiding officer.

December was the traditional social season for the Saints in the Hollywood Ward, with socials planned every weekend. Included among the many events was "a mammoth farewell party" given for President and Sister Richards on Friday, 15 December. The evening began with a program in the Wilshire Ward chapel. President Cannon spoke for stake members when he said of President Richards: "He came to the office with such devotion to the Church and to its ideals and with such a fervent testimony of the gospel that his influence was immediately felt. He has stimulated spiritual growth throughout the entire stake." He concluded that LeGrand Richards's courage and understanding, his fair sense of justice, his knowledge of Church government, and his humility "had endeared him to them all."[18] After the program a dance and reception followed in the recreation hall and lounge, and gifts were given to the Richardses in heartfelt appreciation for their service.

Those stake members who worked with LeGrand Richards had nothing but praise for him. While it was apparent that President McCune's mission and greatest skill was as an administrator in seeing that the Church was well established in a new environment, LeGrand Richards's great legacy was that of spirituality. Katherine Higginbotham later concluded, "Those who followed him worked hard to maintain the level of spirituality which he and his counselors achieved, but they did not surpass it."[19]

The man chosen to succeed LeGrand Richards as the third president of the Hollywood Stake was David H. Cannon. Born in Salt Lake City in 1893, Cannon was the son of Elder Abraham H. Cannon, a member of the Council of the Twelve. He fulfilled a mission to the British Isles from 1912 to 1914 and then married Marguerite Callister. Following graduation from George Washington University Law School in 1917, he became an assistant attorney general of the United States, a position which ultimately brought him to Los Angeles in 1924. He eventually entered into private practice, specializing in postal law.

Elders Rudger Clawson and George Albert Smith of the Council of the Twelve presided at the 24 January 1934 stake conference where David H. Cannon was unanimously sustained to lead the stake. President Cannon chose as his counselors Charles H. Norberg and Wilford G. Edling.

On 24 December 1933, the Presiding Bishop of the Church, Sylvester Q. Cannon, called a special meeting of priesthood leaders in Los Angeles to inform them that the economic situation of the Church had improved to the point where it could once again help local congregations obtain suitable meeting places. When the nation was thrown into the Great Depression, the Church had placed a moratorium on chapel building since the decrease in income experienced by most Church members also resulted in a dramatic decrease in the amount of tithing being paid. This moratorium caused at least a few in Los Angeles to wonder whether they should remain in California, since having an appropriate structure in which to meet was viewed, to a certain extent, as confirmation of Church support of their decision to leave Utah.

Following Bishop Cannon's announcement the southern California Mormon newspaper, *The News 'n' Nuggets*, ran the headline, "Permanency of Mormons in Southern California Assured." The accompanying article concluded, "the restraint under which the Church in this section of the country seems to have been held by the officials with regards to building has been dispelled."[20] The article also stated that because chapels could again be erected, divisions which were badly needed in many of the wards would finally be made, thus assuring the vitality of the Church in Los Angeles.

In 1934 the California gubernatorial election became a major issue in the Mormon community. By this time Church leaders generally shied away from the kind of partisan politics that had characterized the Church before Utah statehood, though they occasionally entered the political scene when they felt that moral issues were clearly involved. President Heber J. Grant usually refused to express himself on political matters for fear that the Church might be accused of interference in politics, but in this case he believed that moral considerations compelled him to take a stand.

Upton Sinclair, a socialist with a controversial economic platform, was running for governor on the Democratic ticket. Disagreeing with his economic solution to the nation's woes, President Grant, a Democrat, fearlessly commented on the California election in the October 1934 general conference and came out in opposition to Sinclair; however, his moral opposition extended beyond the basic economic issue:

> I do not want to be accused of engaging in politics, but . . . I am willing to have it said that this is politics, if they want to make politics of it. Any Latter-day Saint who sustains or votes for a man to be governor of a state who had ridiculed in print the Savior of the world, is doing that which I as President of the Church hereby condemn.[21]

President Grant also sent a letter to California Church leaders stating his opposition to Sinclair, which letter was widely published in California newspapers. Needless to say, such a strong political stance by the President of the Church caused controversy among the members in California. Many continued publicly to support Sinclair, feeling, evidently, that

Church membership did not compel them to follow their leader on this issue, and some became even more vocal in their support of Sinclair. Consequently, President Alonzo Hinckley, the California Mission President and a recently sustained member of the Quorum of the Twelve, was asked to meet with California Church leaders to further discuss the matter. On 24 October 1934 he met with Hollywood Stake leaders, quoted from President Grant's address, and read President Grant's letter. Elder Hinckley told stake leaders that "President Grant spoke in the last conference as President of the Church," and then sadly noted that "the ears of some of our people are more open to the politician than they are to the prophet."[22] It cannot be determined how Church members actually voted, but Sinclair lost the election to incumbent Governor Frank Merriam.

In 1934 baptized membership in the Hollywood Stake exceeded 8,000 members, a doubling in size since the creation of the stake six years earlier. Units within the stake ranged in size from El Segundo Branch with 114 members to Wilshire Ward with 1,813 members. Statistical reports suggested, however, that much needed to be done to encourage progress among the Saints. For example, only 20 percent were attending sacrament meeting, still above the Church-wide average, but a far cry from the record 67 percent of December 1923.

On 1 January 1935, the San Fernando Branch of the California Mission became the seventeenth unit of the Hollywood Stake. Later that month the eighteenth unit was added with the creation of the Arlington Ward. On 20 January 1935 a special high council meeting was held in conjunction with the bishopric of the Wilshire Ward at which both President Grant and Presiding Bishop Sylvester Q. Cannon were in attendance. The meeting was called to discuss the division of the Wilshire Ward to relieve its crowded conditions, and it was decided to divide the ward at Adams Boulevard. Those residing south of Adams became members of the new Arlington Ward, while those to the north continued in the Wilshire Ward. On 27 January the Arlington Ward was officially created at a meeting of the Wilshire Ward, and Lyman H. Robison was sustained as bishop. When the Arlington Ward first met in March 1935, meetings were held at the Masonic lodge on Western Avenue.

The eighteen wards and branches in the Hollywood Stake were well beyond the optimal number for an effective stake organization. Consequently, the decision was reached to split the stake at its April 1936 quarterly conference. Not only had the Hollywood Stake grown but so had the Los Angeles Stake, which contained sixteen units, and a decision was made to split that stake, also, at its May quarterly conference.

President David O. McKay, Second Counselor in the First Presidency of the Church, was the presiding authority at the division of Hollywood Stake, and Elders Reed Smoot and John A. Widtsoe of the Council of the Twelve were also in attendance. The wards and branches to be part of the new stake were Alhambra, Burbank, Elysian Park, Garvanza, Glendale, Lankershim, Pasadena, San Fernando, and Hollywood. The wards and branches remaining in the Hollywood Stake were Arlington, El Segundo, Inglewood, Mar Vista, Santa Monica, Boyle Heights, Wilshire, and Redondo. When the Los Angeles Stake was divided the following month and the Long Beach Stake created, the Redondo Branch was transferred to the new Long Beach Stake and the Boyle Heights Ward was transferred to the Los Angeles Stake.

The announcement concerning the proposed division of the Hollywood Stake was made in the Saturday evening priesthood session of stake conference. Following the meeting the Melchizedek Priesthood quorums of the new stake were asked to meet in the recreation hall. President McKay then asked each of the 119 men present to submit two names for the new stake and the names of three brethren for the new stake presidency. These recommendations were then prayerfully studied.

As the last speaker during the Sunday morning session of conference, Wilford Edling was giving his farewell address as an outgoing member of the Hollywood Stake presidency when he was handed a note that President McKay wished to speak to him immediately. Cutting short his remarks, President Edling left the conference to meet with President McKay, who had been his mission president in England ten years earlier. During their meeting, President McKay asked President Edling if he were called as stake president, would he choose as counselors any of a list of people he then named. President Edling replied that he probably would not unless President McKay recommended it. President McKay then informed him that the Lord wanted him to be the new Hollywood Stake president and that he had two hours to choose his counselors and seven members of the high council, the minimum number needed to make a quorum.[23]

At the Sunday afternoon session, President McKay pre-

sented the proposed division of the stake along with the name of
Pasadena for the new stake. David H. Cannon was sustained as
the president of the new stake with Rulon H. Cheney and LeRoy
J. Buchmiller as his counselors.

Wilford G. Edling was unanimously sustained as the new
president of the Hollywood Stake with Preston D. Richards and
Jesse R. Pettit as counselors. Katherine Higginbotham continued for a time as stake clerk. At the same time the Adams
Ward was received into the Hollywood Stake by a vote of the
people.

Thirty-three year old Wilford Edling, a native of Ogden,
Utah, was a tax consultant and certified public accountant by
profession. Following his mission to England, he had attended
George Washington University in Washington, D.C., before
finishing his schooling in southern California. He came to California in 1927 and the following year married Relia Schade in
the Salt Lake Temple. His accounting training would later be
put to service in the Church when he accepted the position as
chairman of the Church Finance Committee. For many years he
read the auditor's report at each April general conference.

Concerning the division of the Hollywood Stake, the
California Intermountain News wrote:

> It is now evident that Pres. McKay and his associates, Elder Reed
> Smoot and John A. Widtsoe, members of the Quorum of the
> Twelve, were authorized to administer extensive surgical treatment
> to the stakes in Southern California. And they did it—with a free
> hand and without anesthetics. . . . Hollywood Stake was cut
> squarely in two. . . .
>
> One of the startling surprises of the division and reorganization
> effected last Sunday was the ruthless kidnapping of Adams Ward
> by the Hollywood Stake. . . .
>
> The most amazing of all the surprises, was the selection of
> Wilford G. Edling as President of the Hollywood Stake. Even the
> wisest of the prognosticators overlooked this young man. . . .
>
> An evidence of his wisdom is found in his selection of Preston D.
> Richards, and Jesse R. Pettit as his counselors. It would have been
> difficult to find two abler men. Each of them has had wide and
> varied experience in church activities.[24]

And as President Edling pointed out, each was also old enough
to be his father.

Not only did President Edling have two able counselors to
assist him in his new assignment, he also had the benefit of
Elder John A. Widtsoe of the Council of the Twelve, who was

spending a year in Los Angeles while teaching at the University of Southern California. In the summer of 1935 the university offered an opportunity to the Latter-day Saints, Catholics, Jews, and Protestants to teach about their religious doctrines as a regular subject of instruction for credit, provided the churches would provide qualified instructors. This opportunity was largely the result of the work of Dr. Eugene L. Roberts, an LDS member of the USC faculty.

When word of this opportunity reached the Brethren in Salt Lake, they considered it of sufficient importance to ask Elder Widtsoe, former president of Utah State Agricultural College and of the University of Utah, to inaugurate the program. The classes taught by Elder Widtsoe were well attended and marked the first time that Mormonism was taught formally in a non-Mormon university for academic credit. It was noted that the classes dealing with Mormonism had the largest attendance of any of the classes under the new program. The initial course, "The Church and Its Program" proved so popular that additional courses were offered, including "The Doctrine and Covenants of the Church," and the "History and Philosophy of Mormonism." Consequently, what originally was intended as a partial year assignment became a year's assignment. In addition to classes offered for credit, classes were also taught in the evening for the benefit of local Church leaders.

One result of Elder Widtsoe's visit was that a spirit of tolerance toward the Mormons was built up among the clergy in Los Angeles, and many prejudices began to disappear. Dr. Carl S. Knopf, for example, dean of the school of religion at USC, was one of those touched by Elder Widtsoe and his successor, G. Byron Done. Nicholas Smith, president of the California Mission, later told a general conference audience of his astonishment when he attended a lecture on the Mormons by Dr. Knopf and heard him declare that the man who wrote the Book of Mormon must have been inspired of God or he could not have said such things.[25]

In addition to his work at the university, Elder Widtsoe helped inaugurate the fireside program during his time in the Hollywood Stake. Almost every Sunday evening, special theological lectures were held at a different ward, followed by refreshments. One of the favorite topics of discussion was also one of Elder Widtsoe's favorite subjects: the Word of Wisdom.

Throughout the 1930s the nation remained in the grips of depression. At the April conference of 1936, President J. Reuben Clark announced the particulars of the Church's new welfare plan, called "The Church Security Plan." Prior to this time, however, the essence of the program had already been implemented in the Hollywood Stake and throughout Los Angeles, both through local initiatives and the special emphasis placed upon the area by the Church's Welfare Committee, under the direction of Harold B. Lee.

One of the first steps taken by the stake was the establishment of an employment committee. In 1932 Alice H. Osborn of the Adams Ward, one of the wards hardest hit by the depression, opened an inter-stake employment and relief office which operated out of her home until room was obtained at the Adams Ward chapel. In addition, each ward was asked to make work, where possible, for its unemployed and underemployed members. Charles H. Norberg was appointed work director for the stake. At first the elders quorums and Relief Societies undertook drives to bring clothing and furniture to the storehouse, but in time this program was taken on by the unemployed.

Initially, each ward provided the means for distributing clothing and furniture, but for better efficiency and service a bishop's storehouse was created in the old mission home. A storehouse was also created for food items, which initially were distributed at ward houses or from the homes of local leaders. At first anyone could come and select items from the storehouses, but as time progressed and abuses were noted it was decided that materials could be obtained only with an order from a bishop or Relief Society president. Requiring such an order helped ensure that the worthy poor received the benefits. As abuses continued in the system, such as non-Mormons contacting all the bishops in Los Angeles for assistance, Leona Fetzer was appointed by the Church to work with the Relief Society in clearing applications for assistance.

In March 1938, the Hollywood and Pasadena stakes opened a cooperative self-help salvage program in Glendale, which, by the end of the year, proved so successful that it was taken over as part of the Church's southern California welfare efforts and its scope expanded to include all the Saints in Los Angeles. In October 1939, this effort at helping people to help themselves became the Deseret Industries of southern California.

The welfare efforts of the Saints were a model of cooperation and good will. Fast offerings actually increased, and storehouse provisions came not only from these funds but also from other contributions, such as Relief Society canning projects. Within its first six months of operation the new storehouse provided food for 265 families. The next year saw various wards and quorums establish programs for milling flour and growing fruits and vegetables. Many LDS physicians and dentists donated their services, wards financed men who wanted to set themselves up as gardeners, the Adams Ward Relief Society made fifty quilts, and the Inglewood elders quorum helped one of its needy members build a home. In truth, there were few who were not involved in the welfare effort.

Following the announcement in late 1933 that chapel construction could once again begin, the Hollywood Ward began looking for a permanent meeting place, and a lot was purchased in the eastern portion of the ward. Since this was not the most ideal location, however, building plans were delayed. During a further search for a better location, it was discovered that the Mt. Olivet Methodist Church on Normandie Avenue was for sale. This structure, which had been built in 1924 at a cost of $100,000, was for sale for $35,000. While the location and price were right, questions still remained about whether a chapel could be purchased from another church, and Bishop Raymond L. Kirkham contacted President Grant for advice. Upon hearing of the deal, President Grant told Bishop Kirkham that he would personally come down, look at the property, and decide what should be done. After looking the structure over, he told the brethren to buy it immediately.[26] On 5 November 1937 the Hollywood Ward met in its new home for the first time. Two weeks later, on 18 November, the purchase was consummated. This building became one of the few chapels in the Church that was not built initially for the use of its members.

When the Wilshire Ward was dedicated, President McCune announced that the stake's next major building goal was a temple in the Southland. The feeling that the Saints in Los Angeles needed a temple was also shared by Church leaders in Salt Lake City, and in 1934 a committee of members of the Los Angeles LDS community was asked to make an intensive search for a temple site. Members of the Hollywood Stake on the search committee included David H. Cannon, Charles H. Norberg, and Wilford G. Edling of the Hollywood Stake presidency, Bishop David P. Howells, and Preston D. Richards. During the search President Cannon and his counselors made several trips each month to check on possible locations.

Early in the search for a temple site it became obvious that there were many differing opinions as to where the temple should be located. Most Church members favored a site in the downtown area or in the eastern part of the city, which was more developed than the western section. Several times sites were found, but on more than one occasion desirable properties were taken off the market when the owners learned that the property would be used for a Mormon temple. Other sites the Church could have purchased were not approved by the Brethren in Salt Lake City. These included a location on Pico Heights, another on Los Feliz Boulevard east of Western Avenue, one on Olive Hill in the Hollywood area, and a lot on the corner of Santa Monica and Wilshire Boulevards in downtown Beverly Hills.

Finally, a 24.33-acre site was located in Westwood on the north side of Santa Monica Boulevard between Manning and Selby Avenues and extending to Ohio Avenue. It was the property of the Harold Lloyd Motion Picture Company and contained the old Harold Lloyd estate, a large stucco building with a tile roof that had also been used as the company offices and in 1937 was being used as a sorority house by students attending nearby UCLA. This impressive site was considerably larger than would be needed for a temple. Upon seeing it, however, President Grant emphatically approved the location, observing that it would better serve the needs of the Church than would a smaller piece. In April 1937 the purchase was completed and the title to the property transferred to the Church. The purchase price as reported in the *Deseret News* was $175,000.[27]

Many local Saints, however, questioned the purchase of a site for a temple in Westwood, which was in the northwestern portion of the Los Angeles Basin. Nevertheless, the wisdom of the decision was soon confirmed, for what was then the outskirts of Los Angeles became engulfed by the city as it expanded to the north and west, rather than to the east as most felt it would at that time. Also, the temple is now conveniently located near freeways that were not envisioned at the time, making it accessible to everyone living in the Los Angeles area.

Following the purchase of the temple lot, Bishop Howells was appointed chairman of the California temple building committee. On 8 May 1937 this committee sponsored its first fund raising evening, a turkey dinner at the Wilshire Ward.

By September 1937, Church authorities had appointed a board of temple architects to draw up plans for both the Idaho Falls Temple and the Los Angeles Temple. The six members of this board prepared several possible floor plans, including a one-level temple, separate facilities for endowments for the living and dead, and the use of one room for the endowment ceremony, rather than the four rooms traditional at the time. From the beginning, however, it was difficult for the board to be creative as a group, for its members could seldom agree upon designs. They finally agreed that each would prepare sketches reflecting his own ideas and that all the sketches would be submitted to the First Presidency, who would then choose the design. The First Presidency chose for the temple in Los Angeles the design of board members Lorenzo S. Young and Ramm Hansen, which featured a central tower, and this design was published in Nels Benjamin Lundwall's 1941 edition of *Temples of the Most High*. However, before that temple could be built the decision was made to erect a larger one, though the new Los Angeles Temple architect, Edward O. Anderson, would freely borrow from the Young and Hansen design.

In July 1939, at a high council meeting held at the home of President Wilford Edling, a decision was reached to create a new ward from the western portions of the Wilshire and Hollywood Wards. A. Eldon Rex was approved as bishop of the new Beverly Hills Ward with William F. Jackson and C. Dean Olson as counselors. Estelle Dixon was the first Relief Society president. The first meeting of the Beverly Hills Ward was held on 6 August 1939 at the Beverly Hills Women's Club at 1700 Chevy Chase Drive, where the ward continued to meet until its chapel next to the Los Angeles Temple was completed in 1953.

On 8 November 1939 a special priesthood meeting of the Hollywood Stake was called by Elder Stephen L Richards of the Council of the Twelve. The purpose of this meeting was to discuss another division of the Hollywood Stake. Elder Richards first announced that the Hollywood Ward would be returned from the Pasadena Stake after a three-year absence, and that the Torrance and Redondo Wards would be brought in from the Long Beach Stake. He then recommended that the stake be divided so that one stake would include the Adams, Arlington, Beverly Hills, Hollywood, and Wilshire Wards and the other would include the Santa Monica, Mar Vista, Inglewood, Torrance, and Redondo Wards and the El Segundo Branch. This division was approved by those in attendance. Elder Richards then announced that the stake would no longer be called the Hollywood Stake, but would henceforth be known as the Los Angeles Stake. The name of the existing Los Angeles Stake was changed to the South Los Angeles Stake, and the newly created stake would be the Inglewood Stake. This action was also unanimously approved. A special stake conference was held on 19 November 1939 at which all these changes were made official. The following week Elder Richards officially organized the Inglewood Stake with Alfred E. Rohner as president.

Exactly why the name of the Hollywood Stake was changed and why it was done at a special conference rather than waiting until a regular stake conference does not appear in the official records. However, several reasons have been proposed. Some stake members, such as former presidents Wilford Edling and Winfield Cannon, have suggested that for some time President Grant and President McKay had expressed concern about the atmosphere of the movie industry, which was synonymous with Hollywood in many people's minds. They wanted the name of the stake to be changed so that a stake of Zion would no longer be associated with that industry in the public mind.[28] There seems to be some justification for this, for a week before the special priesthood meeting was called Presidents Grant and J. Reuben Clark spent four days at Twentieth Century Fox consulting with executives on matters relating to the production of the film *Brigham Young*. They had ample opportunity to observe the false glitter and facade of the industry.

Some even recall that President Grant had such a dislike for the movie industry that he vowed there would never be another Hollywood Stake in the Church. However, some who have studied his life feel that he had a great admiration, not dislike, for it, and could separate the acts of a few individuals which gave it such a bad name from the industry itself and the town in which it was located.[29]

Others have suggested that since the stake center was not located in Hollywood, but in Los Angeles, changing the name would be more consistent with the unofficial Church policy of the day of naming Church units according to the areas in which their stake or ward houses were located.[30] For three years Hollywood and the Hollywood Ward had not even been in the stake. Still others have suggested that Church authorities in Salt Lake City did not want to build a temple within the boundaries of a stake named Hollywood, seeing that name as incompatible with what the Church stood for.[31]

Whatever the reason, an important era in the history of the Church came to a close after twelve years with the end of the Hollywood Stake. The preceding twelve years was a time of remarkable growth in Los Angeles, during which many important things were accomplished. Not the least of these was the building of the beautiful Hollywood Stake tabernacle/Wilshire Ward chapel, the creation of three additional stakes in Los Angeles and one in the valley, the instigation of the welfare program to help take care of the Saints' temporal needs, and the purchase of land within the stake boundaries for a temple to help further fulfill the spiritual needs of all the southern California Saints.

As the year 1940 approached and the "new" Los Angeles Stake began its existence, the Church in Los Angeles appeared to have a bright future. While much had been accomplished during the period of the Hollywood Stake's existence, much more needed to be done, and the Saints in the Los Angeles Stake were gearing up to handle the challenges ahead. At the same time it could be seen that the dark war clouds over Europe caused by Germany's invasion of Poland in September 1939 were spreading over the horizon of the United States and would eventually plunge the nation into a new world war. That war would momentarily sidetrack some of the California Saints' hopes and dreams, particularly with regard to their long-awaited temple.

The War Years and Beyond

O n 7 December 1941, a date labeled by the American President Franklin D. Roosevelt as one "which will live in infamy," the United States suddenly found itself actively involved in a worldwide war that had already engulfed much of Europe and Asia. Americans everywhere suddenly became more united than they had been in generations, as they prepared for a time of trial and sacrifice in order to bring the war to an end. "With confidence in our armed forces," President Roosevelt assured them the next day, "with the unbounding determination of our people, we will gain the inevitable triumph. So help us God." Among the Mormons in California, problems arising from a world at war could not be avoided, and the struggle of America to achieve victory also became one of the many important challenges the "new" Los Angeles Stake would face in the 1940s.

Though its name had been changed, little else had as the stake continued to be one of the leaders in the Church in many respects. More important, stake members were continually of service to their fellow Saints throughout the area and were willing to sacrifice to do their part in building the kingdom. Once again stake members pioneered new programs and continued to adapt to the challenge of living the gospel in a growing urban center, a situation made more unique by a world at war.

At the January 1940 stake conference, the first for the "new" Los Angeles Stake, it was reported that 37 percent of the Aaronic Priesthood in the stake attended priesthood meeting, as compared with an anemic Church average of 27 percent. This represented a 15 percent stake-wide increase during the previous six years, but still left much room for improvement. However, attendance of 20–25 percent at sacrament meeting and stake conference essentially mirrored Church averages. Those who attended stake conference heard their leaders address the concerns of both the stake and the Church: ward teaching, tithing, fast offerings, welfare work, the Word of Wisdom, the adult Aaronic Priesthood program, observance of the Sabbath day, missionary work, the *Era* campaign, activity in the Church, marriage within the Church, the law of chastity, and other principles of the gospel.

Socials continued to play an important role in the lives of members of the Los Angeles Stake and, as seen in a sampling of activities, neither quality nor quantity diminished. On 9 March 1940 the opera *La Traviata* was produced at the stake center by the Hollywood Ward and was very favorably received. "Gold and Green Balls" continued to be traditional events, with each ward choosing a Gleaner Girl as its queen, who then entered into a competition at the stake Gold and Green Ball, where one queen was chosen to preside. The Valentine's Dance for 1941, like many other dances, took the form of a girls'-choice dance with the young ladies selecting dancing partners to fill their cards. The stake also sponsored a "hard times" dance for the unmarried adults, with prizes given for best costumes and to the winners of the games and activities. The Adams Ward M Men put on the hilarious M Men Scandals of 1941. Included in the cast was Spencer H. Osborn, later a counselor in the Adams Ward bishopric and still later one of the General Authorities of the Church. A dance followed the play. Each year the M Men and Gleaners also held a barbecue in Griffith Park. The Twenty-fourth of July continued to be observed, often with three-day stake-sponsored carnivals. Each Christmas, the Adams Ward continued to present the *Messiah.*

Because of financial problems associated with the Great Depression, certain changes were made in the operation of stakes and wards. Beginning in 1939, Church authorities in Salt Lake City requested that all stakes and wards implement the budget system. Each organization was to estimate what its operating expenses would be, and then Church members would be asked to contribute enough above their tithing and fast offerings to meet those expenses. In 1940, the first full year of implementation, the stake's first operating budget was set at about $1200 with each ward being asked to pay to the stake thirty cents per capita. Similar budgeting procedures were followed in the wards.

By 1940 plans for the anticipated Los Angeles Temple seemed to have fallen on hard times. One problem was the apparent lack of enthusiasm for genealogical and temple work throughout the Church. In July the Genealogy Committee in Salt Lake City announced that at the rate genealogical work was being done, the Salt Lake Temple could handle all the temple work in the Church by itself. Margaret E. Gordon, supervisor for genealogy work in the California Mission, addressed this matter and what it meant for the anticipated Los Angeles Temple. In an article in the *California Intermountain News* she declared:

> Our people must be awakened to the fact that there is much to be done and that unless we all take an interest in seeking after our kindred and having the work done for them there will be no need for more temples. That is the situation we in California face. Until the Mesa Temple is unable to handle our work why should there be a temple here?[1]

Other reasons for delay were related to the war. In 1941 President David O. McKay was asked when work on the temple would begin. His reply was that it would not begin until after the Idaho Falls Temple was finished, and it was estimated that this would be in 1942. Consequently, funds for the Los Angeles Temple were included as part of the Church's 1942 budget.[2] The 7 December 1941 attack on Pearl Harbor, however, brought the United States into the Second World War and resulted in the delay of all building that was not war related, including the Idaho Falls Temple. As a result, that temple was not dedicated until September 1945, a month following the end of the war.

It would be another eleven years, however, before the Los Angeles Temple would be dedicated. In a way, its history was reminiscent of the Salt Lake Temple, which took the Saints forty years to complete. Various factors caused the delay, including war and the building of other temples. Through all the delays, the Saints remembered that Brigham Young had prophesied that the temple would be built as soon as they were prepared to use it. Likewise, it seems as if neither the Lord nor his prophet were in a hurry to build the temple in Los Angeles until the Saints in California were ready to use it. In the meantime, not only delays associated with the war but also attention given to other aspects of building the kingdom took precedence over the temple.

Although the worst of the Great Depression was past, welfare work continued to be a major theme during stake conferences and continued to receive much of the attention of stake members. On 13 September 1940, a large welfare fair was held at the stake center that featured entertainment by prominent Mormon artists and booths displaying the various welfare activities undertaken throughout the area.

The welfare projects in the Los Angeles Stake covered a wide range. The Wilshire Ward Relief Society made children's clothes, rag rugs, and doll clothes from second-hand materials collected by the Deseret Industries. Adams Ward erected a woodworking shop on the property adjoining its chapel where a variety of projects were undertaken to pay welfare allotments and stake budget, and retire ward indebtedness. This woodshop also provided many people with needed items at reasonable prices. Among the items produced were cabinets for the Los Angeles Stake Center, chests of drawers, tables, book cases, and food dehydrators. One year, thirty thousand Christmas tree stands were made for commercial dealers and for other wards in Los Angeles.

Another welfare project which began in the Adams Ward was a sewing factory. Bishop Jay Grant of the Adams Ward was owner and manager of Grant Apparel Company, one of the leading manufacturers of blouses on the West Coast. Bishop Grant offered employment opportunities to Church members, and all blouses made during the training period were given to the welfare program. This program proved so successful that stake leaders came to feel that clothing production could be a welfare project in which stake members could participate relatively easily. Food production and processing, on the other hand, had proven difficult in an urban setting. In 1948, therefore, a stake sewing center was established in the former California Mission Home next to the Adams chapel. For a number of years, this served as the main welfare project of the Los Angeles Stake, becoming the main supplier of men's and boys' shirts for the welfare system. The "Shirt Factory," as it came to be known, received favorable coverage in the Los Angeles *Times* and continued to help the image of the Church in Los Angeles.[3]

In the late thirties Church leaders continued to express concern that some youth were marrying outside the Church. In an attempt to deal with the problem, Adams Ward projected a plan for improving the piece of property located next to the chapel to be used as a recreational park. The idea was to help LDS youth get together in a desirable atmosphere, with no cost to themselves. At the time young people were having to pay out money for their recreational programs with less than satisfactory results, for when they were taken away from the ward centers their surroundings were not always conducive to good morals and LDS ideals. The Adams Ward recreation center was opened in November 1940.

To improve the property, ward members spent $3,000 for equipment and landscaping. The park, enclosed by a fence, had a basketball standard, volleyball, badminton, ping pong, and tennis courts. There were places for shuffleboard, horseshoes, sand boxes, swings, slides, and jungle bars. Picnic tables were placed under shade trees and a drinking fountain was installed. Fluorescent lights were added to illuminate the park. In addition, a fireplace for barbecuing, rest rooms, and showers were also planned. This park would play an important role in filling the recreational needs of the Los Angeles Latter-day Saint community for many years, and especially during World War II.

On 24 February 1941 the La Cienega Branch was created out of portions of the Wilshire, Arlington, Beverly Hills, and Mar Vista Wards. Although it was created mainly from wards of the Los Angeles Stake, this new branch became part of the Inglewood Stake.

The following month, on 19 March 1941, a testimonial banquet was given at the stake center in honor of the Arlington Ward M Men basketball team which became the second team from the stake to win the all-Church basketball championship in Salt Lake City. The team included three brothers—Collins, Harold, and Talmage Jones—with Talmage the leading scorer in the tournament and its most valuable player.

By the fall of 1941 the United States was gearing up for possible involvement in war, and the Church was making preparations to assist its members in the armed services. Hugh B. Brown, the Church's Religious Coordinator for Servicemen, came to Los Angeles to ask the Saints for help in providing suitable entertainment for LDS boys who come there on leave from the many military establishments on the Pacific Coast.

The Los Angeles Stake responded to the call and sponsored the first dance for servicemen on leave on Saturday, 1 November 1941. Young ladies of the stake who desired to help out were asked to save the evening for a "date with a soldier."[4] That night families in the stake put up the soldiers in their homes and provided them with home-cooked dinners on Sunday. Another dance was held on Armistice Day, 11 November 1941, following MIA, and the servicemen were again provided with home cooked meals that evening.

The events at Pearl Harbor on Sunday, 7 December 1941, brought the United States into full involvement in World War II and brought about many changes for the Church in Los Angeles. Because Los Angeles was located on the coast it was felt that there was the possibility of enemy attack, and local authorities requested that all buildings be blacked out if the air-raid signal sounded. During the first high council meeting held two days after the Pearl Harbor attack, the air-raid signal sounded and the stake center was blacked out. As a result of the possibility that meetings might be disrupted because of air raids, Church leaders in southern California decided that changes should be made in meeting schedules. Most southern California wards and stakes canceled all evenings meetings and began to hold sacrament meetings in the afternoon or immediately following Sunday School. MIA was also moved from the evening to the afternoon.

The Los Angeles Stake adopted a schedule in which priesthood meeting was held from 9:00 to 10:00 A.M. on Sunday, Sunday School at 10:30 A.M., and sacrament meeting at 11:30. This arrangement continued until May 1942, when the First Presidency issued a circular stating that the scheduling of back to back meetings was not the policy of the Church and that the practice should be abandoned. Sacrament meeting was therefore moved back to 6:30 P.M.

Another reason why meetings were scheduled back-to-back was the rationing of fuel. In Utah most members were close enough to travel to Church without much difficulty. In Los Angeles, however, where distances were greater, traveling to meetings several times on Sunday became a burden; consequently, some of the Saints curtailed their Church activities, for they did not have enough gasoline coupons to make attendance at all their meetings possible.

Among the events canceled because of the war was the Church's general celebration of the Relief Society centennial on 17 March 1942. Nevertheless, the Los Angeles Stake continued with its own celebration. The stake Relief Society, under the direction of President Mary S. Jordan, planted a tree at the northeast corner of the Wilshire Ward and placed a marker near it commemorating the important centennial.

The Relief Society centennial was not the only event to become a casualty of war. The traditional June MIA conference was cancelled for the duration and April and October general conferences were shortened from four to two days and then opened only to stake presidencies, high councilors, patriarchs, and bishoprics. A pass had to be obtained to enter temple square during conference time.

Because attendance at general conference was restricted, the Church experimented with prototypical regional conferences. In May 1943 priesthood members throughout southern California met at the Los Angeles Stake Center under the direction of John A. Widtsoe of the Council of the Twelve; Thomas E. McKay, Assistant to the Twelve; and Richard L. Evans of the First Council of the Seventy. Specifically invited to this meeting were the presidencies of Aaronic Priesthood quorums and ward teachers. Nearly fourteen hundred priesthood holders were in attendance.

The war brought other changes. Visits of General Authorities to stake conferences, for example, were reduced. Instead, quarterly bulletins were issued from Salt Lake City outlining changes in various programs and giving messages of hope. Leaders in Salt Lake City also requested that all stake auxiliary meetings, such as conventions and institutes, be discontinued, and that ward activities be curtailed. While some ward Primaries continued to meet at chapels during the week, others were moved to Sundays while others were held in homes. Monthly Relief Society luncheons were still held, but only when enough ration tickets had been gathered to purchase the food.

Initially, because of war conditions, the MIA General Board requested that all stake socials except the Gold and Green Ball be discontinued. However, because of the charge that had been given to provide proper entertainment for LDS servicemen, stake leaders petitioned the First Presidency for permission to hold dances more often. In August 1942 permission was given to hold two dances each month.

When the First Presidency authorized the stake to hold two parties per month, it was with the understanding that they would be opened only to members of the Church and investigators, and that restrictions would be placed upon the attendance of nonmembers.[5] Prior to this time, Church-sponsored dances had been opened to all soldiers, but several unpleasant incidents had occurred which Church officials hoped to avoid in the future. In order to comply with the First Presidency's wish, cards were issued by the various bishops, and admittance to Church-sponsored events was limited to those with cards.[6] A card could be obtained only through an interview with the bishop, or in the case of non members, through the recommendation of someone who possessed a card. Thus, through greater supervision, the goal of providing a wholesome atmosphere where young Latter-day Saint men and women and nonmembers of similar standards could gather was accomplished.

Making the need for appropriate entertainment all the more acute was the fact that southern California beaches were closed for a time because of fears of a possible attack, and most of the parks in Los Angeles were taken over by the military. Consequently, the Adams Ward recreation park was a boon for providing Saturday activities for stake members as well as for servicemen. Beginning in 1944, each Saturday night during good weather a dance was held on the newly built dance floor. Games, activities, and refreshments were also provided, with the Gleaner Girls of the stake serving as hostesses. Thus, while the recreation center had been built initially to serve the needs of the youth of the stake, it also helped fill the pressing need of assuring that LDS servicemen had an enjoyable evening with Church members in an atmosphere conducive to maintaining Church standards.

Stake dances during the early years were used not just for socialization but also for inspiring patriotism. One of the dances presented by the M Men and Gleaners carried the theme "The

Spirit of '42." The stake's Gold and Green Ball for 1943 also followed a patriotic theme with the queens from the various wards dressed to represent American women in times of the Revolutionary, Civil, Spanish-American, and First and Second World Wars.

In November 1942, the only time figures were published, there were 144 men and women of the Los Angeles Stake serving in the armed forces.[7] Many of these were members of the Hollywood Ward, which periodically held "Hollywood Ward Night" during sacrament meeting under the direction of Bishop John M. Russon. At these meetings letters were read from the ward's servicemen and members of the ward were called upon to bear their testimonies.

Under the direction of the stake MIA, headed by Ira L. Hurst, stake YMMIA president, and Mona Kirkham, stake YWMIA president, the Los Angeles Stake furnished a recreation room at Camp Haan, where servicemen not on leave could go during their leisure time. Each of the wards and the various stake organizations accepted specific assignments in furnishing the room. In addition, a project was undertaken to see that meeting times of the various wards were posted in nearby military camps.

LDS servicemen on leave frequently visited Hollywood, a favorite gathering place for many American servicemen. Because there were not enough motels and hotels in the area, they sometimes resorted to sleeping in the streets. When the Hollywood Ward elders quorum became aware of the situation, it encouraged ward members to open their homes on the weekends for LDS servicemen who were visiting Hollywood or who were attending Church-sponsored activities. Edna Lee Hollister accepted the assignment to see that those needing housing were placed with ward members willing to put them up for the night. Once a "guest" had been put up in the home, ward members were encouraged to write to him throughout the war. To help this undertaking, cots were purchased from ward budget funds and stored at the chapel for use by ward members. Nearly two hundred servicemen could be housed any particular evening because of the efforts of the Hollywood Ward.

The members of the Los Angeles Stake were also directly involved in the war effort. The Hollywood Ward undertook a project to sell war bonds, eventually selling bonds valued in excess of $15,000. The stake's MIA joined with other MIAs throughout the Church in selling war bonds to help purchase rescue boats for planes. Stake members responded to Red Cross calls and organized blood drives. The Beverly Hills Ward organized a Victory Garden Committee composed of Rulon Murphy, Bert Dalton, Frank Rolapp, Wilbur S. Thain, and Burton M. Oliver, who supervised four ward garden projects encompassing about seven acres.

The stake's war effort also proved a means for innovative welfare work. The Los Angeles Stake undertook a project in cooperation with the United States Employment Service, the Labor Division of the Department of Agriculture, and the Los Angeles Chamber of Commerce to help harvest Southland crops that might otherwise have remained unharvested because of a lack of labor. When it was learned that there were fields that needed harvesting, stake members organized to help, and those who were not able to work in the fields often furnished the use of their automobiles. Those who worked on this project not only earned credit for Church welfare activity but also helped the war effort by harvesting badly needed food.

As the war progressed, Los Angeles's population grew as people came from throughout the country to work in the rapidly expanding war industries. These industries, in fact, brought not only an increase in population but also an increase in traffic, a greater demand for land, a rise in housing costs, and the beginnings of serious problems with smog. No longer was unemployment a major concern of the welfare program in Los Angeles. However, the increase in the number of Latter-day Saints created a major new welfare concern—finding adequate housing for newly arrived Church members.

To meet the demands for war-related goods, factories began running three shifts a day, and as men were drafted, women began taking their place in the factories, ushering in a permanent change in the work force and contributing to a gradual change in perspective concerning the place of women in society. Because of the increasing population, the accelerated movement of people, and the constant changes taking place in work schedules and the makeup of the labor force, a major problem faced by the Los Angeles Stake and other stakes in the area was filling ward and stake positions and seeing that programs, such as ward teaching, were adequately run. Consequently, a major portion of the energy of stake leaders was spent trying to fill the holes which continually seemed to arise in the organizational structure. In spite of such trying wartime conditions, however, stake officials did a remarkable job of keeping the stake vibrant. They were helped out by the fact that as migrating Saints moved in, there always seemed to be at least one of the new arrivals who could fill a particular vacancy.

When the war finally ended in August 1945 and peace was brought momentarily to the world, it had not been without tragic cost to the Los Angeles Stake. Records indicate that at least twenty-two members of the stake lost their lives as a result of the war.[8]

While the war took a top priority during the early 1940s, there was other work that needed to be done in the stake. In October 1941 ground was broken for the Arlington Ward chapel. The following month construction work commenced and all employable members of the Church in Los Angeles who were receiving welfare assistance were assigned to be part of the labor force. In December 1942 the Arlington Ward moved into its new building, though until the chapel was dedicated services were held in the recreation hall. The dedication service, originally scheduled for April 1943, had to be postponed because of the restrictions Church leaders had placed upon General Authority travel. Finally, in June 1943, President David O. McKay dedicated the Arlington chapel, which had cost nearly $54,000 to build. It would not be until 1948, however, that the beautiful mural of the Sacred Grove, which was the work of Dr. Martella Lane and for which the Arlington chapel was well known, was added and unveiled.

The Arlington Ward was not the only ward to undertake a building program during the war. In May 1943, after six years of planning and fund raising, Hollywood Ward members, under the direction of Bishop Russon, began an intensive and extensive six-month renovation, redecoration, and re-furnishing program for their chapel. The chapel had been purchased at a cost of $35,000 and now an additional $14,000, plus donated labor, was spent to renovate it. The money was raised partially through carnivals and plays sponsored by the ward. On 23 November 1943 the Hollywood Ward chapel was rededicated by Elder George Albert Smith, President of the Council of the Twelve.

Sometimes overlooked in stake histories are those things that are often the most important, yet the most difficult to do justice to. Chief among them are the tireless efforts of the many people who have served as teachers in the Primary, MIA, Sunday School, Relief Society, and priesthood quorums. Through their efforts and examples they set the tone and help establish levels of knowledge on which Church members often build for spiritual growth. Unfortunately, because the Primary is more a teaching organization than an activities organization, its work in setting the proper foundation for little children in the Church is seldom mentioned. Because its activities outside the classroom tend to be few, this organization is given little attention in stake minutes. The same holds true for the work of the Sunday School as well as the classroom activities of the other organizations.

While all the outstanding teachers and memorable lessons that were the strength of the Los Angeles Stake cannot be mentioned, it is at least appropriate to mention one caring teacher as an example of the powerful influence often wielded by such unsung spiritual heros. When Paul H. Dunn, later of the Church's First Quorum of the Seventy, became a priest in the Hollywood Ward in the early 1940s, Charles B. Stewart was his quorum advisor. Of Brother Stewart, Elder Dunn told the audience at a Brigham Young University devotional:

> I suppose he was late in his seventies when he was assigned by the bishop of the Hollywood Ward to be our adviser. And you know what a seventy-year-old man looks like to sixteen-year-olds. I thought Moses had returned. And we weren't about to give him much of a chance—sometimes we were a little cruel the way many teenagers are.
>
> I'll never forget the first morning we went up to our priests' class. Brother Stewart was standing at the door, not in the room, greeting his boys. There were six of us, as I recall, in that little quorum. He stopped us one by one as we made ready to enter the room. And when it came my turn he said, "You're Paul Dunn, aren't you?"
>
> "Yes, sir."
>
> And he told me a little bit about myself. "Now," he said, "we have a requirement in this priests class. You can't enter until you give me a new thought." He said, "Have you got one?"
>
> I hadn't had one in ten years, but he insisted, "We want a new thought." And I couldn't give him one. So he said, "All right, I'll

teach you one. Now you repeat after me, 'Attention is the mother of memory.' " And I stumbled through it and gave it back to him. He said, "That's fine, young man, you may enter my class."

We had a fine class. We were a little disturbing to him at times, I'm sure. I remember he had long, bony fingers. I'll never forget he used to seat us in a semicircle around his feet. . . . He would come along that row and say, "Now, young men, we have invited the Lord to be with us today and he expects our attention. Remember, 'Attention is the mother of memory.' "

And I'll never forget one day as that finger came down the row, he said, "You realize, young men, that you are the future leaders of the Church?" He continued, "Why, in this very circle there may be a future General Authority." And we all laughed. I remember when my call came, some of them were still laughing.

Well, the class period ended. We shaped up a little bit and went to go out, and he stopped us at the door and he said, "You can't leave until you give me another new thought." I didn't have one, and so he taught me another. He said, "Remember, Paul, 'A strong man and a waterfall always channel their own path.' Now repeat it back to me." And I did. He said, "You may go."

The following week I came to class and once more he said, "Do you have another new thought?"

"No, sir." So he taught me another.

I still recall it, "Example sheds a genial ray which men are apt to borrow, so first improve yourself today and then your friends tomorrow." I had a little trouble giving that one back, but he helped me as he did all of his boys.

Soon the class ended and he said, "Have you got a new thought?"

"No, I haven't."

"I'll teach you another, 'There was a wise old owl that sat in an oak, the longer he sat the less he spoke. The less he spoke the more he heard. Oh! Why can't we be like that wise old bird?' " Then he told us that he called these sayings "gem thoughts" and that the time would come in our lives when we would want to draw upon these ideas to help us in our lives. "One day you will find their true meaning."

"Paul," he'd say, "A good name is better than a girdle of Gold.' Remember that!" Well, we left his class finally, after almost two years of association. I can testify to you the impact of his example still remains.

[Others of these gem thoughts included: "There's an odd little voice ever speaking within, that prompts us to duty and warns us from sin. And what is most strange, it makes itself heard, though it gives not a sound and says not a word" and "Oh, what a tangled web we weave, when first we practice to deceive."]

I was on the island of Okinawa, May of 1945, when I received a letter from Mrs. Stewart and attached to the letter was a little obituary column announcing the passing of Charles B. Stewart, my adviser, my friend, my teacher. And honor to his name, in his concluding week of life he had typed a fresh page of "gem thoughts" for one of his priests who was fighting a great battle far away. Included was a half-written letter which said: "Dear Paul, I've been thinking about you in that far-off country, discouraged, I'm sure, and somewhat depressed; and in order to build your spirits, I have included some additional gem thoughts." I still carry the list with me, brother and sisters, and so I admonish you to listen carefully to these great leaders and teachers.

I know some of you get a little discouraged at times when things aren't always going just the way they ought, pressures of the moment, great decisions to make, lots of complications, but listen while you can because I promise you the hour will come in your life when you will draw upon these great words of wisdom as you make greater decisions in the future.

Since my days with Charles B. Stewart I have become a collector of "gem thoughts." I have many thousands because he taught me to think new thoughts.[9]

In August 1944 the Wilshire Ward bishopric, wanting to increase sacrament meeting attendance and at the same time provide an atmosphere for quiet contemplation, initiated a half-hour "vesper service" before each sacrament meeting. This program, reminiscent of "The Spoken Word" program presented over the air each Sunday morning by the Church, was designed to offer "a period for quiet, restful relaxation and enjoyment, being particularly timely in encouraging comforting respite from our generally hectic, war-shadowed daily existence."[10] It lasted for nearly three years, before it was brought to an end at the request of the Brethren in Salt Lake City.

The service usually began with a prelude hymn, "Though Deepening Trials," with organ music provided by several fine organists, including Cicely Adams Brown and Mary Ellen Smith, or by the Wilshire String Ensemble under the direction of Marcellus Smith. The program itself consisted of musical numbers and a speaker. Only occasionally, at first, were outside artists invited to perform, but eventually a different guest artist was featured each week, with a schedule of those who were to perform often being published months in advance. When this happened, the Brethren, many of whom had had misgivings from its inception, felt that the vesper service had passed from the spiritual into the secular and requested that it be discontinued.[11] In addition, the hoped-for increase in sacrament meeting attendance was never fully realized. Although an average of three hundred persons attended the vesper service, many would leave at its conclusion and not stay for sacrament meeting.

With the end of World War II, the Saints helped the nations of the world to pick up the pieces. To help aid the Saints in war-torn Europe, clothing and nonperishable food drives were undertaken throughout the United States. Nearly $60,000 worth of goods was gathered by the Church in Los Angeles and sent for the relief of the European Saints. At the same time, to help pick up the pieces at home, the Los Angeles Stake presidency appointed George W. McCune to visit and administer to Latter-day Saints at the Veterans Hospital at Sawtelle.

Because of the war conditions, the number of young men and women who could serve missions had been greatly reduced. With the end of the war, however, restrictions on the calling of missionaries were lifted and young men and women in the Southland answered the call to preach the gospel in large numbers. Each week the *California Intermountain News* contained many announcements of missionary calls.

The Los Angeles Stake grew rapidly during the war, mostly because of the influx from the Intermountain area for employment in defense industries. At the beginning of 1947, stake membership stood at 5118, an increase of over a thousand since the beginning of the war. All this created the need for a sixth ward in the stake, and on 30 June 1946 the LaBrea Ward was created from portions of the Wilshire, Hollywood, and Beverly Hills Wards. G. Lynn Hogan was sustained as the first bishop and Gunhild L. Beckstead as Relief Society president. Initially the meetings of the LaBrea Ward were held in the Wilshire Ward chapel.

New Year's Day 1947 not only rang in a new year, but also marked Utah's centennial year. Throughout the year celebrations were held both in Utah and California commemorating the arrival of the Mormon pioneers at the Salt Lake Valley. In the 1947 New Year's Day Rose Parade the State of Utah entered a Utah centennial float. It immediately followed the queen's float and was awarded first prize in the state and county divisions.

In March the Wilshire Ward under the sponsorship of the stake presented a Cavalcade of Mormon Music, which was described in the *California Intermountain News* as "a truly worthy contribution to the Utah Centennial Year."[12] In the latter part of June, the Los Angeles Stake staged a Pioneer Ball at the stake center under the sponsorship of the Sons and Daughters of the Utah Pioneers. Prizes were given for the best pioneer costumes. In July the Hollywood and Beverly Hills Wards sponsored a carnival at the Adams Ward recreation center to celebrate the arrival of the pioneers.

A choir from Los Angeles under the direction of Abel J. D. Peterson and made up of members of at least ten wards and four stakes made a tour of Utah during July. At the Twenty-fourth of July Parade in Salt Lake City, the California chapters of the Sons and Daughters of the Utah Pioneers entered a float depicting the contributions of the Mormon Battalion. There were reportedly many Los Angeles Stake members who saw this float, as a large portion of the Beverly Hills Ward went to Salt Lake City for the centennial celebration.

In November 1947 members of the First Presidency came to Los Angeles to visit the temple site. On 15 November, President George Albert Smith announced in the *Church News* that Church leaders were "thoroughly satisfied with the site and if assurances can be had that zoning laws will protect the surrounding area we will be ready to proceed with construction." Preston Richards, a member of the Los Angeles Stake presidency and a former law partner of J. Reuben Clark, was given the responsibility to do the legal work for the temple. Finally, the long-awaited day of having a temple in Los Angeles seemed near at hand. In December the Church took the first formal step when the Los Angeles City Planning Commission was asked to approve construction.

January 1948 marked the twenty-fifth anniversary of the creation of a stake in Los Angeles, and this called for a celebration. On Sunday, 25 January 1948, a commemorative meeting was held at the Adams Ward chapel, where the stake was organized, to which all those who were present at the organization were especially invited. There were 104 in attendance who had been present twenty-five years earlier, including all members of the original stake presidency, four high councilors, one member of the high priests presidency, three bishops, two counselors in bishoprics, one ward clerk, and twenty members of the original young people's chorus. Announcement of the meeting had been made in the *California Intermountain News* for several weeks, and the number present seems to indicate that many members who had helped pioneer the Church in Los Angeles had moved away from the area. In addition to those invited guests, the congregation was approximately the same size as that which attended the services on 21 January 1923—exceeding one thousand. George W. McCune conducted the commemorative exercises.

The growth of the Church in the twenty-five years that had passed since the organization of the stake is seen in the fact that the original twelve wards created the first year were now located in six stakes that included over fifty wards. Church membership in Los Angeles had grown from around 4,000 in 1923 to nearly 40,000.

A major concern among Church leaders continued to be youth marrying outside the Church. During the early months of 1948 Bishop Jay S. Grant of the Adams Ward felt great concern when statistics showed that less than 50 percent of his ward's youth were marrying within the Church. A subsequent survey of all the wards of the stake revealed that nearly 60 percent of the youth of the stake were marrying outside the Church, with a majority of those losing all contact with the Church.[13] Seeing a need to be met, Bishop Grant, with the blessing of President Edling and Howard W. Hunter, president of the Pasadena Stake and chairman of the regional stake presidents' council, set out to find a solution.

Shortly after he had been put in the Adams Ward bishopric, Bishop Grant and his wife, Nina, had held what they called "get acquainted parties." They invited to their home for games and refreshments different groups of long-time ward members plus new move-ins or converts. This program not only proved successful in establishing friendships, but occasionally resulted in the marriage of some of the young people who met at the Grant home. The Grants decided to try the principle with the LDS youth in general by arranging for parties where they could meet each other in a positive, Church-related atmosphere. Using their own home and financial means and a committee of stake members, they set out to establish a "get acquainted party" for the M Men and Gleaners in Los Angeles.[14]

Bishop Grant contacted the leaders of each of the six stakes, who were asked to furnish lists of the unmarried M Men and Gleaners in their stakes. When the names were tallied, there was a total of more than 2200. This number was more than could be accommodated even at the stake center, let alone a garden party at the Grant home, so it was decided to limit attendance to one thousand, with the remainder to be invited to a second party. Personal invitations were sent, and at the first party in August 1948 nearly six hundred showed up, some from as far away as San Francisco. To attend the party, guests had to obtain a card from their bishops, such as those used for dances during the war, verifying that they were members in good standing.

When the young people arrived they found that a wooden dance floor had been set up on the Grant's lawn, and a Hawaiian orchestra was playing the music. The guests were greeted at the door by members of the committee who saw that each of them signed a register, was given an autograph book, and then had a piece of paper pinned on. The autograph books were provided so that those attending the party could keep track of their newly made friends. The pieces of paper helped them to get acquainted. Prior to the party, Bishop Grant's committee met to think of words that were associated in pairs, such as "night" and "day," "salt" and "pepper," and "Jack" and "Jill." Each piece of paper contained one of these words, with a matching word being given to a member of the opposite sex. Those couples who matched their tags were eligible for a prize, and in searching for their matching names they got to know not only each other but other people as well. The names and addresses on the register book were published following the party and sent out to all those in attendance so that they might keep in contact with those who signed their autograph books.

These initial parties proved so successful that the Los Angeles Stake scheduled a "get acquainted dance" at the stake center in the later part of September 1948. Other stakes scheduled similar dances, and hardly two weeks passed without a "get acquainted dance" in one of the stakes in the Los Angeles area. Not only were the youth getting to know other members of the Church whom they might not have known otherwise, but the goal of increasing temple marriages was achieved as at least ninety-three couples who were introduced to each other for the first time at these socials were married in the temple.[15]

At a stake conference held on 16 January 1949, with Elders Spencer W. Kimball and Mark E. Peterson of the Council of the

Twelve in attendance, Wilford Edling was released as president of the Los Angeles Stake after thirteen years of service. John M. Russon, bishop of the Hollywood Ward, was unanimously sustained to take his place. As counselors, President Russon chose Melvin Keller and Orson Haynie, and Ralph T. Rolapp was sustained as stake clerk.

The usual expressions of appreciation given to retiring stake presidents were especially deserved by President Edling. During the last six years of his presidency he lived in Los Angeles while his family lived in Salt Lake City, and only an occasional visit could be made. In 1943 Relia Edling's asthmatic condition had deteriorated to the point that a change of climate was needed to escape the effects of the ocean breezes. For years the Edlings had desired to move to Glendale, partially to escape the breezes, but since that was outside the stake boundaries they remained where they were so that President Edling could fulfill his assignment as stake president. Because Relia had family to stay with in Utah, and relatives there in the medical profession, she finally moved to Salt Lake City for what they initially felt would be only a short separation. As the length of separation grew, however, President Edling approached President David O. McKay on several occasions regarding the possibility of a release so that he could be reunited with his family. Each time he was approached, President McKay discussed the matter with the First Presidency and each time President Edling would be told, "Yes, there will be a change, but not yet."[16] Each time there was also a promise that when he was released, he would receive blessings as a result of his sacrifice.

Consequently, the Edlings tried to make the best of the situation. The family made summer visits to Los Angeles as long as Relia's health would permit and President Edling visited his family in Utah when the occasion would allow. During the war years these visits were especially infrequent because of gasoline shortages. Whatever trips could be made during this time were usually by train.

This was indeed a difficult time for the Edlings, and in describing this period, President Edling once said:

> I have listened intently to many testimonies on the efficacy of prayer. Perhaps I can best telescope this multi-year experience by saying that every such testimony I can strongly affirm, for it was those talks with the Father of us all that made life not only bearable

with its wonderings but at times truly peaceful and joyful. The promised blessings surely did follow.[17]

Following his release, the Edlings did indeed move to Glendale where they found a house that matched the drawing of the home they hoped one day to live in. Although not for sale when they first saw it, eventually they were able to buy it. Later, because of his accounting work, Brother Edling was invited to be chairman of the Church's finance committee and the family moved to a beautiful home in Huntsville, Utah, President McKay's home town, where they continued to live a wonderful life together until the death of Sister Edling in 1986.

On 3 February 1949, the Los Angeles Stake held a special program in tribute to the members of the outgoing stake presidency. Gifts of thanks and remembrance were presented to them, and following the program the Hollywood Ward presented a three act play.

The new stake president, John M. Russon, was born in Salt Lake City and moved with his family to southern California in 1924. After graduating from Hollywood High, he studied at the University of Utah and served in the Swiss-German Mission. He married Mary Anderson in the Mesa Temple on 29 November 1935. Professionally, he worked in the life insurance business, specializing in estate analysis and planning.

As President Russon assumed leadership, the variety and quality of activities in the Los Angeles Stake continued to be impressive. On 20 January 1950, for example, an LDS art exhibit was held in the Wilshire Ward building. This exhibit, sponsored by the Wilshire Ward, was the inspiration of Claire Hobbs Snyder, who also displayed some of her own works along with those of numerous other artists in the Mormon community. A similar exhibit was held annually for several years, receiving favorable coverage in the Los Angeles *Times* and giving many musicians as well as artists a chance to demonstrate their talents.[18] The exhibits were often held in conjunction with the Wilshire Ward MIA's "Evening of Music," a program in the chapel which usually preceded the art demonstration in the cultural hall.

The year 1950 marked California's statehood centennial. While this anniversary did not receive as much attention from most members of the California Mormon community as had the centennial of Utah, for many of them their native state, there was one activity of note. During the spring a group of nearly three hundred descendants of the men of the Mormon Battalion retraced the battalion route, with the men in military uniforms and the women in period dresses. When the group arrived in Los Angeles, a flag-raising ceremony was held at city hall, not far from the original site where the Mormon Battalion first raised the American flag over Los Angeles. Present on the occasion was President George Albert Smith, who spoke to the nearly fifteen hundred people gathered at city hall. As part of the celebration, approval was given to the proposal of May Belle T. Davis that a Mormon Battalion memorial should be erected near the site of Fort Moore as part of the city's commemoration to the state's centennial. This was the culmination of years of tireless effort by Sister Davis, though the memorial would not be finished for several more years.

The welfare needs of the Church in Los Angeles continued to be a concern and shortly after John Russon became stake president, the Los Angeles Stake joined with the South Los Angeles and the Inglewood Stakes in trying to find one location suitable for a welfare center that would meet the needs of the entire area. Shortly, an excellent site was located in East Los Angeles on Soto Avenue, between 11th and 12th streets. The IRS had placed a tax lien upon the buildings and property, and it was to be auctioned to the highest bidder. With the assistance of Elder Henry D. Moyle of the Council of the Twelve, this property was purchased for $175,000, roughly one-third its actual value. Following the purchase, the Church was offered $170,000 for part of the property, but it had an ideal location for carrying out its welfare program and declined the offer.[19] In September 1949 the Church placed funds in escrow, and by January 1950 the property was cleared for the creation of a huge welfare center for the southern California region. The buildings on the property provided nearly 80,000 square feet of space, and remodeling began immediately. By 1951 the Deseret Industries, the bishops' storehouse, and other welfare activities had all been moved to this location.

In June 1950 the Church made its second major welfare purchase of the year in southern California when it bought the 505-acre ranch of Louis B. Mayer in Perris, California, in Riverside County. The Perris property was a beautiful horse ranch complete with ranch house, nine guest cottages, a race track, eleven barns containing horse stalls, a garage, a blacksmith shop, a paint shop, a machine shop, chicken coops, feed sheds, farm land, and complete equipment to operate the farm. The ranch also contained an extensive underground irrigation system, five wells, and thirty-five miles of fencing which had been installed at a cost of $10,444 per mile.

Elder Henry D. Moyle was instrumental in locating the property and persuading the stake presidents in southern California to purchase it as a welfare project. The asking price for the land was $400,000, which Elder Moyle believed was a fraction of its true value. To purchase the property required a down payment of $100,000, and the Saints in the Los Angeles area were given less than one month to come up with the money. The stake presidents were taken aback at the prospect of raising that amount until they were reminded that it was a small step from $100,000 to two dollars, which was the amount that each member in the area would have to come up with to reach the down payment.[20] The stake presidents accepted the challenge and within two weeks had come up with the money. The remaining cost of the ranch was paid outright by the Church, with the region expected to repay the Church over the next five years.

Various projects were envisioned for the ranch, including the raising of beef and dairy cattle, turkeys, and chickens, and these were divided among the various stakes. The Los Angeles Stake was initially given responsibility for the potato project. In addition, volunteers were needed to fix and maintain the ranch. Most of the buildings required new paint jobs and new roofs along with other maintenance projects.

As a welfare farm, however, the Perris ranch failed to measure up to expectations. Within a couple of years most welfare projects gave way to the potato project, since that could be carried out more easily than the daily care required by animal projects. Moreover, the expenditure of manpower and money that it took to operate and maintain the property forced operations in the red. Just to bring water to the land, for example, cost over $5,000 a month. One stake president soon composed a song entitled "Some Day the Ranch Will Pay," which was sung at the various welfare meetings that dealt with the farm and resulted in many a good laugh from the other presidents.[21] Feeling that the efforts of members in southern California could be used more productively, therefore, the stake presidents recommended that the ranch be sold and that other welfare property, such as citrus groves, be purchased. At first the proposal was met with opposition in Salt Lake City, mainly from Elder Moyle who felt that if the region held onto the ranch it could be sold at a substantial profit. It was finally sold at a fair profit and the money was used to purchase other welfare projects, including a citrus grove.[22]

While the Perris ranch failed to measure up as a welfare farm, President Russon saw its importance as extending far beyond the welfare work. Later he said that he felt that the raising of $100,000

> was the Lord's way of preparing the hearts of the people of Southern California to respond to the request to help build the kingdom. . . . I believe that that was the seed that enabled us to have fertile ground in the hearts of the people to gain their sustaining vote and have the overwhelming success that we did when it came to raising the funds for the temple . . . and had it not been for that and the faith of the people demonstrating that they would respond and could raise those sums of money, I don't think we would have had the temple nearly as early as we did in the Los Angeles area.[23]

The first decade of the "new" Los Angeles Stake was one filled with challenges brought about by events not only in Los Angeles but throughout the world. The problems that were met and overcome not only helped strengthen the Church in Los Angeles but also helped prepare the Saints for the blessings of having a temple in their midst. Meeting such challenges as continued population increase, the needs of servicemen, the requirements of the war, the needs of the welfare program, the concerns of youth marrying outside the Church, and the continued filling of a calling by a stake president separated from loved ones showed that while their tasks were not always easy, stake members continued to be anxiously engaged in building the kingdom.

George W. McCune
Stake President
1923–1931

David H. Cannon
Stake President
1934–1936

LeGrand Richards
Stake President
1931–1934

John M. Russon
Stake President
1949–1962

Wilford G. Edling
Stake President
1936–1949

Winfield G. Cannon
Stake President
1965–1968

Arvo Van Alstyne
Stake President
1962–1965

John K. Carmack
Stake President
1972–1977

Merlin W. Sant
Stake President
1968–1972

William W. Tanner
Stake President
1978–present

Rodney H. Brady
Stake President
1977–1978

Adams Ward chapel
Dedicated in 1913

Adams Ward chapel after renovation in 1942

Ocean Park Branch chapel
(presently the Santa Monica Ward chapel)
Dedicated in 1922

Mar Vista chapel
Dedicated in 1928

Wilshire Ward chapel
Dedicated in 1929

Stained glass window in the Wilshire Ward chapel

Glendale Ward chapel
Dedicated in 1939

Arlington Ward chapel
Dedicated in 1943

Hollywood Ward chapel
Built in 1924, purchased by the Church in 1937,
and rededicated in 1943

Westwood Ward chapel
Dedicated in 1953

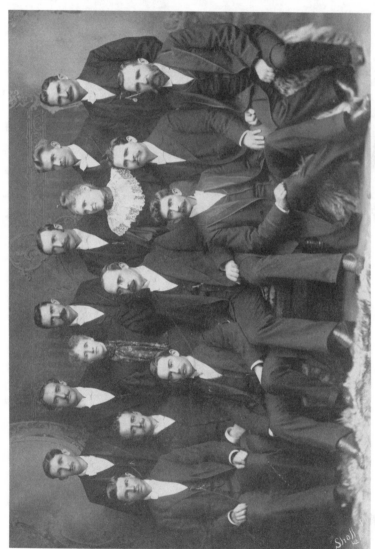

President Henry S. Tanner with the California missionaries
Los Angeles. 1895

William J. Reeve
First Los Angeles Branch president
(1912–1923)

Eliza Woollacott
Early member of the Los Angeles Branch

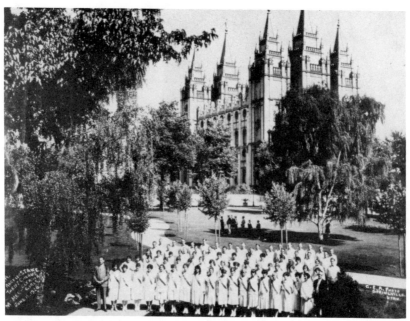

Los Angeles Thrift Chorus Excursion to June Conference, 1926

Los Angeles Thrift Chorus en route
to the Mesa Temple dedication, 1927

Officers, bishops, and counselors of the
newly-created Hollywood Stake, 1927

President Heber J. Grant with
Stake President George W. McCune and
Wilshire Ward Bishop David W. Howells and
their wives at the dedication of the
Wilshire Ward Chapel, 1929

Wilshire Ward basketball team
Regional champions, 1930–1931

Youth of the Wilshire Ward,
approximately 1940

Groundbreaking ceremony for the Arlington Ward chapel,
one of the few buildings constructed during World War II

Social activity at the
Adams Ward recreation center, early 1940s

Originally the California Mission Home next to the Adams Ward
chapel, but in 1948 became a stake sewing center
better known as "The Shirt Factory"

Presentation of proposed Los Angeles Temple
to stake authorities, 1952

A meeting of Elder Henry D. Moyle and stake presidents
in the Los Angeles Temple district

Los Angeles Temple
Dedicated in 1956

President and Sister David O. McKay with the
first Los Angeles Temple presidency

Groundbreaking ceremony at the
Wilshire Ward chapel for a new annex
to become a home for the deaf branch, 1961

Elder George Q. Morris with the first deaf
branch presidency of the Southern California
Branch for the Deaf, 1955

Cast members of the musical
Plain and Fancy, 1959

Cast members of the musical
Meet Me in St. Louis, 1960

Members of the Wilshire Ward M Men and Gleaners, 1960

The stake presidency in 1968 represented three
generations of stake presidents: (from l. to r.)
Charles T. Attwool, John K. Carmack, Merlin W.
Sant, William W. Tanner, and Roy S. Kellogg

Helen Kennedy of the Wilshire Ward,
first black member of the Los Angeles Stake

Leaders of the Los Angeles Third Ward

Leaders of the Los Angeles Fourth Ward

Leaders of the Los Angeles Sixth Ward

Regional representative John K. Carmack and stake
presidency honor Los Angeles Temple presidents and
matrons at the twenty-fifth anniversary of the temple, 1981

Stake Young Women's Award Night, 1986
Recipient: Jennifer Johnston, center

Many Los Angeles Stake members participated in
"Hands Across America," shown here near the
Los Angeles Temple

Youth conference testimony meeting, 1986

Dinner following the general women's broadcast,
prepared and served by priesthood holders, 1986

President Gordon B. Hinckley speaks at a 1987 Fourth of July celebration honoring the 140th anniversary of the American flag-raising over Los Angeles by the Mormon Battalion

President and Sister Myrthus Evans,
Los Angeles Temple
1970–1975

President and Sister Benjamin Bowring,
Los Angeles Temple
1955–1970

President and Sister Robert L. Simpson,
Los Angeles Temple
1980–1982

President and Sister Richard C. Stratford,
Los Angeles Temple
1975–1980

President and Sister Jack McEwan,
Los Angeles Temple
1986 – present

President and Sister Allen C. Rosza,
Los Angeles Temple
1982 – 1986

A Spiritual Renaissance

On 17 January 1949 the First Presidency presided at a meeting of southern California Church leaders at the Wilshire Ward chapel. At this meeting, President George Albert Smith announced that the time was now right for the eleventh House of the Lord in this dispensation to be built in Los Angeles. Finally, the day was at hand that had been prophesied by Brigham Young in an 1847 letter to the Saints in California wherein he said that "in the process of time the shores of the Pacific may yet be overlooked from the temple of the Lord."[1] President Smith also announced that the proposed Los Angeles Temple would be substantially larger than the one envisioned in previous architectural plans. Instead of seating two hundred people, the ordinance rooms would seat three hundred, the same as the Salt Lake Temple. Also, a large priesthood assembly room would be added. When President Smith asked for a sustaining vote on the proposal to build a temple in the Southland, approval was unanimous.

Three weeks earlier, on 27 December 1948, the members of the First Presidency had sent a letter to the eight stake presidents in southern California announcing the meeting and indicating that "it would seem we have come to the point where we may with wisdom go forward with this long desired and antici-pated construction of a House of the Lord."[2] Building the temple had been delayed, the letter said, because of problems relating to World War II and the need to "forestall, if possible, the estab-lishment of industrial and business operations" in the area sur-rounding the temple "which would be undesirable."

The letter also recommended that the stake presidents meet as soon as possible to discuss a fund-raising campaign. When a fund-raising program had been undertaken for the Idaho Falls Temple ten years earlier, the response of the Saints in Idaho had been less than Church leaders had hoped for.[3] Understandably, they were anxious to avoid similar problems in southern Cali-fornia.

Shortly following this long-awaited announcement, local Church leaders sent a letter to the southern California Saints discussing "the benefits, and opportunities afforded the Church membership to make contributions towards the erection of this Temple." It also discussed the advantages of building a temple on Santa Monica Boulevard and President Heber J. Grant's in-spiration in selecting the site. "It is the highest point in elevation between Los Angeles and the ocean, and the great highways and contemplated freeways running north and south and from the east meet within a short distance of the Temple lot, affording excellent transportation facilities." Furthermore, the letter said, the temple "will add greatly to the already developing cultural life of the educational community in which it is situated, giving emphasis to the great truth: 'The Glory of God is Intelligence.' " The letter reminded the Saints that the words of Brigham Young concerning the Salt Lake Temple also applied to the Los Angeles Temple, "It shall be a monument to the City . . . and an acknowl-edgement of our faith and devotion to God."[4]

With the announcement of the temple, it was anticipated that ground-breaking and the fund-raising campaign would take place within the year. However, two years would pass before ground was broken, and three years before fund-raising and construction began. There were several reasons for the delay. One was the need to draw plans for a larger temple. For almost two years Church architect Edward O. Anderson and his staff labored to complete the working plans, which had to be submitted to the city for approval. After that, final drafts and specifications still needed to be prepared. Next, there were legal problems to take care of. Several branches of city government— the planning commission, the city engineer, the building department— had to be consulted and all their regulations met. Preston D. Richards, a former counselor in the Los Angeles Stake presidency and the Church's legal counsel in southern California, worked, at no expense to the Church, to obtain the necessary permits, plan approval, and zoning changes. After nearly two years, Richards's efforts were finally rewarded on 9 January 1951 as the Los Angeles City Council approved construction of the temple. "I thought I knew what red tape was until I ran into the Los Angeles building restrictions and requirements," one member of the Church Building Committee later commented.[5] A final reason for the delay was that shortly following the city's approval of the plans, President George Albert Smith passed away, and the natural delays surrounding the installation of a new First Presidency postponed some of the temple preparations.

On 22 September 1951 ground was broken for the Los Angeles Temple. The ceremony was not publicly announced, but was a small, "brief and more-or-less informal" ceremony with only the California stake presidencies and their wives and city officials invited to attend.[6] Since facilities were not available to accommodate a larger crowd, which Church officials estimated would have been at least 10,000 if all Church members were invited, the numbers were kept small. Also in attendance were more than a score of General Authorities. LeGrand Richards, former Hollywood Stake president and then the Presiding Bishop of the Church, spoke of the great growth in California, reminding those in attendance that when he was stake president twenty years earlier there were only three stakes in all of California and that there were then twenty-two. He also told the Saints that this ground-breaking ceremony would be one of the most important events in the history of the world. President J. Reuben Clark, First Counselor in the First Presidency, reminded the Saints that this ground breaking also brought with it "great responsibility." He urged Church members to consider the sacrifice entailed in building the temple a privilege. "Sacrifice is one of the great principles that build spirituality," he said, and he promised the Saints great joy as they sacrificed to build and maintain a temple "to meet the requirements of God."[7]

President David O. McKay told those present that "a hundred years from now men will read with great interest the happenings of this day."[8] He then led the group to what would be the southeast corner of the temple and, with a gilded shovel, dug into the earth. Other leaders also took turns breaking the earth, which proved to be so hard that President McKay obligingly "softened it up" with his shovel for some of the brethren, much to the delight of those in attendance.[9] Following the ground-breaking, President McKay dedicated the site for a House of the Lord.

Two weeks later the stake presidents in the Los Angeles Temple district were invited to meet with President Stephen L Richards, Second Counselor in the First Presidency, during October general conference to discuss fund raising. President Richards reminded them that it was customary for members in a temple district to make contributions and then informed them that the First Presidency had "decided that possibly a million dollars would be your fair share."[10] President Noble Waite of the South Los Angeles Stake, chairman of the fund-raising committee, later commented that President Richards did not know "how nearly [he] knocked out fourteen stake presidents with that statement. We kept our chins up and it was only afterwards when we got out, and we confided in each other that we were really staggered. But we had received the commission . . . and our instructions were to make a plan, organize, and submit the plan, and get the approval of the First Presidency."[11]

President Richards suggested that the total amount should be divided among the stakes in the temple district and Church members living in the California Mission. However, it was the desire of the First Presidency that no individual assessments be made, but each person should give what he or she was able, on the principle of the widow's mite. President Richards also recommended that a guide be created indicating how much families in a particular income bracket might give. The Brethren were confident that if local members were directed as to possible contributions, local leaders would be able to raise their share.

When the stake presidents returned to California they formulated a plan, which, with a few modifications, was accepted by the First Presidency. The assessments to the stakes and the mission were made according to population, with the

Los Angeles Stake responsible for raising $70,000. A pledge card was created so that "every giver may determine for himself and according to his own circumstances the size of his Temple contribution."[12] The guide recommended that those making two thousand dollars annually donate $72 at two dollars a month for thirty-six months, the estimated time needed to build the temple, and those making over $25,000 annually donate $1980 at $55 a month. Each stake was to see that all Church members received copies of the guide through the wards. The wards were to obtain pledges from their members and turn the total over to the stakes.

President McKay agreed to come to Los Angeles and officially launch the fund-raising campaign. On Sunday, 3 February 1952, the Prophet met with twelve hundred stake and ward leaders and assured them that all was finally in preparation for building a temple, and that construction would shortly begin. He also discussed the fund-raising campaign and commended the group for the spirit of cooperation and unity being shown in this campaign to construct the "largest temple ever built in this dispensation." He urged the leaders to "let the young people, even the children in the cradle, contribute to the temple fund, for this is their temple, where they will be led by pure love to take their marriage vows."[13]

President Waite later told a general conference audience that the fund-raising plan would not have been as successful "if it had not been for the soul-inspiring discourse of President McKay. He electrified those 1200 people, and they went out of that meeting with a determination in their hearts that they were going to consummate that commission that was given by the First Presidency."[14] To help ensure that this determination remained in the hearts of the southern California Saints, President McKay also exhibited a three-foot scale model of the anticipated temple, which would be displayed in the various stakes throughout the fund-raising campaign. Each stake president was given the opportunity to make a few brief comments. President John M. Russon said that since the temple was to be located within his stake boundaries, he hoped it would be the first to subscribe its quota.

Sunday, 17 February 1952, was the day set aside in the Los Angeles Stake for gathering pledges. During the previous week each family in the stake had been sent a pledge card and souvenir folder of the temple. Prior to Sunday each family was to consider a pledge and seal it in an envelope. Between 2:00 and 4:00 P.M. on the appointed day, a representative of the bishopric (priesthood leader, ward teacher, visiting teacher, or other ward officer) visited each home in the stake to pick up the envelope and answer any question the families might have. After totaling their pledges, each ward conveyed its total to President Russon. When all the pledges had been received and the stake's total known, the figure was telegraphed to President McKay that evening. The following morning President Russon received a telegram from the First Presidency: "Congratulations to Los Angeles Stake Membership on being first in Los Angeles Temple District to complete canvass for temple subscriptions amounting to 238 percent of quota. Commendation and Blessing."[15]

Instead of the $70,000 they had been asked to pledge, the members of the Los Angeles Stake pledged $163,450 that Sunday and an additional $18,000 in the next several weeks. Like the widow of old, stake members had searched their hearts and pledged to give not just of their excess. When the pledges of other stakes were received, the same thing had happened throughout California. Over $1,648,000 had been pledged, or nearly 165 percent of what the local Saints had been asked to give.

By July 1952 all preparations for work on the temple were complete, and the following month work began. Each morning the workers opened their day with prayer, and their prayers were answered as the temple was completed without accident. During one stretch of three months it rained hard nearly every weekend, but never hard enough during the week to stop work on the temple. These and other incidents helped confirm to the Saints that the hand of the Lord was in the building of their temple. While most workers on the temple were members of the Church, 20 percent were not. However, before the temple was completed, at least four non-Mormon construction workers and their families joined the Church.

Overseeing the construction was Church architect Edward O. Anderson, who moved his office from Salt Lake City to Los Angeles. He located it first in the old Harold Lloyd estate and then in the basement of the temple's Bureau of Information (Visitors Center) when it was completed. During the time that he oversaw the work on the Los Angeles Temple he also prepared the plans for the London and Swiss temples.

Steadily the temple took shape, with its progress being followed almost weekly in the *California Intermountain News* and the *Church News*. As the work progressed, few were unimpressed with the massive undertaking. President McKay, on touring the recently poured foundations, commented that he could not believe he had approved a project as vast as this one. He mentioned that in the blueprints it just did not look like it would be that huge an operation.[16]

And huge it was. The temple was 364 feet wide, 241 feet deep and contained 190,614 square feet of floor space, or approximately four and one half acres. The concrete foundations were twenty-four feet deep and two feet thick. The excavation for the footings and foundations and the pouring of the foundations took nearly six months. The height of the building, including the tower, was 257 feet, eight and one-half inches, with the tower rising 151 feet, eight and one-half inches above the roof. Atop the sacred building was a statue of the angel Moroni, which weighed 2100 pounds and was fifteen feet, five and one-half inches tall, with an eight-foot trumpet. When the temple was planned only one other building in Los Angeles was taller—the Los Angeles City Building—and when completed, it could be seen by ships twenty-five miles out to sea. During the period it took just to build the Los Angeles Temple, another temple, the Swiss Temple, was planned, built, and dedicated.

As work progressed on the temple, stake members also faithfully progressed toward paying their pledges. Although they had greatly over-subscribed their quota, they worked to meet the amount they pledged, as did those in the other stakes. One young deacon filled out a pledge card for $150. When the bishop saw the amount he felt sure the deacon must have made a mistake. The deacon assured the bishop, however, that he wished to give $150 to the temple and that the amount was within his reach. Whatever money this young man earned from his paper route, mowing lawns or other odd jobs that came his way, he gave to the temple fund. Within two and one-half years he had met his pledge. One unidentified elderly widow, in frail health and nearly blind, pledged $400 dollars and gave that amount and more from her meager savings. As she neared her total pledge in September 1954 she told her bishop: "I hope and pray the Lord will bless me and preserve my life until I can have the privilege of going through the Los Angeles Temple."[17]

These were only two of the many examples that could be given of sacrifices made to build a house of the Lord. Children emptied their piggy banks; families put off making home improvements, buying new cars, or taking vacations to donate to the temple. Stake presidents throughout the temple district reported that donating to the temple was a faith-promoting and testimony-building experience for the members in southern California, and that peace and happiness were the result of taking the opportunity to contribute.

Stake members donated not only their means, but also their time. While full-time laborers did the actual building, Church members helped in other ways. They performed clean-up work on the grounds, for example, and armed with hoes and shovels they assisted in seeding the lawn and landscaping. They also contributed funds for landscaping, beyond their original contributions.

As the Saints in southern California continued to give of their time and financial means, President Noble Waite told a general conference audience:

> We are enthusiastic. . . . We are very happy and proud, and we are very thankful that the First Presidency and the other General Authorities of the Church are building a temple in our area. I am sure it is going to do a great deal of good in Southern California.
>
> I vision a spiritual renaissance in that area. Our people will be spiritually uplifted. It will be a great blessing. We . . . are happy. We are enthusiastic. We are resolute in our determination to fulfill the commission which was given to us. Unflinchingly and unhesitatingly, we shall move forward doing everything in our power to see that everything goes in accordance with the plans of the First Presidency of the Church.[18]

As the temple rose, thousands of interested people came to visit. In April 1953 the Los Angeles Stake high priests quorum was conducted through a tour of its shell. Between sessions of the October 1953 stake conference held at the Westwood Ward, President John Russon led nearly one thousand stake members to the unfinished temple for a tour. But stake members were not the only ones interested, and as the massive structure took shape so many visitors stopped that a temple mission was created to answer their questions and to conduct guided tours of the grounds so that the work could progress uninterrupted.

One visitor, a writer for the *Southwest Builder and Contractor*, wrote, "It is already quite apparent that nothing more impressive has ever been built in Southern California."[19]

By December 1953, the building had risen to the base of the tower, and work had progressed to the point where a cornerstone could be laid. On 11 December ten thousand Church members and nearly all of the General Authorities attended the cornerstone laying ceremony, one of the largest gatherings of Latter-day Saints in California up to that time. Countless others listened by radio as the ceremony was broadcast both in Los Angeles and over KSL radio in Salt Lake City. The ceremony was also filmed and recorded for the benefit of future generations.

Music was furnished by the Mormon Choir of southern California and President McKay conducted the ceremony. The prophet reminded those in attendance that this temple, like all temples, was to be a "house of prayer, a house of fasting, a house of faith, a house of learning, a house of glory, a house of order, a house of God." (D&C 88:119.) President Stephen L Richards laid and dedicated the cornerstone on the east side of the building.

In October 1954, ten months following the cornerstone laying, the imposing angel Moroni statue was placed atop the temple. Originally the statue faced south, towards the front of the temple, but it was turned a quarter turn to face east, the same direction that the angel Moroni on the Salt Lake Temple faces. The story is told of a neighbor to the east of the temple who, when asked if she had visited the temple grounds, replied "No, I'm waiting until the angel turns around and faces me." She later told one of the guides on the temple grounds, "Imagine my surprise when I woke up one morning and discovered that the angel was looking right down my street."[20]

Frederick G. Williams, president of the temple mission, relates some of the other humorous stories associated with people who visited the temple. One well-dressed woman asked if it was the angel Gabriel on top of the temple. When told it was the angel Moroni she replied that her husband had said there were only two individuals who could blow a horn like that, the angel Gabriel and Louis Armstrong, and she was sure it wasn't Louis Armstrong. A man upon seeing the reflecting pool at the front of the temple wanted to know if all the neighbors would be permitted to use the swimming pool or if it would be restricted only to members of the Church. One Jewish visitor told a story that reflected the pride felt in Los Angeles for the new temple even among non-Mormons. When her family visited Salt Lake City, she said, her nine-year-old son told a Temple Square guide, "You should see our temple in Los Angeles. It's bigger and prettier than this one, and it has ninety rooms in it."[21]

As each floor became protected from the elements, work began on the interior of the temple. In the baptistry, creation room, garden room, and world room, beautiful murals were painted. Church leaders wanted a mural depicting Christ's baptism behind the baptismal font, and Joseph Gibby of the Wilshire Ward was commissioned to paint it. Gibby recalled that this was the fulfillment of one of his "life's dreams." He had studied art at Ogden (Utah) High School under LeConte Stewart, who had painted some of the murals in the Hawaiian Temple and had often talked to his students about his experience.

After receiving the measurements for the mural, Gibby made a sketch that was then sent to Salt Lake City for President McKay's approval. Following the prophet's approval, and with instructions to change nothing, Gibby set about to paint the twenty-four-by-nine-foot mural. Within three months he had almost finished it, except for the face of Christ. Not satisfied with his attempts at painting the Savior, he approached temple architect Edward Anderson about his problem. Brother Anderson smiled and replied, "You are in luck. President McKay will be in town tomorrow so we will go to see him at his hotel and you can tell him what's the matter."[22]

The next day they went to see President McKay. When Brother Gibby told him his problem, President McKay placed his hand on Brother Gibby's shoulder and looked him straight in the face "with those great beautiful eyes [which] seemed to look right through" him. After a moment the President said, "Christ had chestnut hair, hazel eyes, and a fair complexion."[23] "What a thrill it was to hear those wonderful words from the mouth of a Prophet of the Lord!" Brother Gibby later recalled. "Now I knew how to paint the Savior's face, and that is the way I painted it [the] next day."

By autumn 1955 the work on the temple was nearly complete, and the building was opened to public tours before dedication. At first it was unclear whether nonmembers would be allowed to tour the temple without a Church member accompanying them, but so many expressed a desire to see it that the decision was made to open the prededication tours to all those who wished to attend. As a trial run, two thousand area Church leaders and their wives were invited to tour the temple on 25 November 1955. On 19 December it was opened for public viewing and it remained open to the public until 18 February. By that time over 662,000 people had visited the temple, far exceeding the number anticipated. The greatest number to tour in one day exceeded 27,000, and the average daily total was nearly 12,000. Often the line of people waiting to enter the temple would form a semicircle around the grounds, four abreast, even though the wait lasted several hours.

Visitors came from throughout the West as chartered buses brought them from as far away as Seattle, Washington, and Utah. Local sightseeing companies made the temple tour part of their tours of the city. Among the visitors was Cecil B. DeMille, then directing the movie *The Ten Commandments,* who was taken through by President David O. McKay; and actor Harold Lloyd, from whom the temple property had been purchased in 1939.

The .61 mile tour usually lasted approximately forty-five minutes once the visitor was inside the temple. At the beginning, a tape-recorded message explained to visitors the purpose of the temple. Guides from the Los Angeles area were stationed throughout the temple to answer visitors' questions. Members of the Los Angeles Stake and the other stakes in the area donated a great number of hours to see that all went smoothly for the visitors. One day Willard P. Burnham of the Wilshire Ward pushed fourteen wheelchair visitors through the temple tour.

The tours eliminated much of the misunderstanding that existed among nonmembers concerning the purpose of the temple. One rumor had surfaced that the Mormons were going to bring their dead to the temple to baptize them; as a result several homes near the temple were put on the market, often at reduced prices. Not only did the tours clear up such misinformation, they also allowed nonmembers to learn of the purpose of the temple and to partake of its beauty. Those who attended often wrote local leaders concerning their feelings. The Board of

Supervisors of the County of Los Angeles adopted a resolution congratulating the Church for its wonderful edifice. The resolution read, in part, "Not only spiritually but architecturally it constitutes one of the notable additions to the life of Southern California."[24] Another visitor wrote: "It was a day we will never forget. The beauty and magnitude were completely overwhelming. One thing we all noted was how friendly and helpful everyone was—always a smile, but then I guess they have so much to be proud and grateful for."[25] From another visitor came this note: "Last evening my husband and I had the rare privilege of seeing your new temple which is truly beautiful and inspiring. . . . I think if you knew what a tremendous spiritual uplift we both experienced you would forgive me for the small contribution I am sending."[26] The opening of the temple was also covered favorably in the local papers as well as national magazines such as *Time*.[27]

Following the last day of tours on 18 February 1956, the temple was closed for nearly two months as workmen finished the last details and worked to get everything in order for the dedication services in April. These final details were supervised by the first temple president, Benjamin L. Bowring, and Sister Leone Bowring, the temple matron. The Bowrings came to this assignment from Hawaii, where they had presided over the Hawaii Temple.

On Sunday, 11 April 1956, the long-anticipated day arrived when the Los Angeles Temple was to be dedicated. Between Sunday and Wednesday, 14 April, eight dedicatory sessions were held. At each session nearly 6,700 Saints were in attendance, seated not only in the assembly hall, but also in the ordinance rooms and other places throughout the temple where the services were carried over closed-circuit television. The services were open to all members of the Church who could qualify for a recommend, and over 50,000 Saints attended.

At the opening session President McKay paid special tribute to three great Church leaders who passed away before construction began: President Heber J. Grant, Preston D. Richards, former counselor in the Los Angeles Stake presidency, and David P. Howells, former bishop of the Wilshire Ward, had carried much of the responsibility for purchasing the temple property and laying the spiritual and legal groundwork allowing for its construction. "They are not occupying seats in any of the rooms," he said, "but I am sure that they are here with us in spirit." In addition, he declared, "a million and a half members of the Church are rejoicing this morning at the completion of this magnificent edifice, and the eyes of other millions are turned towards this great event."

President McKay reminded those in attendance that as a result of having a temple in their midst, they

> will have increased responsibility as never before, in the words of the prophet, "to do justly, and to love mercy, and to walk humbly with their God." (Micah 6:8). . . . [Because of the] congratulatory messages and words of commendation on the magnificence and glory of this sacred edifice, the inspiration of these memorable dedicatory services only combine to increase the responsibility of every member of the Church—the responsibility ever to remember that it is "not everyone who sayeth unto me, Lord, Lord, shall enter into the Kingdom of God, but he that doeth the will of our Father which is in heaven."[28]

Other speakers also made significant comments on that important day. President Noble Waite was asked to represent the Saints in Los Angeles, and noted that their dream had come true. He thanked the General Authorities for building the temple and declared that it had not been a sacrifice for the Saints, but rather a glorious opportunity with many blessings. President J. Reuben Clark, First Counselor in the First Presidency, reminded the Saints that "to the early temples in the days of Israel people brought sacrifices to atone for sin. Since the Saviour fulfilled the Mosaic law, we now bring to temples pure hearts and contrite spirits. We are not here to be forgiven of sin, forgiveness should precede entrance into temples. We are here having forsaken our sins with resultant forgiveness and in a spirit of deep humility; living a life of righteousness, we are here to do the work which is done in these temples and what the Lord commands."[29]

Second Counselor Stephen L Richards suggested that each Church member make two resolutions: First, "honor His priesthood, which in His grace and mercy He has restored to men in the earth in the fullness of the gospel," and, second, resolve that "our children shall be brought to a more perfect understanding of these exalted principles of life, that there may develop within them from their earliest youth an intelligent and passionate longing for the attainment of the highest and best in life."[30]

Following the addresses, President McKay gave the dedicatory prayer:

O God, our Eternal Father, Creator of the earth and of the teeming manifestations of life thereon, we, thy children, assembled in dedicatory services in this house built to thy most Holy Name—plead that we may be accepted by thee.

May we feel thy presence and the presence of thy Beloved Son, Jesus Christ, by whom all things were made and only through whom will the consummation of thy divine purpose pertaining to the inhabitants of this earth be wrought. That we may thus sense thy presence and have assurance that our prayers are heard by thee, may every heart in this edifice this day be clean and pure before thee, and every mind be willing to do thy will and to work for the accomplishment of thy purposes.

When our first parents chose to take upon themselves mortality, they knew that they would be driven from thy divine presence and that their only hope of ever regaining it would be dependent upon thy revealing thyself to them through thy Beloved Son, who would give to them the plan of Salvation. Today, we express heart-felt gratitude to thee for having given in the beginning the gospel plan, and with it man's free agency, a part of thy divinity wherein man may choose the right and merit salvation, or choose the wrong and merit condemnation.

Down through the ages men have been free to accept or to reject thy righteous plan. Thou knowest, and history records, how many in wickedness yield to the enticements of the flesh, and how few, comparatively, follow the path of light and truth that leads to happiness and eternal life.

But thy mercy, thy love, thy wisdom are infinite! And in dispensations past thou hast pleaded, as thou dost now plead, through chosen servants for thy erring children to repent and come unto thee.

We thank thee that thou, O Great Elohim, and Jehovah, thy beloved Son, didst appear to the Prophet Joseph Smith, and through subsequent administrations of angels didst enable him to organize the Church of Jesus Christ in its completeness with apostles, prophets, pastors, teachers, and evangelists, as it was established in the days of the Savior and his apostles in the Meridian of Time.

In keeping with the unwavering truth that thy Church must be established by divine authority, thou didst send heavenly messengers to bestow upon the Prophet Joseph Smith and others the Aaronic and Melchizedek priesthoods, and subsequently all the keys of the priesthood ever held by the prophets from Adam through Abraham and Moses, to Malachi who testifies of the authority of Elijah to "turn the heart of the fathers to the children, and the heart of the children to their fathers," down to the latest generation. For this completeness and consistency of restoration of authority, we express gratitude today and praise thy holy name.

We are grateful for this land of America, "choice above all other lands." The freedom vouchsafed by the Constitution of the United States, which guarantees to every man the right to worship thee in accordance with the dictates of his own conscience, made possible the establishment of the Church of Jesus Christ of Latter-day Saints. O Father, may the American people not forget thee! Help us to see the greatness of this country and to minimize its weaknesses. We express gratitude for the right of the people to resort to the ballot, and for freedom to meet in legislative halls to settle problems and disputes without fear of coercion of dictators, secret police, or slave camps. Help people everywhere to sense more clearly that government exists for the protection of the individual—not the individual for the government.

Bless, we beseech thee, the President of the United States, his Cabinet, the houses of Congress, and the judiciary. Give the President health and wisdom needful for the leadership now placed upon him.

We express gratitude to thee for the men whom thou hast chosen to lead the Church from the Prophet Joseph Smith, his brother Hyrum, and other associates, their successors through the years down to the present General Authorities.

Continue to reveal to the President and his counselors, the First Presidency, thy mind and will concerning the growth and advancement of thy work among the children of men.

We have felt thy presence and in times of doubt and perplexity have hearkened unto thy voice. Here in thy holy house, in humility and deep gratitude we acknowledge thy divine guidance, thy protection and inspiration. This is truly thy work—help us to be able representatives, faithful and true!

Bless the presidencies of stakes, the high councils, the presidencies of missions, the bishoprics of wards, the presidencies of branches, presidencies of quorums—Melchizedek and Aaronic; presidencies and superintendencies of auxiliary associations throughout the world—make them keenly conscious of the fact that they are trusted leaders, and that they are to keep that trust as sacredly as they guard their lives.

This edifice, as eleven other temples dedicated to thy holy name, is a magnificent monument testifying to the faith and loyalty of the members of thy Church in the payment of their tithes and offerings. Not only the building of temples is thus made possible in different parts of the world, but also the proclaiming of the restored gospel, and the carrying out of thy purposes by the building of chapels, tabernacles, and recreation halls wherever needed by churches organized in many lands and climes.

In this respect, we invoke thy blessing particularly upon thy people and their friends in this temple district who have so willingly and generously contributed their means, time, and effort to the completion of this imposing, impressive house of the Lord. May each contributor be comforted in spirit and prospered a hundredfold! May all be assured that they have the gratitude of thousands, perhaps millions, on the other side for whom the prison doors may now be opened and deliverance proclaimed to those who will accept the truth and be set free.

For this purpose thou hast revealed that the gospel is to be preached to those who have passed beyond the veil, as well as to millions now living whose faith in thee and in thy gospel is faltering and unstable, who are now being influenced by false ideologies, which are disturbing the peace of mind and distorting the thinking of honest men and women. May the temples, tabernacles, churches, wherever a branch or ward of the Church is organized, declare even in silence that Jesus Christ is the way, the truth, and the light, and that . . . 'there is none other name under heaven given men, whereby we must be saved.'

Guide us, O Lord, in our efforts to hasten the day when men will renounce contention and strife, when '. . . nation shall not lift up sword against nation, neither shall they learn war any more.' To this end we beseech thee to influence the leaders of nations that their minds may be averse to war, their hearts cleansed from prejudices, suspicion, and avarice, and filled with a desire for peace and righteousness.

Temples are built to thy Holy name as a means of uniting thy people in bonds of faith, of peace, and of love.

Today, therefore, we come before thee with joy and thanksgiving, with spirits jubilant and hearts filled with praise that we are permitted to participate in the dedicatory service of this, the twelfth temple to be dedicated since the organization of thy Church. Millions have had their attention drawn to it—many through curiosity, some because of its beauty in structure, others because of its lofty purpose. Help all, O Father, to realize more keenly and sincerely than ever before that only by obedience to eternal principles and ordinances of the gospel of Jesus Christ may loved ones who died without baptism be permitted the glorious privilege of entrance into the kingdom of God. Increase our desire, therefore, to put forth even greater effort towards the consummation of thy purpose to bring to pass the immortality and eternal life of all thy children.

To this end, by authority of the Holy Priesthood, we dedicate this, the Los Angeles Temple of the Church of Jesus Christ of Latter-day Saints, and consecrate it for the sacred purposes for which it has been erected.

We ask thee to accept this edifice and to guard it from foundation to statue. Protect it from earthquakes, hurricanes, tempestuous storms, or other devastating holocausts. We dedicate the ground on which it stands and by which it is surrounded. May the baptismal font, the ordinance rooms, and especially the sealing rooms be kept holy that thy spirit may be ever present to comfort and inspire. Protect all mechanical parts pertaining to lighting, heating, ventilating system, elevators. Bless the persons who are charged to look after all such installations and fixtures that they may do so faithfully, skillfully, and reverently.

Bless the president of the temple, and his wife as matron. Let humility temper their feelings; wisdom and kind consideration their actions. May they, and others who will be appointed as assistants and custodians, maintain an atmosphere of cleanliness and holiness in every room. Let no unclean person or thing ever enter herein, for "my spirit," saith the Lord, "will not dwell in unclean tabernacles"; neither will it remain in a house where selfish, arrogant, or unwholesome thoughts abide. Therefore, may all who seek this holy temple come with clean hands and pure hearts that thy holy spirit may ever be present to comfort, to inspire, and to bless. If any with gloomy forebodings or heavy hearts enter, may they depart with their burdens lightened and their faith increased; if any have envy or bitterness in their hearts, may such feelings be replaced by self-searching and forgiveness. May all who come within these sacred walls feel a peaceful, hallowed influence. Cause, O Lord, that even people who pass the grounds or view the temple from afar, may lift their eyes from the groveling things of sordid life and look up to thee and thy providence.

Now, dear Lord, our Eternal Father, through love for thee and their fellow men, faithful members of thy Church, and others who believe in thee, by tithes and other generous contributions, have made possible the erection and completion of this thy holy house, in which will be performed ordinances and ceremonies essential to the happiness, salvation, and exaltation of thy children living in mortality and in the spirit world. Accept our offering, hallow it by thy presence, protect it by thy power. With this prayer we dedicate our lives to the establishment of the kingdom of God on earth for the peace of the world and to thy glory forever, in the name of thy Beloved Son, Jesus Christ. Amen.[31]

Following the prayer, those present joined in singing "The Spirit of God like a Fire Is Burning," a hymn that had been sung at the dedication of the Church's first temple at Kirtland, Ohio, and at every temple dedication since. They also gave the traditional "Hosanna Shout," a shout echoed in spirit by members throughout the Church.

By the time of the Los Angeles Temple dedication, the spiritual renaissance envisioned for the Saints in southern California had already begun. For several years the entire Latter-day Saint community had worked with the common goal of seeing the temple to completion. The Saints had sacrificed both time and money, but they saw that their efforts had brought forth great blessings, including a noticeable increase in spiritual strength. One observer has commented that because of the temple within its boundaries, the Los Angeles Stake progressed from being a "social stake" to becoming a spiritual stake. While it cannot be said that spiritual matters were not emphasized earlier, it was nevertheless clear that because of the temple spiritual matters took on a new importance and direction. There were several reasons for this.

As discussed earlier, when Church finances would not allow for the building of chapels during the depression, some members in California had doubts as to whether they were to remain there. When Church leaders announced a short time later that chapel building would resume, few could doubt that the Church was in California to stay. Such can be the power of a building. Since the Los Angeles Temple was the most expensive and most sacred Church building in California, its construction strongly affirmed that the Church was now firmly entrenched.

No longer need southern California Church members be concerned about establishing their identity through socials and stage productions; these now become more a source of fellowship than identity. Now the Saints could gather to the house of the Lord and gain an even more special identity and unity with each other through performing eternal ordinances for the living and the dead. They could also gather on the temple grounds as family, friends, ward members, and fellow Saints and simply enjoy the spirit of the imposing temple reaching heavenward, taking their thoughts with it.

All this helped remind Church members that having built the temple they were obliged to work even harder than before to fulfill the mission of the Church. Thus the temple became a blessing to member and non-member alike as renewed emphasis was given to that mission. Before long it was clear that missionary work had increased, temple and genealogical work had increased, and greater emphasis was being placed on preparing the youth for temple marriage and on preparing all the Saints to enter the house of the Lord.

Finally, the temple provided an opportunity to participate more often in the sacred temple ceremonies that always enhance the lives of the Saints. Previously only a few trips could be taken to the nearest temple each year, but now the Saints could attend on a monthly, even weekly basis. While the Spirit is often overshadowed by the hustle and bustle of everyday life, for members to enhance their spiritual lives, a new source of spirituality and a new means for building the kingdom was created with the completion of the Los Angeles Temple. With the varied opportunities for service associated with both building and visiting the temple, it is little wonder that the Church in southern California would experience a great rebirth of the Spirit.

An Era of Transition

The spiritual renaissance that came from anticipating a temple in their midst began early among the Los Angeles Saints, as donations of both time and money, as well as other evidences of deeper, more wide-spread commitment to building the kingdom, increased. Early in his presidency, for example, John M. Russon introduced a three-fold campaign in the stake which was intended to create a greater feeling of understanding and achievement among the members and also increase their spirituality. Basing his campaign upon the Savior's admonition to Peter that if he loved Him he would feed His sheep, President Russon asked stake members to (1) feed their neighbors spiritually through home teaching, (2) feed their neighbors physically through increased fast offerings, and (3) feed themselves through regular Church attendance. The result was a 50 percent increase in fast offerings during the time the temple was under construction. Tithing donations also increased, in spite of the many other contributions stake members were asked to make. These included donations to the temple, other building funds in the stake, and an increased welfare assessment resulting from the unprofitable nature of the Perris ranch. Attendance at meetings also increased, and in 1952 the stake was in ninth place in the Church for priesthood meeting attendance. Among the Aaronic Priesthood, where the greatest increase came, 72 percent regularly attended priesthood meetings and 60 percent attended sacrament meeting.

Anticipating the completion of the temple, stake leaders also increased their emphasis on preparing for and attending the temple. In 1954, two years before the temple was dedicated, there were sixty-one marriages in the stake. Forty, or 66 percent, were temple marriages, and among nineteen of the remaining twenty-one couples, one of the partners was not a member of the Church. This represented a remarkable increase over a few years earlier, when 60 percent of the youth were marrying outside the Church and among the rest there were few temple marriages. In addition, members continued to make the trip to the Mesa Temple, both in stake and ward groups, often taking the youth of the stake who performed baptisms for the dead.

Another concern was welfare. At the dedication of the Welfare Center, President J. Reuben Clark, Jr., gave a special challenge to those in attendance: "This building cannot carry on the great welfare program. It can neither wreck nor make successful the work to be done here. We members of the Church are the ones who can either make or mar. Let us dedicate ourselves, rather than the building to the task."[1] The Los Angeles Saints took this instruction to heart. In addition to more than 22,000 hours of labor contributed at the Perris ranch during the next year, 20,000 hours were contributed to fixing up the Welfare Center, besides the numerous canning assignments filled. Many additional hours were donated at the Perris ranch in mending fences and roofs, painting barns, and clearing weeds. Other projects were also undertaken, such as cutting and selling cordwood to benefit the welfare program and salvaging and selling materials from the old Harold Lloyd estate on the temple grounds.

Meanwhile, other events were taking place that would have important and long-lasting consequences for the Saints in the Los Angeles Stake. During the 1950-51 school year, Ray L. Jones, principle of the Logan (Utah) Seminary, was appointed by the Church Educational System to introduce the seminary program into the Los Angeles area. After examining all possibilities, Jones concluded that, because of the numerous after-school activities, the only time available for seminary was before school. He proposed, therefore, an early-morning seminary program, even though such programs had not been highly successful when they had been tried in other places.[2] Original plans called for establishing three or four early-morning classes at LDS meetinghouses located near high schools with large numbers of LDS students. Interest was so great, however, that when the school year began, six classes were operating within the boundaries of five different stakes, two hundred students were enrolled, and an equally large number were anxious to attend. Halfway through the year seven new classes were added and enrollment exceeded 450.

At the beginning of the following school year, twenty-six early-morning seminary classes were being taught in various ward meetinghouses throughout the Los Angeles area. This meant that LDS high school students often had to leave home as much as two hours earlier than normal in order to be transported to seminary, go to class, and then make it to school on time. But it was not just the students who demonstrated the commitment and sacrifice necessary to support the new program. Stake and ward leaders worked diligently to arrange for adequately equipped seminary rooms in their chapels, to promote enrollment, and to find and recommend to the seminary administrators people who would be well prepared and inspiring teachers. The teachers themselves were usually professional people who were willing and able, in addition to their full-time jobs, to put in hours of special preparation, be in their classrooms early, and provide instruction that was academically sound as well as spiritually uplifting. They received a small stipend and were supervised in their work by administrators in the Church Education System. But the program could not have been a success without the marvelous support of faithful parents throughout the area who helped get their children up early each morning, organized car pools to transport them to seminary and then to high school, and helped out the program in any other ways they could. The continual struggles involved in all this will probably never be fully told, but the generally enthusiastic response to early-morning seminary assured Church authorities of its viability and eventually the program was introduced throughout the Church.

On 13 January 1951 the Beverly Hills Ward broke ground for its new chapel, located on Ohio Avenue, on the back portion of the temple property. LeGrand Richards, Presiding Bishop of the Church, was in town to attend the Los Angeles Stake conference, and he turned the first shovelful of dirt. By coincidence, the City of Los Angeles had given approval for the building of the temple earlier that week.

The ground-breaking ceremony marked the end of a ten-year struggle to obtain a chapel for Beverly Hills Ward. It began in 1940, under the direction of Bishop A. Eldon Rex, when the bishopric asked permission to build on what seemed the best location—the property purchased for a temple.[3] The request was denied, however, for the Brethren in Salt Lake City felt that to allow the ward to use that property would give it an unfair advantage over others, for no other ward in the Church shared property with a temple.

With the coming of World War II, any thought of a building for the Beverly Hills Ward was put on hold. Following the war, however, the new bishop, Marvin L. Saunders, and other ward leaders continued to look for property in Beverly Hills, the geographical center of the ward. When they approached the city council about the possibilities of building a chapel, however, they ran into unexpected difficulty. Most members of the council felt that there were enough churches in the city already, and they refused to give their support. The ward eventually turned its eyes back to the north end of the temple lot and finally secured two acres of that land from the Church prior to the announcement of the building of the temple.

Harold M. Burton, architect for the Wilshire Ward chapel, was enlisted to draw up the plans, which were then sent to Church headquarters for approval. An interesting sidelight to this story is seen in the fact that the original design did not call for a balcony in the chapel, for at the time this was against Church policy. During construction, however, various changes were made in the plans and, without official approval, a balcony was added in order to obtain the proper architectural effect.[4]

In 1949 C. Dean Olson became bishop of Beverly Hills Ward and it was his responsibility to oversee the chapel's construction. Like the Wilshire Ward before it, however, Beverly Hills Ward faced a major problem in raising funds as the Church would pay only around 20 percent of the cost of the building. Fund-raising became such a concern for Bishop Olson, and he worked so hard at it, that he suffered a heart attack before the building was dedicated.

The ward tried many fund-raising projects, such as fairs, carnivals, and dinners at the Beverly Hills Women's Club. Zatelle Sessions, ward Relief Society President, later estimated that during this time she helped cook thousands of meals as part of the effort.[5] However, these fund-raising dinners proved less than successful as only a few hundred dollars was raised at any one time. Those in charge soon recognized that they were probably just "spinning their wheels," since most of those who purchased the meals usually also helped donate the food.

Finally, early in 1952, Zatelle Sessions suggested that the ward take a different approach, such as putting on a major theatrical production. She had a friend, John Marlowe Nielson, who conducted the University of Utah's Glee Club and Men's Chorus and she approached Bishop Olson about inviting that group to come down and perform. The bishop approved, and when Nielson was contacted he volunteered his choral group for the occasion. A time was arranged for in March, during the break between winter and spring quarters at the University of Utah. Bishop Olson, meanwhile, talked with Charles P. Skouras, a Fox-Western executive married to a member of the ward, who arranged for the ward to use one of his company's theaters, the famous Carthay Circle in Beverly Hills, at no cost. Rod O'Connor agreed to serve as master of ceremonies, and for the headline performer Bishop Olson had arranged with a talent pool for a Hollywood star to appear.

As the appointed time approached, however, no headliner had been obtained, and Bishop Olson took it upon himself to try to arrange for one. In addition to being bishop of the ward and a successful businessman, Olson was also the mayor of Beverly Hills. He called the famous comedian Danny Thomas, a resident of Beverly Hills, introduced himself, and asked if he could visit with him. Once they were together, Olson admitted that he had misrepresented himself, for even though he was the mayor he had come to talk to Thomas about the possibility of helping his church raise money for a new building. In the gracious and generous spirit for which he is still known. Thomas agreed.[6]

On 21 March 1952 the Beverly Hills Ward presented an "Evening at Carthay Circle," with Danny Thomas as the featured guest. From ticket sales and advertising in the program, over $20,000 was raised for the building fund. From that time on, according to Bishop Olson, money seemed to flow in.[7] Interestingly, one member of the University of Utah Glee Club, Rodney H. Brady, moved into the Westwood Ward fourteen years later and eventually became bishop of the ward and, later, president of the stake.

Members of the Beverly Hills Ward donated not only their means but also countless hours of labor toward completing the chapel. Some of those who did so still look back and smile at the fact that their best efforts helped the chapel obtain a certain uniqueness, for not all their handiwork turned out plumb or even.

Unfortunately, however, the chapel was not completed without a tragedy. On a Monday morning in November 1951, volunteers were pouring cement for the tower. After four hours of work, the project was still not complete and those on the tower asked for two men working on the ground to come up and assist them. Richard Hunter and Arthur Wallace volunteered. They mounted a platform used to haul wheelbarrows of cement up to the tower, but the platform had risen only about twelve feet when it gave a violent jerk as one of the gears slipped and the pulley wheel went over the restraining blocks, sending both men tumbling off. Wallace landed feet first on the concrete floor, breaking an ankle, but Hunter was pitched off head first, landing on his elbow with such force that it pushed his collar bone through his spinal cord, severing a vertebra in his neck and leaving him a paraplegic.[8]

Hunter was a young, unmarried student at UCLA, studying to become an architectural engineer. Through an agreement worked out with the family, the Church provided him with assistance in laying the foundation for his future life and, in spite of his great tragedy, he has become successful in real estate. He married Mary Fitzell, an LDS girl from the Arlington Ward, who has served as not only a fine companion but also as a great strength to him. They now live in St. George, Utah.

As work progressed on the chapel, local leaders decided that the name of the ward should be changed, since it would no longer be meeting in Beverly Hills. On 13 July 1952 a special meeting was held at the stake center to consider a new name, and among those discussed were Temple, University, Village, and Hilltop Wards. The name eventually chosen was Westwood Ward, which President Russon later officially presented to the members in a sacrament meeting where it was unanimously approved.

On 11 September 1952 the Westwood Ward Primary began meeting in the unfinished building. On 14 December the ward used its chapel for the first time for Sunday meetings. The occasion was the first Westwood Ward conference, where 590 people, including the stake presidency and many stake officers, attended the first sacrament meeting. Four months later, on 12 April 1953, the Westwood Ward chapel was dedicated by Elder Harold B. Lee of the Council of the Twelve.

The Beverly Hills/Westwood Ward was not the only unit to change names or meeting places in this era. On 12 January 1952, a branch for the deaf was organized in the Adams Ward chapel under the direction of President Russon, and it became a unit of the Los Angeles Stake. Its history actually began many years earlier when Joseph F. Evans, a member of the Vermont Ward and a young father, was called on a mission to England. While he was absent, tragedy struck his family in the form of both diphtheria and scarlet fever, leaving two of his children dead and another daughter, Rhoda, deaf.

Later, as the heavy industries of World War II moved into Los Angeles, the deaf were encouraged to come and work in them, both because they were 4-F in their draft ratings and because they could work in the noisy industrial environment with a minimum of discomfort. As the number of LDS deaf grew in Los Angeles, a Sunday School class for the deaf was organized in 1941 at the request of Rhoda Evans Moulder. Her father, Joseph Evans, was the teacher. Seven people—five members and two investigators—began attending, but by November 1942 the number had grown to over twenty-five. The "Silent Class," as it was called, soon became a permanent part of the Vermont Ward Sunday School and met in a specially-built room in the Vermont chapel. As the deaf population grew in the area, Joseph Evans and Rhoda Evans Moulder were called by the South Los Angeles Stake presidency as missionaries to the deaf. By 1946 the number enrolled in the class exceeded one hundred.

As the "Silent Class" grew, its members began to express their hopes for a branch organization and a small chapel of their own. They asked Paul J. Smith, a class member residing in North Hollywood Ward to confer with President Hugh C. Smith of the San Fernando Stake about the possibility of adding a deaf chapel onto the North Hollywood chapel then under construction. Eventually the matter was referred to the First Presidency of the Church, who sent Elder Spencer W. Kimball of the Council of the Twelve to Los Angeles to hold a conference with the deaf. Over one hundred members attended the conference, which was held at the Los Angeles stake center. As a result of this conference, a committee composed of the local stake presidents was asked to draw up recommendations for the creation of a deaf branch. Finally, after approval from Church headquarters, the Deaf Branch was created as a unit of the Los Angeles Stake in January 1952.

Three factors favored locating the Deaf Branch in the Los Angeles Stake. First, the stake was centrally located, an important factor since members were drawn from throughout the Los Angeles area. Second, although few branch members lived within the boundaries of the stake, two prominent members of the Los Angeles Stake had a great interest in the deaf. Wayne McIntire, a member of Hollywood Ward and of the high council, had a daughter who was deaf. When they had discovered this, the McIntires had moved to Los Angeles so she could be helped at the John Tracy Clinic. McIntire became the high councilor responsible for coordinating the branch. The other stake member who worked with the deaf was Ray Jones of the Arlington Ward, who was overseeing the seminary program in the area and who, as a professional educator, had taken a special interest in the problems of the deaf. Both men eventually joined the faculty of California State University at Northridge, one of the best schools for the deaf in the country.

The third factor favoring locating the Deaf Branch in the Los Angeles Stake was the fact that not only individual stake members but also stake leaders were willing to make the deaf feel wanted, loved, and cared for, and did all they could to help them create a strong organization. In fact, providing a home for the Deaf Branch was seen by President Russon as one of the stake's major accomplishments in this period of time.[9]

Joseph F. Evans, father of the "Silent Class," was sustained as branch president with Joe F. Brandenburg, first counselor, Walter J. Huggins, second counselor, and Carl E. Torrell as clerk. While Evans and Huggins could hear, Brandenburg and Torrell were deaf. Torrell was also a recent convert to the Church, having been taught the gospel by members of the "Silent Class" with whom he worked. There were twenty-nine deaf class members present when the branch was organized, including four investigators. The first meeting was held the following week in a building behind the Adams Ward chapel that had once served as the bishops' storehouse. Meetings were scheduled at the same time as the Adams Ward so that hearing children could attend the Adams Ward Sunday School.

Most attempts to make the deaf feel at home in the stake were successful, even though there were a few miscues. At stake conferences the deaf sat in the first few rows on the north side of the chapel where someone would interpret for them, but branch members did not attend the June 1955 stake conference because their normal interpreter, Edward Redmond, an investigator, became ill and no adequate replacement was found. In spite of such momentary setbacks, however, the attitude of the deaf Saints can best be seen in the branch's motto: "Keep Smiling and Keep the Work Going."

Besides the Westwood Ward and the Deaf Branch, another unit made a change in meeting places during this time. Beginning in March 1951, the LaBrea Ward moved out of the Masonic temple on South Arlington and returned to share the stake center with the Wilshire Ward. One result of this move was that the Mutual Improvement Associations of the two wards began holding joint meetings. Since they were sharing the same building, the small number of youths in each ward made one MIA more practical.

On Thursday evening, 19 September 1953, the Mormon Choir of southern California was formally organized in the Wilshire Ward chapel. In a prayer offered on the occasion by President Bryan L. Bunker of the California Mission, the deepest spiritual hopes of those in attendance were well expressed: "Bless this little ripple now beginning that it will grow into a mighty wave, and become a great power in the promulgation of the Gospel of Jesus Christ."[10] Because of the efforts and devotion of dedicated choir members—such as Lois Nicholson, who by 1986 had sung with the choir for over thirty years—this prayer has literally been answered, for the choir has served as a powerful missionary tool and blessed the lives of Mormon and non-Mormon alike both within and without California.

The beginnings of the Mormon Choir of southern California can be traced to January 1950, when Frederick and Marianne Davis and their two daughters, Patricia and Rebecca, moved from Salt Lake City to Whittier, California. Davis, who was born in the Friendly Islands and lived in New Zealand before immigrating to Utah in 1934, had developed a fine reputation for his musical talents, and shortly after his arrival in California he became director of the Whittier Ward choir. He was also instrumental in setting up the Southern California Oratorio Society, and would eventually become the director of the Ellis-Orpheus Club (male chorus), the oldest musical organization in Southern California, and the Los Angeles Women's Lyric Club.

Meanwhile, one of the desires of Roy Utley, bishop of the Wilshire Ward, was to have an outstanding ward choir. Early in 1951, therefore, he contacted Davis about the possibility of moving into the Wilshire Ward and taking over the choir. Harold E. Phelps, president of the choir as well as a successful realtor, had known of Davis's talents when he lived in Salt Lake City, and he quickly began working to find a suitable home for the Davis family within the ward. He soon succeeded, and Davis began to direct the choir.

It was not long before Davis's path crossed that of Kay Gordon Wenzel, a member of the Hollywood Ward. Wenzel had heard the Wilshire Ward choir under the direction of Davis, and described the beauty of his work as having inspired her beyond words. That summer she also met Raymond Stewart, producer of the "Our America" programs held each fall at the Hollywood Bowl, who was attempting to organize a radio series over KMPC with the theme, "Go to Church." When Stewart asked Wenzel if she could recommend a fine choir for his initial program, she recommended the Wilshire Ward choir and negotiated its appearance.

Stewart was so impressed with the choir that he said to Wenzel, "Kay, I want a 300-voice Mormon choir just like that for my program at the Hollywood Bowl on October 7. What are the chances?"[11] After obtaining Davis's consent to direct such a group if it were organized, and with the advice of President John M. Russon, Wenzel approached all the stake presidents and bishops in the area to obtain clearance. She also contacted President David O. McKay about the possibility of organizing such a choir on a one-time basis. After two months of phone calls and letter writing, permission was granted by all concerned.

By October a 309-voice choir had been gathered from throughout the Los Angeles area. Following a highly successful program before an audience of eight thousand at the Hollywood

Bowl, the choir was asked to perform another concert as part of the San Bernardino centennial celebration, which was held nine days later. Following this concert the choir was disbanded, but it was reassembled when choir members received the exciting news that they were invited to participate in the famous Hollywood Bowl Easter sunrise services to be held the following April.

Ironically, this invitation provided the Church with an unusual opportunity for missionary work, for the Hollywood Ministerial Association, upon learning of it, began formal opposition to the choir's participation in that sacred Easter event on the grounds that Mormons were not Christians. This resulted in a meeting between local Church leaders and the ministerial association, where Church leaders had the opportunity to explain the Latter-day Saint views of Christ, and the matter was resolved. As a result of the meeting, in fact, the choir occasionally was asked to perform at the churches of some of the very ministers who had objected, thus helping to foster better good will between the Mormons and the Los Angeles religious community. A few years later when the choir sang at the church of one of these ministers, he afterwards exclaimed: "Almost thou persuadest me to become a Mormon!"[12]

Sunday, 13 April 1952, was an exciting day for members of the choir as they gathered in the famous Hollywood Bowl for the Easter sunrise service. Accompanied by a sixty-piece orchestra, the choir sang the "Hallelujah Chorus" and "Worthy Is the Lamb," both from Handel's *Messiah*.

Many words of praise were given to the choir following the event, including a letter to Frederick Davis from President Stephen L Richards of the First Presidency of the Church:

> Permit me to extend congratulations to you for the beautiful choral music which I had the pleasure of hearing over the radio in the broadcast of the Hollywood Bowl Easter Services. I heard many favorable comments, and my associates in the First Presidency were pleased with the rendition of the numbers your Choir gave and wish to extend felicitations. I am sure that our people in Southern California must have had great pride in this outstanding achievement.[13]

Although originally established for one concert, it became evident that the choir was here to stay as more invitations to perform were received. One of these came from Salt Lake City, and was a request to tape some music for a program called "Faith in Action," which was being broadcast coast to coast over the NBC radio network. Because of all this, suggestions were made to organize the choir on a permanent basis, and in January 1953 the matter was taken up with the stake presidents in the area. They gave the idea their enthusiastic approval. President Russon then wrote the First Presidency requesting permission to create a permanent Mormon choir in southern California whose membership would cross stake lines. The First Presidency granted permission in a letter dated 10 March 1953, which also noted the "unusually commendatory comments from the NBC people" concerning the choir's participation in the "Faith in Action" program.[14]

When the choir was formally organized in September 1953, 186 members were present, though a member ceiling of 150 was later established. At the organization, President Russon was set apart as president of the choir under the direction of the First Presidency, and since that time the Los Angeles Stake president has served either as the choir's president or its priesthood advisor. The Los Angeles Stake has also served the choir by allowing it to use the Wilshire Ward chapel for rehearsals.

Over the years the choir's contributions have been many. It has made over one hundred national broadcasts, and its appearances at stake conferences and other events are too numerous to mention. A few, however, must be noted. In 1954 the choir was asked to sing in the Hollywood Bowl at a non-political rally for President Dwight D. Eisenhower. On 12 August 1955 it gave a fund-raising concert to assist the Mormon Tabernacle Choir's tour of Europe, and in 1956 it sang at the dedication of the Los Angeles Temple. In December 1956 the choir presented its first major performance of Handel's oratorio *Messiah* in the Philharmonic Auditorium in downtown Los Angeles. For thirty years this was an annual Christmas tradition in Los Angeles.[15] In 1960 the choir sang at two sessions of the Church's general conference in Salt Lake City.

From the proceeds of its 1959 performance of *Messiah*, the choir donated $25,000 toward the building of the Dorothy Chandler Pavilion, thus becoming a founding member. In December 1964, during the first week of this great music center's opening, the choir's presentation of *Messiah* became one of the first concerts given in the building.

In addition to its many concerts within California, the choir has given concerts in Hawaii, Nevada, Arizona, and Utah. It has also performed in Mexico, Israel, New Zealand, and Australia.

Following the 1980 presentation of *Messiah*, Frederick Davis retired as choir director and Russell Fox took his place. Accompanists for the choir have been Cicely Adams Brown and Helen Cartwright.

Prior to 1953, Institute of Religion classes for LDS students at the University of Southern California were taught in the Methodist church located near campus. On Friday evening, 11 December 1953, a new LDS Institute of Religion building adjacent to the USC campus was dedicated by Elder Spencer W. Kimball of the Council of the Twelve. Earlier that day, the cornerstone-laying ceremony was held at the temple. The institute building was designed by Douglas W. Burton, son of Harold W. Burton, and featured a chapel, lounge, library, classrooms, offices, kitchen, a large patio, and a clock tower which faithfully chimed the hour for many years. Located just south of campus on the corner of McClintock and 36th streets, the building also served as headquarters for the seminary and institute system in southern California, as the social center for the institute program until other institutes were built at other area universities, and finally as the meeting place for the University of Southern California Ward after it was created.

Some of the problems that confronted stake leaders during the 1950s were reminders that the Latter-day Saints, like everyone else, lived in a secular world with all its secular temptations and diversions. One of these was the frequently recurring problem of juvenile delinquency, which surfaced again even within the Latter-day Saint community. In both the 1930s and 1940s the problem had, at times, become quite severe. In March 1935, for instance, there were over 125 teenage members of the Church in Los Angeles County either on probation or being dealt with for delinquency, an average of over four per ward. Left to their own initiatives as to how to deal with such problems, stake leaders usually organized delinquency committees to work closely with those in trouble and continued to emphasize youth programs, especially Scouting.

In the 1950s Church leaders again became greatly concerned over the number and seriousness of Latter-day Saint juvenile problems. In 1954 Lyman Thompson, a member of the

Hollywood Ward who worked for Los Angeles County at Juvenile Hall, reported that 166 LDS youth were being dealt with by county officials. The following year the number increased to 244. While most of the problems were minor in nature, some were very serious and even included a murder.[16] Even though most of the LDS youth involved were not members of the Los Angeles Stake, stake leaders nevertheless spent much of their time dealing with the problems that existed and trying to prevent others.

Unlike previous times, however, the youth problems of the 1950s were not limited to major urban areas such as Los Angeles, but were a source of concern throughout the Church. The social changes taking place in the country brought many of the youth into a spirit of rebellion against traditional values and institutions, and the Latter-day Saint youth were not unaffected. As a result, the efforts of local leaders were combined with changes in the Church's youth program to help combat trends toward juvenile delinquency by giving the youth a greater sense of involvement in the Church and its activities.

A significant change was made in the Aaronic Priesthood program in 1954 when the Presiding Bishopric announced that the age at which worthy boys could be ordained to the office of teacher had been lowered from fifteen to fourteen, and the age for ordination to the office of priest had been lowered from seventeen to sixteen. This action was taken, it was explained, because fourteen-year-old boys were restless as deacons and did not wish to be grouped with the younger boys. The following year, the "Duty to God" award was established as part of the Boy Scout program, and this distinctive honor recognized achievement in religious activity as well as in Scouting.

The MIA also responded by sponsoring more recreational and cultural programs. In 1954 it began to sponsor regional conferences in which the youth had opportunities to participate in dance, drama, speech, and music festivals. Prior to this time such festivals had been held annually in Salt Lake City, but the new plan was to extend them on a regional basis to all the major areas of Church population. The first of these regional conferences was held in Los Angeles in August. The Hollywood Bowl was the site of the music festival, while the dance, drama, and speech competitions were held at East Los Angeles Junior College. The dance festival took place on the football field while

the speech and drama presentations were held in the auditorium. The importance Church leaders placed on what was
happening was symbolized by the presence of President David
O. McKay, who addressed a huge crowd of several thousand
LDS youth who attended the conference session on Sunday
morning in the Hollywood Bowl.

The large numbers attending the conference created a few
problems for the city of Los Angeles. The music festival featured
a chorus and orchestra of over fifteen hundred, more than the
stage of the Hollywood Bowl could hold without violating fire
codes. The fire marshall tried unsuccessfully several times to
limit the size of the choir but finally gave up, concluding, "Oh,
h——, the Mormons don't smoke anyway."[17] At the Sunday
morning service, the handful of policemen on hand to direct
traffic soon became inadequate, and reinforcements had to be
called in. The conference, however, was a huge success so far as
the Church was concerned, and it established a pattern that
continued for several years.

The stake also redoubled its efforts with respect to the
youth. At stake conferences President Russon spoke of the need
for love and of the necessity of demonstrating affection in the
home in order to combat juvenile delinquency. He also requested that family members meet together on Sunday afternoons in a form of family home evening, and he pledged that no
stake or ward meetings would be held at that time. He also set
aside the third Friday of each month as "Family Recreation
Night," when no stake or ward activities would be held, and
urged families to use the time for participating together in
activities.

Besides asking families to pay increased attention to the
needs of their own youth, the stake undertook additional means
to help. Fathers-and-sons outings continued and Scouting was
given renewed emphasis. In addition, the stake created a soft-
ball diamond in the vacant field behind the Westwood Ward
chapel, which not only gave the youth another wholesome activity to participate in but also prevented the Emerson Junior
High located next to the field from exercising eminent domain
and taking over the property.

While great emphasis was placed upon the young men, who
presented most of the juvenile delinquency problems, the
young ladies were not forgotten. Under the direction of stake

YWMIA president Audrey Snow, the Los Angeles Stake sponsored personal improvement courses at the stake center. Classes were conducted every two weeks for a six-month period, and at the end the girls put on a fashion show in which they were required to model only clothes they had sewn themselves.

If problems arose among the young men that could not be handled effectively by parents, Church leaders, or local authorities, Ettie Lee, a member of the Wilshire Ward who had some special qualifications, was there to provide some needed assistance.

Lee was born in Luna, New Mexico, in 1885. At seventeen she began a teaching career in a one-room schoolhouse in Thatcher, Arizona, where Spencer W. Kimball was one of her fourth-grade students. In 1905 she moved to Los Angeles and entered the University of Southern California to pursue a master's degree in education. She also began a teaching career in the Los Angeles School District that would eventually cover forty-four years. She earned national recognition for her creative teaching methods and authored several textbooks which were used in schools throughout the United States and Europe.

While teaching in Los Angeles, Ettie Lee became deeply concerned over the increasing number of young men among her students who were getting into trouble with the law and being sent to correctional institutions. In studying the problem she discovered that these boys all had one thing in common: they came from broken or troubled homes. Believing that the institutions to which they were sent did not teach young people to become productive members of the community, she concluded, "A boy in trouble does not belong behind bars. He needs love. He needs a mother and father to guide him. Above all, he needs a home."[18] Armed with this firm conviction, she began searching for better solutions.

When she approached authorities concerning alternative care for troubled youth, such as youth homes where boys would live in a family environment and learn to work, Lee discovered that such care was not available, nor was there a disposition on the part of authorities to provide it. Concluding that if something was to be done she would have to do it herself, she put her trust in Jacob's teachings in the Book of Mormon that a person who sought for riches to feed the hungry, clothe the naked, and visit the sick, would be blessed to obtain riches. (Jacob 2:18-19.) While she could do little on her $200-a-month teacher's salary, she could do something, and her desire to help these boys, along with her faith in the cause, more than compensated for her lack of funds.

She checked out books from the library on real estate investments and, following their advice, saved half her salary for investment purposes. In time, she was able to make a down payment on a four-plex, and after school at nights and on weekends, she cleaned, painted, and repaired the apartments. After the apartments were rented, she continued to do the maintenance work herself. It was not long before she sold these apartments for a profit, and with the money she bought a thirteen-unit apartment house, fixed it up and sold it, then bought a thirty-unit apartment complex, and after that a sixty-unit complex. In all, over fifty different apartment complexes passed through her hands. Her pattern was to "buy, improve, sell, work hard, save, invest," and to trust in God.[19] Those who dealt with Ettie were amazed at her hard work, courage, perception, and seemingly unorthodox methods. Often she would excuse herself from an important meeting so that she could pray about a transaction. She would then calmly return, a decision made.

As Lee accumulated properties, she soon owned enough to be able to retire comfortably. However, since she was doing all this for a purpose, and believing that she was guided in her acquisitions and that they were, therefore, not hers, she continued to set aside all her profits for her boys' homes. She lived in one of her smallest apartments, subsisting first on her salary and then on her teacher's pension.

By the time she retired from public school teaching, Ettie Lee had not only the time but also the means to begin her work of rehabilitating wayward boys. In 1950 she purchased her first boys' ranch, a sixty-acre ranch near San Jacinto, after ignoring advice that the ground water supply was inadequate. With her characteristic faith she had a well dug that not only supplied enough water for the ranch, but also produced an excess, which was then sold to neighboring ranches to help cover her own expenses. She named this first boys' home "Waterflow Ranch," after the miraculous development of the well.

Over the next twenty-four years Ettie Lee opened twenty additional homes in California, Utah, and Nevada, each patterned after the home of her youth. Although never married, she had a very large family, and her warm and loving homes have helped thousands of boys—who often arrived unloved, bitter, and despairing—to become productive citizens. The success of Ettie Lee's homes revolutionized the treatment of wayward and neglected youth in America, as many other homes based on her vision and philosophy have been opened.

When she died in 1974, President Spencer W. Kimball wrote of Ettie Lee:

> A woman of vision, selflessness and sacrifice, she has done much for young men who had been deprived, but through her vision and enterprise have found much in life, including opportunity and accomplishment.
> Our world would greatly profit if it had more public spirited sacrificial [men and women] such as this splendid woman. God bless her memory.[20]

In 1954 the Church began what leaders hoped would become a successful program for teaching the gospel to the Jewish people. Because of the large number of Jews in Los Angeles, especially in the western portion of the Los Angeles Stake, a pilot program was inaugurated there, and it later spread to other large cities with sizeable Jewish populations. Instrumental in establishing the program were LeGrand Richards, who had become a member of the Council of the Twelve, and swimsuit designer Rose Marie Reid, a member of the Westwood Ward.

Elder Richards had always had a great love for the Jewish people and once told his father that "if the Church ever undertook the work in earnest among the Jews," he "would certainly like to have a hand in it."[21] As a result, he wrote a work entitled *Judah! Do You Know?*, but later, at the suggestion of Rose Marie Reid, changed the name to *Israel! Do You Know?* Reid felt that the Jews might not readily understand the implications of the reference to Judah.

Born and raised in Alberta, Canada, Rose Marie Reid showed an early talent for design. Following the death of her husband, she moved to Los Angeles and opened her famous swimsuit company. Through her business in an industry dominated by Jewish people, she naturally made many Jewish friends. A descendant of Orson Hyde, who in 1841 had dedicated the land of Palestine for the preaching of the gospel, she had a great personal interest in the Jewish people and recalled that as a young girl her father had often told her that during her lifetime the Jews would return to Jerusalem. All this led to the development within her of a great desire to share her religion with them.

In 1953 Sister Reid met Michael Silver, a Jewish accountant with whom she had business dealings, and eventually she began to teach him the gospel. When he asked for literature, however, she hesitated, for almost everything written in the Church had been written for Christians. She felt that the Jewish people could be appealed to more effectively through literature designed especially with their background and religion in mind. She was delighted, therefore, to learn from Elder Richards's daughter of the book he was writing, and she was able to obtain a copy for Michael Silver.

Following the publication of *Israel! Do You Know?* in 1954, the moment that Elder Richards and Sister Reid were waiting for arrived when the First Presidency gave permission for the establishment of an experimental "Jewish Mission" in cities with large Jewish populations. This mission was to function without full-time missionaries. Rather, proselyting efforts were to be the responsibility of Church members already living in the cities who would be called as part-time missionaries.

In November 1955 Elder Richards contacted President Russon and asked if he would organize and supervise a trial Jewish Mission in Los Angeles. Elder Richards recommended that two missionaries be called from each stake to work specifically with the Jewish people. Fifteen people from six stakes, including Rose Marie Reid, Herond N. Sheranian, and J. Leland Anderson of the Los Angeles Stake, accepted such calls. A recent Jewish convert, Jerome Horowitz, was also recruited to help out in the Los Angeles Jewish mission.

Before these missionaries could begin active proselyting, methods for teaching Jews still had to be developed. For some time Reid had been experimenting with ways of presenting the gospel to her Jewish friends, and both she and Horowitz drew upon their experiences and wrote suggested door approaches for the missionaries. In addition, at the suggestion of LeGrand Richards, Reid wrote a sixty-five page booklet entitled *Attention Israel* as an introduction to Elder Richards' *Israel! Do You Know?* These publications served both as the primary literature to be read by the Jewish people and as the Jewish mission's plan for teaching the gospel. Later, Reid wrote a detailed plan to be used by the missionaries, *Suggested Plan for Teaching the Gospel to the Jewish People.* It was almost two hundred pages long and included ten lessons for teaching the gospel. When sent to Salt Lake City, however, it failed to receive Church approval, which left the Jewish missionaries to devise their own proselyting methods. Most continued to rely upon the writings of Rose Marie Reid, which she published at her own expense.

According to one account, even after several months of the Jewish Mission, "virtually no missionaries had been adequately trained, little actual proselyting had been done, and few Jewish persons were close to accepting Mormonism."[22] Reasons for these problems included a general lack of knowledge among the missionaries as well as differences of opinion as to how the gospel should be presented to the Jews. There was also the lingering question as to whether it was proper at all to organize special proselyting activity just for the Jewish people.

During the summer of 1956, Leo J. Muir was appointed as coordinator of the Jewish Mission. To raise interest in the mission, Reid, Horowitz, and Muir began speaking at the various wards in Los Angeles about Jewish proselyting activities. By the end of the year the number of missionaries serving in the mission had grown to nearly fifty.

Proselyting activities included parties frequently given by Church members to help friendship their Jewish acquaintances. The *California Intermountain News* recounts one of these, held at the home of Dr. and Mrs. Herond N. Sheranian and sponsored by the Sheranians and Rose Marie Reid, to which 125 Jewish friends and guests were invited. The entertainment portion featured Reid Nibley, noted Mormon pianist, and a program of Israeli folk dances performed by the Israeli Dance Group.[23]

The mission continued to function until March 1959, when the First Presidency issued a statement that missionary efforts directed specifically at the Jewish community should be discontinued. Instead, each stake was to have two missionaries who could teach the Jewish people if the need arose. While the Jewish Mission was not as successful in bringing Jewish converts into the Church as had been hoped, it met at least with some success as nearly two dozen Jewish people were converted.

Los Angeles Stake, meanwhile, continued to face its own internal challenges, one of which was the unfortunately low morale in LaBrea Ward. From the time of its creation, this ward had not done as well as stake leaders had hoped, and at least three problems seemed to be involved. One was a feeling prevalent among some members that it had been a mistake to create the ward in the first place. Such negativism cast a shadow over the ward from the beginning, for many who were assigned to attend refused to do so and simply continued going to their old wards. The fact that the La Cienega Ward of the Santa Monica Stake was closer for many than were the meeting places of the LaBrea Ward did not help, and some simply yielded to the temptation to attend there.

Another problem was that some members of the ward began to feel amost as if they were merely step-children of the stake and that, at least to some degree, the ward was being used as a pawn in dealing with stake problems. When certain changes were made in ward boundaries, for example, some members complained that stake leaders were simple gerrymandering in order to locate leaders or to keep a good balance in other wards. When attendance at the Arlington Ward exceeded capacity, for instance, portions of that ward were transferred to LaBrea. Later, however, after many members refused to attend LaBrea because the Arlington Ward chapel was closer, this section was transferred back. Soon afterward, Merlin Sant, who lived in the area in question, was made bishop of Arlington Ward. Although the stake presidency clearly explained why the action was taken, there were those who believed that the transfer had taken place only so that Sant could be the new bishop.[24] In addition, after 1952 the LaBrea Ward was the only ward in the stake without a chapel. Consideration had been given to the possibility of building one, and a site had been selected, but when it became clear that city zoning could not be changed to accommodate the chapel the plans were abandoned. The LaBrea Ward thus became a permanent resident of the Wilshire chapel, but some ward members felt discriminated against because they did not have their own.

A third problem was the fact that almost from the beginning the vitality of the ward was gradually sapped as many families, especially young families, began moving out of the ward and few moved in to replace them. These families were joining the "white flight" to the suburbs, which was occurring not just in Los Angeles but in most major American cities. The problem was both social and economic and reflected a major crisis in American race relations as well as in American urban development. As black families began moving into formerly all-white neighborhoods, racial bias induced many whites to move out, often selling their property at less than market value. This resulted in dramatic drops in property values, and as whites who may not have otherwise moved saw economic disaster on the horizon they also put their property up for sale. This only provided more opportunity for the usually less affluent blacks to move into the vacuum, and the cycle continued in neighborhood after neighborhood.

The effect on the Church was foreseeable. As blacks began moving into the boundaries of LaBrea Ward, many members, not immune from the prejudices of the day, began moving out and ward membership declined dramatically. Between January 1954 and May 1955 it dropped from 650 to 430. Part of the problem, of course, was the fact that at the time blacks were not allowed to receive the priesthood and its accompanying blessings, and this fact alone made members reluctant to allow their children to associate with other young people who would not eventually be eligible to marry in the temple. Church policy even prohibited active proselyting among blacks, which provided little incentive for blacks themselves to investigate the Church, though if any inquired concerning the gospel they could be taught. Though all this would change later, the reality of the time was that "white flight" was creating an administrative disaster so far as LaBrea Ward was concerned.

While LaBrea Ward was the hardest hit, it was not the only ward in the stake affected by racial and other issues. With changes in the inner city resulting not only from the growing black population but also through expanding industrialization, young couples began settling in more outlying areas, such as within the boundaries of Westwood Ward. As a result of a series of housing acts passed by Congress, new housing was available within the ward which required little or no down payment, unlike older homes in some of the more well-established areas. All this only helped hasten the decline of Church membership in the older parts of the city. Most wards in the stake, therefore, except the Westwood Ward and the Deaf Branch, had been losing membership for several years, and between 1950 and 1955 total membership in the stake declined by over six hundred, from 5,000 to 4,400.

Because so many young families were leaving, the social structure of the wards also began to change. In 1950 there were only twenty-one Aaronic Priesthood holders in the Wilshire Ward among a total membership of over one thousand. In the Adams Ward there were only fourteen Aaronic Priesthood holders. This reflected the fact that in these wards, as in LaBrea and Arlington, there was a preponderance of older members, especially widows. As a whole, the stake averaged two members per family, with a low of 1.7 in Adams and Wilshire and a high of 2.3 in the Westwood Ward. There was also a shortage of Melchizedek Priesthood in the stake as 60 percent of the families had no Melchizedek Priesthood holder in the home, a statistic that reflected not only the growing number of widows but also the consequence of so many marriages outside the faith. This not only left many families without the blessing of the priesthood, but it also had a potentially devastating effect upon the potential for leadership in the wards and the ward teaching program.

Since 1950 stake leaders had done their best to deal with these problems by occasionally realigning boundaries in order to help the wards remain viable. No sooner was one problem solved, however, than others arose, and it became apparent to President Russon and his counselors that these frequent changes were disruptive to the smooth functioning of the wards. Consequently, they decided that a major reorganization of the stake was needed in order to alleviate the need for so many future changes.

At the March 1955 stake conference, the matter of shifting populations was discussed with Elder Joseph Fielding Smith of the Council of the Twelve, who recommended that the stake study the situation carefully and then submit recommendations to the Brethren in Salt Lake City. In April 1955 a survey was conducted to determine exactly where stake members lived and what changes in ward boundaries would be needed to best keep the wards functioning and properly staffed and to ensure that each ward had adequate Melchizedek Priesthood. As a result, stake leaders determined that the best way to reach this goal was to dissolve LaBrea Ward, distribute its four hundred members to surrounding wards, and change the boundaries among the remaining wards in the eastern part of the stake. At the same time, the increase in population of the Westwood Ward to over eleven hundred, along with an adequate number of Melchizedek Priesthood holders, allowed for the division of that ward.

Near the end of May, the stake presidency submitted their recommendations to the First Presidency, who, in turn, assigned Elders Marion G. Romney and George Q. Morris of the Council of the Twelve to study the proposal at the Los Angeles Stake conference in June.[25] Following their visit, the Apostles approved the recommended changes. President Russon then called an unprecedented meeting of stake members to be held at the stake center on 3 July 1955.

An air of expectation filled the 845 stake members who gathered in this special meeting. President Russon told them that changes in boundaries must be made from time to time, mentioning the shifting population and the influx of blacks into portions of the stake as major contributing factors.[26] He then announced a complete reshuffling of boundaries. The most important changes were the dissolution of the LaBrea Ward and the creaton of the Westwood Second Ward. In addition, portions of the Hollywood Ward went to Adams, Hollywood and Wilshire Wards exchanged selected areas, and a portion of Arlington was made part of the Adams Ward.

When the dissolution of the LaBrea Ward was presented and the membership of the ward was called upon to sustain the stake presidency in this matter, about seventy-five members stood in the negative.[27] Even though some of them had felt that the creation of the ward was a mistake in the first place, and continued to think so through the years, their trials had created such a special unity among them that even the thought of being split up among adjacent wards was distasteful. Nevertheless, the LaBrea Ward was disbanded, and its members residing south of Adams Boulevard became part of the Arlington Ward, while those north of Adams were assigned to the Wilshire Ward.

The Westwood Ward was divided at Santa Monica Boulevard, with the Westwood First Ward north of that line and the Westwood Second Ward south of it. William F. Jackson was released as bishop of the First Ward to become bishop of the Second Ward, with John T. Bernhard and Eston H. Clarke as his counselors. Arvo Van Alstyne became the new bishop of the First Ward, with J. Grant Brazier and J. Wallace Frame as his counselors. Except for the Deaf Branch, the Westwood Second Ward was the smallest unit in the stake, with 520 members, and next to it was the Westwood Ward, with about 580. With the temple and the UCLA medical center under construction, however, and with this being one of the few areas with undeveloped land, the area covered by these wards was seen as the only part of the stake where substantial growth was still possible. The Wilshire Ward was now the largest unit in the stake, with membership in excess of nine hundred. Each of these changes were effective as of 17 July 1955.

By October 1955 it became apparent to the stake presidency that having a temple within the stake presented a golden opportunity for missionary work in the area. To emphasize this, President Russon released four high councilors living near the temple to serve stake missions: W. Wayne Austin, senior member of the high council; Mervin L. Saunders; Romney Stewart; and Varnell R. Rosa. President Russon explained this action to the *California Intermountain News*: "This is an example to the entire stake of our recognition of the tremendous missionary opportunity afforded us at this time. We are calling to stake missions some of our top leadership. . . . Surely our mission program deserves the finest people if it is to achieve the desired results."[28]

This emphasis on missionary work paid dividends as eighty-six converts were made in the Los Angeles Stake Mission during the first nine months of 1956. There were eighty-one stake missionaries at the time, and while they found converts, their success did not come without great effort. In August alone, they held 195 cottage meetings, placed twenty copies of the Book of Mormon, passed out 389 tracts, and had four baptisms.

When the Los Angeles Temple opened in April 1956, only four sessions were held each day. At the first session, the stake presidencies and their wives were joined by President David O. McKay; Elders Delbert L. Stapley and Richard L. Evans of the Council of Twelve; and Gordon B. Hinckley, Assistant to the Twelve. Also that first day, twelve marriages were performed.

Unfortunately, during the first few months of its operation, attendance at the temple was significantly less than anticipated. In Los Angeles Stake, President Russon had encouraged each member to prepare to enter the House of the Lord, but even though many did so, and were worthy, few had what was called the "temple habit."[29] Having lived some distance from a temple for so long, many had gotten out of the habit of regular attendance, and it took awhile before the Saints in general acquired the "temple habit" and increased their attendance.

John M. Russon was a goal-oriented stake president, and even though his predecessors also set goals for the stake, he was more vocal than most in expressing them. At the beginning of each year he sequestered himself for several days in a hotel room or some other place where he could not be disturbed by visitors and phone calls. There, in prayerful and contemplative solitude, he evaluated his past year's performance and planned out what he wanted to accomplish during the coming year in his family, in his profession, and in the Church. He then set goals for himself and also arrived at possible goals for the stake. These he discussed with his counselors, and the three of them then set stake goals. President Russon also coined phrases which helped people to remember the goals and helped him determine procedures to follow. Some of these slogans were "Follow through in '62," "Our attitude determines our altitude," and "Every calling is great when greatly pursued."

At the January 1957 stake priesthood meeting, President Russon presented the stake goals for 1957, calling them "The Three Ps." This was taken from a phrase he used in his business, known as the "Four Ps"—"Proven Process Prevents Problems." The stake presidency had given considerable thought to what the goals should be and concluded that the responsibility of each stake member was, first, to preach the gospel; second, to perform vicarious ordinances; and third, to perfect the Saints.[30] It is interesting to note that nearly a quarter of a century later, in 1981, these same goals were identified by President Spencer W. Kimball as the three-fold mission of the Church.

The Los Angeles Stake presidency was also concerned about the spiritual well being of the many college and university students within the stake boundaries, and watched with great interest what was happening in connection with the Deseret Clubs and the institutes of religion. Following the dedication of the new institute building at the University of Southern California, Sunday services began to be held in its chapel and students living near the campus were free to attend either these meetings or the Adams Ward. With experience, however, stake leaders saw that such an arrangement was unsatisfactory, for many students were becoming "neither fish nor fowl," shifting between the two units and not developing a feeling of responsibility toward either. The lack of ties to any one ward was reflected in low tithing and fast offerings and in a lack of concern among many students for the inactive Latter-day Saints on campus. Without these things as part of their lives, the students could hardly enjoy the full blessings of the gospel.

At the time there were 204 LDS students at USC, and since many of them were married, the number of people tied to the university was much larger. Although USC is a "commuter school" and many of its students come from some distance to attend classes, sixty students lived within walking distance of the campus. When their families were counted, approximately one hundred young people were close at hand, and stake leaders felt this was enough to justify the organization of a campus branch of the Church. Attendance at the institute's priesthood meetings and Sunday School already averaged sixty-five, and it was anticipated that attendance at a branch would be substantially larger. After much consideration, therefore, the stake presidency determined that the needs of students at the University of Southern California could best be served by their own branch, and in January 1957 wrote the First Presidency of the Church about such a possibility.[31] The recommendation was favorably considered; President Henry D. Moyle wrote of the First Presidency's approval and gave the stake presidency authority to create a ward rather than a branch if that should seem best.[32] On 17 March 1957 a ward was established for students at the University of Southern California, under the direction of President Moyle. It was named the University Ward; and Melvin Keller, a member of the USC dental school faculty, was sustained as the first bishop. His counselors were Winfield Q. Cannon, a local business executive, and Herman Allenbach, a dental student.

While many students continued to attend their home wards, a large percentage came to the new University Ward, and during the early years membership averaged 150-200. To give students a sense of responsibility for the success of the ward as well as all the other experiences necessary to operating a regular ward, they were asked to contribute to a ward budget, and the ward was charged $70 per month for the use of the institute building.

For the students, the organization of the ward meant many things. Most were enrolled in graduate programs at the university or in one of its professional schools, such as medicine, dentistry, or law. Others were enrolled in the Southern California School of Optometry or in other nearby professional schools. Demands on their time were extremely heavy, so married couples, especially, found great strength and comfort in the new ward through their close association with others who were experiencing similar academic pressures and financial struggles. Some felt that other Church members may not have fully understood their special problems, and the understanding of the University Ward leaders as well as supportive stake leaders helped all of them feel closer to the Church. Their social lives, too, were enhanced through ward activities geared especially to their needs.

In addition, the intellectual lives of students were enhanced as they found that their testimonies and faith were not drawn into question just because they wanted to discuss in some detail some of the new ideas they were being exposed to. One former elders quorum president recounts an incident that exemplifies what this meant to at least one member of the new ward. In a personal priesthood interview, a quorum member who was also a recent convert to the Church told him that the creation of the ward had strengthened his testimony of the truthfulness of the Church. When he attended the Adams Ward, he said, he felt that some of the older members treated him almost as if he were an intruder and that they seldom recognized him when he raised his hand in Sunday School or priesthood classes. More important, few people in the ward were willing to discuss with him the kinds of questions that were being raised in his mind as a result of his intellectual training at the university. They seemed to feel, he said, that raising such questions was evidence of lack of faith, so they should not even be discussed: he felt, however, that such questions should be discussed openly by people with faith, for that was the only way faith could be sustained by people who were being trained at the university to ask questions. Now that he was associating with people in similar circumstances, he felt the Lord had answered his prayers and made a place for him in His Church.[33]

By 1958 the shifting population of the stake had again become a problem. Although the stake population had fallen by only fifty-six since 1955, the population of the Adams Ward had fallen by more than 250 and ward membership stood at less than 450. Average family size was less than 1.6, as many members were single and/or elderly. By contrast, the Westwood Ward averaged 2.5 members per family, with the Westwood Second Ward close behind, reflecting the fact that most of the young families remaining in the stake chose to reside in the Westwood area.

The downward trend in the Adams Ward was not likely to reverse itself, for the residential area in the ward was fast becoming blighted through increasing industrial and commercial development. This had been spurred by the beginning of the construction of the Interstate Highway System in 1956, including the Harbor Freeway which ran near the Adams Ward chapel and cut the chapel off from the major residential portions of the city. As business and industry moved into the area, families moved out and ward membership declined, making it increasingly difficult to staff the ward and conduct all ward programs adequately. In addition, the growing black population in the area resulted in the same "white flight" experienced in LaBrea Ward.

Adams was not the only ward undergoing changes. Both the Wilshire and Arlington Wards were also losing membership, primarily through "white flight" but also because of industrialization. The makeup of the Hollywood Ward was also changing, but its problems resulted from an apartment building boom within its boundaries that caused its population to mushroom. The nature of the new arrivals, however, was different from those in other wards, for many of them were star-struck singles who were attracted to the romance associated with Hollywood. Others viewed Hollywood as a stopping point until they found in a "house or spouse." The makeup and stability of the ward was changing, then, for apartment living gave no real tie to the area and the ward was becoming highly transient and somewhat unwieldy for one bishop to manage.

As business and industry accompanied the freeways into the area around the Adams Ward, property value jumped and as early as 1956 the Church received lucrative offers for the Adams Ward property.[34] Although stake leaders saw that the demise of the ward was imminent, they felt it premature to sell at that time and declined the offers. Even if the ward was disbanded, the location was ideal for the Deaf Branch, which shared the property, for it was near the freeways and the branch's membership came from the entire Los Angeles area. Branch membership, moreover, was growing. In addition, in 1957 the Church Education System's administrative offices for the huge early-morning seminary program moved out of the USC institute building and located in one of the buildings behind the Adams Ward. Thus the Adams property appeared to have continuing value to the Church, even if the Adams Ward were disbanded.

As the area around the Adams chapel became more commercialized, however, the desirability of holding that property for Church use diminished. When lucrative offers to purchase the property came again early in 1958, stake leaders gave them more serious consideration. They were faced with the inevitable conclusion that the Adams Ward must soon be disbanded, that the stately old chapel was not essential for Church use, and that, in the long run, the best use of the property was for commercial purposes. Such a decision was not to be made lightly, however, for the Adams Ward had been the mother ward in California, and its chapel had served as a landmark for forty-three years. This tradition weighed heavily on many ward and stake members, and considerable emotion was attached to it. Nevertheless, recognizing that the Arlington, Hollywood, and Wilshire wards could use the increased membership that would result from dissolving the Adams Ward and that the Church would benefit economically by selling the Adams property, the stake presidency recommended all of this to the First Presidency.[35] In November 1958, the First Presidency and Quorum of the Twelve gave their approval to disbanding the Adams Ward and disposing of its chapel.[36]

An agreement was reached with the Lightolier Corporation through Zion's Security Corporation, the real estate and investment arm of the Church at the time, and within a very short time a branch of the United Bank of California was built on part of the property. Originally some long-term leases were involved, but eventually all the property was disposed of. Part of the stake's share of the transaction was used for building an addition onto the Wilshire Ward chapel for the Deaf Branch, and the Church's portion became the basis for further transactions with the Lightolier Corporation through which the Church was able to obtain the property on which the Salt Palace was built in Salt Lake City.[37]

A special meeting was called at the stake center for 30 November 1958, at which time the approved changes were presented to stake members. President Russon began by telling those present that this was, in reality, a continuation of the special meeting which had been held in 1955. The necessity for calling it grew out of the seemingly relentless changes taking place in the eastern portion of the stake. It was an emotional meeting, but to relieve tensions concerning the demise of the Adams Ward, President Russon quipped that any similarity between the stake presidency's recommendations to cut up the stake and the rite of carving the Thanksgiving turkey, which occurred the previous Thursday, was purely coincidental.[38]

The first order of business was presenting to the congregation for its sustaining vote the dissolution of the Adams Ward after thirty-five years of active life plus a history dating back to the organization of the Los Angeles Branch in 1895. The proposal was approved, but the Adams Ward left behind a legacy that has extended throughout southern California. In a sense, Adams Ward gave birth to almost all the wards within the Los Angeles area, and they became a magnificent progeny.

The membership of the Adams Ward was transferred to other wards, with 120 members going to the Arlington Ward, 260 to the Wilshire Ward, and sixty to the Hollywood Ward. In addition, 120 members were transferred from Wilshire to Hollywood, most of whom had been transferred to Wilshire in 1955.

The announcement then was made that the Hollywood Ward would be divided along a more-or-less east-west line, principally along Normandie Avenue. Those residing west of the line were members of the Hollywood Ward, with Sullivan C. Richardson as bishop; those east of the line became members of the Hollywood Second Ward, with Edward C. Nadle as bishop. As a result of the changes, Arlington had 820 members; Wilshire, 845; Hollywood, 570; Hollywood Second, 585; and the two Westwood Wards each had nearly seven hundred members.

Finally, President Russon announced the selling of the Adams property. Although most members knew that the sale of the building was inevitable, few were untouched by the announcement. This, after all, was the first chapel erected in southern California and the second built in California. Within the building the first stake in a major metropolitan area was created, as was Hollywood Stake, forerunner of the present Los Angeles California Stake. During the early days of the Church in Los Angeles this chapel was one of the first places new arrivals from Utah would seek out. Here many couples met for the first time, many Church stalwarts were baptized and instructed in the gospel, and it was not uncommon to hear a sermon from the President of the Church or another General Authority or to meet such leaders informally in the chapel's hallways. It was known in Los Angeles as a monument to Mormonism, and most deservedly so.

Selling the Adams chapel and disbanding the Adams Ward exemplified more than anything else the transition that was taking place in the Los Angeles Stake. At the same time that stake leaders were making changes in order to assure the viability of the remaining wards, their actions were also dissolving two of their strongest links to the past. In some ways, both the Adams Ward and its chapel epitomized the early twentieth century white, Anglo-Saxon church, deeply intertwined with Utah Mormonism. Their demise epitomized the fact that Mormonism was no longer a Utah church, but a church for all people and that it must relate to its surroundings if it was to remain viable. In 1958 the actions taken by the stake presidency were necessary to maintain the Church's vitality, but they were also partly influenced by both national and Church policy toward the black minority. As time has passed, however, and racial views and practices have changed, members of the Los Angeles Stake have adopted new policies in order to fulfill their stewardship regarding all the inhabitants of Los Angeles.

The Deaf Branch continued to meet in the chapel until it was demolished in January 1959, and then it moved to the Wilshire Ward chapel. Before the chapel was razed, the beautiful stained glass window was saved with the thought of placing it in the Deaf Branch chapel when it was built. However, the First Presidency recommended that the window be placed in storage, and Ralph Rolapp's Beverly Hills Transfer and Storage Company stored it free of charge for many years.[39] Eventually, this window became part of the permanent stained glass collection at the Church Museum of History and Art in Salt Lake City.

The month after the closing of the Adams Ward, the stake presidency, following a recommendation of Ray C. Colton, LDS institute director at UCLA, wrote the first presidency for permission to organize a ward at UCLA.[40] Such action had been delayed to determine how the program would work at USC and also because the membership at UCLA was smaller than that at USC. In addition, the students at UCLA did not have their own building, but shared the university's Religious Conference Center.

On 11 January 1959 a special meeting of UCLA students and their families was held at the Westwood Ward chapel. The organization of the new University UCLA Ward was approved and Arvo Van Alstyne was sustained as bishop, with Stanley R. Borquist, first counselor; Earl S. Becker, second counselor; and John K. Carmack, clerk. Van Alstyne was assistant dean of the UCLA law school.

Almost all of the students attending UCLA at this time were enrolled in graduate programs or professional schools and were, therefore, old enough to be married and have children. At its creation, in fact, the UCLA ward had more children per capita than any other ward in the stake. Within a year of its creation, however, almost half of the ward was comprised of single students, as the married ones had finished their schooling and single students were more seriously considering UCLA for undergraduate studies.

As a result of all these changes, a great measure of stability was brought to the stake. For over a decade no major changes were undertaken other than the establishment of a Spanish branch in 1966. Occasionally, boundary changes would be made, such as when seventy members were transferred from the Westwood Ward to the Hollywood Ward in 1961. These, however, were minor as compared with the major changes that took place in the stake between 1955 and 1959.

The changes in the wards combined with President Russon's insistence that the recreation halls become sports centers for the young people also brought about changes in the Hollywood, Wilshire, and Westwood chapels. In July 1958 ground was broken by President Russon for remodeling the

Hollywood Ward and constructing a new recreation hall. Following the creation of the Hollywood Second Ward, an additional bishop's office was added to the renovation project. At Wilshire basketball standards were added to the recreation hall. At Westwood ground was broken in December 1959 to add six new classrooms, another bishop's and clerk's office, a colonnade, and a patio.

On 12 June 1962 President Russon read to the high council the official notice of his release as president of the Los Angeles Stake and his new call as president of the Swiss Mission. During his thirteen years as stake president, the stake had undergone a tremendous transition. His administration witnessed the end of an era of Church stability in Los Angeles and the beginning of a new era brought about largely by changing demographics in the city. Although two wards had been disbanded, the number of units in the stake had increased to nine with the creation of the Hollywood Second, University, University UCLA, and Westwood Second Wards and the addition of the Deaf Branch.

In spite of the many changes, President Russon had skillfully led the stake through times that were trying to most of its members and had helped these members to grow spiritually in the process. Although he would be half a world away when the issues which were just beginning during his presidency were brought to a head, he had helped bring to the presidency the man best suited to help the stake face its continuing challenges.

A Stake for All People

The decade of the 1950s was characterized in America by prosperity and conservatism. Having done without for so long because of the Great Depression and a world war, Americans lost much of their pre-war taste for activism and change and settled down to enjoy the good life. There were still those who saw a need for reform, however, and some important steps were taken, especially in the area of civil rights. In its 1954 *Brown v. Board of Education* decision, the Supreme Court struck down the doctrine of separate but equal education and began the process of breaking down legal segregation throughout the United States. The following year, when Rosa Parks, a black seamstress, was arrested in Montgomery, Alabama, for refusing to give her seat on a city bus to a white man, the outraged black community began a boycott of city transportation, led by the Reverend Martin Luther King. In addition, blacks began moving from the South in record numbers and settling in major urban areas. Instead of immediately bettering themselves economically as they had hoped, however, they frequently found themselves caught in a web of poverty and victimized by prejudice and discrimination. The breaking down of racial barriers was slow in coming, and the reformers of the 1950s were disappointed as they failed to gather the wide support for which they hoped.

In the 1960s, however, more rapid changes took place with respect to the rights of blacks and other minorities. While many Americans were appalled, even frightened, at the prospect of change, most citizens became much more positive toward the idea of eliminating racial inequality. As black leaders adopted passive resistance and nonviolent answers to discrimination, the nation's political leaders were stirred to legislative action against many historic wrongs. Unfortunately, their best efforts could not produce jobs or equality in housing, nor could they eliminate the prejudice that was still widespread. By 1965, therefore, many young blacks, frustrated by the inequalities of the system, were turning towards militancy and aggressive defiance. The tragic result was racial riots over the next several years in many of the nation's larger ghettos.

Not only were young blacks finding themselves disillusioned with their world, but also many white youth questioned society's traditional values and institutions, contrasting the affluence of their parents with the poverty around them. What seemed like selfishness and complacency in the older generation led some young people to search for new traditions and values. Youth of the "beat generation," as it came to be known, gathered to large cities where they shared their rebellion and contempt for middle-class values through a counterculture characterized by "rock" music, a life-style that rejected material possessions, and a manner of dress that included tattered clothes, sandals, beads, and long hair.

As the 1960s began, serious international tensions were also causing divisions at home. Fears of an expanding "red menace," for example, led President John F. Kennedy to send military aid and advisors to support the government of South Vietnam in its fight with communist opposition forces. By 1962 there were over sixteen thousand Americans fighting in Vietnam. Two years later, student protest movements began on the nation's university and college campuses, largely as a response to American involvement in Vietnam. The war continued to escalate, and by 1965 the nation was deeply divided over the morality of its involvement in the conflict.

The Church could hardly escape the problems of the 1960s; and part of its response to the challenges was the establishment of priesthood correlation, which included a renewed emphasis upon the home teaching and family home evening programs. On the local level, the Los Angeles Stake and its members were especially vulnerable to the social problems of the era. Because it was part of a large metropolitan area that already faced problems such as those relating to race and poverty, its challenges were only magnified as tensions in Los Angeles flared and as discontented youth from around the nation poured into the area seeking refuge and like-minded companionship. The stake needed strong leadership in these times of stress and change, and in the minds of the members it was never more evident that the Lord had prepared the right men and women for the needs of the day. Fully aware of the new problems and challenges of their times, these leaders faced them with courage, inspiration, and imagination, concentrating more on the needs of the people than on maintaining traditional programs and procedures.

In 1962 Arvo Van Alstyne, a member of the UCLA law faculty, became president of the Los Angeles Stake. In a sense, he symbolized some aspects of the new age, for, unlike previous stake leaders, he was neither from the Mountain West nor from a family steeped in the LDS tradition. Born and raised in New York City, he was converted to the Church, along with his family, by Ernest L. Wilkinson, later president of Brigham Young University. Valedictorian of his high school class, he also graduated at the top of his undergraduate class at Yale. During World War II he served as a military flight instructor stationed in San Francisco, where he met his wife, Ruth, a native of California. His limited contact with the Church during the war years led him into inactivity. After the war he returned to Yale, where he attended law school and continued the tradition of graduating at the top of his class. Following graduation, he turned down several offers of employment in the East, including one from Ernest Wilkinson's New York law office, accepted a position in southern California, and moved to Hollywood. Wilkinson heard of this and wrote John M. Russon, then bishop of the Hollywood Ward, asking him to be on the lookout for the Van Alstynes. The Van Alstynes, meanwhile, determined they needed a church and decided to give his a try first. They looked up the Hollywood Ward, and Bishop Russon and the ward members welcomed them with open arms. Arvo quickly became active again, and Ruth was baptized. Bishop Russon,

feeling that there was no better way to learn Church government than as the ward clerk, called Van Alstyne to that position.[1]

After a period of time in the Hollywood Ward, the Van
Alstynes moved to Pasadena where the stake president,
Howard W. Hunter, took an active interest in them and helped
further cement their relationship to the Church. When Van
Alstyne accepted a position on the law faculty at UCLA, the
family moved back into the Los Angeles Stake, settling in the
Westwood Ward, where he served as bishop of both the West-
wood and UCLA wards.

In June 1962 while President Russon was preparing to leave
for the Swiss-German Mission, Arvo Van Alstyne was finalizing
preparations for a summer that included a teaching assignment
in San Francisco followed by one in Salzburg, Austria. A week
before the quarterly stake conference, Elder Mark E. Petersen
arrived in Los Angeles to interview possible candidates for stake
president. Following his interview with Elder Petersen, Van
Alstyne became concerned enough about the possibility that he
might be called that he wrote a brief, or memorandum, for Elder
Petersen explaining why he could not be stake president. He
then left for San Francisco a few days before the scheduled conference. As Elder John Carmack later observed, however, his
brief only served as further evidence that Arvo Van Alstyne was
the man the Lord had prepared to lead the stake at this time, for
he was not only worthy and capable but also so well-reasoned.[2]
As final preparations were being made for stake conference,
Elder Petersen reached Van Alstyne in the Bay Area and asked
him to return, for the Lord needed him as the stake president.
This he did, while his family remained in San Francisco.

On 24 June 1962 Arvo Van Alstyne was unanimously sustained as president of the Los Angeles Stake, with Edward A.
Nadle and Winfield Q. Cannon as his counselors. Following the
conference, he returned to San Francisco and then headed for
Salzburg. Nadle, a Chicago native who had joined the Church
after moving to Los Angeles and a man who has served four
times as a bishop, was the virtual stake president while the Van
Alstynes were in Europe that summer. After a little over a year
in the stake presidency, Nadle was called to preside over the
Northern States Mission. Winfield Cannon then became first
counselor and Merlin Sant was set apart as second counselor.

Because he was neither a life-long member of the Church nor steeped in the traditions of the stake, President Van Alstyne was able to bring a perspective to his callings that many could not offer. He knew what it was like to be an outsider who had been given a chance and was accepted on an equal basis by the majority, and he was willing to give all that same opportunity. His legacy to the stake was not in chapels built or wards created, for there were none. Rather, it consisted in the attitude he helped instill in stake members that all men and women are God's children. His strong views concerning the rights of individuals, largely a result of his training as a constitutional lawyer, had an important influence upon future leaders who were responsible for shaping the direction of the stake as it became, in reality, a stake for all people.

One way President Van Alstyne began slowly to make changes was in filling stake leadership positions. While he continued to use men well established in the Church, he did not use them exclusively. Rather, he gave people of different ages, backgrounds, and economic status the opportunity of serving in prominent positions. For example, he called to the high council men in their late twenties and early thirties. This may have lowered the prestige of the high council in the minds of some members, but it gave valuable training to future leaders, such as John K. Carmack and William W. Tanner, who would use that training over the next twenty years as they served in the stake presidency. In addition, the diversity in President Van Alstyne's appointments gave the stake presidency the benefit of a wide range of viewpoints. President Van Alstyne was the perfect leader for the stake during the years of unrest in the early 1960s, for he was level headed, knowledgeable, committed to the Church, and highly regarded by all groups. He also understood the changing situation in Los Angeles, and quietly, but with courage, he was willing to take whatever action was necessary. He worried little about what effect change would have on the traditional nature of the stake, but rejoiced in the advances that were being made toward making it a stake for all people.

Meanwhile, other significant developments were taking place in the stake. At the same conference in which President Van Alstyne was sustained, a new annex to the Wilshire Ward was dedicated as a home for the Southern California Branch for the Deaf. During the afternoon session of conference, seventy-five members of the branch were joined in the chapel of the new annex by ninety-four stake officers and visitors, including the new stake president. The proceedings of the meeting were broadcast into the chapel of the stake center, and Elder Mark E. Petersen dedicated the building.

Permission to use part of the Wilshire Ward property for construction of a chapel for the deaf had been obtained two years earlier, and on 3 April 1961, informal ground-breaking ceremonies were held. The dedication was originally scheduled for sometime early in 1962, but it was delayed because the $100,000 building was not yet paid for. The initial $1,000 had been donated by the branch president, Joseph Evans, and the branch finally was helped over the top by a benefit concert given by the Mormon Choir of Southern California at the Beverly Hills High School in April 1962, just three months prior to the dedication. Designed by Harold Burton, the original Wilshire Ward architect, the annex featured a small chapel, a bishop's office, a Relief Society room, and classrooms.

As an alternative to the counterculture spreading throughout America, stake and ward leaders sought ways to provide members with more and better opportunities both to participate in and to see fine cultural events. As a result, almost all the wards in the stake produced outstanding dramas, with the Wilshire Ward's summer production of the early 1960s deserving particular note.

While bishop of the Wilshire Ward, Irving L. Pratt instigated a series of summer plays, which included the Broadway musical hits *Good News, Plain and Fancy, Meet Me in St. Louis,* and *Oklahoma.*[3] Not only did these plays provide notable cultural experiences, but they also helped unify ward members in a common goal and provided activities for the many transient LDS youth who came to Los Angeles seeking summer employment. Even though they were not regular members of his ward or stake, Bishop Pratt was as much concerned with them as with any other Church members. He also recognized the merits of summer theatrical productions, for they not only made use of the talent already available in the ward but also gave the young transients a full, worthwhile, fun-packed summer where they could sing, dance, act, build sets, make costumes, work lighting and sound equipment, and generally become involved in the ward. For the production of *Plain and Fancy,* a story of the

Amish in Pennsylvania and their encounter with two New Yorkers, a barn was raised on stage each night. For *Meet Me in St. Louis,* a trolley was built. To produce *Oklahoma* required nearly 35,000 hours of dedicated labor.

Initially these productions came under the direction of the ward MIA, and they were usually presented to "standing room only" crowds. In addition, they were seen and favorably reviewed by local theater critics, and the set designs of Kay Russon, first counselor in the Wilshire Ward bishopric, received special praise. One ward member featured in these productions was Jim Pike, later of "The Lettermen" fame.

Wilshire Ward's summer productions not only had the desired effect on young people, but they also helped raise money for the ward budget, welfare assessments, improvements for the stake center, missionary funds, and community service. After running for two weeks in the Wilshire Ward, *Oklahoma* went on the road to San Diego, Whittier, Pomona, and Long Beach to help raise money for projects in these areas.

Ever since the 1949 announcement that a temple would be built in Los Angeles, stake leaders and the Temple Advisory Committee had been anxious to establish a branch genealogical library on the temple grounds. Under the direction of President Van Alstyne such a library was established in the basement of the Bureau of Information (Visitors' Center). It was dedicated on 20 June 1963 by Elder Thomas S. Monson of the Council of the Twelve. Although originally designed as a temporary facility until a larger structure could be built, it continues to be used with modifications and expansions and is the largest branch genealogical library in the Church outside Brigham Young University. It has been not only a great benefit to the temple work in the area but also a service to the community and a missionary tool, since a vast majority of those using the facilities are non-LDS.

In the spring of 1965, President Van Alstyne faced a challenging dilemma when he was approached by Stanford University about serving as a visiting professor in its law school for the 1965-66 school year. Since this was one of the top law schools in the country, he recognized that the invitation was both a great honor and a potential help to his professional career. At the same time, he felt deeply his commitment to the Lord as well as to the members of his stake, and he had been stake president for only three years. Unsure of what to do, he made arrangements to discuss the matter with President David O. McKay, who was staying at the First Presidency retreat then located at Laguna Beach. After hearing the story, President McKay had only one question: "Is there adequate leadership in the stake if you should go?" President Van Alstyne later recounted that as soon as the question was asked the strong face of Winfield Cannon came into his mind, and without mentioning whose face he had seen, he simply replied, "Yes, there is." "Then I think you should go to Stanford," President McKay immediately responded. "We will replace you."[4]

Two General Authorities of the Church, Elder Harold B. Lee of the Council of the Twelve and Elder Sterling W. Sill, Assistant to the Twelve, were present at the June 1965 Los Angeles Stake conference. It was clear that a change in the stake presidency was about to be made, and in anticipation of the large attendance on Sunday morning, 27 June, the Scottish Rite Masonic Temple had been scheduled.[5] Previously, a list of possible candidates had been prepared, and each of them was interviewed, with Elder Sill asking the questions and Elder Lee sitting silently by and seeming to look right through those being interviewed. Following all the interviews, Elder Lee summoned Winfield Q. Cannon back into the office and called him to be the next stake president. President Van Alstyne's initial inspiration had been confirmed. President Cannon selected as his counselors Merlin W. Sant and John K. Carmack, each of whom would one day serve as president, and Evan J. Christensen became stake clerk. They were all sustained unanimously on Sunday morning.

Three months earlier something propitious had happened when John Carmack almost left the stake. Since his law practice was located in Encino, he had made an offer on a home in Woodland Hills where he would be closer to work. The bishop of the ward the Carmacks anticipated moving into was a friend and invited them to speak at his ward's sacrament meeting. The week before they were scheduled to speak, however, a portion of the Los Angeles Stake high council meeting was occupied with the reorganization of the Westwood Second Ward, where Arthur Wallace had been selected to become the new bishop, and when it came time to discuss counselors President Van Alstyne asked Carmack to leave the room. The following Sunday morning Carmack called President Van Alstyne to tell him that his family was to speak that day in a ward they were considering moving into and asked, "Do you have something you wanted to talk to me about?" The stake president replied that he would be right over, and when he arrived he told Carmack that he was being considered as the first counselor in the Westwood Ward and asked him to stay in the stake for at least a year to fill that position.[6] Carmack agreed, and this paved the way for his call in June to be a counselor in the stake presidency.

President Winfield Q. Cannon was born in Rotterdam, Holland, where his father, Sylvester Q. Cannon, was serving his second term as president of the Netherlands-Belgium Mission. After the family's return to Salt Lake City, Winfield grew up there, attended the University of Utah, served for thirty months in the Swiss-German Mission, then went to Utah State University where he graduated with a degree in civil engineering. While attending Utah State he met his wife, Wanda Parkinson, and they were married in the Salt Lake Temple in 1932. It was not long before the Cannons joined thousands of other Saints who were migrating to California because of the Great Depression, and they settled initially in the Hollywood Ward. As their family grew they moved from one place to another in the Hollywood area before eventually purchasing a home in the Wilshire Ward. They became members of the LaBrea Ward when it was created, and Cannon served as its last bishop.

The new stake presidency continued the enlightened attitudes and policies of President Van Alstyne's administration. The complexion of the stake had already begun to change as minorities, especially Hispanics and Koreans, began moving more rapidly into its boundaries. President Cannon and his counselors believed not only that Saints in these minority groups should be taught the gospel in the language they prayed in but also that special organizations should be created for them to help meet their needs. The stake presidency, therefore, initiated various special programs to help these minorities find their places in the LDS community. A Spanish branch and a Korean Sunday School dependent on the Wilshire Ward were organized within a year after Cannon became a stake president. In addition, programs were started to help meet the needs of the increasing number of unmarried adults in the stake, and a solemn assembly was conducted for the benefit of all single young men in the stake who had been through the temple.

Within two months of the installation of the new stake presidency, the racial tensions and frustrations that had been smoldering among the black youth of the nation's ghettos erupted in riots and other violence that continued in the cities of the nation for several summers. In August 1965, in Los Angeles, riots were touched off in the Watts area that lasted for several days and resulted in mass destruction and looting of property. Even though the riots and racial difficulties were centered outside Los Angeles Stake boundaries, they were not just a fringe worry but had a direct effect upon the stake and its members in many ways. Bert Scoll, for example, a member of the high council, was watching television when news of the Watts riot broke. As he sat there he suddenly saw pictures of his own medical clinic in flames from a fire bomb and realized that he was watching the destruction of his own property even as it was happening.[7]

The animosity of many blacks in the ghettos was directed not only at whites but also, at times, against other blacks—especially at those who had become economically successful and had migrated out of the ghetto. Those who lived near the Wilshire Ward tended to be in this class, and a black congregation had purchased a church across from the Wilshire Ward. These people were therefore possible targets of violence, and a curfew imposed by the city extended to the area around the stake center. All this resulted in the cancellation of all Wilshire Ward meetings during the period of the riots, and for some time afterwards no meetings could be held at night. Following one Sunday morning high council meeting, stake leaders felt the ominous implications of the times as they had to pass by the national guard and its armored vehicles on their way home. As President William W. Tanner recalls, they soon understood in a very real way that the fires may have been a few miles away, but emotional flames also raged around the Wilshire Ward.[8]

The Watts riot brought turmoil and stress to all of Los Angeles, and because of its policy against giving the priesthood to blacks the Church found itself the object of some hate and bitterness. As a result, some of its buildings were not safe. One night an assistant stake clerk, Roy Kellogg, was on the temple grounds and felt impressed to walk around it. When he got to the front door, he found several people trying to break in.[9] Threats were made against the USC institute, and it did not make local Church members feel any better that the head-quarters of the militant Black Panthers were located on the corner of Vermont and Exposition, just three blocks from the institute. Around each of the threatened buildings, therefore, security was enhanced. Even after the curfew was lifted, Church members were afraid to go to the Wilshire Ward for meetings, especially at night, because of continuing animosi-ties. Consequently, almost all meetings in the building were held during daylight hours.

During the presidency of Winfield Cannon the Vietnam War escalated, bringing several related problems to the stake. The war became a deeply emotional political issue and, as with the rest of the nation, stake members were divided and unfortunate tensions were created among some of them. In addition, the number of young men eligible for the draft who could serve on missions was limited, by Church agreement with selective service officials, to one per ward. This placed a terrible burden on the shoulders of stake and ward leaders who had to make the final decision as to who could go and who could not go. The task was made even more complicated by the fact that many young men who may not have volunteered for missions if military ser-vice were not the alternative now expressed a great desire to go. At the same time, limiting the number who could fulfill mis-sions also resulted in a decrease in the number of missionaries in the field, including in the California Mission, and this only increased the responsibility of local units for missionary work.

During both World War II and the Korean War, restrictions had been placed upon the number of full-time missionaries who could be called, but missionary activity within the boundaries of the stake was hardly affected because of the great emphasis it previously had placed upon missionary work. The seventies quorums were primarily responsible for missionary work in the stakes and, according to revelation, each quorum was to have seventy members. In the 1930s a second quorum of seventies had been created in the Los Angeles Stake, thus making it one of the few stakes in the history of the Church to have two such quorums. Originally, two quorums had functioned well, but by the 1960s, as a result of the decline in stake population, maintaining them became a serious problem. The total number of seventies in the stake had fallen to a little over seventy, which was not enough to fill two quorums, but too many for one. Stake leaders had exchanged considerable correspondence with the General Authorities about the possibility of eliminating one quorum, but some members of the Church's First Council of the Seventy were adamant that the stake maintain its status quo. Others felt the stake could combine the quorums if the number of seventies fell below seventy.

It may have seemed ironic that, in a time when the Church needed increased stake missionary work, the leaders of the Los Angeles Stake were grappling with the question of how to eliminate one of its quorums of seventy. Given the circumstances of the stake, nevertheless, members of the stake presidency considered this a necessity, and they were determined to find a way to do it. The problem was complicated, however, by the fact that those seventies who were functioning in their calling were doing an outstanding job. Stake leaders, therefore, did not wish to make them high priests just to eliminate one quorum, for without them missionary work would suffer. On the other hand, over one-third of the stake's seventies not only were not doing their jobs, but were inactive in the Church. Curiously, this made it impossible to release them, for the only option when releasing seventies was to make them high priests, and this was not an option for people who were inactive. Occasionally the number of seventies fell below seventy, but by the time the process had begun to combine the quorums, other seventies would move in and take their places.

The irony of the situation became almost laughable. Elder Bruce R. McConkie of the First Council of the Seventy, who was never noted for public displays of humor, was the visitor at one stake conference. At the time there were seventy-two seventies in the stake. As President Cannon later recalled the incident, the matter was being discussed again when suddenly Elder McConkie "in his very somber way, leaned back in his chair in the stake president's office" and said, "You know, President Cannon, if I were you, I would be inclined to go down to San Pedro, and rent a leaky boat, and take some of your seventies on a trip to Catalina Island."[10] When he began speaking, the stake presidency had hung upon his words, expecting him to say something profound that would help them with their problem, so his tongue-in-cheek remark threw them completely off balance and they hardly knew how to respond. After an appropriate length of time, Elder McConkie relaxed a bit and said, "I guess we hadn't better do that." At last, however, the number of seventies fell below seventy and in April 1967 the 355th Quorum of Seventy was dissolved. And, added President Cannon, "we didn't have to send any on that leaky boat."[11]

Stake leaders became involved in a variety of projects in this era, including one that eventually resulted in the construction of Church-owned apartments for retired Latter-day Saints who wanted to work in the temple. As early as 1953, the First Presidency had written President John M. Russon about the possibility of establishing a retirement home for Church members in Los Angeles.[12] The stake presidency recommended that if the Church did build such a facility, it should be placed near the temple, then under construction, so that members could take advantage of the temple. This idea, however, was never pursued. In 1958 the temple advisory committee recommended that the Church construct housing specifically for temple workers on Church-owned property near the temple.[13] This also was not immediately acted upon, but after the temple had operated for a time, attendance began to decline, particularly during the day-time hours. The problem was especially acute for those who had to come long distances and who could not easily afford to stay for any extended time in motels. The various discussions among stake leaders concerning retirement housing, housing for temple workers, the need to increase day-time attendance, and the need to provide inexpensive housing for out-of-town visitors finally resulted in the construction, on temple property, of what has come to be known as the Temple Patrons' Apartments. In 1966 these apartments were completed and the forty-two stake presidents in the temple region signed an agreement with the Church that they would pay off the cost over the next fifty years. Because Winfield Q. Cannon was chairman of the temple advisory committee, his name headed the list, and he often tells people that he has to live at least until 2016 because he signed an agreement with the Church which was to expire then.[14]

Some of the apartments were made available to those who came from long distances and desired to stay an extended period of time. Others were reserved for those who wished to live near the temple more permanently so they could do temple work. In either case each Church member living there must participate in a minimum average of two endowment sessions per day for each day the temple is open. Those living in the apartments initially became part of the Westwood First Ward, but in time they were divided between both Westwood Wards.

Not all the plans and hopes of stake leaders were achieved, however, and one building they wanted deeply but never got was a new Los Angeles stake center and regional culture building, also to be erected on the temple grounds. In December 1963, the temple advisory committee, under the direction of its chairman, President Arvo Van Alstyne, submitted such a proposal to the First Presidency, and the following October permission was given to go ahead.[15] Fund raising had actually begun as early as 1962, and plans for the building included a large auditorium that could seat twelve hundred people, a choir loft seating 150, and facilites for dividing part of the auditorium into a smaller chapel for use by residents of the Temple Patrons' Apartments if they were made into a branch. A cultural hall behind the auditorium would seat an additional thirteen hundred, bringing the total seating capacity to 2,500 and allowing every stake in the region to hold its conferences there. It would also allow for the presentation of large concerts. In addition, the building would contain classrooms, a kitchen, office space, and a baptismal font; and expansion plans would include a genealogical library. It would also contain facilities for movies, musical and dramatic productions, and basketball.

Various concerns convinced stake leaders of the need for such a building. At first the crowded conditions at Wilshire Ward seemed to suggest the need for a new facility, but when it began to appear that the ward might be abandoned altogether because of the changing racial mix in the area, the new project seemed even more imperative. Another factor was a threat to the continuation of the Southern California Mormon Choir, partly because of the dangers involved in going to evening practices at the Wilshire chapel but more specifically because of some suggestions from the management of the Los Angeles Music Center that the choir should no longer perform there regularly.[16] In any case, in 1965 Church leaders put a temporary hold on most building projects and ultimately they withdrew their support completely from the project.

It was during President Cannon's administration that the "hippie" movement moved into full swing, and the Los Angeles Stake was not immune from its consequences. As young people began to wear long hair, beads, and headbands, and began to speak differently, some members publicly expressed their strong disapproval. While some felt that it was best to try to understand the movement, others were aghast and felt that anyone who seemed to show any sympathy for the youthful counterculture was spiritually disloyal. It appears, however, that most stake members steered a middle course, recognizing that it was partly a fad that would pass and that most of those involved were trying to express their individuality and reassess their roles in life. Stake leaders also recognized that simply choosing to dress differently or to listen to different music was not necessarily contrary to God's commandments, and that those involved were still people who needed ministers. They took the position that it was possible to make room for a number of points of view and that it was not wise to make problems over unimportant issues. Rather, they tried to take advantage of the great talent and testimony exhibited by people of differing points of view. The integrity of the Church as an institution had to be maintained, however, and when it came to more important questions, such as drug abuse or premarital sex—things clearly contrary to the commandments of God—stake leaders stood firm.[17]

In addition to the famous Haight-Ashbury district of San Francisco and Greenwich Village of New York City, another gathering place for "hippies" was in Hollywood, along Sunset Boulevard and in the canyons. Many Latter-day Saint youths caught up in the movement left home, often without telling their parents where they were going, and presumably went to the "hippie pads" in the Hollywood area. Stake leaders often received ten to fifteen contacts a month from concerned parents asking for help in locating their children. The major responsibility for trying to locate run-away Latter-day Saint youth fell upon the Hollywood Ward bishop, Farrell Miles, in whose boundaries most of the "pads" were located. Bishop Miles soon established a program of making contacts and identifying possible locations where these youth might be. Consequently, he spent many additional hours above and beyond the normal heavy duties of a bishop in searching for LDS youth in an environment where outsiders were looked upon with distrust, thus making his task all the more difficult.[18] As a result of his untiring efforts, however, many families were reunited.

On 16 June 1968, at a stake conference attended by Elder Mark E. Petersen of the Council of the Twelve and Elder Franklin D. Richards of the First Council of the Seventy, President Cannon was released because he had been called to preside over the West German Mission. At the same meeting Merlin W. Sant was sustained as the new stake president.

President Sant had been a long time resident of the Los Angeles Stake, having come with his family from Idaho in 1920. From 1923 to 1925 he served a mission in the Netherlands, and upon his return he married Edna West. By profession he owned and operated a construction company. At the time of his call to lead the stake he was a youthful sixty-four years old and still included waterskiing among his favorite activities. Not unlike his predecessors, President Sant was not afraid to break with tradition, and he was willing to address the problems of the stake in a straightforward manner. Some of the changes he worked hard for, however, would not be realized until years after his release.

When it came to selecting counselors, Elder Petersen admonished the new president to consider younger men who might be trained eventually to lead the stake.[19] Sant, following Elder Petersen's advice, selected John K. Carmack and William W. Tanner, both young men in their thirties who would later serve as stake presidents. Charles T. Attwoll was sustained as stake clerk.

The story of missionary work among the deaf in this era is a story of unusual faith and determination. Prior to 1968, the work was conducted solely by members of the Deaf Branch, largely because Church policy prohibited extending mission calls to those with severe hearing problems. In 1968, however, the policy was changed and the first deaf missionaries in the Church were called in connection with the Los Angeles Deaf Branch. Initially, eight full-time missionaries were assigned to Los Angeles, five of whom were hearing impaired. For at least two, their calls came in fulfillment of patriarchal blessings which stated that they would serve missions in spite of their handicaps.[20] The other missionaries could hear and had to be trained in sign language. One of these, Elder Jack Rose, himself a convert and a zone leader at the time, specifically asked to be made a junior companion in order to work with the deaf.

It was difficult for the missionaries to contact the deaf, who had been made the victims of so many schemes and con games that they were suspicious of almost everyone. Fearing the motives of strangers, they were often afraid to open the door. It was also difficult to tract since the deaf could not hear a knock on the door or the doorbell. Consequently, the missionaries relied largely upon referrals. In spite of these difficulties, within a year of the organization of the deaf mission eighteen converts had been made, including two brothers who were deaf, dumb, and blind.

These men had been contacted by Elder Rose and his companion, who, through a slow, laborious process, taught them the gospel by drawing out in the palm of their hands the letters of the alphabet. After the second brother had been baptized, the two, with tears streaming down their faces, embraced each other and then the missionaries who had so lovingly and painstakingly taught them the gospel. It was said that when they were first contacted these brothers had the most forlorn, pathetic-looking faces imaginable, but following their baptism, their countenances changed to the point of showing genuine hope and happiness. Shortly following baptism they were given the priesthood and, with the assistance of a member of the branch who could see, began to pass the sacrament.[21]

Partially as a result of missionary work, the Deaf Branch grew in strength to almost three hundred and the decision was made to create a Deaf Ward. In June 1972 Joseph Brandenburg, who had been the first deaf branch president in the Church, was sustained as the ward's first bishop. In addition, a second deaf branch had been established in 1971 in Fullerton.

In the early 1960s many Koreans began coming to America for educational purposes, and soon a sizeable group of Korean Latter-day Saints were attending USC or residing within stake boundaries. Under the direction of President Cannon, therefore, President Carmack organized a Korean Sunday School, which met at the USC institute and had a membership of around fifty. President Carmack had developed a special interest in and love for the Korean people as a result of his military service in Korea and his getting acquainted with some members there during the Korean War. While in Seoul, he had served as leader of the small group of Saints in that city and helped the first missionaries assigned to the country become settled.

Around 1970, a member of the Korean Sunday School approached California Mission President John K. Edmunds for help with missionary work in the growing Korean community. President Edmunds promised to assign two of his finest missionaries if the man would serve as interpreter and share his testimony with those they contacted. The man agreed, and through the ensuing missionary efforts the little congregation continued to grow.[22]

As their numbers increased, members of the Korean Sunday School began to express a desire to become a branch. Stake leaders agreed that a dependent branch should be organized, feeling it important that the Koreans have their own leaders and learn to assume their own Church responsibilities. Church policy, however, required the approval of Salt Lake City before any branch could be created, and the Los Angeles Stake presidency's proposal was turned down. Unsatisfied, stake leaders tried again, this time arranging for a meeting in Salt Lake City at conference time with a committee of the Brethren who handled the creation of new units.[23] During the meeting it became apparent to the stake presidency that the proposal had been rejected because the Brethren had differing opinions as to the proper course the Church should take regarding minority units. Although they had previously approved such units, problems had arisen that caused some of the Brethren to rethink their positions. Some felt that by organizing special language units the Church built in segregation and second-class citizenship, and that if minority families were placed in the mainstream they could be taught the basics of Church government and their children could be brought up with the cultural advantages of the integrated ward. Other members of the committee supported minority units as a way to provide better Church training without the interference of language and cultural barriers. Many Saints simply could not speak English, and it seemed better to provide worship services and other Church programs in their own language than to require them to attend services week after week and not understand them.

As they met with this committee, the members of the stake presidency were given a chance to explain why they felt it was in the best interest of the Koreans to organize a branch. One concern was that because of the more reserved Korean culture, the Koreans would not integrate well into American wards. Another was the language problem, and it was observed that the men, who had come for the purpose of attending school, could function well in English, but their wives could not and therefore probably would be unable to function in a standard ward.

Stake leaders returned to Los Angeles hoping to hear soon from the committee, but nothing came. Some Korean members, meanwhile, became discouraged, feeling that perhaps the Church was uninterested in them, and some gradually became inactive. For the time being, however, the Korean Sunday School continued to function, though with increasing difficulty.

Another concern of the stake was the growing number of single adults. Members of the Church were following the national trend of marrying later in life after establishing a career, which meant that an increasing number of young men and women moving into the Los Angeles Stake because of the many employment opportunities were single. In addition there was a growing number of divorced and widowed members of the Church.

The matter came to a head while William W. Tanner was a member of President Winfield Cannon's high council and had the responsibility for overseeing what had become a large M Men and Gleaner program. He became acutely aware of a growing problem when, on one occasion, a group of single adults was together and several began to criticize stake leaders, arguing that they were not interested in the singles. Deeply concerned, Tanner invited them to his home to explore the matter further, and there, he said, they "really unloaded" their frustrations.[24] Having been a student at USC when Winfield Cannon was bishop, Tanner knew that Cannon had a great love for the singles and young adults, and he tried to convince them that the leaders really were interested in them. He was unsuccessful on that point, but he reported their feelings to the stake presidency.

Stake leaders became vitally concerned with the problem, realizing that many serious needs really were not being met. They also realized that the perception single adults had of their lack of interest was more important than the fact that they actually were interested. Something had to be done to change that perception, provide better support for the singles, and give them greater opportunities for meeting possible mates among Latter-day Saints.

One of the first things the stake did was to reintroduce, on an expanded basis, the "Get Acquainted" program begun by Bishop Jay Grant in 1946. Ensign and Erma Call were assigned as co-chairmen of the stake's new "Get Acquainted" committee, positions they would hold for the next twelve years. The committee planned a dance every three weeks, a monthly square dance, a monthly fireside, a quarterly dinner-dance, and an annual luau. The stake welcomed all LDS singles to these activities, regardless of whether they lived within its boundaries, and the program soon began to attract people from throughout the area. This even led to some criticism from other stakes, but it seemed inconsistent with the aims of the program to keep people away simply because they did not live within certain boundaries. The purpose of the program was to increase the opportunity for single LDS adults to meet each other, and this seemed to be the best approach at the time.

The program was not without its problems, however, as the Calls discovered when they decided to hold the "Get Acquainted" activities in various chapels throughout the Los Angeles metropolitan area. Often they would schedule a building, only to find that when they arrived early to set up before the function the building was dark and the doors were locked. After a frantic search for a bishop, or custodian, or anyone who could open the building, they usually had to put away the chairs in addition to the job of setting up for the dance. After two years the need for a permanent place became apparent and the two Hollywood wards volunteered the use of their chapel, which was both centrally located and close to the freeways. The fact that it was in Hollywood also helped, for the town's reputation made people want to go there.[25]

Singles from throughout the Los Angeles area came to these events, sometimes with the hope of meeting a prospective spouse and sometimes just to socialize. Some marriages resulted, and one that made the newspapers was between a woman with seven children and a man with eight. After their marriage they also had a child of their own.[26] One long-range impact of the program was that it eventually became the basis for a Church-wide "Special Interest" program.

The "Get Acquainted" program was geared primarily toward singles of marriageable age, but, under the direction of President Carmack, the stake also established "Action" for younger single adults. Cosponsored by the institutes of religion, this group met in Sunday evening "firesides" every few weeks and attracted young adults from throughout the area.

While much had been done under President Cannon's administration, much more remained to be done before the needs of the single adults were met. Dialogue continued, and early in President Sant's administration stake leaders learned that the single women wanted to attend Relief Society but couldn't because it was held during the day on weekdays, when most of them worked. The stake presidency quickly recognized, however, that these women needed the association Relief Society provided as much as did the married sisters, and it was decided to organize a Sunday morning Relief Society.

When this proposal was presented to the stake's correlation council some people objected, simply because it was not specified in the handbook. President Sant, however, simply sat back in his chair and said, "Well, I'm the president of the stake, and I have the authority to do what's needed for the people. We feel as a presidency that that needs to be done. Now if the Brethren don't like it, they can always release me."[27] He had the courage to innovate if the situation called for it, and the program proved to be very successful.

The Relief Society was just for the women, however, and the singles of the stake also felt the need for getting together as a group to learn the gospel. Stake leaders, therefore, worked with the institute director at USC and a special evening class was begun.[28] The singles were delighted, and the class proved successful.

As time progressed, the perception once held by many single adults changed as they began to realize that stake leaders really were concerned for their well-being. Perhaps this gave them courage to discuss an even greater concern. They appreciated all that had been done, but they still felt their needs were not being fully met. What they wanted was a ward or branch of their own, where they could meet together on a permanent basis, study the gospel together, and promote regular programs and activities geared to their particular needs and problems. As they talked with stake leaders, the singles pointed out that in the wards they attended they had little in common with other members, for those wards were geared towards families. They were also tired of explaining why they were not married and trying to convince people that they were not really "abnormal." As a result of such problems, many had become partially or totally inactive.

In addition, even though the "Get Acquainted" activities were going well, many singles were finding them less than satisfactory so far as finding LDS marriage partners was concerned. Some succeeded, but others were marrying outside the Church or not getting married at all. Many complained that they were being expected to choose marriage partners simply by attending dances or eating punch and cookies in the cultural hall following firesides, where association was often limited to looking at each other. As one single man put it, the situation had created "an army of lookers."[29]

Stake leaders agreed that a ward or branch exclusively for single adults could be extremely valuable, and that this was the right way to go. In March 1969, therefore, they petitioned the First Presidency of the Church for the creation of such a ward.[30] They gave many reasons. There were several hundred unmarried persons between the ages of twenty-one and forty who, because of the high concentration of apartment dwellings and the convenience of urban employment, resided in the stake. Most were concentrated in the Wilshire and Hollywood wards. These, stake leaders pointed out, were also the wards with the greatest administrative problems and some of the lowest statistics, for the singles felt they had little to contribute, that the wards had little to offer them, and that if they were seeking mates they wanted to go "where the action was." Church attendance by single adults in their own wards, if at all, averaged about 20 percent. Too many were marrying outside the Church, and while the M Men and Gleaner programs provided some social contact, it was not effectively meeting the marriage needs.

A ward especially for these single adults, stake leaders argued, would help many of them come back into Church activity. It would serve as a center where they could unite in an atmosphere that would also provide the social contacts that could lead to temple marriage. They proposed that the new unit be called the Beverly Hills Ward, that it meet at the USC institute, and that its membership be limited to those between twenty-one and forty. They recognized that this was a deviation from the Church norm, but argued that it was nevertheless necessary because circumstances in the stake were not normal. They also felt that they would be derelict in their calling if they failed to take action to solve the problems they were facing. In July 1969, however, the First Presidency wrote back that after much discussion the Brethren had rejected the proposal, for they felt that it presented too many problems.[31] As with the Korean proposal, stake leaders did not give up after one attempt and again approached the Brethren. Again, however, they were unsuccessful and finally the matter had to be dropped.[32] Unfortunately for the singles, many more became inactive, and the question as to whether the proposed ward would have helped remained unanswered.

In the late 1960s and the early 1970s the Church's practice of not allowing blacks to hold the priesthood again became a heated issue. Several universities, including Stanford, refused to participate in athletic events with BYU because of this policy, and as BYU teams traveled to other universities they experienced both threats and acts of violence. When priesthood days were held at the Los Angeles Temple, protestors showed up. There were also bomb threats against some of the Church's property, including the temple and the USC institute, and the life of President Joseph Fielding Smith was threatened when he came to Los Angeles for a solemn assembly.[33]

The priesthood issue had a direct effect on Los Angeles Stake. For one thing, the Church ran into problems with the Los Angeles Redevelopment Agency over the institute of religion at USC. The area around the university had been designated by the City of Los Angeles as part of the nation's urban redevelopment campaign to help restore the decaying central cities. As a result of the 1964 Civil Rights Bill, however, businesses or private organizations involved in the targeted area must sign a master plan development contract (an owner's participation agreement) with a nondiscrimination clause. Since the institute was located in the heart of the area, there was a question as to whether the Church would have to sign the agreement in order to keep the institute open, though some in the legal profession held that the Church was not subject to the agreement because it did not receive federal funds. The major problem, however, was connected with the fact that the institute building had been enveloped by the expansion of the university and was thus effectively located on campus. The university had expressed interest in the property, and local leaders feared that unless the Church signed the agreement the rights of eminent domain would be exercised by the redevelopment agency on behalf of the university and the Church would not be adequately compensated.[34] With the agreement, local leaders felt they would have sufficient leverage with the university that it would assist in locating an acceptable new site for an institute building if the property were taken.

On the other hand, both President N. Eldon Tanner of the First Presidency and the Church's legal counsel felt that the Church should not sign the agreement, but, rather, surrender the building if it was required. They were concerned that by signing this agreement, the Church might put itself in a tenuous legal position if a discrimination suit were filed.[35] Local leaders felt, however, that the institute would have no difficulty living within the simple and standard nondiscrimination clause, since all races were welcome in any of its classes. The problem, they recognized, was with the ward that shared the building, even if it was only as a guest of the institute. If necessary, they reasoned, it would be rather simple to differentiate between the institute, which was open to all, and Church organizations, where priesthood was an issue, simply by moving the ward to another location. Afraid of possibly losing a valuable piece of property without receiving anything in return, and possibly losing the institute program as well, stake leaders recommended that the agreement be signed.[36] In the end, however, the Church did not sign it. The university, nevertheless, did assist the Church in finding a new location and, until new facilities were finally obtained, neither the university nor the redevelopment agency expressed any desire to force the institute out of its building.

During the 1960s, blacks continued their expansion into the southwest portion of the stake and white families continued their exodus from the area. As a result, stake membership declined to around 4,000 people in 2,500 families, or an average of 1.6 members per family. As families moved out, membership in the Wilshire, Hollywood, and Arlington wards became characterized by a preponderance of older members, especially widows and women who had never married. This presented a problem to the wards, since the priesthood, already depleted, had to spread itself even more thinly.

No ward was more troubled or depleted than the Arlington Ward. Its building was located in the middle of a depressed black community, and soon it was unsafe even to attend Church services. In addition, ward membership, which at one time had been as high as fourteen hundred, had been declining for several years, and when C. N. Schaap was called as bishop in March 1969 he was told by President Sant that most likely it would be for only a short time.[37] When the decision was made to disband the ward, membership had dwindled to around 150, and a good percentage of this number had actually moved from the ward but returned on Sundays to fill their assignments and keep the ward functioning. Many of those who remained were widows who could not afford to move and who had set up a program of calling each other regularly to make sure everyone was all right. Priesthood leaders were few, as were youth and children. While the ward's Scout troop had twenty-six scouts, only one was a member of the ward. There were only nine in the Primary until a newly baptized black family moved into the ward and then the numbers swelled to eleven.

When it became unsafe to walk the streets after dark, meetings were held in daylight hours. Nevertheless, some sisters were knocked down and had their purses stolen as they left Relief Society. Vandalism became a problem at the chapel as windows were broken almost weekly and the building was broken into at least three times. Following one funeral a group of youth congregating on the steps outside the chapel refused to move aside for the casket and had to be physically removed. One night outside the chapel Bishop Schaap had a gun placed against his head by two men demanding money and his watch. Acting as if he were taking off his watch, Schaap put the car in gear, stepped hard on the gas and took off. On another occasion the ward received a letter from the "Black Panthers" demanding "eight million dollars." Other congregations in the area had their meetings disturbed by militant groups and, as a result, ward members were instructed that if any of their meetings were disturbed, even if during the sacrament, they were to leave the building quietly, go home, and have a closing prayer there; only the bishopric was to stay.[38] Fortunately, nothing untoward ever happened.

Serious as they were, these problems produced at least one positive result as members of the ward drew especially close to each other, with everyone taking an interest in the well-being of everyone else. Also, partly because some of the most faithful members continued to attend the ward, it was often on top of the stake percentages during its last years.

Nevertheless, the dwindling numbers coupled with concerns for the safety of ward members led stake leaders to propose to the First Presidency that the ward be disbanded. On 16 June 1971 the stake presidency, with deep regrets, dissolved the Arlington Ward, transferring those living in the ward boundaries to the Wilshire Ward and asking those who had been returning on Sundays to attend their home wards. Initially, the chapel was rented to another congregation, but with the approval of the First Presidency it was sold in 1972 to the Galilee Baptist Church, which has maintained the mural of the sacred grove.

Even before the Arlington Ward was dissolved and its chapel sold, stake leaders had been giving consideration to selling the Wilshire Ward chapel. As with Arlington, there was a question of safety. Some of the feeling may have been the result of prejudice, for the chapel was in a black neighborhood, but a few incidents involving stake members made safety a real concern. As a result, many members and ward leaders began to say that they would neither go there nor let members of their wards go there, especially for night meetings, and finally night meetings were curtailed.

Unlike the situation at Arlington, however, little thought was being given to disbanding the Wilshire Ward. Under the direction of President Sant, nevertheless, the stake presidency began looking for potential chapel sites within ward boundaries that would reduce the risks Church members were subjected to in going to the chapel.

After considering several locations, the stake presidency selected a parcel of land on the corner of Wilshire Boulevard and Muirfield Road, near the Los Angeles Country Club in the Hancock Park area, as the best location for a new chapel. Asking price for the property was $1.1 million, but in the fall of 1970, after Elder Marion G. Romney of the Council of the Twelve had been shown the various properties available, the Church purchased it for one million dollars.[39] Stake leaders were confident they would be able to get the property rezoned for building a chapel.

The building envisioned for the Muirfield property was similar to the highrise which the Church had recently purchased in New York City to serve as home to the Manhattan

Ward and as a stake center. Stake leaders hoped that the new building would house not only Wilshire and other wards but also the stake center, a mission office, the Church's Los Angeles regional offices (including social services), a branch campus for BYU, and the USC ward. It might also contain offices for the USC and Los Angeles Community College institutes of religion, though classes would continue to be held at the campuses.[40] This, however, was only one of the options being considered, and it was never taken past the discussion stage.

The Los Angeles Stake was not the only one undergoing change. All the surrounding stakes were also declining in population. The membership of the Inglewood and Santa Monica Stakes dropped, for many members could no longer pay the high taxes required to live in those areas. Like the Los Angeles Stake, Huntington Park was also losing population as the racial makeup of its membership changed. During the last part of President Sant's administration and the first few years that John K. Carmack led the stake, therefore, it was not only the future of the Wilshire chapel and ward that was in question, but also, in the minds of some, the future of the stake. The suggestion was even made that the stake should be dissolved, with the eastern wards being placed in Huntington Park Stake and the western ones in the Santa Monica Stake, thus creating two strong stakes out of what were becoming three weak stakes.[41]

Other solutions to the problems created by change were proposed by committees called to consider possible alternatives for changing the boundaries of the stake. One suggestion was that wards be created not on the basis of geographic boundaries but, rather, on the basis of special needs, such as ages of children.[42] Everyone had to travel to Church meetings anyway, so it was suggested that such an arrangement would make little diffference to the members of the stake so far as their time was concerned. Theoretically, these new kinds of wards, like special wards for single adults, could better meet the special needs of all members. As with the building of a highrise structure, however, these ideas were never carried past the discussion stage.

These and other uncertainties concerning the future of the stake as its membership continued to decline only added to the many challenges stake leaders had to confront in these rapidly changing times. While the challenges related to a declining Anglo population did not go away, they would be exchanged for another challenge when President John K. Carmack and his counselors made a commitment to keep the Church strong within the stake boundaries, regardless of the skin color or national background of those residing therein: a commitment exemplified in what happened later in the Wilshire Ward chapel, which the stake continues to use.

Even though the decade of the 1960s was a most trying and challenging period for the Los Angeles Stake, it was, in a special sense, also a time of progress. There are those who might argue that because of declining population, the stake failed even to hold its own. Its achievement, however, was in the fact that in this time of conflict and rapid change it met its challenges straight on. It helped serve as an anchor and calming influence in a time of turmoil and adversity by making its members as comfortable as possible with the situation in which they found themselves. In addition, its leaders were preparing the stake for future growth.

Unity in Diversity

I n June 1972 Elder Howard W. Hunter of the Council of the
Twelve, a former member of the Los Angeles Stake, returned
as the visiting General Authority at stake conference. He had
been assigned to reorganize the stake, for President Merlin W.
Sant had been called to preside over the New Zealand South
Mission. After all the priesthood leaders had been interviewed,
Elder Hunter called John K. Carmack back and said, "The Lord
wants you to preside over this stake, and I concur." He also indicated that the feelings of those he had interviewed were nearly
unanimous in this move, which, he commented, spoke well for
the unity of the stake.[1]

It was on 16 June 1972, exactly four years from the day he
was sustained as stake president, that Merlin W. Sant was
replaced by John K. Carmack. This was also Father's Day and
both stake presidents' fathers were in attendance and were invited to speak. William W. Tanner and Romney Stewart were
sustained as counselors.

Elder Hunter told President Carmack that the Los Angeles
Stake was one of those key stakes which the Brethren in Salt
Lake City watched closely, and he counseled him to take full ad-

vantage of the inspiration that would come in the months and years ahead. He also suggested that the new president not be too efficient, reminding him that one of the most important roles of a stake president is to meet with the people, to work with them, to feel their spirit, and to be accessible to them. Elder Hunter also recommended a few changes in the way things had been done in the stake.[2]

John K. Carmack was born in the small railroad town of Winslow, Arizona, in 1931. During World War II his family moved to California, eventually settling in Santa Barbara. Following a mission to Montana and Wyoming he attended Brigham Young University, where he graduated with a political science degree. He then entered the army and served among the U.S. occupation troops in Seoul, Korea. There he also became group leader for the small group of Saints in that city. While still in the military, he applied for admission to the master of public administration program at USC and, as a back up, to the UCLA law school. Following his release, he went to Los Angeles to stay with a brother while looking for employment and waiting for school to start at USC. During this time, however, he became acquainted with Arvo Van Alstyne, who helped persuade him to attend the UCLA law school instead. While attending UCLA, he met Shirley Fay Allen, whom he married in the Los Angeles Temple in 1958.

A friend at BYU once called young John Carmack "CCC," "Complete Control Carmack," for he was always in control of his feelings and he took full responsibility for any job he was assigned. This was also characteristic of him as stake president, for through study and prayer he seemed almost always to understand just what needed to be done. It has been said of him that the Lord could always trust him to be on the right side of the issue.[3] One of his strengths, nevertheless, was the fact that through his legal training he had learned that there are at least two sides to every question, and he would listen with patience and understanding to points of view other than his own.

President Carmack was known for his great love of people and for his willingness to give of himself freely. One stake member, for example, who was confronting some serious personal challenges, often called her local priesthood leader late at night and talked until 1:00 or 2:00 A.M. This leader finally complained about the situation to President Carmack, only to discover that when that member finished talking to him, she would then call President Carmack and talk for the remainder of the night. Instead of becoming upset with the calls, however, President Carmack demonstrated his love and patience by observing, "Isn't it wonderful that the Lord provides someone to help this person at the time of need?"[4]

President Carmack and his counselors continued the important traditions of the stake, maintaining great respect for those who had gone before, but they also recognized that the stake and its needs were changing. Their greatest responsibility, they realized, was to make a unified stake out of one that was being fragmented by many different nationalities and backgrounds. They tried, therefore, to teach by both word and example that the stake existed for all people, including a number of different ethnic groups as well as members of all ages. They also taught through examples that the stake existed to serve, unify, and love everyone and that all members could make the adjustments necessary to work in close harmony with those of different languages and cultures. Thus, the stake effectively left behind its traditional past in which members were basically one in background and language, and stake leaders taught that the present, although greatly different, was also a glorious reality. President Carmack later expressed the feeling that the greatest accomplishment of his administration was the instillation of a feeling of "unity in diversity."[5]

In October 1972, the First Presidency of the Church, under the direction of President Harold B. Lee, sent a letter to the stakes and missions requesting that "adequate attention be given to members of the Church who do not speak the language of the majority where they live."[6] The letter reminded local leaders that they had the responsibility for members of different racial, language, or cultural groups within their boundaries, and suggested that language barriers should be broken down through translation. It encouraged priesthood leaders to foster the welfare of foreign-language minorities through Sunday School classes taught in their own languages, while still trying to integrate them into the mainstream if possible. The letter also authorized specialty units, but only where there was a sufficient minority living within a stake's boundaries.

Leaders of the Los Angeles Stake welcomed the interest Church leaders were expressing in minority members, for it only confirmed what they had been trying to do for years in breaking down barriers. They also recognized, however, that the new guidelines for dealing with minorities were not completely adequate for their stake.

Supreme Court Justice Oliver Wendell Holmes once stated that the life of the law was not logic, but experience. Such, stake leaders found, also held true regarding minority units in southern California. While it seemed logical to say that minorities should be integrated into regular wards, their experience had taught them not only that "adequate attention" usually required specialty units for minorities with language and cultural barriers, but also that adequate units could be created only by going beyond stake boundaries. They had already tried other means, including offering English classes for Spanish-speaking brothers and sisters and providing translators, but experience indicated that the best way to nurture the minorities further along was through love, enfranchisement, and eventually encouragement to learn leadership through leading. Stake leaders adopted this attitude not because it was logical, but because it was right.

Bringing some of the minorities into what were essentially Anglo-American wards often deprived them of the leadership training they needed. Specialty branches, on the other hand, gave opportunity for personal growth to members who might otherwise do little more in the Church than sit on the back row at meetings they barely, if at all, understood. To help them become leaders in the Church did not require teaching them English as much as it did giving them firsthand experience in administering Church programs by organizing them into specialty units and then allowing them to interact with the English-speaking majority in the stake through translators. In addition, having a branch president who understood both the language and the culture of a particular group greatly improved the capability for counseling branch members and assisting in their spiritual welfare.

At the same time, stake leaders recognized that specialty units should be created only if they were really needed. A large number of Armenians, for example, lived in the Hollywood area and the Hollywood Ward created an Armenian Sunday School for their benefit. Most of these members, however, had little problem with the language or culture and a majority had a greater desire to be part of the Hollywood Ward than to have their own unit. The Armenian Saints continued to attend that ward, therefore, where they learned the gospel in English.

In addition to organizing specialty units, stake leaders tried to become aware of the special challenges faced by members of different cultures. Minority members were invited to participate in stake leadership meetings and conferences, and special training meetings were held on both the stake and ward levels for those units with members with special needs.

The emphasis was not only upon minorities but also upon those with special needs, such as the deaf. When better communication facilities were made available for the deaf, stake leaders readily took advantage of the new technology. Telecommunication devices were placed in the homes of both the stake president and the branch president so that deaf members could more easily communicate with their leaders without having to show up on their doorsteps or use interpreters.

Throughout its history the Los Angeles Stake has been plagued by the problem of transiency, along with the directly related challenge of keeping stake and ward positions filled. It has been estimated that some 50,000 Saints have lived within the stake boundaries, and because so many have stayed for only a short time before moving out into the suburbs or back to Utah, someone once dubbed it a "hotel stake."[7] During the administration of President Carmack the entire stake seemed to be in a constant state of motion. Every bishopric and branch presidency was reorganized at least once because one of its members left the stake. The high council turned over almost completely. When openings did arise, new members of the stake, minority members, and singles were often called upon to fill the openings and to receive the training that went with them.

Hollywood Ward was a dramatic example of the problem, with an average turnover of about 10 percent each month. Members would be trained in Church callings but, after functioning only for a short time, move from the ward and usually from the stake. The problem of keeping the ward staffed became so acute that the bishopric began meeting new arrivals at the door on Sunday morning, finding out where they were from, calling their former bishops to discover if they were in good standing, issuing them a call, and then introducing them and sustaining them in their new callings that afternoon in sacrament meeting.[8] Instead of attempting to visit each new arrival immediately, the bishopric was forced to contact new members and welcome them to the ward through registered letters.

The entire urban area of Los Angeles was having difficulty maintaining Church population during the 1970s, particularly with respect to young families who were moving from the city to Orange County or to San Fernando Valley. People left not only to escape the changing patterns of the neighborhoods, but also to avoid the growing practice of busing in order to achieve integrated schools. Others left because of inflated property values and the accompanying rise in property taxes. One of the areas of the stake hardest hit by these problems was Bel Air, in the Westwood First Ward, where parents were not only paying high taxes to support the schools, but were also having their children bused downtown to integrate the inner city schools. While many of those who moved from Bel Air left the stake, others tended to move into the Cheviot Hills area of the Westwood Second Ward where schools were integrated and the threat of busing was removed.

As a result of the highly controversial busing issue, a number of private schools were established in the Los Angeles area. Some groups within the Church requested the use of Church buildings for such schools. To consider the request, a special meeting was held in Salt Lake City between Elder Vaughn J. Featherstone, the area administrator for California, and some of the priesthood leaders from Los Angeles. The matter was debated thoroughly, but the conclusion was that Church buildings could not be used for private schools.[9] This decision was probably the wisest possible at the time, but it may well have contributed to the continuing exodus from the western portion of the stake.

The wards in the eastern part of the stake were also experiencing great changes, but for different reasons. The area encompassing Wilshire, Hollywood, and Hollywood Second Wards was becoming a high crime area, and an increasingly undesirable place to live. So many families were moving from these wards, in fact, that few youth remained, and in order to have thirty or forty in attendance at MIA meeting the three wards combined for that activity. It was a difficult time for these wards, but in a way it proved a blessing as the members who remained intensified their support for each other and a special spirit and unity developed among them.

Many parts of Hollywood had deteriorated badly, and the city was no longer the attractive place for families it once had been. There were many apartment dwellers in the Hollywood wards as well as many welfare problems. There was also a growing drug problem in the city, and Church membership rolls included a number of people who were trying to straighten out their lives. All these things contributed to the fact that even though many good, faithful, and active people remained in Hollywood, there were fewer established families. At one point the ward included 440 families but only 560 members, or an average of 1.3 members per family.[10] Many of these were singles, while others were married to non-Mormons.

The demographics of Wilshire Ward were also changing, as many younger families moved out, leaving a larger population of older singles. At one time, for example, there was a total membership of over 600, but more than half were members of the Relief Society and these were mainly widows over sixty-five. An unusually large share of the responsibility for the success of the ward, therefore, fell upon the ward Relief Society president, Marion Pinkston.

Active members in these wards especially Melchizedek Priesthood holders, found themselves spread very thinly. The Hollywood Ward, for example, had only twenty-four high priests and the Hollywood Second Ward had only thirteen, in spite of the fact that the membership of both wards exceeded five hundred. The average attendance of elders was 21 and 28 percent, respectively, with over 60 percent of the elders in each ward not attending any meeting. Seldom, if ever, therefore, were two Melchizedek Priesthood holders assigned together as home teachers, and seldom were home teachers assigned less than six or eight families. Occasionally a home teacher was assigned fifteen or eighteen families and instructed to try to visit the whole group every other month.[11]

One significant result of all these changes was the fact that when the Hollywood and Wilshire wards celebrated their fiftieth anniversaries in 1973 and 1977, respectively, they were substantially different wards than those that had been created a half-century earlier. The fact that Wilshire Ward's celebration featured ethnic foods symbolized much of what was happening.

Some older members of both wards, of course, remembering the different atmosphere of former days, were still uncomfortable with what was taking place around them, and a few were heard to say that while they had not left the ward, the ward had left them. Others, however, not only accepted what was happening but also glorified the changes as the only way for the Church to accommodate both the present and the future.

Amid all the changes taking place in Los Angeles Stake, the two Westwood wards remained the strongest and were largely self-sufficient. As a result, they were required to assume an increasing share of the responsibility for the success of the stake, and their members were called upon more frequently to fill stake leadership positions. The changes also meant that President Carmack and stake auxiliary heads spent relatively little time with the Westwood wards. Instead, most of their time and the time of their successors was spent with the struggling minority units and the rapidly changing wards in the eastern part of the stake, training future leaders.

Recognizing the great diversity among the wards, the stake presidency began assessing the stake budget on the principle of the widow's mite. Budget was assessed not according to membership, but in relation to the amount of tithing paid in each unit. As a result, the Westwood wards still pay over half the stake budget, while the minority wards pay but a small fraction.

One of the first and most important decisions made by the stake presidency under President Carmack was to keep the Wilshire Ward chapel. During the early months of President Carmack's administration, he and his counselors continued to ponder the building's future. Conventional wisdom still held that it was only a matter of time before it would be sold and a new one built in a better neighborhood, but as they evaluated the situation they began to see the future of the chapel as sound and exciting. They noticed that, in actuality, it was being used more than ever before, and by a wider variety of people. While Anglos were moving from the Wilshire Ward, other groups such as blacks, Koreans, Filipinos, and Latins were filling the void. For stake leaders, whose responsibility was not just to think of the present but also to consider the future, it was clear that the chapel's best days could still be ahead, serving the wide variety of minorities living nearby. In addition, there was artistic and historical value in the magnificent structure that also argued for its retention. Thus, the longer they analyzed the situation the more the members of the stake presidency moved towards keeping the chapel. Not only did they deliberate its future, but they also spent considerable time petitioning the Lord to discover his will.

Finally, on one occasion while President Stewart was out of town, Presidents Carmack and Tanner were earnestly praying about the matter when they received the inspiration that it was not the Lord's desire that the chapel be sold. The spiritual impression was that whatever happened the stake should not abandon it, for the Lord needed it in that location, not only because those Saints still living in the area needed a place to meet, but also because there were going to be converts made from among the people who had moved in. The Wilshire chapel might be disposed of later, but it was not supposed to be done away with at that time.[12]

After receiving this inspiration, the stake presidency determined to restore the building as much as possible to the condition it was in when dedicated by President Heber J. Grant. Because it had been felt that the building might be sold, it had become sadly neglected and hardly a room did not need some work.

When the stake presidency presented its decision to refurbish the building to the high council and bishops, the ensuing discussion revealed a wide range of opinions, including the feeling that it may not be wise to put money into a building that logic said would have to be sold. But the stake presidency pressed the issue, feeling that as a stake they "should have more faith than fear" and follow the inspiration of the Lord.[13] As a result, when stake leaders were asked to pledge their support of the stake presidency they did so, even though some continued to question the wisdom of the decision. They gathered behind the stake presidency because President Carmack had presented the decision for what it was—the will of the Lord. The message was also sent throughout the stake that the Wilshire Ward chapel would continue to serve those who lived near it, who would most likely constitute an entirely different group from the one it originally served.

Stake leaders then forced the issue. In June 1974 the stake presidency asked that the Muirfield property be sold, for the stake no longer had an interest in building in that area.[14] In

November 1974 they wrote to the Church Building Department for permission to place the Wilshire Ward complex again in good repair.[15]

Even though the stake had decided to keep the chapel, there were still those who continued to say that it was too dangerous to attend meetings there. Stake leaders, therefore, recognizing that there were some dangers, tried to minimize them and make it as safe as possible for all. A back-to-back meeting schedule for all units using the Wilshire Ward was approved so that all Sunday meetings were held during daylight hours. Feeling that it would also be less dangerous if lighting around the chapel was improved and more parking made available, the stake also took steps in that direction. When a convalescent hospital immediately south of the building was put up for sale in November 1974, it was purchased and the property was made into a parking lot, thus allowing almost everyone who came to the chapel to park on Church property.

In October 1975 the Wilshire Ward renovation project was approved by the Church Building Department and work began immediately. C. Dean Olson headed a committee to raise $100,000, the stake's share of the cost. Thomas Andersen and Garn Wallace, as stake physical facilities representatives, oversaw the project during construction while two other stake members, Robert Little and Donald Peart, served as supervising architects. E. Myron Pinkston provided many fine finishing touches on the building and its furnishings, and Joseph Gibby painted a picture to hang above the chapel's baptismal font similar to the one he had painted for the Los Angeles Temple.

This major renovation project included installing beautiful red carpeting, similar to that originally in the building. The chairs on the stand were redone, as was a portion of the woodwork inside the chapel. One of the original painters who helped paint the many geometrical patterns in the chapel, Eddy Lundquist, was located, and he produced the original stencils so that even the walls and ceilings were restored as they were.[16] A new roof was placed on the building and extensive repairs completed throughout. Indeed, few efforts were spared to restore the Wilshire Ward to the very beautiful building that it was—and still is.

As work began on the building and before the great numbers of Hispanics began swelling the ranks of the stake, President

Carmack received a powerful spiritual confirmation of the decision stake leaders had made. A vision came to him in which he saw that while the building then served as a home for only one Spanish-speaking branch, it would one day serve many Spanish wards and be a center of Spanish activity.[17]

Another Church unit which received a permanent home was the UCLA Ward. From the beginning the university's Religious Conference Center had been used by both the ward and the institute of religion, although that arrangement had proved less than ideal. The desire had always been for an institute building that the ward could also use, but efforts to acquire one had been unsuccessful. Such a building had to be within walking distance of the campus, be easily converted into a chapel, and have adequate parking. The Church owned property near the campus, but it was not adequate by itself for an institute building. Other potential sites were examined, but the Church was unable to obtain zoning variances. Finally one day in 1970, when most Church leaders were despairing that a suitable location could be found, Bishop John H. Webster was traveling along the Santa Monica Freeway when he felt inspired to drive down Hilgard Avenue and stop at the sorority house next to the Church's property.[18] Visiting the house was its owner, who, when asked, said she would be willing to sell.

Unfortunately, building a parking lot required a zoning variance, which Church leaders were uncertain they would be able to obtain, and when the matter was presented at a public zoning meeting, all those who spoke opposed the change. Near the end of the meeting, however, the county's representative conducting the meeting called Bob Little, the Church's representative, to the stand and asked him two questions. First, he wanted to know, was Little aware that the property was zoned for highrise apartments? Second, would the Church sell the property to someone who desired to build a highrise? Little answered that if the Church could not use the property it would sell to the highest bidder, even someone wishing to build apartments. When the floor was opened for more comments, all those who had opposed the variance came forward and gave their support, realizing that a parking lot that they could look down upon was preferable to a highrise that would block their view.[19] The zoning was changed and by the summer of 1972 the sorority house was converted into an institute building suitable for ward use.

Now that the Church had its own building near UCLA, the single adult institute program was moved there. That change was made not only because of concerns over the future of the USC institute, but also because of the great love which the new UCLA institute director and newly appointed bishop of the UCLA Ward, Alan K. Parrish, had for the singles. In addition, this new location was more favorable to the needs of the singles, for it was closer to Santa Monica and the San Fernando Valley, where many were living. The number of singles attending the institute classes as well as the UCLA Ward soon mushroomed, and the stake ended up with what was essentially a singles ward meeting in connection with the UCLA Ward. The singles, many of whom were professionals who had come to the area to start their careers, found that the UCLA Ward was uniquely able to satisfy their desires to associate with people of their own faith and circumstances. It was also evident to stake leaders that these single Saints desired not only to have an enjoyable time, but also to participate fully and responsibly in the Church, and that this desire was best being met at UCLA.

As word of the opportunity at UCLA spread, the building soon was filled to capacity each Sunday with students and non-students alike from throughout the Los Angeles area, some from as far away as San Bernardino. The main chapel could seat around 150 people, and there were people standing in the back, sitting on the steps that led into the chapel and in the various rooms throughout the institute where the services were transmitted. While all were welcome to attend the activities and Sunday services, only students could become ward members and receive callings. Consequently, many singles became part-time students so they could have an opportunity to become a part of the ward and to serve in an environment that met both their spiritual and social needs.

Changes were also taking place on a Church level to help meet the needs of the increasing number of single adults. In 1972 President Harold B. Lee observed: "We have found that we have been neglecting some of our adult members—those over eighteen who have not yet found their companions, or who are perhaps widowed or divorced. . . . but we are endeavoring to reach those for whom we have had no adequate programs."[20] Elder James E. Faust was appointed to head up the Church-wide effort to provide for greater involvement of singles in Church activity, which included the establishment of the Young

Special Interest Program for singles under forty. As part of the new emphasis, a singles ward was organized in the Emigration Stake in Salt Lake City. Shortly after its creation, Elder Marion D. Hanks, whom Los Angeles Stake leaders had approached previously about the need for a singles branch, called President Carmack, telling him that if the stake would again apply he would personally walk the application through the process and recommend its approval to the First Presidency.[21]

On 27 January 1974 a special meeting of the UCLA Ward was held at the Westwood chapel to organize the first singles unit outside Salt Lake City. President Carmack presided and Bishop Parrish conducted the meeting. In attendance also were stake presidents from surrounding stakes and Russell M. Nelson, Church Sunday School general president. Earlier in the week President Nelson had called President Carmack to tell him that he would be in town over the weekend for a medical conference and volunteered his services if they could be of help to the stake. His offer was accepted and he was the principal speaker at this meeting.[22]

The new unit was called the Los Angeles First Branch, and Richard Stratford was sustained as branch president. Stratford, recently released as bishop of the Westwood Ward and retired as a partner in the Touche Ross accounting firm, had been contemplating spending a considerable amount of time in Palm Springs, and when President Carmack asked him to take responsibility for the branch he sat silently for so long that his wife, Sally, finally went over to him to ask what he was thinking. He was thinking how this was going to change their lives, he replied, and then he said, "It's time to roll up our sleeves and get to work!"[23]

Membership in the single adult branch was limited to those singles residing within the confines of the Los Angeles Stake. It was initially recommended that membership should be open to all who desired to attend, regardless of where they resided. Leaders of some surrounding stakes, however, opposed the creation of the branch on such a condition for it would continue to draw members away from their stakes. Those singles residing outside Los Angeles Stake boundaries were asked to return to their home wards, though they could become members of the branch if they received written permission from their home ward and stake as well as from President Stratford and President Carmack.

As one member of the branch recalled, however, this policy was not without its problems:

> On the first Sunday of the new branch, it appeared that there could possibly be a slight problem—within a month it was confirmed: the majority of the women lived within the stake, and the majority of men lived outside of the stake.
>
> Within six months, President Stratford, seeing that he had a crisis on his hands, was busy buttonholing single male visitors from outside of the stake to obtain the necessary signatures to become a member of the branch. He was very successful in this endeavor. Within a year or so, most of the banished had returned to become members of the branch.[24]

The establishment of the singles branch presented some challenges, one of which was adapting Church curriculum and programs to the needs of the singles. Thus, a Sunday School class developed by branch members focused on the problems peculiar to single adults, such as dating, self-esteem, loneliness, and marriage, instead of the traditional family focus. Branch members were also organized into home evening groups that met every Monday and served the function of "Family Home Evening" in building unity and concern among group members. Nearly every other week the Stratfords invited one of these groups to their home for dinner and swimming.

The creation of the branch produced great rewards for its members and for the Church, many unexpected. All who wished could now be involved, since nearly everyone in the branch could hold a position of responsibility. Thus branch members, the majority of whom were professional and well-educated people, were able to develop their abilities in ways that often were not open to them in traditional wards, where their broad talents were frequently not utilized. The branch also brought single people out of inactivity, many of whom had been unknown to Church leaders. At the branch's initial tithing settlement, for example, President Stratford found that almost half were attending Church for the first time in their adult lives.[25]

Stake leaders also found that the branch was a marvelous vehicle for encouraging repentance and helping many single adults come to grips with the need to put their sins behind them. Since these singles felt that they now had a place in the

Church and that Church leaders cared for them, the number of cases handled by the branch president was not insignificant.[26] The branch, therefore, accomplished a great purpose in helping people bring their lives more fully in tune with the principles of the gospel.

When they proposed the creation of the singles branch, stake leaders envisioned it as something more than just a fun-filled experience for its members. They saw it as an opportunity for singles to develop their talents, enjoy the blessings of serving in important capacities, and get to know each other in "low-risk activities."[27] Dances, for example, are "high-risk activities," in the sense that few single women like to go to them wondering if they are going to spend the whole evening without dancing. Church assignments, on the other hand, are "low-risk activities" where the singles can get to know each other by working together without getting hurt.

In that spirit, therefore, stake leaders put the talents of the singles to use in providing help for other special groups within the stake. At the Deaf Ward, for example, there were problems in teaching Primary and Sunday School to the youth and children, most of whom could hear and needed to have the gospel communicated to them verbally. The singles, therefore, were asked to accept responsibility for providing both leadership and teachers, and as a regular assignment they taught Primary classes as well as classes for the young men and women in the Deaf Branch. The talents of the singles were also employed among the Spanish-speaking Saints, as single adults who could speak the language worked with them in the area of music. Not only did they enjoy themselves, but they utilized their talents, experienced the blessings of service, and were made to feel that they were an important part of the stake. In addition, all this helped foster the feeling of togetherness among branch members.

Part of the goal in establishing this branch was to create alumni, so to speak, who would "graduate" to family wards by getting married. While no complete record has been kept, the fact that between 1979 and 1984 seventy-eight marriages took place between branch members suggests that this goal has been met, at least in part.[28]

Within a year of the creation of the Los Angeles First Branch, the Santa Monica Stake followed suit and created a singles ward. Other stakes then also created singles wards, and by 1987 there were nine such wards in the Los Angeles area. In 1978 the Los Angeles First Branch became the Los Angeles First Ward.

As the Church continued its worldwide expansion in the 1970s, certain administrative changes were made. In 1974, for example, the names of stakes and missions were changed to more consistently reflect their geographic locations. The name of the Los Angeles Stake was changed to the Los Angeles California Stake, which conformed to the uniform pattern being established. Church leaders believed that such a change would make it easier to keep track of the nearly 140 missions and more than 700 stakes throughout the world.

The August 1974 statistical report listed the membership of the stake as 3,571, a decrease of 1,600 members in twenty-five years. These members, however, were contained in a larger number and greater variety of units than existed in 1950: Hollywood I and II Wards, Los Angeles Spanish Branch, Los Angeles First Branch, Los Angeles Ward for the Deaf, University UCLA Ward, University USC Branch, Westwood I and II Wards, and Wilshire Ward. Of the total membership, almost one thousand belonged to the student wards, the singles branch, the Deaf Ward, or the Spanish Branch.

The decrease in stake membership would have been far greater had it not been for missionary efforts. Beginning in the mid-1970s the Los Angeles California Stake led the mission in baptisms, largely as a result of missionary work among the Spanish. This increase in missionary momentum, however, presented a new problem, for, in effect, the stake was trading older experienced members for new and inexperienced converts. As a result, many who might otherwise not have received great responsibilities quite so soon were given assignments and challenges relatively early in their Church careers. Their lack of experience was more than made up for, however, by the fresh insights and enthusiasm they brought to their callings.

As part of its continuing commitment to the city of Los Angeles, the stake joined with other stakes in sponsoring the "Good Samaritan Awards" in the mid-1970s. On 22 April 1975, the first Good Samaritan Awards Banquet was held at the Marriott Hotel in Los Angeles, with 350 in attendance. The awards, based upon the parable of Jesus, honored individuals and groups who had assisted their fellowmen through acts of heroism or charity during the previous year. Members of the community were encouraged to nominate those they felt deserving of this honor, and from the hundreds of names submitted fifteen were chosen to receive the award. Two were Latter-day Saints.

This awards ceremony had been initiated because Church leaders believed that in spite of the negative aspects of society stressed so frequently in the news, the good in people outweighs the bad and that people not only want to, but do get involved in helping others. Stated President Carmack: "All we hear about is problems in the news. There are many today who exemplify the Biblical Good Samaritan and demonstrate by their actions that we are all brothers and sisters. These people represent the wave of the future and we want to honor them."[29]

In May 1975 the Vietnam War ended with the collapse of the South Vietnamese government and the withdrawal of American troops from the country. Following the end of the war, thousands of Vietnamese refugees hastily fled to the United States to begin a new life. As these refugees arrived in the country, a call went out for private assistance to help them, and some members of the Los Angeles Stake responded. One family adopted two Vietnamese orphans, and the stake answered the call by assisting seventeen families to settle in the United States. While some of those assisted were members of the Church, the majority were not, although some would later join. Most of the refugees preferred to settle around the Long Beach area, although a few families found homes in the stake.

In an effort to carry the gospel message to as many people as possible, the regional communication council was given permission by Church authorities to enter a float in the 1976 Tournament of Roses Parade held New Year's Day in Pasadena, California. This float expressed the Church's emphasis on the family and featured the well-known Osmond family. As chairman of the committee, President Carmack was given the responsibility to head a fund-raising drive to pay for the design and construction of a first-rate float, which, it was estimated, would cost $34,000. No assessment was to be made to Church members, however; money was to be raised on a voluntary basis with each stake in the area pledging its support.

As usual, President Carmack approached his assignment prayerfully, and as the result of an anonymous donation from a stake member he was able to raise the first $12,000 when it was needed in July 1975.[30] Other funds for this first float came from the sale of a six-unit apartment building donated by Nadine Dennis, a nonmember of the Church, and from direct voluntary contributions by Church members, most of whom resided in the stake. A float was also entered the following year.

By 1977 the Korean Sunday School was still in operation, although its numbers remained small. Its members continued to express their desires for a branch, however, and stake leaders continued to recognize that need. During the January 1977 stake conference, Bishop Victor L. Brown, Presiding Bishop of the Church, was the visiting General Authority. As the stake presidency outlined for him the challenges in the stake, they mentioned the situation with the Koreans and what the stake had done to hold them, though mostly without success. Bishop Brown then informed the stake presidency of a recent change in the Church's handbook of instructions.[31] While stakes still could not organize independent branches without permission from Salt Lake City, the policy had been changed so that permission was no longer needed to organize a dependent branch. The stake presidency determined that this branch should be tied to the Wilshire Ward where it would receive tremendous support from the ward's bishop, Stephen Eldredge, whose wife, Yoshie, was Japanese.

On 6 March 1977 the long struggle to provide a special unit for the Koreans came to an end when a dependent Korean branch was organized at Wilshire Ward, with Tae Mun Lee as branch president. The Koreans now had the identity and place in the Church they sought. Attendance revived, and many members who had been inactive came back into full activity. The branch received a needed boost with the calling of Korean-speaking missionaries to labor in Los Angeles. The first of these missionaries had been reassigned to the area for health reasons, but before long other missionaries were called to labor in the area known as Korea Town, not far from the Los Angeles stake center.

As the membership grew, approval was given for the creation of an independent branch. In a meeting in the high council room of the stake center on 18 December 1977, the Korean Branch was reorganized as the Los Angeles Second Branch with President Lee continuing as branch president. This meeting demonstrated that the branch had sufficient priesthood, as the majority of Koreans present were priesthood holders. A major concern, however, was the lack of sisters, and only two attended the first Relief Society the following Sunday. Members of the branch came from throughout the area, however, and before long the number of women increased. The attendance, growth, and percentage of individual participation of the Korean Saints was excellent as attendance was often nearly 100 percent.

In the spring of 1977, President Carmack was called to be one of the Regional Representatives of the Twelve, with initial responsibility for the Downey and Santa Barbara regions. Consequently, on 12 June 1977, at a stake conference presided over by Elder Robert D. Hales of the First Quorum of the Seventy, Rodney H. Brady was sustained as president of the stake. Robert H. Millard and Stephen Eldredge were selected as counselors.

President Brady was born in Salt Lake City in 1933 and raised in Sandy, Utah. After completing a mission to the British Isles, where he had the privilege of teaching the gospel to Winston Churchill, he attended the University of Utah, where he received a B.A. in accounting as well as an M.B.A. degree. He then went on to Harvard University and earned a doctorate in business administration. In 1966 he accepted a position with Hughes Tool Company in Los Angeles and moved into the Westwood Ward. He served as a member of the high council and in the Westwood Ward bishopric before becoming bishop of the ward in 1968. In December 1970 he accepted a position as assistant secretary of the U.S. Department of Health, Education, and Welfare. In 1972 he returned to Los Angeles as executive vice-president of Bergen Brunswick Corporation, a chemical and pharmaceuticals conglomerate. Shortly thereafter he was called as second counselor to President Carmack when President Stewart moved from the stake.

Like President Russon before him, President Brady was very vocal about goals, often showing members charts of the progress of the stake. The goals he established were expressed not so much in absolute numbers as in the idea of striving for improvement, realizing that if the stake was moving in the right direction it would eventually get to where it should be. President Brady also demonstrated great belief in people, which included confidence in the ability of people whom many regarded as not unusually talented. He recognized that some never shine only because they are never given a chance.

By March 1978, the Wilshire Ward and the two Hollywood wards had diminished in strength to the point that it was apparent that two stronger wards should be maintained as opposed to three weaker ones. Consequently, the Hollywood Second Ward was disbanded and its membership transferred to the other two wards.

The Deaf Ward, on the other hand, continued to grow to the point that it outgrew its facilities in the Wilshire Ward annex. A decision was made to split the ward, but it had become apparent that most of its membership lived outside stake boundaries, either in the San Fernando Valley or in the Torrance area. It was decided, therefore, that wards ought to be established in those areas. On 16 April 1978 the Los Angeles Ward for the Deaf was disbanded and the San Fernando Valley Ward for the Deaf and the Torrance North Ward for the Deaf were created. This change not only better served the deaf, but also freed the Wilshire annex to become a permanent home for the Korean Branch.

For years, the stake had benefited from the vitality of the Deaf Ward members, who refused to let their handicaps prevent them from doing such things as fielding basketball teams, putting on plays and roadshows, and attending the many stake activities and dances. While the example and enthusiasm of the deaf were missed by the stake, most stake members agreed that the one thing they disliked most about losing the Deaf Ward was its wonderful singing mothers' chorus.

As was common throughout the Church in the 1950s, the deaf had established a Relief Society singing mothers' chorus, which continued as long as they were part of the stake. Even though it was difficult to translate songs directly into sign language, several were so translated for the sisters. While they signed the songs for the audience, they would be accompanied by a vocalist. Often these singing mothers were asked to perform at stake conferences, which added a very special spirit. President Russon remembers that when the deaf choir sang it was a "touching, marvelous experience. . . . They won the hearts of the people throughout the stake."[32] One particular conference weekend when the deaf sisters sang, Dick and Sally Stratford had planned to be out of town, but, to their initial disappointment, events had kept them from leaving. After attending the conference, however, their changed attitude was reflected in a letter to the stake presidency: "When the deaf ward sisters sang in their own language with that beautiful voice of the soloist, I felt an emotional stir that I have never known before. I'm so small and God has given me so much! I looked up at Dick and he had taken off his glasses to wipe his eyes. Truly it was a heavenly experience." Remarked President Stratford, "My, wasn't it fortunate we didn't go to Palm Springs!"[33]

Three months following the division of the deaf branch, one of the most important events in the history of the Church took place. On Friday, 9 June 1978, the First Presidency held a press conference to read a letter dated the previous day that announced that the Lord had heard the pleadings of the Brethren "and confirmed that the long-promised day has come when every faithful, worthy man in the Church may receive the holy priesthood, with power to exercise its divine authority, and enjoy with his loved ones every blessing that flows therefrom, including the blessings of the temple."[34]

Over the previous several months the General Authorities had discussed the possibility of extending the priesthood to all worthy male members, and President Spencer W. Kimball had often sequestered himself in the Salt Lake Temple to plead for guidance from the Lord on the subject. After extended meditation and prayer, President Kimball received a revelation that this was the time. On 1 June 1978 in a meeting with the First Presidency and Council of the Twelve, President Kimball again brought up the subject, expressing hope that all might receive a clear answer. All present were asked to express their feelings on the matter, and after two hours of discussion it was clear that the Brethren were of one mind. They then prayed, with President Kimball serving as voice, and during the prayer the revelation came and the First Presidency and Council of the Twelve "all heard the same voice, received the same message, and became personal witnesses that the word received was the mind and will and voice of the Lord." Those present later stated that none of them "had ever experienced anything of such spiritual magnitude and power as was poured out upon the Presidency and the Twelve that day in the upper room in the house of the Lord."[35]

By the following Thursday, 8 June 1978, a letter had been written to local leaders announcing this change in policy, and this letter was later incorporated into the Doctrine and Covenants as Official Declaration–2. The following day, the First Presidency held its news conference.

Few will forget where they were when they first learned of this grand new revelation. Some were at home and heard it on radio or television. Some were driving in their cars, others were in the temple, and still others learned of the change through the phone calls and personal visits of excited friends, both members and nonmembers. Many of those in their cars pulled over to the side of the road to consider what it meant and to offer prayers of thanksgiving. Many Saints wept tears of joy; others hugged each other and jumped about their rooms with unbridled happiness. Some leaders first heard of the revelation from local members. Robert L. Jachens, bishop of the Wilshire Ward, heard it from Andrew Pulley, a young black member of his ward who had heard it from another ward member. "Don't you believe it," Jachens told Pulley. "Someone has played a very cruel joke." The bishop called Salt Lake City, however, then hurried to tell Pulley it was true, rejoicing that the black members of his ward could now enjoy all the blessings of the Church.[36] Naturally, there were those who said they really could not believe it until they saw a black member blessing and passing the sacrament or a black couple being married in the temple—all of which happened a short time later.

One of the first black members to receive her temple endowments was Helen Kennedy of the Wilshire Ward, the first black member of the stake. She had joined the Church in March 1969 while an employee at Hill Air Force Base in Ogden, Utah. In 1972 she followed her daughter to Los Angeles, but not before being warned by members in Ogden that she would not be as readily accepted as a member of the Church in her new home. She initially approached the Wilshire Ward, therefore, with fear, but she was given a warm welcome and made very much at home. She had such a great testimony of the gospel and faith concerning her place in the Church that she was able not only to accept the limitations on blacks as momentary but also to give strength to others whose testimonies were shaken by this policy. She had such a great love that she refused to allow prejudice to trouble her and won over the hearts of almost all who knew her. With other black members in the area, Kennedy formed a "Special Destiny Group" that met together regularly.

The new revelation was also the direct fulfillment of a prophecy made to a member of the stake. A couple of months earlier, President Brady had an opportunity to counsel a recent female convert who, after her baptism, had learned that blacks could not hold the priesthood. This upset her greatly because the father of her young daughter was black, and she realized that when her daughter reached marriageable age she might be denied the blessings of the temple or, at the very least, her children might not be able to hold the priesthood. After discussing the matter at great length with her, and realizing that he was going out on a limb, President Brady felt inspired to tell her, "This may appear to us to be a problem now, but I assure you that by the time it makes a difference to that young lady it won't be a problem."[37]

By coincidence, two days following the announcement of the revelation on the priesthood, the Los Angeles California Stake was scheduled to hold stake conference, and as part of that conference the Wilshire Ward chapel was scheduled to be rededicated. The building was originally scheduled for dedication in July 1977 but this had been postponed for nearly a year because of delays in the building schedule. This combination of events, however, served almost as a confirmation of the decision of stake leaders not to sell the beautiful, stately building, but to keep it as if it was intended to be used by minority members. Elder LeGrand Richards had been invited back to the stake for the conference and to rededicate the building he had known and loved as stake president. On Friday he called President Brady to inform him of the details surrounding the revelation and to ask him to read the First Presidency letter as part of stake conference.[38]

Present at this memorable conference were about ten black members of the stake and the sister who had been promised by her stake president that the restriction on the priesthood would not affect her daughter. At the conclusion of the meeting these Saints were among the first to reach the stand. There they threw their arms around President Brady and Elder Richards with emotion-packed gratitude, and shared a special spiritual moment with an Apostle of the Lord.

Since the rededication, all the members of the high council who initially fought against the decision to keep the Wilshire Ward have said to the stake presidency, "We're glad you hung tough, and you didn't give in to our objections."[39] The Wilshire Ward is used more today than it ever was, and by more diverse groups. The importance of the decision can also be seen in the fact that over the last several years the neighborhoods around the chapel have started on the upswing and the building has been a convenient gathering point for the minorities in that area. Perhaps President Carmack best summed up the outlook of stake leaders and members about the importance of the stake center when he wrote for the rededicatory program:

> The Savior, Jesus Christ, loves this stake and guides its leaders and members as they seek Him. We don't look back in this stake. There are too many young people to train, saints to serve, converts to baptize, organizations to perfect and create. Our faith and energy are equal to our challenges. The Los Angeles Stake center stands as a symbol of the solid faith of our people in this great community which is Southern California. This is its center historically and the signal continues to go forth from here.[40]

A Vision That We Must Cause to Be Fulfilled

E ven though it was natural that the greatest growth of the Church in southern California should come among the Anglo-Saxon, English-speaking population, the large Spanish-speaking minority was not forgotten. The history of the Hispanic Saints in Los Angeles is one of small beginnings, sporadic growth, exemplary faith, questions over how to deal with linguistic and cultural differences within the Church, and, finally, the organization of a Spanish-speaking stake.

Missionary work among the Spanish-speaking people in Los Angeles began in the mid-1920s. By 1929 a Spanish branch, later known as the Dittman Branch, had been established, but it was under the jurisdiction of the California Mission. In the early 1950s the Dittman Branch and other Spanish-speaking branches were placed under the jurisdiction of stakes. However, these branches were located in the eastern portion of the city, outside the stake boundaries, where the vast majority of the Hispanic population resided. Since few stake leaders spoke Spanish, the Saints attending these branches were left virtually to themselves to carry on as best they could, except for the occasional stake leader who spoke Spanish and was willing to work closely with branch leaders. The branches were also helped, though infrequently, by Spanish-speaking missionaries assigned to Los Angeles. Most contact was limited, however, for while the Spanish American Mission was in operation, nearly all its missionaries were assigned to Texas or to border towns.

In the early 1950s missionary work among the Hispanics in Los Angeles gained new vitality, and by 1953 at least six full-time missionaries were working with them. Because the Spanish-speaking population in the western half of the city was so small, most efforts continued to be directed towards the eastern half. In April 1953 the missionaries tried to conduct a Spanish Sunday School class at the Adams Ward. Very few people attended, however, and those who did seemed to be more interested in hearing Spanish spoken than in hearing the gospel in Spanish.

In time other branches were established, including the Arroyo Branch in Glendale and the Belvedere Branch in the East Los Angeles Stake. Those few Spanish-speaking Saints who lived within the Los Angeles Stake usually had their memberships transferred to the Arroyo Branch or else were required to attend the English-speaking ward in whose boundary they resided. At the same time, the Spanish-speaking population was growing throughout the western United States, and in 1958 the Church established the West Spanish American Mission, with responsibility for missionary work among the Spanish-speaking population in the Western states. The Hispanic community was also growing in the western half of Los Angeles and missionary work was undertaken there, but no effort was made to open a branch of the Church in that part of the city. Instead, as new converts were made, their records continued to be transferred to the Arroyo Branch.

The story of Trinidad Reyna and her family, who moved from El Salvador to Los Angeles in 1963, suggests the difficulties faced by some Spanish-speaking Saints in southern California during this time. Seven years earlier, Trinidad and her daughters, Carmen and Yolanda, had been baptized members of the Layco Branch of the Church in Ilopango Lake. Trinidad was sustained as the Layco Branch's Relief Society president shortly following her baptism, and her daughter Yolanda fulfilled a mission in the Central American Mission.

Once in Los Angeles, the Reynas became members of the Arroyo Branch, but attended only a handful of times because of transportation difficulties. Nevertheless, still having a strong desire to continue fellowshipping with the Saints in their new country, the family occasionally attended the Wilshire Ward, in whose boundaries they resided. Since Trinidad spoke no English, however, and her daughters very little, they became irregular in attending their meetings.

In 1964 Josefina Gallardo, who had known the Reynas in El Salvador, came to Los Angeles to attend her daughter's wedding and sought out the Reynas to renew acquaintances. When Sunday came Josefina was interested in how the Church functioned in the United States and asked the Reynas to take her to the ward they usually attended. Trinidad admitted that they could not attend the Spanish-speaking branch because it was too far away and that they attended the local ward's services only infrequently because they were conducted in English. Josefina suggested, nevertheless, that they should be attending every Sunday to partake of the sacrament and feel the Spirit. Josefina and the Reynas not only began attending the Wilshire Ward but they contacted members of the Arroyo Branch living in the area and invited them also to attend.[1]

Some began to do so, and it was not long before they met Orestes Rodriguez, a ward member who spoke both Spanish and English. He not only made them welcome but also arranged with Wilshire Ward Bishop Varnell Rozsa to organize a Spanish-speaking Sunday School. This class met in the baptismal room of the Wilshire Ward and Rodriguez served as teacher. Attendance at these early Spanish-speaking Sunday Schools averaged about ten.

Anxious to increase their numbers, members of this Sunday School began doing door-to-door missionary work in the evenings and on weekends.[2] These early missionaries included Rosario Salazar, Carmen Franco, Lilian Chanelo, Yolanda Reyna, and Trinidad Reyna. They worked dutifully for two years and were rewarded with success as membership increased.

By the end of 1964, the Spanish-speaking Saints were holding their own sacrament meeting, and the members of the Spanish-speaking Sunday School class had organized themselves into the Spanish Group. Edward T. Aaron, a returned missionary whose wife was from El Salvador, served as group leader with Quenten P. Goodman, first counselor, and Mario Russo, second counselor.

As the Spanish-speaking population grew, an important step for the Hispanic Saints in the Los Angeles Stake was taken on 12 June 1966 when the Spanish Group was organized into a dependent Spanish-speaking branch of the Wilshire Ward. Acting under the direction of stake President Winfield Q. Cannon, his counselors, Merlin W. Sant and John K. Carmack, officiated at the organization. Mario Russo of Argentina was selected as the first branch president. Described as both a spiritual giant and a humble man, President Russo served as a stabilizing influence for branch members during the days of its beginnings. Carlos Vivanco of Chile served as first counselor with Roberto de Leon of Central America, second counselor, and George Solorzano of Mexico, secretary. Josefina Gallardo, who was so instrumental in laying the groundwork for the branch, was sustained as its first Relief Society president. The branch continued to meet in the baptismal room. During these early days, Spanish-speaking Saints came from throughout the western portion of Los Angeles County and from the San Fernando Valley to attend branch services. Because of the distances they had to travel, many were forced to make a day of it, bringing lunches to eat between meetings and giving their children naps on the floor.[3]

On 30 October 1966, only four months after the dependent branch was created, President Sant presided at an all-important meeting where the Spanish-speaking Saints were organized into the independent Los Angeles Spanish Branch. Mario Russo continued as branch president with Mario Vivanco, first counselor, Alberto Medina, second counselor, and Orestes Rodriguez as branch clerk. Luisa Lopez was sustained as Relief Society president. As a result of this important change, these Saints were able to worship together more fully in the language in which they prayed, and had the opportunity for greater growth through Church callings.

They could also worship in an environment relatively free of prejudice. Unfortunately, however, some stake members, recalling the stake's glory days, publicly objected to associating with the Hispanics and to the changes they were bringing to the stake. In the Wilshire Ward, for example, prejudice had grown to the point that a few ward members even suggested that the bishopric should not accept tithing from the Spanish-speaking Saints.[4]

Even after the creation of the Los Angeles Spanish Branch,

there was still opposition to the Hispanic Saints. Because minor problems arose, such as crumbs left on the floor after they ate their sack lunches, some members of the Wilshire Ward tended to blame the Spanish for all problems at the meetinghouse. Charges ranged from causing the ceiling tiles in the recreation hall to come loose because they played so much basketball to stealing the microphones from the chapel.[5]

In spite of such opposition from some Anglos, however, and in spite of all the other challenges associated with being a minority attempting to live the gospel in a new land, this small but enthusiastic group of Spanish-speaking Saints was determined to make their new branch a success. Their efforts were made easier through the steady support given them by the leadership of the Los Angeles Stake and through Spanish-speaking missionaries, although for a time the structure of the missionary program often hindered the work as much as it helped.

Four full-time missionaries of the West Spanish American Mission were assigned to the Los Angeles Spanish Branch. At the same time there were also English-speaking missionaries who often labored in the same area. The feeling at the time was that missionaries who spoke different languages, such as Spanish and English, should be in separate missions even though they might be laboring in the same area. As a result both the California Mission and the West Spanish American Mission operated on an overlapping basis in Los Angeles.

In theory, whenever English-speaking investigators were found they were to be taught by missionaries of the California Mission, and Spanish-speaking investigators were to be taught by missionaries of the West Spanish American Mission. In practice, however, things were far from ideal. Potential investigators were often lost in the process of sending the names between the missions. In addition, cooperation between the missions often got lost in competition over which mission could baptize the most. This resulted in many Hispanic investigators with marginal English skills being taught by English-speaking missionaries in hopes of getting credit for the baptism, regardless of the fact that the investigator would have been better served by Spanish-speaking missionaries. In addition, while each mission's responsibility seemed clear-cut on the surface, there developed a problem of distinguishing which mission would handle missionary work among families in which only one spouse was Hispanic. It was decided that the father's nationality would be the determining factor, but competition again prevented the theory from working in practice.[6]

Such problems associated with operating two missions in the same area were not limited to Los Angeles, and in 1970 the decision was made to disband the West Spanish American Mission. The Spanish-speaking missionaries were then transferred to the various missions in whose boundaries they were working, and this solution seemed to be welcomed by all concerned. As a result, around forty Spanish-speaking missionaries were transferred to the California Mission.

To assist him in overseeing the work of the Spanish-speaking missionaries, California Mission President John K. Edmunds asked David G. Clark, a former mission president in the Guatemala-El Salvador Mission, to serve as his counselor. Clark not only helped the comparatively small number of Spanish-speaking missionaries from being lost in the shuffle, but also helped lay the successful foundation for conducting joint missionary work among Anglos and Hispanics.[7]

During these early days of missionary work among the Hispanics in the Los Angeles Stake, Spanish-speaking people joined the Church at a lower rate than those who spoke English. The Los Angeles Spanish Branch, nevertheless, experienced a steady growth, largely as a result of immigration from Latin America. Some came for economic reasons, some for family reasons, and others to escape political upheaval. But whatever the reasons for coming, many found life in their new land enhanced by their conversion to the gospel.

Within a year of its organization, the Los Angeles Spanish Branch had outgrown its quarters in the baptismal room under the Wilshire Ward chapel. The branch then moved into the annex of the stake center, which it shared with the Deaf Branch.

Late in 1968 President Russo, unable to find suitable employment, returned with his family to Argentina. William F. Jackson, a former missionary in the Spanish American Mission, former bishop of both Westwood Wards, a man of financial means who could greatly assist the struggling branch, and a man greatly respected in the English-speaking community, was sustained as branch president. Because he was so well respected, Jackson further aided in giving the Spanish-speaking Saints a greater feeling of identity with the rest of the Saints in the area as well as an image of legitimacy in the minds of Anglos. He also helped the Spanish Branch become permanently established at the Wilshire Ward chapel.

Shortly after Jackson became branch president, attendance at sacrament meeting often exceeded one hundred. The decision was then made to move branch meetings into the Wilshire Ward chapel. Because their numbers were small relative to the capacity of the chapel, the first ten rows were roped off for sacrament meeting. While this move better served the general needs of the Spanish, the fact that there was no office space available for the branch created a major problem. Consequently, President Jackson, a successful contractor by profession, moved his construction crews into the Wilshire Ward and built offices for the branch in a classroom across from the chapel.[8]

In 1968 another important Anglo leader, A. Marden Duke, became associated with the Spanish-speaking Mormon community. Duke was a local chiropractor, a member of the Hollywood Second Ward, one of the first missionaries to serve in Argentina, and a member of the Los Angeles Stake high council. When President Sant became aware that he had an ex–Spanish-speaking missionary on his high council, he assigned him to oversee the Spanish Branch.[9] Although Duke had not made a concentrated effort to maintain his Spanish, he had found occasion to use it infrequently when Spanish-speaking Saints visited the Hollywood Second Ward. Because so few Anglos spoke Spanish, a high council representative whose Spanish needed refreshing was better than one who spoke none.

Calling Duke to oversee the growth of the Hispanic Saints within the Los Angeles Stake proved to be an important boon to them. In addition to serving as the branch's high council liaison, Duke served twice as its president. He also served as bishop of the Spanish-speaking Los Angeles Fourth Ward. While many Anglos have exhibited great love towards the Hispanics, most of the Spanish-speaking Saints living within the boundaries of the Los Angeles California Stake would agree that few have shown that love as deeply as has Marden Duke. It has been reciprocated fully.

Because the stake's efforts to provide translation services during the early days of the branch were less than adequate,

Anglo leaders such as Jackson and Duke were important in teaching the Hispanic Saints how to manage all aspects of local Church organization. To help him refresh his Spanish, Duke read whatever Church handbooks and other publications he could find that had been translated into the language. As a result, he not only remastered Spanish but also became an expert on the programs of the Church.[10]

On 7 June 1970 William Jackson was released as branch president and A. Marden Duke was called to serve in his place. Under his direction, the branch was more fully organized as efforts were undertaken to establish a Primary and a seminary program. When the branch was organized, there were almost no children and few youth, but by 1970 there were seven Primary-aged children.[11]

Efforts to organize a Primary in the branch were frustrated more than once. Because most parents worked, Primary could not be held on weekday afternoons, as were most Primaries throughout the Church. At the same time, after the MIA was organized in the branch, it met on Friday night and, as in many of their homelands, most members attended. MIA thus became an organization for those from twelve to 102, not just for young people. With experience, it eventually became an activity just for the youth, but meanwhile, since many children were already coming with their parents, it was decided also to hold a Primary that night, and Florentin Bustillos was called as Primary president. It soon became clear, however, that holding Primary at such a late hour was unsatisfactory for the children. Primary was then tried on Saturday mornings, but so many other activities conflicted that the parents did not always have time to bring their children to Primary. Next, the branch tried holding Primary and Relief Society on Sunday at the same time as priesthood meeting, and this proved to be very successful. However, after one member of the General Primary Board in Salt Lake City found that the branch was holding Primary on Sunday, a strong directive was received by stake leaders stating that it was not Church policy to hold Primary on Sunday and also that it was not being done anywhere else in the Church.[12] Consequently, Primary was again tried on Saturday morning, and again it was unsuccessful.

President Duke finally brought to the attention of the stake presidency the difficulty branch leaders were having in starting a Primary and presented a plan to hold it on Sundays after all. President Sant understood the problem and, in spite of Church tradition, authorized the branch to do so. Beginning in the early 1970s, therefore, the Los Angeles Spanish Branch adopted a form of consolidated meeting schedule with all meetings, except youth activities, held on Sunday. The meetings were also scheduled back-to-back to better facilitate the attendance of the many Spanish-speaking Saints who came great distances. Otherwise, they would have to spend all day at the Wilshire Ward or miss some of their Sunday meetings. As a result, the only change the branch needed to make when the Church later adopted the three-hour consolidated meeting schedule was to shorten the time branch members spent in Sunday meetings.

In 1971 early morning seminary was instituted for the youth of the Los Angeles Spanish Branch. To make sure that the program was successfully implemented, President Duke and his counselors, Miguel Rodriguez and Roberto Ojeda, began picking up students early each morning and transporting them to the stake center by 6:45 A.M. Following seminary, they would then take the students to their various schools. This caused many problems, however, and the branch eventually changed to a home-study seminary, which met each Saturday.

Just as the Los Angeles Branch served as an important source of spiritual and social strength in the early days of the Church in Los Angeles, so also have the Spanish branches and wards. There, through association with others, the Spanish-speaking Saints have found great comfort and spiritual hope amid the problems of an everyday life often associated with minimum wages and consequent substandard living conditions. Association with the Church has become at least a partial replacement for family left behind. At the same time, even though they share the bond of a common language, and most share the experience of starting over in a new land, the Spanish-speaking Saints represent many different cultures and countries. Their great diversities, therefore, must be bridged, but without undermining their ties to the best aspects of their native cultures. Because of these special social and cultural needs, certain unique activities have been given great emphasis.

One important activity, begun by President Duke, continues to help the Spanish Saints fulfill their social needs and share their different cultures. This is the annual Fiesta Folklorica. Here, in a colorful atmosphere of native dress and decorations, food typical of the various countries is served, and this is followed by a program of traditional folk dances and music. Often this program ends with the singing of the national anthem and "God Bless America."[13]

Over the years this fiesta has served four important functions. First, it has helped the Spanish-speaking Saints to overcome differences through sharing cultures and backgrounds. Second, it has served as an important missionary tool. Church members often bring non-member relatives and friends to the fiesta where they are not only treated to an enjoyable evening, but are also exposed to the gospel. Next, as the Anglo community has begun attending these activities, the talents of the Hispanic members and the beauty of their heritage has helped to erode many prejudices against them. Finally, the fiesta has served as an important fund-raising activity for branch and ward budgets.

In October 1972 A. Marden Duke was released as branch president and called again to the high council. He continued to associate with the branch, however, serving again as high council liaison. Antonio Feliz was sustained as the new branch president, but after a year his work took him out of state. Duke was appointed in November 1973 to supervise the branch until a new president could be called, and in February 1974 President John K. Carmack called Duke to serve as branch president for a second time.

During this time the Church implemented a policy with respect to missionary work that, at least for a time, slowed down the spread of the gospel among Hispanics in the American Southwest. In Texas the Church had run into problems with U.S. immigration officials when it was discovered that some of its missionaries were actually illegal aliens as were many of those they were baptizing. Many converts had been made from among those who were entering the United States illegally in order to escape the trying economic and political conditions at home and whose circumstances had made them especially receptive to the gospel. This was interpreted, however, as Church encouragement of illegal immigration, and American officials threatened legal action to stop it. In order to avoid further problems, therefore, Church leaders adopted a policy that missionaries were not to work with those illegally in the country.[14] Instructions were issued that missionaries were not to baptize those who could not prove their citizenship or demonstrate that they were in the country legally. Missionaries then began asking for green cards and proof of citizenship. The result was that the number of baptisms greatly declined.

Following the implementation of this policy, however, many local leaders began to question its wisdom. The gospel was meant for all people, they said, regardless of where they might be living. They also observed that under the new policy missionaries were, to a certain extent, assigned to act as immigration officials and enforce the laws of the nation by checking up on citizenship. Furthermore, they said, the Church had taken too drastic a step, for under the old policy it was not really encouraging illegal immigration, it was only providing immigrants with the blessings of the gospel once they had come. If they should be required to leave the country, they would at least take those blessings with them.[15]

For their part, local Spanish leaders saw the situation as somewhat analogous to the dilemma faced by Adam and Eve in the Garden of Eden. At the same time that Adam and Eve were commanded not to eat of the forbidden fruit, they were also commanded to multiply and replenish the earth, yet these commandments were contradictory in nature. Hispanics observed that even though the immigrants had broken man's law by crossing the borders, remaining in their native countries often kept them from obeying a higher law, that of providing for their families.[16] Such cruel dilemmas were not easy to resolve, either in or out of the Church.

In 1976 the matter was reconsidered by the Brethren in Salt Lake City, and the policy was changed.[17] Once again the gospel was made available to all Spanish-speaking people in Los Angeles, regardless of their status in the country, and the work among them was accelerated. In 1977 there were 158 baptisms in the Spanish Branch, and in the first four months of 1978 there were fifty-eight.

As political unrest became more intense throughout Central and South America, the branch, as well as many wards, received greater strength in numbers and Church experience from members fleeing to the United States. Many came as political refugees, others to improve their economic conditions and to find a better life, while still others came to be reunited with family members who had already come. All came with great hope, regardless of the fact that they were unable to speak English and had no prospects for employment. Almost all found themselves in difficult situations when they arrived, and the stories of hardship will probably never be fully told. Most came without legal papers or money and with only the few personal items they could carry, and many were robbed of the few possessions they began with. Others were exploited by ruthless "coyotes" (unscrupulous people who bring illegal aliens over the border for profit), while others were abandoned in the deserts by those who were supposedly helping them.

Somehow many made their way to Los Angeles, and once they arrived they sought out the Church, relatives, friends, and shelter. Because most of the Hispanic Saints already there had once been in similar dire circumstances, they looked out for the new arrivals with the kind of special love that grows only out of hardship. Apartments already crowded, as several families shared to economize, always had room for the new ones until they could get established. There was always room for one more at the table no matter how meager the day's meal might be. One sister often greeted those in need by leaving money in their palms without a word of explanation, or wanting a word of gratitude.[18] She did this although she was not much better off than those she was helping.

By April 1978 almost five hundred people were regularly attending the sacrament meeting of the Los Angeles Spanish Branch, an increase of three hundred over five years earlier. As a result, the decision was made to divide the branch, and on 23 April 1978 the Los Angeles Third Ward and the Los Angeles Fourth Branch were created by President Rodney Brady. Rafael Seminario, who had been in the Church for only five years, was made bishop of the new Los Angeles Third Ward, while President Duke was retained as president of the Los Angeles Fourth Branch. The Third Ward continued to meet at the Wilshire Ward, but the Fourth Branch moved into the Hollywood Ward. At the time of its division, membership in the Third Ward was over four hundred, while the membership of the Fourth Branch was around two hundred. Five months later, on 17 September 1978, the Fourth Branch became the Los Angeles Fourth Ward and Duke was sustained as its first bishop.

Those who made up the leadership of the Los Angeles Third Ward presented a very interesting picture as almost all, including Bishop Seminario, had been converted in the Los Angeles Spanish Branch. A few had been members when they arrived in Los Angeles, but only Samuel Robles, the ward executive secretary, had been born in the United States.[19]

The story of Bishop Seminario is not unlike that of many Spanish-speaking members of the Church. Natives of Peru, the Seminario family first encountered the Church through missionaries in their native land. Being more interested in the missionaries as Americans than as Church members, however, they did not listen to their gospel message. Because of political and economic conditions at home, they had a desire to come to the United States to better their lives. In 1963 Jorge, the oldest son, arrived. Once in Los Angeles he began working in the kitchen of the Queen of Angels Hospital, and a portion of his wages was used to help bring other family members. One by one each son followed the same pattern as each accepted work in the kitchen of the Queen of Angels Hospital, until the entire family had arrived by 1970. Not only did family members work full-time, but they also went to school full-time; and while they had to struggle, they found the better life they had sought. This included the gospel of Jesus Christ, for within nine months they were again contacted by missionaries in California, and all members of the Seminario family were baptized.

Three important events took place between June 1978 and May 1980 which helped the Spanish-speaking Saints feel that they had finally become well integrated into the Latter-day Saints' community while in Los Angeles. The first occurred at the June 1978 stake conference when the Wilshire Ward chapel was rededicated. The Los Angeles Third Ward and Fourth Branch combined choirs, under the direction of Dwight Over, furnished the music at the conference. The invitation to participate helped the stake's Spanish-speaking members feel that indeed they were fully accepted as part of the Los Angeles Stake.

The second event was the stake roadshow festival that took place in July 1979. The Los Angeles Fourth Ward presentation, written and directed by Jaime Espinosa and Rolando Arroyo, won first place as the best roadshow in the stake. The award not only brought the warmth of justifiable pride to the stake's Hispanic population, but it also increased their confidence in the fact that they were not considered inferior by the Anglos in the stake.

The third important event occurred during the May 1980 Southern California Area Conference held at the Rose Bowl. There, before a huge audience, President Spencer W. Kimball gave a memorable address in which he commented warmly on the place of the Hispanic Saints:

> More than thirty years ago, while in Arizona, I caught something of the vision of the future of our Hispanic brothers and sisters. At that time they were few in number, had very little education, and very little of this world's goods. They were struggling to find their way in the Church. In my heart and in my mind's eye I could see a better day dawning for them. Lately I have begun to see some fulfillment of that vision, for we find these brethren and sisters coming to the temple in great numbers. They are loving fathers and mothers. Many of them are well educated and excelling in many of the areas of business, industry, and education. But this is just the beginning. They are but a vanguard of the vast numbers who will follow in their footsteps. We must do our part to help them, to lift them up, to call them to the positions of responsibility and leadership, and give them opportunities to serve so that they and their people can come into the Church by the thousands and then tens of thousands, for that is my vision, and it is a vision that we must cause to be fulfilled.[20]

When President Kimball spoke of his vision and gave this charge concerning the Hispanic people, it provided, in a way, dramatic support for the direction the Los Angeles Stake was already taking in promoting their growth and development. Some stakes in the area seemed to view the Hispanics almost as a plague, feeling that they ought to learn English and attend English-speaking wards.[21] Even if Spanish-speaking units were created, the Hispanics were often left on their own, with little energy being exerted to explain to them how the Church should be run. Early in their association with the Spanish-speaking Saints, however, Los Angeles Stake leaders adopted the attitude that while one might complain about the inconveniences caused by the Hispanic Saints, they were here to stay and should be treated as brothers and sisters in the gospel. The Church was for all people, they believed, and these Saints had just as much right to its blessings as did anyone else. Because they had special needs and problems, therefore, the stake must accommodate them, not vice versa.

Stake leaders adopted this attitude because they recognized that even though Hispanics could learn English and attend English-speaking wards, many would fall away before that would happen. Because of the size of the Los Angeles Spanish-speaking community, it was more difficult to bring them fully into American society than it was with other minority groups, for the only time they really needed English was when they attended Church. Since everyone in their neighborhoods spoke Spanish, signs were often posted in the Spanish sectors of the city which read "English is Spoken." With little motivation for learning English, therefore, there was also little desire to learn it, and many would not go through the struggle, preferring instead to drop out of Church activity.

Los Angeles Stake leaders placed great emphasis on trying to meet the special needs of the Hispanics. Following President Kimball's address, many stake members began to catch his vision, and stake leaders caught it to an even greater degree. There were some in the stake who had opposed expending so much energy working with the Spanish Saints. Stake leaders had listened patiently to their complaints, but then pushed ahead in spite of the objections, and the area conference provided warm confirmation that their decision was right.

In the Wilshire Ward, where the Anglos had the greatest contact with the Spanish and where the opposition was strongest, ward leaders were selected from among members who not only had the necessary leadership abilities but also exhibited a willingness to work with the minorities and to treat the Spanish-speaking occupants of the building as equals, rather than just tolerating them. The stake also arranged for the boys of the Los Angeles Spanish Branch to meet with the Boy Scout troop of the Wilshire Ward until the branch could organize a troop of its own.

Spanish-speaking members of the stake were given assignments at the stake level, not just for what they could do for the stake, but also because of what the calling could do in training them to be leaders. Initially, most of those who filled positions on the high council and auxiliary boards were bilingual, such as Rafael Seminario, who was called as a member of the high council in 1976. However, as means of translation improved, non-English speaking members were also called, and a translator was provided at any meeting that even one non-English speaking person was to attend.

From the beginning, stake conference sessions were translated, but this required the Hispanics to sit in special areas, such as the balcony of the Wilshire Ward chapel where special earphones were installed. Eventually, however, the stake purchased new receivers that allowed the Spanish-speaking members to sit anywhere in the congregation rather than forcing them to sit as a group. These receivers contributed greatly to their growing sense of belonging to the stake as a whole rather than being an isolated part of it.

Many hours were also put into training the Spanish-speaking Saints in all the programs of the Church, even if this required additional time and meetings. The stake Relief Society, under the direction of Ella Farnsworth, for example, held additional training meetings just for Hispanics. Farnsworth was bilingual and had spent much of her married life in Spanish-speaking countries. Shortly after she moved into the stake, President Tanner called her as president, a position with which she was very familiar, for she had served several times previously as a ward or stake Relief Society president.

After analyzing the situation concerning the Spanish, Farnsworth instructed her board to provide low-cost teaching aids, such as posters made from brown grocery bags and crayons, and to prepare for leadership meetings to be held entirely in Spanish. The Anglo sisters on the stake board were apprehensive as they prepared for the first all–Spanish-speaking leadership meeting, but they were given the names of members who could translate for them and could coach them on correct Spanish pronunciation. Also, many prayers were offered for the success of the meeting.

The training meeting and its prayer meeting were conducted entirely in Spanish; most attending did not understand a word. Later, however, board members reported that this experience had helped them to understand more fully the problems of the language barrier, and a member of the Spanish Relief Society presidency commented, "At last we can finally understand what you have been trying to teach us to do."[22] Through this and subsequent meetings, the bonds between Anglo and Spanish sisters were made stronger.

The stake presidency, high council, and other stake organizations also devoted many extra hours to help in the training process. Because Bishop Seminario had no experience in running a ward, he called upon stake leaders to help him; they willingly responded, often meeting with him until 1:00 A.M. During the first part of President William W. Tanner's administration, a great portion of his time and that of other stake leaders was spent working with the Spanish-speaking Saints. President Tanner counts as one of the greatest achievements of the stake the way so many stake members unselfishly responded to the call, and how all this not only helped create a solid core of well-trained leaders but also contributed to the growth of an impressive spiritual strength in the Spanish-speaking LDS community.[23]

Initially, because of their difficult economic situation, the Spanish Saints were not asked to pay into branch or ward budgets for maintaining local meetinghouses. A few years after the creation of the branch, however, the film "The Windows of Heaven" was shown throughout the Church. This impressive production focused on President Lorenzo Snow's special revelation in the early twentieth century on tithe paying. After watching it, stake leaders felt that if the Hispanics were to grow spiritually they must also begin to assume their full financial responsibilities.[24] Consequently, the branch was assessed a budget, though one that was substantially lower than those of English-speaking wards.

As might be expected, raising the budget money was difficult, but the stake refused to let the branch off the hook and seemed almost unmerciful in its demand for the money. At the same time, the stake presidency recognized that most Hispanic Saints simply could not give more from their meager incomes and informed the Spanish leaders that they would leave it up to them as to how they raised the money. Stake leaders recognized that the Church handbook contained a provision against wards or branches going outside their own boundaries to raise funds from Church members in other areas, but they also recognized that, if strictly enforced, that provision could cripple the Spanish branch. Realistically, therefore, they authorized and supported a modification of the rules. When branch leaders proposed inviting the stake as a whole to its annual fiestas as fundraising activities, the stake presidency, after obtaining the unanimous support of the bishops, enthusiastically encouraged stake members to come out and support the branch. It was not long before stake members found themselves eagerly looking forward to the fiestas, now packed to capacity, and often gave more for their meals than the ticket price. These fiestas continued to be effective fund-raising activities, even after several Spanish-speaking wards were created in the stake and after these wards were transferred to the Huntington Park West Stake.

The Spanish-speaking Saints also sponsored other projects to help them meet their financial responsibilities. One was collecting old newspapers. After the newspapers were collected, young and old alike gathered at the church, in homes, and in a garage rented specifically to store the papers, and rolled them into twenty-five pound rolls, which were then sold to a pottery company.

Once they started paying toward maintenance of their chapel, the Hispanic Saints also started taking greater pride in ownership. The minor problems of water left running in the bathrooms, food in the chapel, and graffiti on the bathroom walls—things which Wilshire Ward members had complained about—disappeared.[25] As a result, the Hispanic Saints were also accepted and appreciated much more readily by the Anglos.

Lacking financial means also hurt the Spanish-speaking Saints in other ways, including their involvement in youth activities. Stake leaders felt it essential, however, that the young Hispanics be involved in all activities for the youth, including Scout camps, girls' camps, and youth conferences. To facilitate this, they often invited more affluent members of the stake to help them obtain the needed funds. In connection with one youth conference held at Brigham Young University, for example, the Spanish youth who wanted to go raised over $4,000 toward the cost of attendance. Their efforts still fell short, however, so the stake presidency called people to go throughout the stake and ask those with the means to do so to provide additional assistance. The goal was met, and since then this procedure has been repeated often in support of other youth events.

When it became apparent that many Hispanic youth were not fulfilling missions because they could not afford it, the stake presidency took additional action. They promised the Spanish leaders that if they would prepare their young people to go on missions, the stake would see that they were supported in the mission field. Funds were raised through many generous—and often anonymous—donations, several Hispanic youth went on missions who otherwise would have been unable to do so, and the stake maintained its commitment to them even after the Spanish units were transferred to another stake. The faithful support by stake members to this call for funds was exemplified by one widow who donated $15,000, and then came back later to make another contribution nearly as large even though her own financial resources were hardly enough to allow it.[26]

At one time members of the Los Angeles Stake contributed more fast offerings than were needed to care for the poor in the stake. However, as the number of Spanish-speaking Saints grew, the stake presidency and stake Relief Society presidency made arrangements with Spanish leaders to assist families as they arrived, recognizing that whether they were legally in the country or not they were still brothers and sisters who must be cared for. New arrivals were furnished with their first and last month's rent and a food order. Rarely, however, have those assisted turned up again on the Church's welfare rolls. This fact has made the leaders of the Los Angeles California Stake enthusiastic believers in helping the Spanish Saints as they try so hard to help themselves.[27]

The work of the Los Angeles Stake with the Spanish-speaking Saints has extended far beyond its boundaries as they, like other groups, have continually moved in and out of the stake. Because of its central location—the bus station is within the boundaries of the Third Ward—the stake has been home at least temporarily for most of the Hispanics arriving in Los Angeles. While some stay only briefly, many remain long enough to be trained in some aspect of Church leadership before leaving for better employment in other parts of the city or in other cities.

By June 1983 the number of Spanish-speaking Saints in the stake had grown to almost one thousand, with the majority residing in the Los Angeles Third Ward. The decision was made to create three Spanish-speaking wards. At a special meeting of the Los Angeles Third and Fourth Wards on 26 June 1983, the boundaries of the wards were changed and the Los Angeles Sixth Ward was created from the southern portion of the Los Angeles Third Ward. Like the Third Ward, the Sixth Ward also shared the Wilshire Ward chapel. Gustavo Velasquez, a former high councilor in Guatemala who came to the United States to escape political persecution, was sustained as bishop of the new ward. At the same meeting, Bishop A. Marden Duke was released after twelve years of presiding over the Los Angeles Spanish Branch and the Los Angeles Fourth Branch and Ward and was again called to be a member of the high council. Mario Mendoza, former second counselor in the Los Angeles Fourth Ward, was sustained as the new bishop.

Not only was work increasing among the Spanish-speaking people in the Los Angeles Stake, but it was also growing in the surrounding stakes. In 1969 a Spanish Branch was established in the Santa Monica Stake. The Huntington Park Ward was organized as a Spanish-speaking ward on 16 April 1978, with English-speaking members transferred to other wards in the Huntington Park Stake. Three years later, in August 1981, the Grant Ward was created from a division of the Huntington Park Ward. In the Inglewood Stake, the Inglewood Second Ward was organized 21 December 1980. In addition, ten other Spanish-speaking units were operating in the greater Los Angeles area, a total of seventeen units scattered between Torrance and Hacienda Heights.

Because of the tremendous growth among the Spanish-speaking, the need for special leadership training became apparent, and a special multi-regional auxiliary training meeting was held at the Los Angeles stake center on 10 December 1983. This meeting demonstrated that there were sufficient numbers of strong Hispanic leaders who could assume stake leadership positions. As a result, the stake presidencies of the Huntington Park, Inglewood, Los Angeles, and Santa Monica stakes began taking the steps necessary for the creation of the first Spanish-speaking stake in the United States.

As early as 1972 a recommendation was made that a Spanish-speaking stake should be created in Los Angeles.[28] No action was taken at the time, however, for even though there were enough members, sufficient leadership had not been developed. Nevertheless, it was the general feeling that it would be only a matter of time until the first Spanish-speaking stake was created, and that this would take place in the eastern portion of Los Angeles, where the Hispanics were more well established. The Spanish-speaking Saints in the western portion of the city, however, had greater support from English-speaking leaders who envisioned their potential and had prepared them for that day.

In 1984 the Brethren in Salt Lake City finally gave approval for the creation of a Spanish-speaking stake on an experimental basis.[29] On 3 June the Spanish-speaking Saints from the Huntington Park, Inglewood, Los Angeles, and Santa Monica stakes gathered in the Huntington Park Stake Center for the momentous occasion. In attendance were Elder Howard W. Hunter of the Council of the Twelve, Elder Robert L. Backman of the First Quorum of the Seventy and the Executive Administrator of the Southern California Area, and Elder John K. Carmack of the First Quorum of the Seventy and a member of the Los Angeles California Stake presidency when the Spanish branch was organized. Local leaders present included the Regional Representative, Elder Nile A. Sorenson; President Robert T. Pratt of the Huntington Park California Stake; President Lloyd E. Carlson of the Inglewood California Stake; President William W. Tanner of the Los Angeles California Stake; and President Herb T. Patten of the Los Angeles California Santa Monica Stake. Sadly, many of the Anglos who had worked hard for this day were not able to attend because of a lack of room.

The new stake, with a membership in excess of 2200, consisted of seven wards: Grant, Huntington Park, Inglewood, La Cienega (its name changed from the Santa Monica Spanish Branch at this time), and the Los Angeles Third, Fourth, and Sixth Wards. The new stake was named the Huntington Park West Stake, and its offices were located in the Huntington Park stake center. The stake presidency consisted of President Rafael N. Seminario, former bishop of the Los Angeles Third Ward; First Counselor Francisco Yanez, former bishop of the Grant Ward; Second Counselor Ramon Riquelme, former president of the Santa Monica Spanish Branch; and Edger Orellana as stake clerk.

President William W. Tanner of the Los Angeles Stake was one of those who had worked long and enthusiastically for this historic occasion. The love and hope he and other stake members felt for the Hispanic people were well expressed in his statement published in the program issued that day: "We will miss the life the Los Angeles Third, Fourth, and Sixth Wards have given to the Stake. Their warmth, affection, brotherhood and sisterhood, has been shared with love and respect. Today is the realization of a dream, and the way to the fulfillment of a vision."[30]

During the meeting, President Seminario expressed gratitude for the efforts of Anglo Church leaders and the faith the General Authorities had placed in the abilities of the Hispanics:

> We're happy the Brethren have seen fit to form the stake, giving us the opportunity to be in leadership positions.
>
> We are going to have many challenges, but we think we have a lot of brothers and sisters who are ready and willing to put forth the extra effort that it requires to bring forth the work now in this new stake.
>
> We have had the opportunity to work in the Anglo wards. We have learned a lot and this is probably the best test for everybody to see how much we have learned.[31]

While very excited at having a stake for the Spanish-speaking people, President Seminario later noted that he was also sad that the Anglos and Hispanics had been split because both groups had something to share and to teach.[32] The Anglos had taught the Hispanics how to run the Church on a ward and stake level and had shared of their abundance. The Hispanics had taught many Anglos humility, a humility resulting from life's experiences, as well as lessons in sacrifice. They had also shared an enthusiasm for life and a devotion to the gospel which they would not allow trials to diminish.

An example of the give-and-take between the two groups is seen in a Christmas tradition in which members of the stake "adopted" Spanish-speaking families for Christmas to ensure that they would have an enjoyable day. Prior to one Christmas, Bishop Seminario received a phone call from the father of an Anglo family wondering what was the best way to get the presents and food they had purchased to their Hispanic family. "Should we leave it at the chapel?" he was asked. Bishop Seminario replied that while the family did not live on the best street in Los Angeles, the area nevertheless could be visited safely before dark. He urged the man, therefore, to take his entire family to visit the Spanish family, who lived in a rundown building in a very poor part of town and consisted of a young mother and seven children who had been abandoned by their father. A few days later, Bishop Seminario received another call from the same man, who gratefully told him how much he appreciated being asked to visit the family. He said that after seeing how little the family had, the great love family members exhibited, and the good-natured way they accepted their plight, his family had come to better appreciate what they had and realized that they had taken too much for granted.[33]

As the number of Hispanics in Los Angeles continues to increase, many projections concerning the Church suggest that they will become the largest group in the central city, and that the Anglos will, to a certain degree, turn the guardianship of the Church in that area over to the Spanish-speaking Saints. If the past is any indication, they will be equal to the task, in spite of the many challenges they face.

After one stake conference, President Seminario found one of his stake members, an older sister, standing on the corner. When he asked her what she was doing still there, she told him that she had come to the conference on the bus, that this had required several hours and numerous transfers, and now she could not remember how to get back home.[34] This sister's faithfulness in coming to stake conference regardless of the inconvenience is typical of that seen throughout the Spanish-speaking population in the Church, and it has helped the Hispanics average over 60 percent attendance at sacrament meeting before the stake was created and over 65 percent following its creation. These figures stand in stark contrast to the surrounding wards and stakes, where the average is around 40 percent.

Since its organization, the Huntington Park West Stake has averaged over half of the region's baptisms—enough to create a ward a year. Many of these new converts, however, move out of the stake following their baptism. Nevertheless, the stake has a fine record of retaining its converts in the Church, largely through the dedication of such men as Luis Arteaga, the Los Angeles Sixth Ward mission leader who has visited as many as thirty new families each month. Such fellowshipping efforts are essential to the vitality of the Church, and here the Hispanics take a back seat to no one.

The accomplishments of the Spanish Saints are truly amazing when the challenges they have had to overcome are considered. At the same time, major problems and challenges remain, some of which are unique to the stake. The greatest of these is its poor economic situation. When the Huntington Park West Stake was created, a majority of the poorest Saints from the Huntington Park, Inglewood, Los Angeles, and Santa Monica stakes were brought together into one stake. Consequently, the four stakes from which it drew provided the new stake with a sizeable financial base from which to operate.

However, this base will not be sufficient for all the expenses, and the Hispanic Saints eventually must find a way to make their stake fully self-sufficient.

Since most members do not speak English and many are relatively undereducated, they often do not earn more than the minimum wage. As a result, many are forced to work two jobs, often up to sixteen hours a day, just to make ends meet, with little money left over to give to the Church. There are other members, especially new arrivals, who, like other Hispanics, are exploited by ruthless elements in the economic system. When some have gone to pick up their paychecks, for example, they have been greeted not with money but with threats of deportation. Others have been underpaid. One young man worked fourteen hours a day and received fifteen dollars for his labors.

The need to work up to sixteen hours a day just to survive, and then still having constant financial worries, leaves precious little time for Church work. This lack of time, in fact, has been more damaging to the strength of the Hispanic wards than lack of money. Unlike most wards, where members are well established and have most evenings and weekends free for Church work, the Spanish Saints, as a rule, are simply unable to give as much time to the Church as other members. Consequently, many programs, such as home teaching and visiting teaching, have suffered, as around 50 percent of the families are visited each month.

Those who have analyzed the situation suggest that the stake's greatest long-range need is for the members to obtain college educations.[35] It is only through an education that the Hispanic Saints can move into better neighborhoods, have greater financial stability, and have better working hours, thus allowing them to give more time and means to the Lord. Stake leaders stress that obtaining an education is the only way to escape the vicious economic environment in which Hispanics find themselves, and the best way for a man to help himself, his family, and his Church. To do this on top of everything else poses a formidable challenge, but one that must be met before the Hispanic Saints can achieve their full potential either as individuals or as a stake.

Another problem facing the stake is that almost half its families are single-parent families. Most of these families are headed by females with several children. As a result, in most wards there is a shortage of priesthood, and some wards assign ten families to each pair of home teachers.

This shortage of priesthood holders is especially critical because, as President Seminario explains, each day the young people confront a literal hell as they face problems such as gangs and drugs, which are greatly magnified in the Spanish sections of the city.[36] Because of these evil influences, it is especially important that someone, such as a bishop or Scoutmaster, care for these fatherless youth and help them overcome the challenges. It is the large number of youth that has helped to keep the Spanish wards vibrant, and there is great hope for the future of the Church among Hispanics if they can hold onto their youth.

In the early days of the Los Angeles Spanish Branch, some members of the Wilshire Ward complained that the Spanish youth were always present at the building, and asked if they did not have homes to go to. It was difficult for them to realize that for many, because of poor conditions in their neighborhoods and homes, spending the evening at the meetinghouse was often better than going home, and certainly preferable to being on the streets.[37] As a result, on most nights except Monday, the Spanish youth have met together at the chapel. Basketball, new to most of them, has become a favorite sport. Indoor soccer, volleyball, and dances have also become important. Along with being helpful in keeping the LDS youth in close contact with the Church, these activities have also brought non-Mormon youth off the streets and into a favorable environment, with many new converts as a result.

Another challenge leaders must address is related to the fact that as the youth have become acculturated to the American way of life, some have lost the desire to attend Spanish-speaking wards and branches.[38] For parents who speak English, this presents only a minor problem, but for those who do not, this could become a major problem.

The idea of organizing a Spanish stake was, of course, controversial, but everything that has happened so far suggests not only that it will work, but also that it was the desirable thing to do. Hispanics still need patience as they strive to reach their full potential, but the vision of President Kimball is beginning to be fulfilled. With the continued patience and understanding efforts of Hispanic and Anglo alike, that vision will be realized. Already prophecy is being fulfilled in a grand and humbling way.

Microcosm of a Worldwide Church

Following his release as a counselor in the Los Angeles Stake presidency, William W. Tanner was called as executive secretary to Ralph Chalker, Regional Representative of the Twelve. At a regional meeting held a week after the rededication of the Wilshire Ward chapel, however, President Rodney H. Brady told Tanner that he had accepted the position of president of Weber State College in Ogden, Utah. At that point, President Tanner recounts, the Spirit came over him and he was impressed that he was to be the next stake president.[1] Subsequently, on 30 July 1978, William W. Tanner was set apart by Elder L. Tom Perry of the Council of the Twelve as the eleventh president of the stake.

President Tanner retained Robert H. Millard and Stephen Eldredge as counselors. When President Eldredge was released to complete his Ph.D. at New York University in 1979, Royal Peterson was called to take his place, and when President Peterson died of cancer in 1980, David Youkstetter was called into the stake presidency. Lynn O. Poulson succeeded President Youkstetter, and later Howard B. Anderson replaced President Millard.

President Tanner, a native of Salt Lake City, was the grandson of Henry S. Tanner, the mission president who established the Los Angeles Branch. From 1956 to 1958 he served a mission in the central Atlantic states, where his grandfather and brother had previously filled missions. Following his mission, he graduated from the University of Utah and then was accepted into the USC dental school, where his brother was on the faculty. In August 1959, shortly before moving to Los Angeles, he married Elizabeth Findlay in the St. George Temple.

Two major events in these early years had great impact on the shaping of President Tanner's life. The first occurred between his first and second year at USC, when he was spending most of his time working on Sundays and was unable to attend church regularly. This led him to feel that he would put aside his church activity until after graduation. The Sunday following this decision, however, he was called by President John M. Russon to preside over the elders quorum in the USC ward. "This really had to be the hand of the Lord," he thought, for he had made a conscious decision not to go to church.[2]

The second event occurred while he was a member of the stake high council under President Winfield Cannon and held the assignment as advisor to the stake M Men. Elder Paul H. Dunn had arranged a solemn assembly at the Los Angeles Temple for all single endowed men. President Tanner attended in his high council capacity. Those in attendance sat silently for at least half an hour before the meeting began, and as he sat there he thought, "Bill Tanner, here you sit in probably the most sacred place you will ever be, the house of the Lord, the place where perhaps even the Savior himself has walked, and yet outside the temple is a city that could be called a real Sodom and Gomorrah." At that point he made a renewed commitment never to be involved in activities inappropriate to the Spirit.[3]

When L. Tom Perry spoke at the stake conference where President Tanner was sustained, he summed up the situation in the stake very well by saying that it represented a microcosm of the world, since natives of many of the nations of the world were found within its boundaries. He further urged stake members to take the gospel to those people, so that they could then take it to their homelands.[4]

By the 1980s the diversity within the Los Angeles Stake indeed made it a microcosm of a worldwide Church. Within Hollywood Ward, for example, at least twenty-seven languages were spoken. Often, the first impression one received of the stake was its international flavor. For example, when a stake Primary children's chorus sang "I am a Child of God" at stake conference, they seemed to represent all races and nationalities. This variety gave true meaning to the song, which was co-authored by Mildred Tanner Pettit, a one-time member of the stake and an aunt of President Tanner. Her patriarchal blessing told her that her music would be an influence throughout the world, and this song has been a direct fulfillment of that prophecy. She woke up one night with the music running through her mind and immediately wrote it down. The next day when she contacted Naomi W. Randall, she learned that Sister Randall had received the words to the song in a similar way.[5] Today, not only in the stake where Mildred Pettit once lived but throughout the world, children of different races and national origins sing that song together, reinforcing its truth that all are God's children. Such an attitude did not come easily in Los Angeles, but in the two decades before 1987 the stake watched prejudices melt away as people of various races and nationalities were brought together and learned to know and love each other in spite of differences.

Stake leaders under President Tanner continued to strive to develop a sense of pride in the "microcosm" makeup of the stake and to teach the value of all people, regardless of skin color or nationality. They were concerned that the gospel remain relevant in the lives of members by having the stake serve all the people who lived within its boundaries. Following this leadership, the members took increasing pride in their stake, recognizing that its ethnic diversity made it unique among stakes in the Church. The challenge, they recognized, was to become unified in action and faith, not dress and language.

Because of these efforts in the stake, most of the minorities were made to feel that they were loved, wanted, accepted, and important to the success of the stake. It was clear that any criticism of a minority would not have a sympathetic reception among stake leaders. If tensions arose, stake leaders tried to respond quickly by expressing love and support. The minority groups, because of their enthusiasm, became the life-blood of the stake.

The changing nature of the stake, however, created some significant challenges. It became difficult, for example, not only to keep positions filled, but to keep them filled with experienced

Church members. One of the things stake leaders had to learn was to do away with the classical image of a leader in the Church: older, married, financially secure, and steeped in the LDS tradition. The situation was somewhat reminiscent of the time when a young, inexperienced John Taylor said to Joseph Smith during the infancy of the Church, "We're the very best that the Lord has to give you." As President Tanner put it for the modern Church:

> You have to come to the point that you understand that this is the Lord's Church, that all of these people are His children, and that the Gospel reaches into the hearts of every man regardless of his status in life or his educational level and . . . it is for all of them. Therefore, there has got to be someone there that the Lord is preparing for the call. . . . It is amazing what happens because the Lord really blesses the individuals that are called. If they have the right attitude and the right spirit, the Lord fills in the gaps.[6]

The changing nature of the stake also had an impact upon its finances. For years, the stake had a very strong financial base, but this slowly eroded as families from the upper economic brackets moved away and were replaced by many with modest financial means. Thus, while members of the stake responded to Church teachings concerning fast offerings and substantially increased their contributions, their efforts often were not sufficient for the changes taking place. Where the stake once had a regular surplus and was a major contributor to the general Church fast-offering fund, there were times in the 1980s when the stake had to rely upon Church funds to meet its needs.

There were many other important activities and changes in the stake during President Tanner's administration. In April 1979 the new Institute of Religion building adjacent to USC was opened at 1057 W. 30th Street. At services held on 26 April, Elder Paul H. Dunn dedicated the building. Another major change: in March 1980 the Church put a new consolidated meeting schedule into operation Church-wide. Prior to this time, however, several of the wards and branches in Los Angeles Stake had adopted a form of consolidated schedule in order to adjust to the problems and realities of living in a huge metropolitan area. In these cases the only change needed was shortening the time spent at Church.

Sunday, 6 April 1980, marked the sesquicentennial of The Church of Jesus Christ of Latter-day Saints. The Los Angeles

California Stake joined in celebrating this milestone by partici-pating in two major events. One, appropriately, was an "ethnic dinner" held at the stake center, along with a lecture by Leonard J. Arrington, former Church historian. Entitled "Church History from a Different Point of View," the lecture reviewed 150 years of Church history through the lives of lesser-known Saints. The other event was a dance festival held at the Rose Bowl in Pasadena in July. Nearly ten thousand dancers performed before some seventy-five thousand spectators, in-cluding celebrities and civic and religious leaders.

With the continued growth of the Church it became ever more complicated to have representatives from around the world gather at the semiannual general conferences in Salt Lake City. Church leaders, therefore, began a series of area con-ferences, whereby Church leaders would go to various parts of the world to meet with the Saints. Initially they were held only outside North America, with the first one in Manchester, Eng-land, in 1971, but beginning in 1979 they were also held in the United States. Rapidly improving technology, however, soon re-sulted in the increased use of satellite broadcasts, and these provided greater access to general conference. Area conferences were discontinued, therefore, by 1981.

In May 1980 an area conference was also held at the Rose Bowl. Church leaders in attendance included Presidents Spencer W. Kimball and Marion G. Romney of the First Presi-dency; Elders David B. Haight and Howard W. Hunter of the Quorum of the Twelve; Bishop Victor L. Brown, Presiding Bishop of the Church; Elder Vaughn J. Featherstone, California Area Supervisor; Elaine Cannon, president of the Young Women; and Barbara B. Smith, president of the Relief Society. This was the largest gathering of Mormons in history as over 30,000 attended the Saturday women's session and more than 80,000 people filled the Rose Bowl for the Sunday sessions. A four-thousand-voice choir provided the music on Sunday. The conference was translated into seven languages and gave new impetus to the work of the Los Angeles Stake in its multi-ethnic diversity.

In his keynote address, President Kimball charged leaders and members to reach out to the minorities and to increase their missionary efforts. This included not only preparing every young man for a mission and praying that the Lord would touch the hearts of the leaders of nations so that missionaries might be allowed to enter, but also carrying the gospel message to the people of California:

> There is a great possibility that we, the members of the Church, may not have been doing our total duty. To some extent we have been bypassing our neighbors. There are millions of great and wonderful Protestants and Catholics and others and they need and want the gospel. They may not know they want it, but they want it just the same. And you and I—only we can give it to them. The gospel is without price. . . . The Lord has said that when you have been warned, warn your neighbor. Now that comes as a command to you and me. It is not left to our discretion or to our pleasure or to our convenience. Every man and woman should return home from this conference with the determination that they will take the gospel to their relatives and their friends. And if they do not, they must consider that they are not in total favor of their Heavenly Father, because he has commanded us to do so.[7]

Immediately following the conference, the wards and stakes throughout the Los Angeles region took President Kimball's message to heart and held informal open houses in their chapels to introduce non-Mormons to the Church's family-oriented way of life.

Even prior to the area conference, the changing makeup of Los Angeles gave missionary work an added importance. The fact that many Saints had moved out and so few had moved in meant an increased potential for missionary work. For the seven years prior to the creation of the Huntington Park West Stake, while the Spanish-speaking Saints remained members of the Los Angeles California Stake, it led the California Los Angeles Mission in baptisms. Even after the creation of that Spanish-speaking stake in 1984, the Los Angeles Stake was consistently the second highest baptizing stake in the area.

Much of the missionary success was due to the leadership of Michael Grilikhes, stake mission president. President Grilikhes, a successful television and movie producer, upgraded the stake mission program, and through his efforts the Saints were motivated to move forward with missionary efforts. When Roy Richardson was bishop of the Wilshire Ward, for example, his goal was twenty stake missionaries from his ward, and one year there were over seventy baptisms in the ward. To help missionary work move forward in the UCLA Ward, a Book of Mormon project was begun. In each sacrament meeting, a ward member related his or her experience in giving out a Book of Mormon.

Those who were reluctant to pass out books soon gained courage, and before long nearly everyone in the ward was giving out copies of the Book of Mormon to non-LDS friends and acquaintances.[8]

Because of the affluent nature of some areas in the western portion of the stake, such as Beverly Hills, Westwood, Bel Air, and Cheviot Hills, most non-members there were satisfied with their position in life and saw no need for a change, especially regarding religion. As a consequence, the results from regular missionary work, such as tracting, were not highly successful in these areas. A major missionary effort was made, therefore, among the part-member families and this became an effective program. In the Westwood wards, for example, several counselors in bishoprics—John B. Cahoon, David L. Scoll,—originally came from part-member families.[9]

While the stake worked to bring new members into the gospel, it also worked to ensure unity among the stake family, something that was becoming more difficult to maintain as the stake grew to become like a miniature United Nations. Unfortunately, people from different cultures not only were the victims of prejudiced Anglo-Americans, but also often held biases against each other. Just as Brigham Young had struggled in the early days of the Church to unify English, Danish, and Swedish converts in Utah, so also Los Angeles Stake leaders worked to unify the Spanish-speaking, the Orientals, and the Anglos. Their philosophy was that if you get to know someone, you learn to love him. If there were problems with prejudice, they felt, they could be overcome if the Saints in the stake could really get to know one another.[10]

To accomplish this, the stake adopted several "low-risk" multicultural activities. One was a series of "International Food Fairs," which were actually an extension of the Spanish fiestas and focused attention on the fact that there were many cultures represented in the stake. These were initially started by the stake Young Women's presidency under the direction of Louise LaCount. The first one was held 14 May 1983.[11] They brought together people from many of the cultures in the stake and allowed them to demonstrate the special qualities of their cultures. In addition, wards such as USC and UCLA were assigned different countries to represent with food and artifacts. A growing group of Filipinos from the Wilshire Ward roasted a pig on a spit. Other nationalities, including Chinese, Koreans, Guatemalans, Salvadorans, Peruvians, Argentineans, and Armenians demonstrated their culture. Helen Kennedy of the Wilshire Ward came dressed in colorful clothes and a red bandanna, looking like she just came off an old Southern plantation, and served food such as corn bread and ribs and talked about her culture. In addition to the food fairs, Wilshire Ward sponsored an "All Nations Night" which continued the tradition of native costumes and unique and exotic cuisine.

At Christmas time, the stake Primary sponsored an international Christmas party at the stake center where the different nationalities decorated Christmas trees in the traditional manner of their country. Holiday foods from a variety of nations were served as examples of Christmas as celebrated in many countries. The first was held in December 1980 and all those who came were asked also to donate a wrapped present for the needy.

Another event that helped unify the various ethnic groups was the stake priesthood dinner meeting. In 1951 President Russon introduced this tradition in hopes of increasing attendance at the monthly priesthood meetings.[12] The dinners proved so successful that they were continued until President Carmack was installed, at which time Elder Howard W. Hunter suggested that they might have outlived that purpose. Under President Tanner, however, they were reinstated as opportunities for stake members to get together for brotherhood.[13] By that time the Church had changed its priesthood meeting schedule so that these stake meetings were held only twice a year on Saturday night. As the dinners were re-inaugurated, responsibility for them was rotated among the wards. When the Korean branch had the responsibility, the stake ate Korean food; when the Hollywood Ward had its turn, it often prepared Armenian food; the Spanish wards served Mexican food and the Chinese branch served Chinese food. These dinners provided marvelous opportunities for priesthood members to get to know one another better and were appropriate preludes to the priesthood meeting, which was held in the chapel.

One man who provided tremendous help to the stake in its work among the minorities was President Briton McConkie of the California Los Angeles Mission. He had a great vision of what could be done. Missionary work among the English-speaking people was not going very well when he took over the mission in 1978, so he decided to focus his attention on the minorities. He believed that one of his special missions was to strengthen existing minority units and establish new minority ones in Los Angeles.[14] He worked diligently to carry forward that work.

Following the revelation on the priesthood, missionary work among members of the black community increased, and there was a rapid influx of black members of the Church. President McConkie was anxious to have a branch of the Church established in the Watts area, the center of the black community in Los Angeles, just as branches had been established for other minority groups. He felt that blacks would gain a great deal of strength from such an organization and thus lay the groundwork for continuing the great strides being made in their community.[15] Eventually, a thriving branch, the Southwest Branch of the Huntington Park Stake, was established there.

When the Southwest Branch was initially organized, black members from throughout Los Angeles were invited to attend in order to give it sufficient strength. President Tanner and his counselors recognized that such a branch was necessary in the Watts area, but they also felt that the strength provided by black members was greatly needed in the Los Angeles Stake. They felt that as the complexion of the community changed, the complexion of the ward should also change. Because there were no language barriers that would discourage blacks from functioning in traditional wards, stake leaders felt that these members should attend the wards in whose boundaries they lived and receive leadership training in an established ward.

When the Southwest Branch was organized, wise and proper procedures were not always followed in recruiting potential members. As a result, some black Saints in the Los Angeles Stake became disenchanted with the Church, interpreting the invitation to attend this branch as an attempt to segregate them.[16] In spite of such problems, however, the Southwest Branch proved a blessing to the blacks in the Watts area, and in the Los Angeles Stake the Wilshire Ward in particular soon began to enjoy the blessings of its growing black membership.

Another ethnic group to be incorporated into the Los Angeles Stake was the Chinese, though the branch actually had its beginnings in 1978 in the Elysian Park Ward of the Glendale

Stake.[17] A member of that ward, David Honey, had recently returned from a mission to Hong Kong and had come to live in Chinatown. Honey, whose thoughts and actions were more consistent with Chinese culture than were those of most Americans, was one of the few non-Asians to be fully accepted into that community. There were several Chinese members of the Elysian Park Ward, and Honey took the initiative to organize a family home evening group for the Chinese-speaking members of the ward. The lessons were taught in Chinese with each member taking a turn teaching the others. Shortly thereafter, permission was given to start a Chinese Sunday School class in the ward.

President McConkie had served as the Church's legal counsel in Asia, where he developed a great love for the Asian people; as with the blacks, he had a special desire to strengthen the work among the Asians in Los Angeles. Under his direction, Cantonese-speaking and Mandarin-speaking missionaries were transferred from Hong Kong and Taiwan to labor in Los Angeles.

By 1979 the nucleus of the Chinese group had moved from Elysian Park Ward to Huntington Park Ward. Under the direction of President McConkie, and with the approval of President R. Don Smith of the Huntington Park California Stake, a Chinese group was organized in February 1979. The Chinese retained membership in their home wards but attended meetings with the group. The first meeting was held on 19 February 1979, with Elder Kent Flake, a full-time missionary, serving as presiding elder.

Following its organization, the group struggled to maintain its existence—it had little local leadership and the missionaries were unable to give the necessary time and still do the required missionary work. In addition, meeting in Huntington Park had proven less than ideal. Realizing the importance of helping to improve the situation for the Chinese Saints, however, the Los Angeles California Stake gave its assistance. Among other things, the stake provided a more central location for investigators and members, and the group moved into the annex of the Wilshire Ward. Shortly after that, on 3 August 1980, the Los Angeles Fifth Branch, the first independent Chinese branch in southern California, was organized. Branch boundaries included the confines of the California Los Angeles Mission and drew membership from the San Fernando Valley on the north to Orange County on the south. Fifty-one people attended the organizational meeting, held under the direction of President William W. Tanner, Ted Hi Ong, an American-born Oriental who was serving as a counselor to Wilshire Ward Bishop Roy Richardson, was sustained as branch president, with David Honey and Da Wei Zhang as counselors. Mo Ping Mo was called as Relief Society president. On 31 December 1980, membership stood at twenty-five.

Through these difficult times, the branch maintained its progress largely because of the hard work and sacrifices of Ted and Amelia Ong and Anglo-Americans such as David Honey and James and Donna Jean Moore. The Moores had developed an initial interest in the Chinese branch because their son had served a mission to Taiwan. Because the Chinese lacked priesthood, James Moore helped them prepare the sacrament each Sunday following his regular meetings at the Wilshire Ward. He then told the stake presidency that he and his wife had developed a great love for the Chinese and wondered if there was something they could do for them.[18] James was soon called to be branch clerk. Donna Jean Moore was called to be the branch Primary president, and a successful Primary program began. Although the active Primary membership in the branch had been only four or five children, the ranks occasionally reached twenty-five or thirty as members brought their friends. It was at this Primary, in fact, that many Asians were taught of Jesus Christ for the first time. The Moores were a great strength to members of the branch, most of whom were comparatively young, as they provided counsel, stability, and the comfort of an older generation. They also brought the open, warm affection common among Americans to a culture noted for its discipline and where affection was shown through personal sacrifice rather than emotional expression.

By early 1982 the branch was still struggling, as attendance at sacrament meeting was often as low as thirteen persons, including children. Thought was given to dissolving the unit, but during the summer a number of strong priesthood holders moved into the branch. As a result, the branch moved from having only two Melchizedek priesthood holders when organized to sufficient numbers for full priesthood leadership, including a full elders quorum presidency. The Relief Society also grew to a strong membership with an excellent spirit. By the end of the year the Chinese branch was a viable unit as sacrament meeting attendance averaged forty people.

With the growing numbers of Hispanics using the Wilshire Ward chapel, it soon became apparent that the Chinese branch would again have to search for a permanent home. Bishop Nadle of the Hollywood Ward offered assistance. As a result, the members of the Hollywood Ward put their arms around their Chinese brothers and sisters, making them a part of the larger great work. Frequently, for example, they included the Chinese branch in their activities and invited the Chinese to their meetings. In May 1982 the branch began meeting in the Hollywood chapel on Sunday morning, simultaneously with the Hollywood Ward, and this allowed the children of the branch and the ward to meet together in Primary and Sunday School classes. This arrangement was also more favorable for investigators and members alike and made it easier for those who had to use public transportation to come to meetings. The Chinese youth also began to meet with the youth of Hollywood Ward for their various activities.

The Chinese branch is noted for the positive attitude of its members and their great esprit de corps and brotherhood. On stake temple nights the Chinese often have 100 percent of their temple recommend holders in attendance. In October 1983 the branch sponsored "An Evening in China," which featured a Chinese dinner and show. This event stemmed from the Chinese Saints' desire to make a contribution towards the building of the Taiwan Temple, to share the temple blessings they enjoyed in Los Angeles. Through their efforts, the branch raised over $1500 for the Taiwan Temple fund.[19]

March 1981 marked the twenty-fifth anniversary of the Los Angeles Temple, and special activities were planned to mark that event. The temple president, Elder Robert L. Simpson of the First Quorum of the Seventy, asked the Los Angeles Stake to serve as host. Invited guests included the former temple presidents and matrons: Benjamin and Leone Bowring, Myrthus and Mae Evans, and Richard and Sally Stratford. On Saturday 14 March, a reception was held for the former temple presidents at the Westwood Ward, and special temple sessions were planned for stake members that weekend. As a special part of the commemoration, the temple remained open for thirty-six continuous hours. Beginning Friday, 20 March, at 7:30 A.M., sessions started throughout the day and night at half-hour intervals with the last session at 6:30 P.M., Saturday, 21 March.[20] When the temple first opened, only four daily sessions were offered; By the mid 1980s the number had grown to twenty. It was not unusual during the evenings and on Saturdays for all the parking on the temple grounds to be filled and members desiring to attend the temple having to park outside the complex.

Over the years the temple has, indeed, blessed and enriched the lives of the members of the Los Angeles Stake. They have been able to attend the temple to perform baptisms, endowments, and sealings for themselves and for the dead. By the mid 1980s, most active members of the stake married in the temple. In addition, stake members volunteered their time to work in the genealogical library and spent countless hours extracting names from microfilm records.

During June 1983, several changes took place to enhance further the "microcosmic" makeup of the Los Angeles Stake. In addition to the creation of the Los Angeles Sixth Ward, the Korean branch was split for the second time, with the new branch becoming part of the Chatsworth California Stake in the San Fernando Valley. The branch had been divided previously, when membership reached about 150, and the second branch became part of the Torrance Stake, though later it was transferred to the Cerritos Stake. This initial division was undertaken without the knowledge of President Tanner and in so doing reduced the critical mass, and hence the strength, of the branch in Los Angeles and slowed its growth rate.[21] The Chatsworth branch grew at a faster rate because many Koreans saw better opportunities for integrating themselves into American culture and helping their children become Americanized by moving into the suburban areas in the valley. By 1987 the number of Koreans in the three branches had grown to around 250 members. They frequently came together for social activities. Soon they proposed that a district-type organization be established for them in preparation for a Korean stake.

Another major challenge to the Los Angeles Stake has been meeting the needs of the youth. One youth program for which it has become well known is Scouting. In 1963, for example, Wilshire Ward was chosen as the best scout troop in the Church and President John M. Russon was awarded the Silver Beaver award, one of the highest awards given by the Boy Scouts in recognition of service to youth.

There was a period of time, however, when Scouting did not enjoy such a high level of achievement in the Los Angeles Stake. Considerable credit for the renewed emphasis goes to Walt Parker, an administrator in the Los Angeles school system and, in the late 1960s, the non-LDS Scoutmaster of the Arlington Ward where his wife was a member. His Scout troop was composed largely of young men who were wards of the court and, as part of their penalties, were required to participate in Scouting. In spite of this, Walt Parker had a marvelous troop and one superior to the others in the stake.[22]

As a result, members of the stake presidency carefully examined the Scouting program and the needs of the youth and decided they were going to make the program work. They determined that the greatest work they could do was in the area of preventing the youth from becoming inactive and building future leaders.[23] They resolved to put a high priority on the youth program, particularly Scouting, and place high quality leaders in these programs. As a result, several prominent leaders were released to work in Scouting. Lynn O. Poulson was a member of the Westwood Second Ward bishopric when he was released to be that ward's Scoutmaster. Paul Weenig and C. Burton Stohl were released from the high council. Thomas M. Anderson, who had become an Eagle Scout as a youth in the Wilshire Ward, was put on the high council with the responsibility of overseeing the Scouting programs. In addition, the youth programs also had two strong advocates in the stake presidency in William W. Tanner and Rodney H. Brady. Both men were avid Scouters. Each had received the Silver Beaver Award and served at the local, regional, and national levels of the Boy Scouts in addition to their duties in the stake presidency. President Tanner served on the Los Angeles executive board of the Area Council of the Boy Scouts of America and as chaplain at several national jamborees. President Brady served on the national council and was also the Cub Scout leader in the Westwood Ward.

Because of the limited number of youth in the stake, stake leaders had gone outside stake membership to keep Scouting functioning. If there were only two or three ward members of Scouting age, the stake reached out into the community and brought non-LDS boys into the program. In doing this, it developed strong troops that met the needs of the youth both inside and outside the Church. In the Wilshire Ward in the summer of 1986, for example, only three of a troop of thirty-two Scouts were Church members. Significantly, the troops of Los Angeles Stake were themselves microcosms of the world, with blacks, Koreans, Chinese, Armenians, Caucasians, and Hispanics all enjoying the benefits of Church-sponsored Scouting activity.

The renewed efforts to build Scouting were time consuming, but, as President Brady has stated, "When you speak of sacrifice, you really have to compare the cost versus the results and the cost in time and effort was certainly far less than the result."[24] In the Wilshire Ward, Roy Richardson became virtually a father to a wide variety of underprivileged boys, most of them non-LDS. Most of the Los Angeles Stake Scouts came from low income families and single homes. Others had parents who seemed not to care about them. Some had become involved with various evils of the world, including drugs, and many, by the standards of the world, might have been considered failures. In many cases, however, the Scouting program of the Los Angeles Stake turned these young men into real achievers. So close did some of them become to the Richardson family that they often showed up at the Richardson house early in the morning and stayed the day, eating meals with the Richardson family. The Richardsons realized that the meals they gave them might have been the only meals they would have had that day.[25]

Several young men joined the Church as a result of their scouting experiences, and so also did several nonmember Scoutmasters, including Walt Parker, Glen Johnson, Thor Dockwiler, and John Stockman. The latter eventually became bishop of the Wilshire Ward.[26] Thus, as stake members served the Los Angeles community through Scouting, they also served the Church both through bringing about convert baptisms and through helping the young men acquire skills as Scouts. For stake leaders, the emphasis on improved Scouting also had other measurable effects as almost every LDS Eagle Scout eventually filled a mission. President Tanner summed up the attitude of stake leaders toward scouting this way:

> I don't know of a better laboratory for young men to learn the skills of the priesthood. . . . Scouting has something for every boy. It can appeal to the quiet scholarly boy as well as the athletic boy. . . . Becoming an Eagle Scout is not the ultimate goal of an LDS Scout.

Missionary service, temple marriage, an eternal family and a life-time of Church service are the goals we try to instill in our young men. . . .[27]

The thing that I have seen in Scouting is that we have to be sure we keep a balance between what our mission is and what Scouting's mission is. Our mission is to provide missionaries. There were troops who were really outstanding Boy Scout troops, who would have fifteen Eagle Scouts, but no missionaries. And from my way of thinking, that's no good. I want fifteen Eagle Scouts, but I want fifteen missionaries. And so, we have to keep that goal as to what this program is for. This program is to teach our young men to be citizens, to be responsible, to pay their duty to God and to other people, to keep themselves morally clean, and to serve their Father in Heaven. So that's been the emphasis here and that's really been our goal.[28]

Even though special emphasis was placed upon the Scouting program, the Explorer-age boys were not forgotten. For one thing, the stakes in the Los Angeles area instituted the Seagull Award to honor young men in each stake. It recognized seniors in high school who made noteworthy achievements in their community, in Scouting, in school, and in the Church, and each was given a special plaque.[29]

Fathers and sons' outings also played a prominent role in the stake activities for youth, and the young men—whether members or non-members of the Church—who had no fathers were often taken to these outings by stake members who volunteered to be their fathers for those occasions. At the 1986 outing at least twenty non-LDS youth who belonged to LDS Scout troops and their fathers attended.

The young women's program also received considerable attention. As with the young men, stake members share great concerns about rearing young women in an urban environment. When Frances W. Richardson first moved into the stake, she was called as Young Women's president in the Hollywood Ward. Raised in suburban California where there were highly active families, and where the Church functioned much as it did in Utah, she was not prepared to deal with inner-city youth who came from broken homes or part-member families, who were exposed to the world in some of its worst forms, and who were often headed for serious trouble. Many of them had no parents at all, and other had parents who simply did not support the efforts of leaders. Ward leaders tried everything they could think of, but in spite of their best efforts and the hours they spent, they tasted failure more often than not.[30]

To help bring the girls of the stake together so they could get to know each other and also to show them that stake leaders were interested in them, two stake-wide slumber parties were held in 1982. The first, in February, was for the Beehive girls and the second, in May, was for all girls in the stake. In July 1985 the young women of the stake attended a camp at Big Bear, much like Boy Scout camp, which featured whitewater rafting, boating, water-skiing, swimming, wind-surfing, and other activities designed for good, wholesome fun.

On 9 November 1984 a special leadership meeting was held at the Westwood chapel. In attendance was Ardeth G. Kapp, general president of the Young Women in the Church, who counseled local leadership on how to build the young women's program. The following day a tri-stake conference for young women and their mothers from the Inglewood, Los Angeles, and Huntington Park stakes was hosted by the Los Angeles Stake Young Women, under the direction of Rynna S. Barner, stake Young Women's president, at the Westwood Ward. The theme of the conference was "Let Me Soar." In addition to Ardeth Kapp, the conference featured workshops on improving self-esteem and physical self-improvement. These were followed by a luncheon and fashion show put on by the young women of the Los Angeles Stake. They had made all the clothes modeled in the show and in that way achieved goals in their personal progress program. Workshops were also held for mothers on how to more effectively communicate with their daughters, and in the evening a tri-stake dance was held at the Westwood Ward.[31]

In August 1985 Sister Kapp returned to the stake for a special awards dinner held in connection with the Young Women's personal progress program. After a lovely dinner, she favored the young women with a talk and then presented awards for their personal progress.

A special award was reserved for the girl who completed all of her goals and went beyond to earn special distinction. In 1985, for example, it was a college scholarship. The 1986 special-award winner completed sixty-five goals and also received a letter from President Ronald Reagan, similar to what Eagle Scouts receive, recognizing her accomplishments. In addition, all the young ladies who earned the personal progress awards in 1985 and 1986 participated in a special excursion to Palm Springs.[32]

The Los Angeles Stake suffered, in comparison with other stakes in the area, from a shortage of youth. Because of this, it became a leader in bringing together the youth of all stakes in the region for youth conferences, dances, and special youth outings so that they would have a larger LDS group from which to gather friendship and strength.

During these years the Relief Society of the Los Angeles Stake also developed new programs for the benefit of the adult sisters. On 12 October 1985, for example, it hosted a "Voyage of Discovery," which consisted of a lovely program and dinner. The purpose of the event was to present the talents of women in the stake and to honor those who had achieved through music, poetry, and other artistic activities. It had the effect not only of honoring the women who had worked in the Pursuit of Excellence program during the year, but also of bringing considerable talent out of the closet.[33]

Not only did the Relief Society honor their own, but the priesthood of the stake also honored them. When the Church instituted a general women's meeting prior to its annual general conference and broadcast it over the Church satellite systems, members of the stake presidency decided that they wanted full participation on the part of the sisters. They also made it a special event. Borrowing from the success of the stake priesthood dinners, the stake priesthood quorums began hosting beautiful banquets for the sisters in the stake at each of these meetings. The only responsibility the sisters had was to determine the number who would attend and then show up for a fine dinner, prepared and served by the priesthood, which featured flowers on the tables that the sisters could take home.

At the first dinner, held in September 1983, there were 420 sisters present. The following year there were over 550. In coordinating this event the stake presidency asked the brethren in each ward to participate, so that it soon became a group effort and brought together in a special kind of fellowship members from all the wards, including singles and students.

Stake leaders felt that these dinners helped stake members feel good about the stake and also helped the stake's sisters acquire a more positive attitude towards the priesthood. Often the perception of the priesthood was one of a willingness to delegate assignments to the Relief Society. Through these dinners stake leaders began to change that perception to exhibit the priesthood as a group of brethren willing also to serve.[34]

As the Los Angeles California Stake began its sixtieth year in 1987, it was apparent that it was a microcosm of a worldwide Church in ways other than its racial diversity. One way in which the stake has become a microcosm has been in the effort of the Saints to build up Zion where they reside. For there to be Zion in Los Angeles, the Saints must stay and stand strong in that area. It is not an easy place for them to live, but the members have felt a commitment to helping the Church remain strong and at the same time to make a commitment to improving the community. The well-being of Los Angeles, they have felt, is directly related to whether the Church remains strong as a bulwark against evil. When the Saints first came to southern California they were told that they must be the leaven in the loaf. Through the activities of the Los Angeles California Stake they have indeed been a leaven. While the Church in Los Angeles was quite different in many ways from the Church found on the east bench of Salt Lake City, it was meeting the needs of a wide variety of people in a large metropolitan, cosmopolitan area.

Stake members have done the best they could with what they have and are not trying to emulate more traditional stakes, realizing that their environment necessitates a certain uniqueness. Indeed, the stake has survived and grown because it has done whatever is necessary to adjust to the special conditions prevailing in the stake environment. Conditions in the inner city have made it difficult and often dangerous to do visiting teaching and home teaching. Some members lived in areas where it was not safe for women to go out after dark. Many of the sisters in the Wilshire Ward were not able to get out because of age and lack of transportation. To overcome this problem, the ward developed a system of telephone networking to replace the standard visiting teachers. Under this system the sisters were each assigned to call other sisters each month, to see how they were doing and to make sure that their needs were met. While not the traditional approach, the percentage of sisters contacted each month usually exceeded 90 percent.[35]

Between 1950 and 1987 there was an average 2.4 percent annual decrease of membership in the Los Angeles basin. While the Los Angeles Stake did not escape this trend, after 1970 the trend in the stake was reversed largely because of the growth of the Church among minority groups and the changing nature of the inner city. In 1982 only the Wilshire Ward and the minority wards and branches showed growth or maintained population, and yet this growth was substantial enough to produce overall growth in the stake. Membership at the end of the year stood at 4,372, nearly a 25 percent increase over a decade earlier, when membership barely exceeded 3,300. Projections in 1982 of future growth estimated membership living within stake boundaries would reach five thousand by the end of 1987, but that figure was exceeded a year earlier than expected.[36] Although stake membership was just over 3,300 on 31 December 1986, the members of the three Spanish language wards who were living within the stake boundaries but assigned to the Huntington Park West Stake brought the total Church population to over five thousand. The total membership within stake boundaries had almost reached the level of the early 1950s, although the ethnic mix was considerably different. This unprecedented growth led to preparations for building a new chapel for the first time since the dedication of the Westwood Ward chapel nearly thirty-five years earlier. It was anticipated that, when completed, this chapel would be used by the Huntington Park West Stake and a steadily growing Spanish membership. Not only did the Spanish membership grow, so also did Los Angeles Stake population, increasing by over two hundred in the two and a half years between the creation of the Huntington Park West Stake and the end of 1986. Activity of stake membership as measured by sacrament meeting attendance also rose to over 40 percent, up from the 37 percent average recorded after the Spanish had been separated from the stake.

It is difficult to anticipate what the Los Angeles California Stake will be like ten, twenty-five, or fifty years from this writing. When the stake was organized sixty years ago, no one envisioned the diversity that characterizes it today. It is likely that other groups will join with the Saints living in the area, making the stake even more a microcosm of the world. As in the past and the present, those strong in testimony and leadership ability and financial capability will still be desperately needed for the Church to remain strong in the area. While there has been a trickle of membership, particularly young Anglo families, moving into the stake over the last few years, it is far from a stream. Missionary work must still be a major concern not only to increase numbers but also to fulfill the charge the Saints have been given to take the gospel to all people.

If the past is prologue, the "microcosmic" Los Angeles California Stake will continue to be a vital force in the Los Angeles metropolitan area as its members work to meet the needs of the Church and its people. As its leaders learn from the past, remain relevant to the present, and maintain a vision of the future, the stake will continue to weather the storms and grasp the great opportunities that lie before it.

Appendix: The Buildings of Los Angeles Stake

Buildings reflect the people who build them. They are a visual statement of the time, place, and concerns of their builders; by examining buildings we learn what a society holds important.

The buildings of the Los Angeles Stake are no exception; indeed, they present an outstanding chronological example of the religious architectural trends of the first half of the twentieth century. The buildings are innovative and individual; and each sought to be the best the stake was capable of erecting at the time.

The chapels and stake tabernacle are the work of five differeent architects. Three of the architects who designed for the Los Angeles Stake have received national recognition for their work: Harold W. Burton, Louis A. Thomas, and Georgius Y. Cannon. These men, along with Robert M. Taylor and Francis D. Rutherford, have left a legacy in bricks and mortar of beauty and a determination not merely to shelter the Saints but to inspire and improve their worship as well.

The first building constructed by the Church in Los Angeles was the Los Angeles Branch chapel, later known as the Adams Ward chapel, at 153 West Adams. The building, designed by Robert M. Taylor with the assistance of building contractor Samuel Dailey, was dedicated by President Joseph F. Smith on 4 May 1913. The cost of the lot and the building came to $25,500, a substantial sum for the time. The typically Edwardian red brick architecture included sandstone detailing imported from quarries at Manti, Utah. The chapel was large with a commodious choir loft and rear balcony. The acoustics of the building were outstanding, especially for music. The central feature of the interior was a large art glass window depicting Joseph Smith's first vision. The window cost $600, most of which was donated by Adam Patterson of Ogden, Utah. This beautiful window was removed before the demolition of the building, carefully stored, and is part of the permanent collection of Latter-day Saint stained glass in the Museum of Church History and Art in Salt Lake City, Utah. The Adams Ward chapel was the center of Mormon activities in Southern California for many years. A mission home was constructed just north of the chapel and, along with a sports field and other recreational facilities, provided a magnet to the Mormons living in southern California. Glenn Evans recalls, "If you wanted to know who was in town from Utah, you just went to the Adams Ward and there they would be."

The building was modified and expanded over the years: the three most radical changes were remodeling the chapel interior by Bishop David P. Howells, lowering the tower after a 1933 earthquake, and painting the building white about 1942. This splendid chapel survived remodeling, massive growth of the Church, earthquakes, and just about everything else, except the change of the neighborhood. The chapel was built on West Adams Boulevard, one of Los Angeles's most desirable locations at the time of construction. The years passed and what had been residential became commercial and what nearby housing was left deteriorated. Still, the chapel endured. However, a nail in the coffin for the Adams chapel was the Harbor Freeway, which isolated it from the better sections of Adams Boulevard to the west. In 1959 it was sold along with its valuable property with the proceeds forming the nucleus of the funding for Salt Lake City's Salt Palace development.

Just as Brigham Young sought the warmth of southern Utah at St. George during the last winters of his life, his successors sought the healing sea breezes of southern California, specifically those of Santa Monica and what was then called Ocean Park. The oldest Latter-day Saint chapel still in use in southern California is located at 2303 2nd Street in Santa Monica. The periodic influx of General Authorities, including the President of the Church, plus substantial local growth, warranted a building of beauty and substance. The Ocean Park chapel was designed by Francis D. Rutherford. The architecture of the chapel as originally designed was a very fine example of Mission Revival. Once again, great care was taken to create a structure of great beauty as well as function.

The focal point of the chapel is the beautiful stained-glass window of Moroni delivering the Golden Plates to Joseph Smith. This window, a gift of Mrs. A. W. McCune of Ogden, Utah, is copied from an original painting by the famous Mormon artist Lewis A. Ramsey (1875–1941) and is one of only two windows of that painting still existing. The window was copied in transparency for the visitors' center at the restored Peter Whitmer Farm at Fayette, New York, when that center was dedicated in 1980.

The Ocean Park Branch chapel, now the Santa Monica Ward chapel, was dedicated 24 September 1922 by President Heber J. Grant. The building was heavily remodeled and enlarged in 1961, at which time the architecture was changed from Mission Revival to a form of Colonial then popular in the Church. The building still boasts excellent acoustics in the chapel, its splendid window, original pews, and a fine Reuter pipe organ installed around 1930. The Santa Monica Ward chapel is still a landmark and one in which the Latter-day Saints can take pride.

In 1922 an exuberant group of local Mormons organized to develop a tract of land later known as Mar Vista. The focal point of this "Mormon" subdivision was to be the ward chapel. The chapel is perched high on the top of a hill at 3655 Centinela Avenue. The architecture of the building is Spanish Mediterranean with tower, patio, and arcades. If a building could be described as happy, then the Mar Vista chapel is it. This is a perky, delightful structure with its wrought-iron pennant atop the tower perpetually blowing in the breeze off the ocean. The building has an unusual chapel interior boasting a sacrament table in an alcove at the highest point behind the pulpit and podium chairs in something like a "high-altar" position. The building is equipped with a pipe organ and, like many of these early chapels, has excellent acoustics. The chapel was built from start to finish in four months at a cost of $70,000. It was dedicated 23 September 1928 by President Heber J. Grant.

The Mar Vista chapel was designed by Louis A. Thomas, a Swiss by birth who also received his early training in Switzerland. He came to the United States as a young man and settled first in Pennsylvania, then moved to Idaho where he joined The Church of Jesus Christ of Latter-day Saints and married Mary Alice Davis. He moved with his family to Los Angeles in 1921 and began work as an architect in the office of C. M. Winslow.

Thomas's first Latter-day Saint building in Los Angeles was the Mar Vista chapel, but he went on to design over seventy other chapels throughout California and Arizona. He also designed many non-Latter-day Saint churches and many municipal structures, for example, Fullerton Junior College, Eagle Rock public schools, Miramonte public schools, and Los Angeles public schools. An outstanding example of his religious work is the beautiful St. Mark's Episcopal Church in Glendale, California. Thomas never forgot his European heritage, and all of his chapels have excellent detailing reminiscent of Europe. He also incorporated Mormon historical design into his buildings, and many of the towers and steeples on his chapels hark back to the Kirtland and Nauvoo temples. The original San Diego Stake tabernacle by Louis A. Thomas won national recognition and was featured in the prestigious *Architectural Forum* magazine. Thomas passed away in 1955, and his funeral was held in the Mar Vista chapel.

Another important architect to leave a legacy in Los Angeles is Georgius Y. Cannon. Cannon designed two buildings for the stake, the original Glendale Ward chapel at 1200 East Carlton Drive, Glendale, dedicated by President Heber J. Grant 8 January 1939; and the Arlington Ward at 3220 48th Street, Los Angeles, dedicated by President David O. McKay 6 June 1943. Paul L. Anderson, in his excellent article "Mormon Moderne: Latter-day Saint Architecture, 1925–1945" (*Journal of Mormon History* 9 [1982], pp. 71–84), gives this description of Cannon's work on the Glendale building:

> The Great Depression of the early 1930s created a building slump that provided some reading time for unemployed architects. One such architect was Georgius Young Cannon, a Salt Lake City man who had studied at MIT and established a practice in Pasadena, California. He read *The International Style* in a library where he spent much time between commissions and was favorably impressed. Soon thereafter he got the chance to try his hand at the new style when he was selected as architect for the Latter-day Saint meetinghouse in nearby Glendale. His design, published in the *Deseret News Church Department*, now the *Church News*, in January 1935, centered on an elliptical chapel with a flat roof and plain white walls. The cultural hall and classroom wings flanked

the chapel and surrounded an open courtyard. An entire wall of glass in each classroom looked into the court. The classrooms were connected to each other and to the chapel by a covered outdoor walkway, an early use of a circulation system that later became common in California schools. The building was a fine example of International Style ideals and a startling departure from conventional Latter-day Saint architecture.

Shortly after its completion, Cannon entered the Glendale meetinghouse in a national competition sponsored by the Pittsburgh Plate Glass company and *Architectural Forum* magazine to recognize innovative use of glass. The prestigious competition was announced in early 1937 and awards were made in the August issue of the magazine. The Glendale meetinghouse won first prize in the institutional category. Several pages of photographs appeared with a glowing caption: "One of the first American examples of the application of the modern style to church building, this example is a worthy successor to the best of its European progenitors." Pictures of the meetinghouse and other award-winning buildings also appeared in several other architectural and engineering publications. . . .

Notwithstanding this award, however, the Glendale meetinghouse was not universally appreciated. According to Cannon, some Church leaders found it too modern for their tastes. The award certificate was never hung in the building nor was the honor reported in the Mormon press. Despite this mixed reception, Cannon did another modern chapel for the Arlington Ward in Los Angeles a few years later.

The Arlington Ward chapel was a reworking of the basic ideas of the Glendale chapel, but this time very much in the spirit of the famous Los Angeles modern architect Richard Neutra. The chapel had no tower but was faced with beautiful Arizona sandstone. The interior of the chapel was graced by an oil-painted mural of the Sacred Grove on the three walls of the choir loft. The mural was the work of Dr. Martella Lane, a distinguished California artist who became a convert to the Church in 1944.

The Glendale Ward chapel and the Arlington Ward chapel were both modern, functional buildings of the highest quality of design. They are proof that simple, efficient structures need not be ugly and uninviting, but that even radically advanced design can inspire. The fate of these two buildings reflects much of what has happened to the Church not only in Los Angeles but also throughout the world. The Glendale area grew rapidly and the Latter-day Saint population warranted a stake of their own. The original Glendale chapel was sacrificed to this growth. It was sold in the 1960s and a new stake center erected nearby. The building still stands, though a pale shadow of its original self. It is now St. Mary's Armenian Apostolic Church. It has been extensively remodeled, and Cannon's original design is now hard to see. The Arlington Ward chapel is still much as it was. It was sold in 1971 and now houses a Baptist church. The current owners maintain it well and, surprisingly, have retained the mural of the Sacred Grove.

The fate of the Arlington Ward was dictated by the fate of the entire South Los Angeles Stake: white flight. The white population of Los Angeles fled from the influx of minorities into south-central Los Angeles, and along with the rest went the Mormons. The beautiful ward chapels of Matthews, Vermont, Miramonte, and Manchester were all sold and now accommodate various Protestant congregations.

Hollywood Ward chapel at 1552 North Normandie in Los Angeles is a unique exception to the policy of Church-designed and constructed chapels. This building was purchased in 1937 from the Mt. Olivet Methodist Church, which had built the structure in 1924. The chapel has been enlarged and remodeled several times, the first work being done by Harold W. Burton soon after its purchase. Brother Burton adapted a Mediterranean/Spanish design for the uses of the Hollywood Ward. He retained the beautiful stained-glass window depicting Jesus Christ and many other choice features of the building. The chapel interior he created is a late example of what is known as Stream Line Moderne. The chapel, equipped with a Möeller pipe organ, has retained much of Burton's design.

Harold W. Burton began as an apprentice architect at age fifteen in Salt Lake City. In 1910 Hyrum Pope asked Burton to form a partnership with him, and together they created Pope and Burton Architects of Salt Lake City. Pope was aged thirty, Burton twenty-three. These two young men would become the leading modern architects of Salt Lake City and of the Church. Burton designed the Alberta Temple in 1912 and the Hawaiian Temple in 1915 and literally hundreds of other chapels, schools, and mission homes. He was Church architect from 1955 to 1964.

In 1950 Burton was asked to design a chapel for the Beverly Hills Ward, later the Westwood Ward. The building he designed is described in the manuscript biography of Harold W. Burton by Paul L. Anderson:

> The exotic feeling of Burton's buildings in Hawaii and Tahiti also appeared in the design for several Latter-day Saint church buildings slightly later in California. The most exotic of Burton's ward buildings for the mainland was the Beverly Hills Ward (later Westwood Ward) [dedicated in 1953] at 10740 Ohio Avenue, near the site for the Los Angeles Temple. As in some of the earlier California churches, the plan included a long chapel which was entered from the street through a foyer, a recreation hall which opened off the side of the chapel, and an enclosed courtyard. These elements had some unique features, however. The chapel had shallow transepts on each side and a raised alcove for the choir in front. The courtyard, depressed a few steps from the colonnade which surrounded it, was beautifully landscaped with tropical plants. As in the Papeete, Tahiti building, the walls were built of concrete block and the parapet of the chapel was perforated in a decorative pattern. In addition, the main facade of the chapel had a shallow entrance

porch which was a simplified version of the building at Papeete. The name of the church appeared along the top of the porch just as in the earlier Tahiti building, but the columns were removed and the corner finials replaced with smaller acroteria. The large wall area around the front door was covered in a checkerboard pattern of gold and light green glazed ceramic tile. The tower was located at the side of the chapel, a simple rectangular element with a perforated pointed spire. Decorative grills inside the chapel also recalled the pierced screens at Papeete.

The detailing at the top of the tower with its perforated spire was to reappear in Burton's last great work, the Oakland Temple of 1964. The Westwood chapel has been enlarged and remodeled several times, but despite changes in the architect's color scheme for the building, much of the beautiful exterior detailing and the basic integrity of the design has been retained. In 1984, after over thirty years of discussion, a fine Schoenstein pipe organ of nine ranks was finally installed in the organ chamber.

In 1927, due to ill health caused by the severe Utah winters, Brother Burton, his wife, Evelyn, and their children moved to Los Angeles. Pope and Burton Architects opened a branch in Los Angeles, and Burton was, for the most part, based in Los Angeles for the rest of his life. The first major commission Harold W. Burton received upon moving his family in 1927 was the Wilshire Ward/Hollywood Stake tabernacle. Brother Burton's wife, Evelyn, in a 1984 interview, recalled:

> Bishop Howells was bishop of the ward and his wife, Adele Howells, was Addie Cannon, a relative of mine. Her grandmother and my grandmother were sisters. Bishop Howells was a businessman and quite, oh, a very wealthy man I would say. Adele Howells invited my husband and me to go over to spend the evening and just out of the clear sky he said, "We want you to be the architect of the Wilshire Ward." The people were poor. They didn't have any money, the Wilshire people, but Emily Sims was a go-getter. So we would organize big dinners. People would come and pay maybe two-and-a-half for their dinner. And the husbands would be dressed in their tuxedos in the evening and the ladies in their long dresses and we'd give these beautiful dinners in the big amusement room—we didn't call it a cultural hall then—and to the tune of a marching band the husbands would come and march around the room. . . . Oh, we did everything under the sun to help raise the money to pay for the building.

The building Burton created at 1209 South Manhattan Place, Los Angeles, is a 32,000-square-foot L-shaped structure in reinforced concrete in a style Burton described as Modern Gothic. With the passage of time, it is more recognizable as Art Deco than as Gothic and has Spanish-style details. The tower is reminiscent of the Nebraska State Capitol, and the chapel wing is not unlike the West Point Chapel of the U.S. Military Academy. The building is monumental in concept but has been blunted somewhat by white paint (Burton intended that it be left gray concrete) and an annex.

It is the interior, however, that parts company with what most people consider a Mormon chapel. The chapel, itself in a splendid state of repair thanks to the 1978 restoration of its original color scheme and decoration, is one of only two Art Deco churches in Los Angeles. The walls are hand-stenciled in bright Deco colors and patterns. The chandeliers are handmade to an original design. The pulpit benches are original in solid oak upholstered in deep red velvet. It is a massive room which can seat 900 if the balcony is used. The chapel boasts an Austin pipe organ of eighteen ranks.

Perhaps the most distinctive features of the chapel are its stained-glass windows. These were important in their own right but are also rare examples of Art Deco church windows. The windows on the north side of the chapel represent Latter-day Saint and Christian themes, including sego lilies, beehive, sheaves of grain, dove, and chalice. The crowning glory of the windows, however, is the large east window behind the pulpit and choir. This is a stained-glass rendering of Christ as the Light of the World from the Victorian painting of the same name.

The chapel is the only part of the building's interior that has been restored to its original state, and one may only look at the rest of the building and imagine how spectacular it all once was. In the July 1929 issue of *The Improvement Era,* there is a description of each room. One of the features that has been modified is the reception room, now the high council room. A description of the reception room will illustrate the care taken in constructing the entire building:

> The reception room for use during social functions is beautifully furnished in the Italian manner featuring a handsomely carved gilt mirror imported from France for a splendid old Los Angeles home now dismantled, an intriguing antique chest, large Italian wall chairs, inviting davenports, consoles, with matching mirrors, fine tables, a soft apple-green carpet providing a lovely setting for the henna brocade draperies and the gold, green, amethyst and blue upholstered pieces. The room is lighted with crystal chandeliers, crystal girandoles for the consoles, and gold torcheres.

This room overlooks the cultural hall and once formed a balcony along the south end of the cultural hall. The reception room was but one of many, including the baptistry, to have received such care and attention to decoration and detail.

The building was dedicated 28 April 1929. At the dedication, President Grant said it was the finest building the Church possessed with the exception of the temples and Salt Lake Tabernacle, and at a cost of $250,000, one of the most expensive chapels built in the Church to that time.

The building's high quality was due to the work of many, but particularly the efforts of two men: President McCune, the stake president, and Bishop Howells of the Wilshire Ward. These were cultured men of taste determined to see a building of substance and quality that would say to the Los Angeles community that the Mormons were not ignorant, polygamous farmers but were people of taste and refinement. To quote from the dedicatory program, President McCune writes:

> A large cheap structure could have been erected in a comparatively short time, but in so doing the greatest opportunity that has yet been given the Church would have been lost—that is, to preach the Gospel to the world by means of a structure that would place Mormonism on a par with her sister churches. Los Angeles has become a city of beautiful churches. Should the Church of Jesus Christ of Latter-day Saints be satisfied with the commonplace when others are dwelling in marble halls? The people of Hollywood Stake have answered these questions by erecting the finest and most costly edifice yet erected by the Church with the exception of its temples. Where much is given much is expected. The catacombs or the fields of Mars were sufficient for meetings of the early Christians—it was the best they could afford. The tiny church is sufficient for the small village where the people can afford no more. The worship of God is just as acceptable in the smallest church in the smallest community as in a mighty temple—but here where opportunities are great and we have so much—could we give less?

The historical department of the Church, according to Paul Anderson, lists the Wilshire Ward chapel as number twenty-one on its list of significant historical sites and buildings. It is ironic that even so important a structure as the Wilshire Ward chapel came dangerously close to being sold. The neighborhood surrounding the Wilshire chapel deteriorated over the years. The Church had purchased a piece of property at Muirfield and Wilshire Boulevard on which it wished to build a highrise building which would include space for the Wilshire Ward. The local stake leaders debated long and heatedly among themselves over what to do, before determining to retain the Wilshire Ward. The Wilshire Ward is built to last and there is no reason why it cannot continue to serve as it has for over fifty years.

Harold W. Burton died in 1969, and, like Louis A. Thomas, this great Mormon architect's funeral was held in a building he had designed, the Wilshire Ward chapel.

The buildings of Los Angeles Stake represent a legacy. The structures are architecturally significant, soundly built, and in an age in the Church of computer-designed, modular, standard chapels, they are a welcome contact with a more individualized and personal age.

A building is more than its design and materials. It is an expression of those who built it and those who use it. It is impossible to calculate the endless hours of volunteer labor in each building, the sacrifices of money, time, and health that were made in order to see that the buildings were built and paid for.

The great British historian Sir John Betjeman speaks of "the spirit of the place." The spirit of a building is the intangible link between those who built it and those who have used and now use it. To sit in the

Wilshire Ward chapel is to worship in the present and share with the past. It is inspiring to think of how many babies have been blessed in that chapel, how many funerals held, how many missionary farewells and homecomings presented, how many sermons preached, how many great leaders of the Church have stood at the pulpit, how many concerts given, and how many quiet moments of inspiration gained from just being in that beautiful place and gazing up at the east window.

MICHAEL ENSIGN EVANS

Notes

Chapter 1: One of the Great Fields in Which the Church Would Thrive

1. Andrew Jenson as cited in Leo J. Muir, *A Century of Mormon Activity in California 1847–1947*, 2 vols. (Salt Lake City: Deseret News Press, 1951) 1:34–35. (Hereafter cited as Muir, *A Century of Mormon Activity*.)

2. Ibid. 1:38.

3. Eugene E. Campbell, "A History of the Church of Jesus Christ of Latter-day Saints in California, 1846–1946" (Ph.D. dissertation, University of Southern California, 1952), 131–35. (Hereafter cited as Campbell, "History of the Church in California.")

4. Ibid., 142.

5. Ibid., 165.

6. Jesse C. Little to Brigham Young, 6 July 1846, as cited in Muir, *A Century of Mormon Activity*, 1:50.

7. W. Ray Luce, "The Mormon Battalion: A Historical Accident?" *Utah Historical Quarterly* 42 (Winter 1974): 33.

8. Daniel Tyler, *A Concise History of the Mormon Battalion in the Mexican War* (n.p., 1881), 118. (Hereafter cited as Tyler, *A Concise History*.)

9. Ibid., 252.

10. Muir, *A Century of Mormon Activity* 1:58.

11. Tyler, *A Concise History*, 290.

12. Muir, *A Century of Mormon Activity* 1:61.

13. Zatelle Sessions Dictation, 1, Los Angeles Stake Collection.

14. Muir, *A Century of Mormon Activity* 1:462.

15. Manuscript History of Brigham Young, as cited in Campbell, "History of the Church in California," 191.

16. Ibid.

17. Parley P. Pratt, "Mission to California, 1851," *California Historical Society Quarterly* 13 (March 1935): 74.

18. B. H. Roberts, *A Comprehensive History of the Church of Jesus Christ of Latter-day Saints*, 6 vols. (Provo: Brigham Young University Press, 1967) 4:239.

19. Campbell, "History of the Church in California," 282.

20. Los Angeles *Star*, January 1860, as cited in Muir, *A Century of Mormon Activity*, 93.

21. Campbell, "History of the Church in California," 282.

22. James B. Allen and Glen M. Leonard, *The Story of the Latter-day Saints* (Salt Lake City: Deseret Book Co., 1976), 69–70.

23. Wilford Woodruff, Journal, 25 September 1890, as cited in Roberts, *Comprehensive History*, 6:220.

24. California Mission Manuscript History, introduction to vol. 2, Archives, Historical Department of The Church of Jesus Christ of

Latter-day Saints, Salt Lake City, Utah. (Hereafter cited as the LDS Church Archives.)

25. Ibid., 20 July 1890.

26. Ibid.

27. Wilford Woodruff to J. W. Pickett and Mark Lindsey, (n.d.), copied into Ibid., 11 December 1890.

28. Ibid., 14 June 1891.

29. Ibid., 31 December 1893.

30. *Campbell's Illustrated Magazine*, (n.d.), copied into Ibid., 12 June 1893.

31. California Mission Manuscript History, 21 January 1895.

32. Laura Tanner to Leo J. Muir, 6 December 1946, Los Angeles Stake Collection.

33. Ibid.

34. Norman B. Phillips, "Historical Sketch of the California Mission," 12, as copied into California Mission Manuscript History, vol. 2, LDS Church Archives.

35. Laura Tanner Reminiscences, undated, Los Angeles Stake Collection.

36. *Deseret News*, 3 December 1896.

37. Tanner to Muir, 6 December 1946.

Chapter 2: A Sunday School, a Branch, and a Mission Conference

1. Muir, *A Century of Mormon Activity* 1:109.

2. *Deseret News*, 20 October 1897.

3. Thomas G. Alexander, *Mormonism in Transition: A History of the Latter-day Saints, 1890–1930* (Urbana: University of Illinois Press, 1986), 135. (Hereafter cited as Alexander, *Mormonism in Transition.*)

4. California Mission Manuscript History, 17 October 1897.

5. Ibid.

6. *Deseret News*, 12 April 1896.

7. Ibid., 26 April 1897.

8. *Conference Report*, April 1902, 35.

9. *Conference Report*, April 1901, 60.

10. Ibid.

11. Richard O. Cowan, *The Church in the Twentieth Century* (Salt Lake City: Bookcraft, Inc., 1985), 76.

12. Allen and Leonard, *The Story of the Latter-day Saints*, 463.

13. *Deseret News*, 20 October 1897.

14. *Conference Report*, April 1901, 44.

15. *Deseret News*, 4 August 1900.

16. Joseph E. Robinson to L. N., 11 January 1907, Joseph E. Robinson Letterpress Book, LDS Archives.

17. Joseph E. Robinson to Mrs. Theodore Klein, 8 February 1908, Joseph E. Robinson Letterpress Book, LDS Church Archives.

18. *Deseret News*, 3 February 1923.

19. Cowan, *The Church in the Twentieth Century*, 75.

20. Joseph E. Robinson to George D. Pyper, 11 January 1911, Joseph E. Robinson Letterpress Book, LDS Church Archives.

21. Elsie Conover Dyer talk to Westwood Ward Relief Society, 1976, untranscribed audiotape, Los Angeles Stake Collection.

22. *Conference Report*, October 1913, 115.

23. *Liahona: The Elders Journal* 16 (27 May 1919): 1448.

24. *Liahona: The Elders Journal* 16 (10 June 1919): 1464.

25. Ibid.

26. Ibid.

Chapter 3: Exodus and Promised Land

1. Based on figures published in the *Deseret News 1987 Church Almanac* (Salt Lake City: Deseret News, 1986), 253.

2. Ibid.

3. The *California Intermountain News* began publication in 1935. In 1937 its name was changed to the *Ensign* and was published under that name for a year. In 1940 the *California Intermountain News* again began publication and continued until 1985. The plane, car, and train were deleted from the masthead in 1947 and its format became more southern-California oriented.

4. Muir, *A Century of Mormon Activity* 1:104.

5. Ibid. 1:465–466.

6. Ibid. 1:116.

7. *Conference Report*, April 1922, 149.

8. Russell R. Rich, *Ensign to the Nations* (Provo: Brigham Young University Press, 1972), 542.

9. Edna West Sant to Frances W. Richardson, 22 March 1984, Los Angeles Stake Collection.

10. *Salt Lake Tribune*, 9 October 1921, as cited in Journal History, 9 October 1921.

11. Ibid.

12. *Conference Report*, October 1922, 33.

13. Cowan, *The Church in the Twentieth Century*, 263.

14. Ibid., 266.

15. As cited in *Rededication Program of the Los Angeles California Stake Center*, (n.p., 1978), 3.

16. Heber J. Grant to George W. McCune, 29 May 1922, George W. McCune Collection, LDS Church Archives.

17. *Conference Report*, October 1922, 152.

18. Ibid.

19. Muir, *A Century of Mormon Activity* 2:72.

20. Heber J. Grant to George W. McCune, 11 January 1923, George W. McCune Collection, LDS Church Archives.

21. *Rededication Program*, 3.

22. Evarard L. McMurrin to George W. McCune, 24 May 1952, George W. McCune Collection, LDS Church Archives.

23. The Los Angeles Stake has often been labeled the first stake outside the Intermountain area after the main body of the Church

moved to Utah. Other stakes, however, preceded it outside the conventionally defined Intermountain area. In addition to the San Bernardino Stake, other short-lived stakes were created in the 1850s, including one in St. Louis, Missouri. In the 1880s stakes were established in Mexico and Canada, with the Canadian stake still in existence today. In 1901 the Union Stake was created in central Oregon. In each instance, these were rural stakes where Latter-day Saints were either in the majority or were a large minority. The creation of the Los Angeles Stake, however, was the first attempt to establish a stake in an urban area where Church members were a small percentage of the population.

Chapter 4: The Los Angeles Stake of Zion

1. *Deseret News*, 3 February 1923.
2. *California Intermountain News*, 8 February 1973.
3. *Deseret News*, 3 February 1923.
4. Gustave Larson, "The Los Angeles Stake of Zion," *Improvement Era* 26 (March 1923): 468.
5. *Deseret News*, 3 February 1923.
6. Ibid.
7. Ibid.
8. Ibid.
9. Larson, "The Los Angeles Stake," 469.
10. Ibid.
11. *Deseret News*, 24 January 1923.
12. "Greetings from the Presidency of the Los Angeles Stake to You and Your Family," (n.p., n.d.), George W. McCune Collection, LDS Church Archives.
13. Muir, *A Century of Mormon Activity* 1:240.
14. Ibid. 1:245.
15. Alexander, *Mormonism in Transition*, 125.
16. Monies raised for the maternity home were later transferred to the stake's building fund. Muir, *A Century of Mormon Activity* 1:152.
17. Alexander, *Mormonism in Transition*, 126.
18. *Deseret News*, 12 April 1924.
19. Ibid.
20. Cowan, *The Church in the Twentieth Century*, 69.
21. Alexander, *Mormonism in Transition*, 114.
22. *Deseret News*, 12 April 1924.
23. Ibid., 14 June 1926.
24. *Conference Report*, April 1925, 142.
25. Ibid.
26. Los Angeles Stake Presidency to Heber J. Grant, 25 January 1927, George W. McCune Collection, LDS Church Archives.
27. *Conference Report*, April 1927, 175.
28. *Washington Independent Herald*, 18 April 1927, as cited in the Journal History of The Church of Jesus Christ of Latter-day Saints, 18 April 1927. (Hereafter cited as Journal History.)
29. *Brooklyn Times*, 29 March 1927, as cited in the Journal History, 29 March 1927. Newcastle is the county seat of Northumber-

land, England, and an export center for the British coal industry. The saying "carrying coals to Newcastle" has the connotation of wasting time and effort and the use by the *Brooklyn Times* most likely refers to the belief that the state of the movie industry at the time was not compatible with religion.

Chapter 5: Forward Hollywood

1. *Deseret News*, 25 May 1927.

2. Stake minutes mention no eastern boundary, but rather state that the line dividing the two stakes extended "indefinitely." Hollywood Stake Manuscript History, 22 May 1927, LDS Church Archives.

3. Hollywood Stake Manuscript History, 30 September 1927.

4. First Presidency to Leo J. Muir, 29 August 1927, as cited in the Hollywood Stake Manuscript History, 30 September 1927.

5. Hollywood Stake Manuscript History, 30 September 1927.

6. "Dedication Program for Hollywood Stake Tabernacle," *Hollywood Stake Herald*, April 1929, 2.

7. Ibid.

8. Alexander, *Mormonism in Transition*, 122.

9. Ralph R. Rolapp Oral History, interview by Chad M. Orton, 1986, rough transcript, 2, Los Angeles Stake Collection.

10. Journal History, 14 November 1927.

11. *Deseret News*, 29 November 1927. The article fails to mention who dedicated the site.

12. Samuel H. Hanks Questionnaire, Los Angeles Stake Collection.

13. Zatelle Sessions Oral History, interview by Chad M. Orton, 1986, rough transcript, 14, Los Angeles Stake Collection; Lucile C. Tate, *LeGrand Richards: Beloved Apostle* (Salt Lake City: Bookcraft, 1982), 150.

14. Samuel H. Hanks Questionnaire.

15. *Hollywood Stake Herald*, July 1928, 6.

16. "Souvenir Book" prepared by the Hollywood Stake for President Heber J. Grant, 1932, Los Angeles Stake Collection.

17. Ibid.

18. Hollywood Stake Manuscript History, 15 April 1928.

19. *Memory Book for Wilshire Ward Annual Reunion, 19 January 1945*, (n.p., n.d.), 1.

20. Ibid., 1, 3.

21. Hollywood Stake Manuscript History, 1 April 1928.

22. Samuel H. Hanks Oral History, interview by Chad M. Orton, 1986, untranscribed audiotape, Los Angeles Stake Collection.

23. *Hollywood Stake Herald*, July 1928, 5.

24. *Hollywood Stake Herald*, October 1928, 7.

25. Helen Wooley Jackson Oral History, interview by Chad M. Orton, 1986, untranscribed audiotape, Los Angeles Stake Collection.

26. Ibid.

27. George W. McCune to First Presidency, 9 April 1929, photocopy, G. W. McCune Collection, LDS Church Archives.

28. Ibid.

29. Ibid.

30. First Presidency to George W. McCune, 12 April 1929, photo-copy, G. W. McCune Collection, LDS Church Archives.

31. *Hollywood Stake Herald,* October 1928, 11.

32. *Memory Book for Wilshire Ward Annual Reunion,* 3.

33. *Deseret News,* 29 April 1929.

34. Ibid.

35. *Conference Report,* October 1928, 4.

36. Hollywood Stake Manuscript History, 22 November 1929.

37. Tate, *LeGrand Richards,* 156.

38. Zatelle Sessions Oral History, 14–15.

Chapter 6: Hollywood Stake Part II

1. As the Church was being established in Chicago, the story circulated among the city's Church members that the next branch president would have arrived on the last train from Utah.

2. Tate, *LeGrand Richards,* 141.

3. Ibid.

4. In the 1978 rededication program of the Wilshire Ward, many stake members who worked closely with President Richards in the Hollywood Stake learned for the first time that he had been called to Los Angeles. Samuel H. Hanks Questionnaire.

5. Tate, *LeGrand Richards,* 144.

6. George W. McCune to President Heber J. Grant, 18 April 1931, as cited in First Presidency to G. W. McCune, 22 April 1931, George W. McCune Collection, LDS Church Archives.

7. First Presidency to George W. McCune, 22 April 1931.

8. Tate, *LeGrand Richards,* 147. While having members vote on a possible stake president was not a common practice in the Church, it was not unknown. See Alexander, *Mormonism in Transition,* 107–108.

9. Tate, *LeGrand Richards,* 147–148.

10. Ibid., 148.

11. Ibid.

12. Ibid., 155.

13. Ibid., 150.

14. Ibid., 156.

15. G. Byron Done, "The Participation of the Latter-day Saints in the Community Life of Los Angeles" (Ph.D. dissertation, University of Southern California, 1939), 229.

16. Ibid.

17. Hollywood Stake Manuscript History, 22 January 1933.

18. Tate, *LeGrand Richards,* 164–165,

19. Ibid., 156.

20. *News 'n' Nuggets,* September 1934.

21. *Conference Report,* October 1934, 131.

22. Hollywood Stake Manuscript History, 24 October 1934.

23. Wilford Edling Oral History, interview by Chad M. Orton, 1986, typescript, 2, The James Moyle Oral History Program, LDS Church Archives.

24. *California Intermountain News*, 23 April 1936.

25. *Conference Report*, October 1936, 35.

26. John M. Russon Oral History, interview by Chad M. Orton, 1986, typescript, 2, The James Moyle Oral History Program, LDS Church Archives.

27. *Deseret News*, 6 March 1937. Ralph R. Rolapp recalled that his father-in-law, Preston D. Richards, who served as the Church's legal counsel in southern California, stated that the purchase price was only $41,000. Ralph R. Rolapp Oral History, 10.

28. Wilford Edling Oral History, 5; Winfield Q. Cannon Oral History, Chad M. Orton, 1986, rough transcript, 24, Los Angeles Stake Collection.

29. Interview with James V. D'Arc, archivist of film and sound, Brigham Young University Archives, 1986.

30. John M. Russon Oral History, 1.

31. Huntington Park California Stake, "Sixtieth Anniversary Souvenir Booklet," 8, LDS Church Archives.

Chapter 7: The War Years and Beyond

1. *California Intermountain News*, 26 July 1940.

2. Ibid., 17 October 1941.

3. Los Angeles *Times*, 5 July 1952.

4. *California Intermountain News*, 17 October 1941.

5. Los Angeles Stake Manuscript History, 5 August 1942.

6. Edling Oral History, p. 15.

7. *California Intermountain News*, 27 November 1942.

8. Los Angeles Stake Presidency to Mark E. Petersen, 12 June 1946, Los Angeles Stake Collection.

9. Paul H. Dunn, "Have You Inquired of the Lord?" Devotional Address, Brigham Young University, 8 April 1969, as printed in *Speeches of the Year 1968–1969* (Provo: Brigham Young University Press, 1969), 3–5.

10. *Memory Book for Wilshire Ward Annual Reunion*, 7.

11. Russon Oral History, 17.

12. *California Intermountain News*, 14 March 1947.

13. Notes of a conversation with Jay S. Grant, June 1986, Los Angeles Stake Collection.

14. *Church News*, 1 September 1948.

15. Jay S. Grant Conversation.

16. Wilford G. Edling Questionnaire, 6–7, Los Angeles Stake Collection.

17. Ibid., 7.

18. Los Angeles *Times*, 26 January 1952.

19. Jay S. Grant Conversation.

20. *California Intermountain News*, 4 July 1950.

21. John M. Russon Questionnaire, 7, Los Angeles Stake Collection.

22. Russon Oral History, 18.

23. Russon Questionnaire, 6–7.

Chapter 8: A Spiritual Renaissance

1. Brigham Young and Willard Richards to the Saints in California, 7 August 1847, as cited in the *Improvement Era* 56 (April 1953): 802.

2. First Presidency to the Stake Presidents of Southern California, 27 December 1948, Los Angeles Stake Collection.

3. Ibid.; Minutes of Los Angeles Temple Committee, 28 February 1949, Los Angeles Stake Collection.

4. David H. Cannon to the members of the Los Angeles Temple Committee, 1949, Los Angeles Stake Collection; Los Angeles Stake Presidency to Saints in Southern California, undated typescript, Los Angeles Stake Collection.

5. *California Intermountain News*, 27 September 1955.

6. First Presidency to John M. Russon, W. Noble Waite, and Howard W. Hunter, 14 September 1951, Los Angeles Stake Collection.

7. *California Intermountain News*, 27 September 1955.

8. Ibid.

9. Ibid.

10. *Conference Report*, October 1952, 75.

11. Ibid.

12. Los Angeles Temple Fund Pledge Card, Los Angeles Stake Collection.

13. *California Intermountain News*, 5 February 1952.

14. *Conference Report*, October 1952, 76.

15. First Presidency to John M. Russon, 18 February 1952, Los Angeles Stake Collection.

16. Russon Oral History, 13.

17. *Conference Report*, October 1954, 73.

18. *Conference Report*, October 1952, 77.

19. As cited in the *California Intermountain News*, 3 November 1953.

20. *California Intermountain News*, 8 March 1956.

21. Ibid., 27 September 1958.

22. Joseph Gibby Questionnaire, 5, Los Angeles Stake Collection.

23. Ibid.

24. *Improvement Era* 59 (March 1956): 156.

25. Ibid., 159.

26. Ibid.

27. *Time*, 16 January 1956.

28. *Improvement Era* 59 (April 1956): 230.

29. *California Intermountain News*, 15 March 1956.

30. Ibid.

31. Taken from the April 1956 *Improvement Era*, pp. 225–227.

Chapter 9: An Era of Transition

1. *California Intermountain News*, 12 June 1951.

2. *Latter-day Sentinel*, 5 January 1985; Cowan, *The Church in the Twentieth Century*, 249–251.

3. Beverly Hills Ward Bishopric to the Presiding Bishopric, 17 December 1940.

4. C. Dean Olson Oral History, interview by Chad M. Orton, 1986, untranscribed audiotape, Los Angeles Stake Collection.

5. Zatelle Sessions Dictation, 18.

6. Olson Oral History, untranscribed.

7. Ibid.

8. Arthur Wallace Oral History, interview by Chad M. Orton, 1986, untranscribed audiotape, Los Angeles Stake Collection.

9. Russon Questionnaire, 2.

10. Frederick Davis, "History of the Beginning of the Southern California Mormon Choir," 5, Los Angeles Stake Collection.

11. *California Intermountain News*, 28 November 1957.

12. Davis, "History of the Beginning of the Southern California Mormon Choir," 2.

13. As cited in Ibid., 3.

14. First Presidency to John M. Russon, 10 March 1953, as cited in Ibid., 4.

15. The 5 December 1986 performance of *Messiah* was the last for the Southern California Mormon Choir in the famous Dorothy Chandler Pavilion. Because of the popularity of the Music Center, difficulties arose in scheduling the *Messiah* performance and no plans have been made to continue the tradition in a new location.

16. Notes of a conversation between Edward B. Nadle and John M. Russon, 1987, Los Angeles Stake Collection.

17. Wallace Oral History, untranscribed.

18. Ettie Lee Homes, *Fireside* 6 (May 1974): 2.

19. Ibid., 3.

20. Ibid., 4.

21. LeGrand Richards, *The Dawning of Israel's Day* (Provo: BYU Extension Publications), 1, as cited in Arnold H. Green, "A Survey of Latter-day Saint Proselyting Efforts to the Jewish People" (Master's thesis, Brigham Young University, 1967), 50.

22. Green, "A Survey of Latter-day Saint Proselyting Efforts," 74.

23. *California Intermountain News*, 31 July 1958.

24. First Presidency to Los Angeles Stake Presidency, 20 August 1953, Los Angeles Stake Collection; Winfield Cannon Oral History, interview by Chad M. Orton, 1986, rough transcript, 13, Los Angeles Stake Collection.

25. Los Angeles Stake Presidency to First Presidency, 27 May 1955, Los Angeles Stake Collection; First Presidency to John M. Russon, 9 June 1955, Los Angeles Stake Collection.

26. John M. Russon, Notes for talk given 3 July 1955, Los Angeles Stake Collection.

27. Cannon Oral History, 13.

28. *California Intermountain News*, 26 October 1955.

29. To help encourage members obtain the "temple habit," the Los Angeles Temple Advisory Committee established quotas for each stake in the temple region. *California Intermountain News*, 22 November 1956.

30. Russon Oral History, 2–4.

31. Los Angeles Stake Presidency to the First Presidency, 8 January 1957, Los Angeles Stake Collection.

32. Henry D. Moyle to John M. Russon, 19 February 1957, Los Angeles Stake Collection.

33. Notes of a conversation with James B. Allen, July 1986, Los Angeles Stake Collection.

34. Los Angeles Stake Presidency to A. M. Foutaine, 13 November 1956, Los Angeles Stake Collection.

35. Los Angeles Stake President to the First Presidency, 20 October 1958, Los Angeles Stake Collection. The decision to sell the Adams chapel had been made by early 1958 as portions of the property were in escrow by April 1958.

36. Although the official letter from the First Presidency giving approval for the disbanding of the ward and the selling of the chapel is dated 2 December 1958, two days after the ward was disbanded, stake leaders had received verbal clearance before undertaking such an important step.

37. Russon Oral History, 11.

38. John M. Russon, "Proposals to the Membership of the Los Angeles Stake," 1, Los Angeles Stake Collection.

39. Russon Oral History, 10.

40. Los Angeles Stake Presidency to the First Presidency, 9 December 1958, Los Angeles Stake Collection; Stephen L Richards to John M. Russon, 18 December 1958, Los Angeles Stake Collection.

Chapter 10: A Stake for All People

1. John K. Carmack Oral History, interview by Chad M. Orton, 1986, rough transcript, 9–13, Los Angeles Stake Collection.

2. Ibid., 8.

3. Mabel Russon, Scrapbook of Wilshire Ward productions, private possession.

4. Carmack Oral History, 15.

5. At the Saturday afternoon leadership meeting, on 26 June, Elder Lee joked about the fact that two General Authorities were in attendance. He said to stake leaders, "When they [the Brethren in Salt Lake City] send one General Authority, it's a stake conference. When they send two, it's a reorganization, generally. When they send three, all hell's going to break loose!" Ibid., 16.

6. Ibid., 17.

7. William W. Tanner Oral History, interview by Chad M. Orton, 1986, rough transcript, 31, Los Angeles Stake Collection.

8. Tanner Oral History, 31–32.

9. Ibid., 29–30.

10. Winfield Q. Cannon Dictation, 19–20.

11. Ibid., 20.

12. First Presidency to Los Angeles Stake Presidency, 20 July 1953, Los Angeles Stake Collection.

13. Los Angeles Temple Advisory Committee to the First Presidency, 7 May 1958, as cited in First Presidency to Los Angeles Temple Advisory Committee, 2 June 1958, Los Angeles Stake Collection.

14. Cannon Oral History, 4.

15. Los Angeles Temple Advisory Committee to the First Presidency, 12 December 1963, Los Angeles Stake Collection.

16. Los Angeles *Times*, undated newsclipping, Los Angeles Stake Collection. The announcement of the proposed ban, directed largely at the choir's *Messiah* performance, promoted one member of the standards committee to remark: "I don't see how they could have deteriorated so much since last Christmas."

17. Carmack Oral History, 33–34.

18. Cannon Dictation, 14.

19. Merlin W. Sant Questionnaire, 2, Los Angeles Stake Collection.

20. *California Intermountain News*, 16 May 1970.

21. John K. Edmunds Oral History, interview by Gordon Irving, 1980, typescript, 120–123, the James Moyle Oral History Program, LDS Church Archives.

22. Ibid., 126.

23. Tanner Oral History, 47–48.

24. Ibid., 136–137.

25. Erma Lunt, "The Southern California Group," 1, Los Angeles Stake Collection.

26. Ibid., 2.

27. Tanner Oral History, 138.

28. Ibid., 139–140.

29. Mike Ownby to Daken K. Broadhead, 25 November 1969, Los Angeles Stake Collection.

30. Stake Presidency to the First Presidency, 26 March 1969, Los Angeles Stake Presidency.

31. First Presidency to the Stake Presidency, 3 July 1969, Los Angeles Stake Presidency.

32. Tanner Oral History, 140–141.

33. Ibid., 29–30.

34. John K. Carmack to John H. Vandenberg, 29 August 1972, Los Angeles Stake Collection.

35. Wilford W. Kirton to John K. Carmack, 5 September 1972, Los Angeles Stake Collection.

36. Carmack to Vandenberg, 29 August 1972.

37. C. N. Schapp Questionnaire, 1, Los Angeles Stake Collection.

38. Ibid., 3.

39. Tanner Oral History, 34; First Presidency to Los Angeles Stake Presidency, 4 September 1970, Los Angeles Stake Collection.

40. John K. Carmack to Church Building Committee, 27 December 1972, Los Angeles Stake Collection; Tanner Oral History, 33.

41. Alan K. Parrish Oral History, interview by Chad M. Orton, 1986, rough transcript, 1, Los Angeles Stake Collection.

42. Ibid., 2.

Chapter 11: Unity in Diversity

1. Carmack Oral History, 21.

2. Ibid., 21–22.

3. "John Carmack and Bill Tanner in the Memories of Others," 4, Los Angeles Stake Collection.

4. Jim Jacobsen, "My Most Influential Teacher," Los Angeles Stake Collection.

5. John K. Carmack Questionnaire, 2, Los Angeles Stake Collection.

6. First Presidency to Presidents of Stakes and Missions, Bishops of Wards, and Presidents of Branches, 10 October 1972, Los Angeles Stake Collection.

7. Notes of a conversation with Arthur Wallace, 1986, Los Angeles Stake Collection.

8. Notes of a conversation with Bob Little, 1987, Los Angeles Stake Collection.

9. Tanner Oral History, 87–88.

10. Cannon Oral History, 23.

11. Ibid.

12. Carmack Oral History, 23.

13. Tanner Oral History, 35.

14. Los Angeles California Stake Presidency to Building Division of The Church of Jesus Christ of Latter-day Saints, 19 June 1974, Los Angeles Stake Collection.

15. John K. Carmack to Church Building Division, 13 November 1974, Los Angeles Stake Collection.

16. *Rededication Program*, 16.

17. Tanner Oral History, 34–35.

18. Bob Little Conversation.

19. Ibid.

20. As cited in Cowan, *The Church in the Twentieth Century*, 356.

21. John K. Carmack Questionnaire, p. 4, Los Angeles Stake Collection.

22. Rodney H. Brady Oral History, interview by Chad M. Orton, 1986, rough transcript, 22, Los Angeles Stake.

23. Richard and Sally Stratford Dictation, 8, Los Angeles Stake Collection; Kathleen P. Allyn, "The History of the Los Angeles First Ward," 3, Los Angeles Stake Collection.

24. Allyn, "The History of the Los Angeles First Ward," 5.

25. Stratford Dictation, 8.

26. Brady Oral History, 25.

27. Tanner Oral History, 148–149.

28. Allyn, "The History of the Los Angeles First Ward," 11.

29. Los Angeles *Herald Examiner*, 26 April 1975.

30. Los Angeles California Stake Manuscript History, 31 December 1975.

31. Carmack Oral History, 29.

32. Russon Oral History, 7–8.

33. Sally Stratford to John K. Carmack, 21 October 1973, Los Angeles Stake Collection.

34. The First Presidency to all general and local priesthood officers of The Church of Jesus Christ of Latter-day Saints throughout the world, 8 June 1978, Los Angeles Stake Collection.

35. Bruce R. McConkie, "The New Revelation on the Priesthood," *Priesthood* (Salt Lake City: Deseret Book Co., 1981), 128, as cited in Cowan, *The Church in the Twentieth Century*, 391.

36. Frances Whitney Richardson, Questionnaire, 3, Los Angeles Stake Collection.

37. Brady Oral History, 18–19.

38. Ibid., 17–18.

39. Tanner Oral History, 38.

40. *Rededication Program*, 11.

Chapter 12: A Vision That We Must Cause to Be Fulfilled

1. A. Marden Duke, "History of the Los Angeles Spanish Branch," 1, Los Angeles Stake Collection.

2. Rosario Salazar Questionnaire, Los Angeles Stake Collection.

3. Mario G. and Anabella Vivanco Oral History, interviewed by Chad M. Orton, 1986, untranscribed audiotape, Los Angeles Stake Collection.

4. Ibid.

5. A. Marden Duke Oral History, interview by Chad M. Orton, 1986, untranscribed audiotape, Los Angeles Stake Collection; Frances W. Richardson, "South of Olympic," *Dialogue* 15 (Winter 1982): 120. The ceiling tiles had actually been loosened by water damage caused by the Wilshire Ward's state of disrepair.

6. Edmunds Oral History, 137.

7. Ibid., 138.

8. Tanner Oral History, 35–36.

9. Duke Oral History, untranscribed.

10. Tanner Oral History, 37.

11. Duke, "History of the Los Angeles Spanish Branch," 2; Vivanco Oral History, untranscribed.

12. Duke, "History of the Los Angeles Spanish Branch," 4.

13. A. Marden Duke, "History of the Los Angeles Fourth Branch and Ward," 3, Los Angeles Stake Collection.

14. Ibid.; Williams Oral History, 30.

15. Frederick S. Williams Oral History, interviewed by Chad M. Orton, 1986, rough transcript, 30, Los Angeles Stake Collection.

16. Rafael N. Seminario Oral History, interview by Chad M. Orton, 1986, rough transcript, 32–33, Los Angeles Stake Collection.

17. Williams Oral History, 31; Duke Oral History, untranscribed.

18. Duke, "History of the Los Angeles Fourth Branch and Ward," 4.

19. A. Marden Duke, "History of the Los Angeles Third Ward," 1, Los Angeles Stake Collection.

20. President Spencer W. Kimball, Address to the Southern California Area Conference, 18 May 1980, as cited in "Conferencia de Organization Estaca Para Miembros de Habla Hispana de Los Angeles, California, 3 de Juno de 1984," (n.p., 1984), 1.

21. Tanner Oral History, 44; Notes of a conversation with Skip Drinkwater, 1986, Los Angeles Stake Collection.

22. Mareen Keeler Questionnaire, Los Angeles Stake Collection.

23. Tanner Oral History, 65.

24. Ibid., 36.

25. Ibid., 39.

26. Ibid., 84–85.

27. Notes of a conversation with William W. Tanner, 1986, Los Angeles Stake Collection.

28. Williams Oral History, 15.

29. First Presidency to the stake presidencies of the Los Angeles California Stake, Los Angeles California Inglewood Stake, Los Angeles California Santa Monica Stake, and Huntington Park California Stake, 1 May 1984, Los Angeles Stake Collection.

30. "Conferencia de Organization . . . ," 8.

31. *Latter-day Sentinel,* 23 June 1984.

32. Seminario Oral History, 14.

33. Ibid., 16–17.

34. Ibid., 26.

35. Ibid., 25.

36. Ibid., 20.

37. Duke Oral History, untranscribed.

38. Vivanco Oral History, untranscribed.

Chapter 13: Microcosm of a Worldwide Church

1. William W. Tanner Dictation, 1, Los Angeles Stake Collection.

2. Tanner Oral History, 12.

3. Ibid., 99–100.

4. Notes of a conversation with William W. Tanner, 1986, Los Angeles Stake Collection.

5. Tanner Oral History, 104.

6. Ibid., 143–144.

7. President Spencer W. Kimball, Address to the Southern California Area Conference, 18 May 1980, as cited in Ferren L. Christensen to Stake Presidents in the Los Angeles and Ventura Regions, 10 June 1980, 3.

8. Tanner Oral History, 130–131.

9. Ibid., 134.

10. Ibid., 57.

11. *New Era* 11 (November 1981): 22–27.

12. *Church News,* 3 January 1951.

13. Tanner Oral History, 154–155.

14. Ibid., 40.

15. Ibid., 111.

16. Ibid., 112.

17. Ted Ong, "History of the Los Angeles Fifth Branch," 2, Los Angeles Stake Collection.

18. James Moore Oral History, interview by Chad M. Orton, 1986, untranscribed, Los Angeles Stake Collection; Tanner Oral History, 42.

19. Ong, "History of the Los Angeles Fifth Branch," 18.

20. *Church News*, 28 March 1981.

21. Minority Unit Report for the Los Angeles Second Branch, 1, Los Angeles Stake Collection.

22. Tanner Oral History, 17.

23. *Latter-day Sentinel*, 15 February 1986.

24. Brady Oral History, 8.

25. Frances W. Richardson Oral History, interview by Chad M. Orton, 1986, untranscribed, Los Angeles Stake Collection.

26. Tanner Oral History, 110.

27. *Latter-day Sentinel*, 15 February 1986.

28. Tanner Oral History, 25–26.

29. Ibid., 73.

30. Richardson Questionnaire, 1, Los Angeles Stake Collection.

31. *Latter-day Sentinel*, 24 November 1984.

32. Tanner Oral History, 75; Shirley Peart Oral History, interview by Chad M. Orton, 1986, untranscribed audiotape, Los Angeles Stake Collection.

33. Wallace Oral History, untranscribed.

34. Tanner Oral History, 155–157.

35. Notes of a conversation with Lois Boswell, 1986, Los Angeles Stake Collection.

36. Five Year Plan, 1982, 1, Los Angeles Stake Collection.

About the Sources

On the day that The Church of Jesus Christ of Latter-day Saints was organized, a revelation was received by the Prophet Joseph Smith that "a record shall be kept among you" (D&C 21:1). Since that time, records have been kept by the various units throughout the Church. Until 1978 stake and mission minutes and selected ward minutes were to be sent into the Church's Historical Department where they were placed into one of several series for each unit. In addition, each unit was to send in a quarterly historical report. From the minutes a summary of historical events was compiled by the Historical Department, combined with the quarterly reports, and became the "manuscript history" of the unit. The manuscript history often not only records listings of officers and events, but also lists subjects discussed in presidency meetings and conferences and includes newspaper clippings concerning the unit. For this book the manuscript histories of the California Mission prior to 1923 and the Hollywood/Los Angeles Stake have been the major source for gathering facts, compiling a chronology, and understanding the important issues. In addition, several of the stake's early publications were also sent in to the Historical Department and are available on microfilm.

Beginning in 1978, as the Church continued its growth and the feasibility of storing all the records of the various units diminished, wards were no longer asked to send in reports; and only a "Historical Report," compiled by the clerk at the end of the year, was to be sent in, greatly limiting the information available to the historian.

Additional records of events, dates, statistics, and names have been supplied by the Church-owned *Deseret News* and *Church News,* and through member-operated LDS newspapers in southern California such as the *California Intermountain News, News 'n' Nuggets,* and *Latter-day Sentinel.* During the first thirty years of the stake's existence, the *Deseret News, Church News, News 'n' Nuggets,* and *California Intermountain News* regularly carried articles on the stake, often in great detail. In the 1950s, for example, the *California Intermountain News* ran a biweekly column on happenings in the Los Angeles Stake. However, as the Church has expanded throughout California and the world, happenings in the stake are now seldom mentioned in the Church-owned newspapers; and the only southern California newspaper still in publication, *Latter-day Sentinel,* must cover an increasing number of stakes in the Southland. Indexes are available for both the *Deseret News* and the *Church News.*

Church magazines and publications have also been an important source. *Liahona: The Elders Journal,* the official publication of the missions of the Church during the first quarter of this century, reported major events in the missions and featured a regular column on the California Mission. Frequently, the Saints in Los Angeles were the

subject of general conference talks, which addresses were then published in the semiannual Conference Reports. Prior to 1925 mission
and stake presidents were often invited to report on happenings in their
area. The *Improvement Era, Ensign,* and *New Era* have also run
articles concerning the stake. The most helpful of these have been
Gustive O. Larson, "The Los Angeles Stake of Zion," *Improvement Era*
26 (March 1923), pp. 467–476; Adele Cannon Howells, "Forward
Hollywood," *Improvement Era* 32 (July 1929), pp. 751–755; Richard
Romney, "A Feast for All the World," *New Era* 11 (November 1981),
pp. 22–27; and a series of articles in the *Improvement Era* concerning
the Los Angeles Temple, which not only chronicled its construction
and detailed its dedication but also covered such diverse subjects as the
history of the temple site. Except for the *Liahona,* indexes are available
for these publications.

A wide variety of information has been furnished by present and
past stake members who have filled in questionnaires provided by the
stake, gathered programs printed for important stake events, sat for
oral histories, provided scrapbooks, and written histories on various
aspects of the stake. Among these histories is Michael Evans Ensign's
"The Buildings of the Los Angeles Stake," included here as the
appendix. A wide range of materials was also gathered from the files in
the stake president's office and included correspondence of the stake
presidency, statistical reports, and financial records. At the time of
publication, these materials have not been placed in a depository, and,
therefore, are designated only as being part of the "Los Angeles Stake
Collection." Under agreement with the Family and Community History
Center at Brigham Young University, materials donated by stake members will eventually be deposited at BYU. Stake records and copies of
materials generated by stake members will also be placed in the Historical Department in Salt Lake City. Under arrangements with the Historical Department several of the oral histories have been or will
become part of its James Moyle Oral History Program.

In addition to stake and mission records in the Historical Department, the Joseph E. Robinson and George W. McCune Collections were
valuable sources of information concerning their administrations. The
Journal History, a daily history of the Church composed largely of
newspaper clippings, contains several references to the Church in Los
Angeles. The John K. Edmunds Oral History was helpful in understanding the challenges associated with missionary work among the
minorities.

While much has been published regarding the Church in the nineteenth century, little has been published concerning the Church in the
twentieth century. The narrative literature dealing with the twentieth
century focuses largely on the Church in the Intermountain area and
mentions Los Angeles and California only in passing. However, four
works have been helpful in placing the stake within the framework of
events in the Church at large. Russell R. Rich, *Ensign to the Nations: A
History of the LDS Church from 1846 to 1972* (Provo: Brigham Young
University Press, 1972) was written as a college-level text and focuses

largely on the nineteenth-century Church in Utah. James B. Allen and Glen M. Leonard, *The Story of the Latter-day Saints* (Salt Lake City: Deseret Book, 1976) is a scholarly one-volume overview of the history of the Church from 1830 to 1976. An important aspect of this work is its extensive chapter bibliographies. Richard O. Cowan, *The Church in the Twentieth Century* (Salt Lake City: Bookcraft, 1985) is an in-depth study of the administration of the contemporary Church. Thomas G. Alexander, *Mormonism in Transition: A History of the Latter-day Saints, 1890–1930* (Urbana: University of Illinois Press, 1986) concentrates on trends, accomplishments, and problems in the Church and the social and intellectual life of Latter-day Saints during this pivotal period.

Two helpful overviews of the Church in California have been Eugene Campbell, "A History of The Church of Jesus Christ of Latter-day Saints in California, 1846–1946" (Ph.D. diss., University of Southern California, 1952) and Leo J. Muir, *A Century of Mormon Activity in California*, 2 vols. (Salt Lake City: Deseret Press, 1951). Campbell concentrates largely on the Church during the first ten years in California and presents the essential histories of the *Brooklyn* Saints, the Mormon Battalion, the Mormons and the Gold Rush, the San Bernardino colony, and the establishment of the California Mission, but only briefly discusses the re-establishment of the California Mission and the expansion of the Church in the state. Muir focuses on the Church in southern California since the re-establishment of the California Mission. Volume One is largely a compilation listing officers and important dates of wards and stakes, miscellaneous events, and professional activities of selected members through 1950. Volume Two is a collection of biographies of California Saints.

A number of miscellaneous works deal specifically with Los Angeles or the Hollywood/Los Angeles California Stake. Chapter 10 of Lucile C. Tate, *LeGrand Richards: Beloved Apostle* (Salt Lake City: Bookcraft, 1982), gives valuable insights into the tenure of LeGrand Richards as stake president. The development of LDS religious education at the universities in Los Angeles is briefly covered in G. Homer Durham, "University Religious Training and the Latter-day Saints Deseret Clubs," *Week-Day Religious Education* 1 (March 1937), pp. 1–2. An important source for the Church in Los Angeles in the 1930s is G. Byron Done, "The Participation of the Latter-day Saints in the Community Life of Los Angeles" (Ph.D. diss., University of Southern California, 1939), which is based largely upon surveys taken among stake members in 1937. The Board of Temple Architects is briefly discussed in Paul L. Anderson, "Mormon Moderne: Latter-day Saint Architecture, 1925–1945," *Journal of Mormon History* 9 (1982), pp. 70–84. A scholarly look at missionary endeavors among Jews in Los Angeles is found in chapters 4 and 6 of Arnold H. Green, "A Survey of Latter-day Saint Proselyting Efforts to the Jewish People" (Master's thesis, Brigham Young University, 1967). An outstanding personal essay on the challenges facing stake members is Frances W. Richardson, "South of Olympic," *Dialogue* 15 (Winter 1982), pp. 116–122.

Index